THE DONG WORLD
& IMPERIAL CHINA'S
SOUTHWEST SILK ROAD

JAMES A. ANDERSON

THE DONG WORLD & IMPERIAL CHINA'S SOUTHWEST SILK ROAD TRADE, SECURITY & STATE FORMATION

University of Washington Press / Seattle

The Dong World and Imperial China's Southwest Silk Road was made possible in part by a grant from the Traditional Chinese Culture and Society Book Fund, established through generous gifts from Patricia Buckley Ebrey and Thomas Ebrey.

Additional support for this publication was provided by the Chiang Ching-kuo Foundation for International Scholarly Exchange and the Office of Research and Engagement at the University of North Carolina at Greensboro.

This book will be made open access within three years of publication thanks to Path to Open, a program developed to bring about equitable access and impact for the entire scholarly community, including authors, researchers, libraries, and university presses around the world. Learn more at https://about.jstor.org/path-to-open/.

UNIVERSITY OF WASHINGTON PRESS / uwapress.uw.edu

LIBRARY OF CONGRESS CATALOGING-IN-PUBLICATION DATA

Names: Anderson, James, 1963– author.
Title: The Dong world and imperial China's southwest Silk Road : trade, security, and state formation / James A. Anderson.
Description: Seattle : University of Washington Press, [2024] | Includes bibliographical references and index.
Identifiers: LCCN 2023054139 | ISBN 9780295752778 (hardcover) | ISBN 9780295752792 (paperback) | ISBN 9780295752785 (ebook)
Subjects: LCSH: China—Foreign relations—Indochina. | Indochina—Foreign relations—China. | Silk Road—History. | China—History—Song dynasty, 960–1279. | China, Southwest—Economic conditions. | Indochina—Economic conditions. | China, Southwest—Commerce—History. | Indochina—Commerce—History. | Vietnam—History—939–1428. | Vietnam—Relations—China. | China—Relations—Vietnam.
Classification: LCC DS740.5.I55 A53 2024 | DDC 327.5105909/02—dc23/eng/20240315
LC record available at https://lccn.loc.gov/2023054139

♾ This paper meets the requirements of ANSI/NISO Z39.48-1992 (Permanence of Paper).

CONTENTS

MAPS

ACKNOWLEDGMENTS

The image of the three white pagodas of the Chongsheng Temple against the dazzling blue springtime sky and the looming Cang Mountains behind the complex was breathtaking, but I couldn't take my mind off my aching feet. I felt as though I had walked the entire way from distant Kunming, miles to the south on the Yunnan-Guizhou Plateau, although most of my journey had been by bus. With this trip in 2011, I had finally connected the dots between the historically powerful center of trade at the gateway to the Tibetan Plateau and the numerous upland polities spread across the river valleys of modern-day southwest China, northern Vietnam, and beyond. After researching the Tai-speaking communities along the eleventh-century Sino-Vietnamese frontier for my first monograph, I began to see similarities between these communities and the kingdoms described by Chinese court chronicles that were located farther west and beyond the territory Song dynasty (960–1279) authorities wished to claim as their own. Although the Dali kingdom (937–1253) received much less attention from Song scholars than its southern neighbor the Vietnamese Đại Việt kingdom under Lý (1009–1225) and Trần (1225–1400) leadership, the two kingdoms on the edge of the Song empire interacted frequently with each other and with the distant Chinese courts through the communities that resided in the frontier areas between these three larger states. Trade was the glue that held this region together in a network that would be later titled "the Southwest Silk Road," and it was the grassroots nature of this trade that attracted me to this new project.

This book has taken many forms over the course of its writing, and I wish

Three Pagodas of the Chongsheng Temple, Dali, Yunnan (ca. ninth century)

to acknowledge and thank everyone who helped shape it into its current form along the way. With this second monograph, I still feel the generous support of all those individuals who helped with my first monograph, *The Rebel Den of Nùng Trí Cao*, on the eleventh-century Dong World leader Nùng Trí Cao and his three failed uprisings.

Research for this book took me overseas several times, but the COVID-19 pandemic put a damper on such activities at a critical point. I must thank all those persons who helped me via email and virtual meetings to keep my project on track when we were all huddled in our offices, wondering if we'd ever see the light of day again.

I would like to thank the late John Whitmore for the work we did together on mapping and understanding the Dong World. I hope that John would endorse my development in this book of ideas he and I first discussed years ago. I also want to thank Kathlene Baldanza, Bradley Davis, as well as friends at academic conferences, in which I presented my ideas for this project, and my colleagues at the University of North Carolina at

Greensboro. This project has benefited immensely from their comments and criticisms. Ben Pease of Pease Press deserves special thanks for the excellent set of detailed maps he created for this project.

Regarding the funding of this book, I benefitted from a Fulbright Scholar Fellowship, which allowed me to spend a year at the Academy of Social Sciences in Beijing. During this time I took trips to Yunnan and Guangxi to visit the library collections in Kunming and Nanning, and to photograph archaeological evidence of the prominent historical sites in my study. Professor Fan Honggui at Guangxi Normal University for Nationalities and Professor Fang Tie at Yunnan University provided me with wonderful research guidance at this time. Several years later I received a Taiwan Fellowship to spend a year at the Academia Sinica's Institute of History and Philology (IHP) in a fruitful scholarly interaction with the researchers there. Supported by this fellowship, I also made use of the historical gazetteer materials held in the Center for Chinese Studies (CCS) at National Central Library (NCL). I want to thank Dr. Tseng Shu-hsien, the Director General of the NCL, and Peter Chang, Assistant for Taiwan Fellowship, for making my stay in Taiwan a very pleasant one. More recently in 2019, I was invited by Dr. Đỗ Thị Thùy Lan from Vietnam National University, Hanoi, to present ideas from this book to her colleagues and students, and during my extended stay I visited the Sino-Nom Institute, where the staff were extremely helpful, as always. I also took a trip by bus to the borderlands city of Cao Bằng to meet with Mr. Đinh Ngọc Hải, former director of the Cao Bằng Provincial Association for the Protection of Nature and the Environment (Hội Bảo vệ Thiên nhiên và Môi trường tỉnh Cao Bằng), who took me and my wife to revisit the historical sites on the Sino-Vietnamese border that I had first seen twenty years earlier. I am happy to report that historical preservation efforts around Cao Bằng have received the resources to protect these sites well for future generations of scholars and visitors.

Regarding the editing and production of this book, I want to thank my two anonymous readers commissioned by the University of Washington Press for their extremely valuable comments. The editorial staff at UWP, especially my acquisitions editor Caitlin Tyler-Richards, offered amazing assistance throughout the publication process. I especially want to thank

Lorri Hagman, the recently retired executive editor at UWP, for all her guidance in bringing this book to press.

Finally, I want to thank again my parents Frederic and Anita Anderson, my siblings Haideen and John, my wife Yueh-miao, and our daughters Quai and Svea for their support, encouragement, and love.

Parts of chapter 1 appeared in James A. Anderson, "China's Southwestern Silk Road in World History," *World History Connected* (March 2009), http://worldhistoryconnected.press.illinois.edu/6.1/anderson.html. Parts of chapter 3 appeared in James A. Anderson, *The Rebel Den of Nùng Trí Cao: Loyalty and Identity along the Sino-Vietnamese Frontier* (Seattle: University of Washington Press, 2007). Parts of chapter 5 appeared in James A. Anderson, "Commissioner Li and Prefect Huang: Sino-Vietnamese Frontier Trade Networks and Political Alliances in the Southern Song," *Asia Major* 27, no. 2 (2014): 29–51, and James A. Anderson and John K. Whitmore, eds., *China's Encounters on the South and Southwest: Reforging the Fiery Frontier over Two Millennia* (Leiden: Brill, 2015).

CONVENTIONS

I have chosen *Vietnamese* and *Vietnam* as terms to describe persons and places associated with political power situated in the vicinity of the Red (Hồng) River Delta. I have rendered the Chinese characters for these persons and places in their Vietnamese (*quốc ngữ*) readings. Moreover, I have used the term *Chinese* to describe persons and places associated with courts and political centers north of the Red River Delta, and I have rendered the characters for these persons and places in their modern (Mandarin) Chinese readings. This practice circumvents the issue of Tai names, but I do not mean for these terms necessarily to indicate modern ethnic identity. The terms *Tai* and *Tai-speaking* are used primarily as linguistic distinctions to mark the Sino-Tibetan language family spoken by the communities of indigenous people, who claim descent from the powerful frontier clans in the period under study.

Wherever possible, I have used dynastic terms to indicate a person's political affiliation.

CHRONOLOGY OF DYNASTIES AND KINGDOMS

QIN DYNASTY

(221–206 BCE)

HAN DYNASTY

Western Han (206 BCE–9 CE)

Eastern Han (25–220 CE)

Period of Disunion (220–581)

Three Kingdoms period (220–280)

Jin dynasty (265–420)

Sui dynasty (581–618)

Tang dynasty (618–907)

Nanzhao kingdom (653–903)

SONG DYNASTY

Northern Song (960–1127)

Southern Song (1127–1279)

Lê dynasty (980–1009)

Lý dynasty (1009–1225)

Dali kingdom (937–1253)

Trần dynasty (1225–1400)

Yuan dynasty (1279–1368)

Ming dynasty (1368–1644)

Latter Lê dynasty (1428–1788)

Qing dynasty (1644–1911)

Nguyễn dynasty (1802–1945)

THE DONG WORLD
& IMPERIAL CHINA'S
SOUTHWEST SILK ROAD

INTRODUCTION
BORDERLANDS ENGAGEMENT
IN IMPERIAL CHINA

The Dong World and Imperial China's Southwest Silk Road: Trade, Security, and State Formation contributes to the newly energized field of borderlands studies by providing the first English-language study of the Southwest Silk Road during China's pivotal Middle Period, from the eighth to the fourteenth centuries. The Sinitic term *dong*, usually translated "grotto," actually means "mountain valley settlement" in the context of this study.[1] As John K. Whitmore and I coined this term to describe a particular region, the Dong World in physical terms is an ecological upland zone defined by the Tibetan Plateau's alluvium-rich streams, which flow to the lowland coastal regions of southern China and Mainland Southeast Asia through rugged mountain valleys, as fertile as they are remote. The political history of the Dong World was shaped by borderlands encounters between distant and locally appointed imperial authorities from both southern and northern lowland regimes and the region's mountain valley polities. The force that held these states together, at several altitudes, was trade. As this book argues, any scholarly work on the Dong World entails the study of a variety of principalities, chiefdoms, and market nodes that emerged and flourished in the overlapping network of trade routes, which modern scholars have labeled the Southwest Silk Road, which passed through China's rugged southwestern borderlands. This network of trade is revealed in a system of markets that supported and legitimized local claims to regional control. Moreover, the region of south China was intricately linked to the economic and political shifts occurring in Mainland Southeast Asia.

This book joins a corpus of scholarship with a long lineage. Borderlands

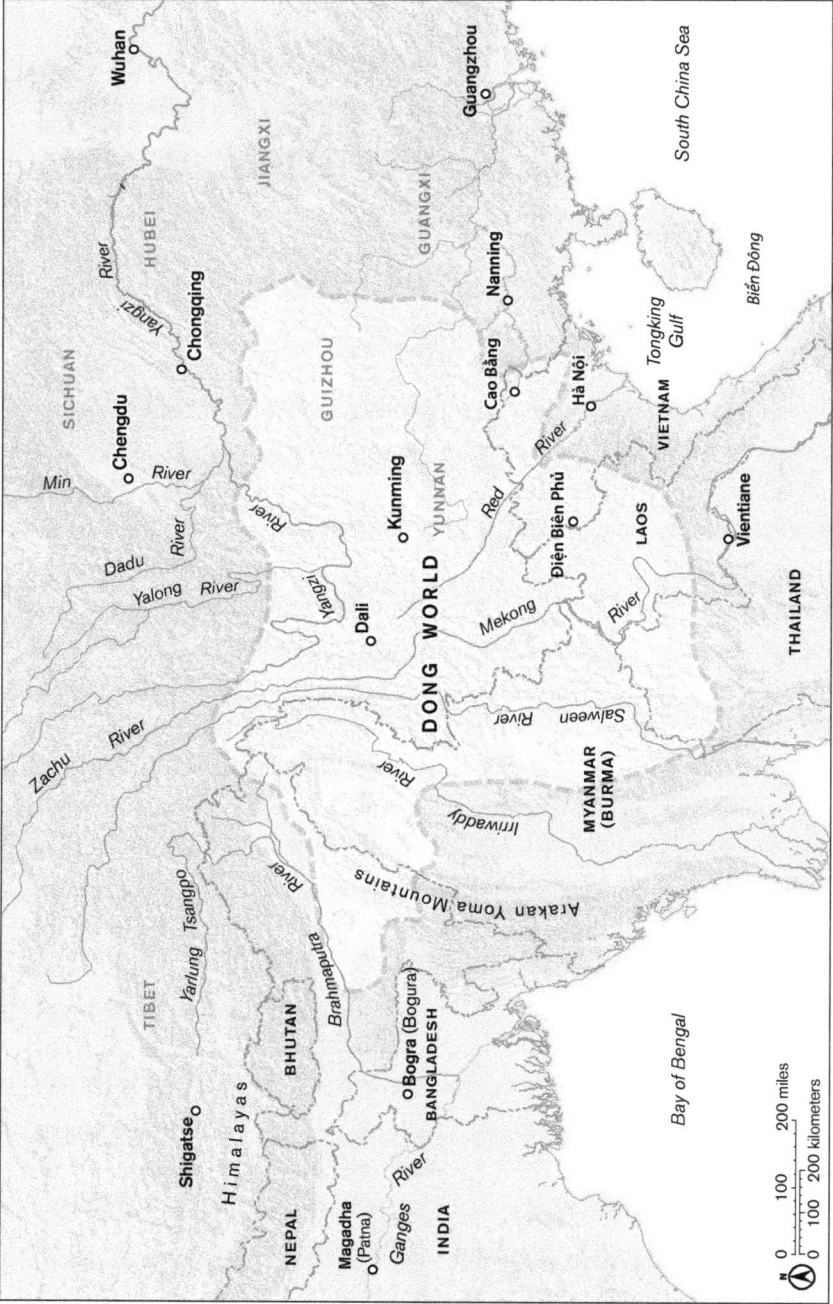

The Dong World

encounters have long captivated the interest of historians of many regions of the globe.[2] Recent work in European medieval frontier studies has critiqued an earlier reliance on the Turner Thesis of the American West, and critics have shifted focus from cultural confrontations between the fourth and the twelfth centuries to cultural interchanges along contact zones between Christian, Muslim, and indigenous communities.[3] Borderlands scholarship on other regions features creative shifts in perspective on interactions between central authorities and frontier communities. As historian of Europe Nora Berend asks, "To what extent did medieval observers see a frontier between themselves and other groups, and how did real interaction compare with ideological and narrative formulations of such interactions?"[4] Modern scholars have called for studies of European frontiers that shift between the "macroscopic" view of political and diplomatic history and the "molecular" view of historical ethnography to understand fully the encounters made over time between states at their common frontier areas.[5] Similar questions and issues must be addressed by scholars examining the Chinese southwestern borderlands in the premodern period. This book draws comparatively on the aforementioned work.

The study of Chinese frontier areas is not a new subject of research, but the field has become revitalized by current events. The rush to explore the strategic and policy implications of the Silk Road region, evidenced by the tremendous international interest in China's Belt and Road Initiative to promote Eurasian infrastructure, has allowed modern Chinese nationalist narratives to obscure more complex dynamics. Restoring the Dong World to the center of the narrative challenges the conventional Chinese scholarly assumption that China's south and southwest became integrated parts of the larger Chinese empire as early as the Qin dynasty (221–206 BCE), and only briefly separated from the imperial order in periods of semiautonomous rule by "separatist" regimes, such as the Nanzhao kingdom of the Tang period (618–907). The dynamic nature of the Dong World region complicates our understanding of the southern expansion of Chinese states, revealing a highly coordinated and cooperative transregional trading network that existed as early as the eighth century.

The Dong World, a network of Tai-speaking polities in the upland valleys (*dong*) of Southeast Asia and southern China, encompassed crucial intermediaries of trade and contact along the Southwest Silk Road.[6] In the eleventh through the thirteenth centuries, such communities were major players in relations between the Song empire, the Vietnamese Đại Việt kingdom, and the Dali kingdom. Culturally, the Dong World was a zone of hybridity and adaptation, or a "middle ground," as historian of the American West Richard White terms the phenomenon.[7] In our coedited volume *China's Encounters on the South and Southwest: Reforging the Fiery Frontier over Two Millennia*, John Whitmore and I coined the term "the Dong World" to describe the social impact this significant cultural zone had on the region described here.[8] This region played a significant role in the economic and political transformation of this corner of Eurasia. Following the waves of Mongol conquests in the thirteenth century, outsiders sought to differentiate among and classify the various Tai-speaking peoples of the area as their contact with lowland authorities increased. By exploring the political and trade activities of these smaller polities in their engagements with the Chinese empire, the Dali kingdom, and the Đại Việt kingdom, this book provides a more nuanced picture of modern-day Yunnan, other sections of southwest China, and northern Southeast Asia in the period preceding Mongol efforts to impose a new administrative order in the region. The dynamic nature of these states is convincing evidence that they shared a regional identity and a lively history of interaction well before northern occupiers in the modern era entered this land and created classifications of "national minorities" from its original inhabitants.

The Dong World was a broad autonomous zone in which the local rulers (native chiefs) contended with each other for influence and manpower from valley to valley. The expansion of neighboring states would present new challenges to those polities. The Dong World, this extensive mountainous region ranging from the Yangzi Valley to the lowlands of Mainland Southeast Asia, has seen increasing intervention from lowland states since the late Warring States period (475–221 BCE). As historian George Moseley wrote years ago, "Divergent cultures persist in the uplands areas which [lowland regimes] could not penetrate, while poor communications have tended to isolate wet-rice cultivators who inhabit small valleys and basins physically remote from the main centers of population."[9] These encounters with the Dong World are at the heart of this study.

However, the Dong World was not the anarchic Zomia described in the work of political scientist James C. Scott.[10] Zomia, a region "beyond the state," as represented in Scott's book *The Art of Not Being Governed: An Anarchist History of Upland Southeast Asia* (2009), was an area of southwest China, peninsular Southeast Asia, and a wide section of Southwest Asia that lay between the imperial orders of the premodern age.[11] Scott described Zomia as a region of political refuge, lying beyond the control of neighboring states to provide those persons tired of the obligations of sedentary governments with an escape. In fact, a multitude of smaller polities existed throughout the imperial periphery. The Dong World revealed in the present volume resembles less a zone of anarchy and more a galaxy (think S. J. Tambiah's "galactic" state) of smaller upland polities orbiting, or avoiding the gravitational pull of, larger lowland states.[12] Rather than existing beyond the state, the Dong World was a complex network of states, fueled by trade, that held at bay the advance of lowland regimes until a series of Mongol conquests, beginning in the mid-thirteenth century, reordered power consolidation in the borderlands areas, and more firmly linked local control to the centralized governance of the Yuan court.[13] The political complexity of the Dong World was the beauty of the system and the subject I explore in this book.

Regarding the naming of the indigenous inhabitants of the Dong World, ethnographer Nguyễn Chí Buyên has noted in the edited volume *Nguồn Gốc Lịch Sử Tộc Người Vùng Biên Giới Phía Bắc Việt Nam* (History of the origins of ethnic groups of northern Vietnam's border areas; 2000) some name-related issues in the ancient Chinese chronicles that contain these references. We must keep in mind that such references were projected on local communities by distant observers from the centers of imperial power and authority. Among court references are general ethnonyms for communities resident in the wide region extending south from the Yangzi River, such as Baiyue, Baipu, Yuepu and Dongyi, and a subsequent division of this network by geographical location relative to existing Han communities, such as Southern Man (Nanman), Eastern Yue (Dongyue), Southern Yue

(Nanyue), Western Yue (Xiyue), Eastern Ou (Dong'ou) and Western Ou (Xi'ou).[14] The names that local elite leadership chose for themselves were transcribed imperfectly into Sinitic script as Miao, a once derogatory term that included both Hmong communities and three unrelated ethnic groups, and the term Manyi, which referred to all indigenous peoples who resided south of the Central Plains.[15] The Sinitic court chronicles classified subgroups within these larger communities by cultural activities, such as the "White Dress Man" (Baiyi Man), the "Tattooed Face Man" (Xiumian Man), the "Gold Teeth Man" (Jinchi Man), the "Silver Teeth Man" (Yinchi Man), and the "Muong-dwelling Man" (Mang Man), among others, which would all today be classified as Tai-speaking groups. Nguyễn Chí Buyên writes that the Dao/Yao ethnic groups called themselves Kìm Mun or Kìm Mẫn (translated as "mountain people") and the Lolo ethnic group in the northern borderlands of Vietnam, classified in the PRC as Yi, called themselves Mùn Chí. Regarding the La Hụ ethnic group, La translates as "hunting" and Hụ as "tiger," so according to La Hụ legends, their ethnonym translates as "those who hunt tigers."[16] To understand this system of naming, we need to move beyond the preserved text as the sole authority and to reach out to other disciplines. As scholar of comparative literature and history Tamar Chin has written, "[We] now look to Chinese frontier archaeology to enrich, to decenter, and to positively correct the worldviews circumscribed by the classical Confucian canon."[17] More work gained from archaeological sites will further complicate the distinctions between the people occupying this region of the Dong World and outsiders who described these communities in court chronicles.

In this book I argue that trade allowed local elite within the Dong World to accrue political leverage with their lowland neighbors, and I begin with an overview of the network of trade known as the Southwest Silk Road. From earliest times, three main routes connected China with the outside world: overland routes that stretched across Eurasia from China to the Mediterranean, known collectively as the Silk Road; the Spice Trade shipping routes passing from the South China Sea into the Indian Ocean and beyond, known today as the Maritime Silk Road; and the Southwest Silk Road, a network of overland passages stretching from central China through the mountainous areas of Sichuan, Guizhou, and Yunnan into the eastern states of South Asia. Although the first two routes are better known to students of world history, the Southwestern Silk Road has a long ancestry and played a significant role in knitting the world together. Moreover, the Southwest Silk Road has remained relevant even through the present day with infrastructure projects under the umbrella of the Beijing-directed Belt and Road Initiative linking China to Mainland Southeast Asia through new rail, road, and maritime links.

The Southwest Silk Road connections between China and Southeast Asia reached a new peak in the Tang period, and these trade contacts would present new political challenges to the Tang court as it negotiated with the emergent Dong World power, the Nanzhao kingdom. The Nanzhao kingdom's center of power was in the lowland Erhai region, but it was buffered from its neighbors by mountainous terrain to the east and west, inhabited by unincorporated communities of ethnically non-Han peoples. The Nanzhao court benefited from its peripheral location as a political tributary of the Tang empire, while at the same time occupying a space just beyond the direct reach of the Tang state. Through tribute and trade with the Tang, Nanzhao leaders—and later, Dali leaders as well—expanded territorial authority in the face of local competition with their powerful Tibetan neighbor. These efforts also involved negotiations with smaller Dong World communities during this crucial period of change. Despite the emphasis in modern Chinese scholarship on this region's territorial bonds with central Chinese authorities, as expressed in modern nationalist narratives, there is ample evidence that states within the Dong World maintained their autonomy throughout this era.

The Dong World polities had an impact on emergent lowland regimes to its south as well. During two centuries of borderlands expansion by the Lý dynasty (1009–1225), the Đại Việt kingdom consolidated its independent status within the tributary order maintained by the Song empire, while strengthening its own authority on the periphery of the Dong World. When the Dali kingdom, a new political actor, emerged at the center of the Dong World, the Đại Việt coexisted with Dali, but not without periods of unrest. The fates of the two states became intertwined, especially after Đại Việt annexed Vị Long and other Dong World native prefectures, which directly bordered the Dali kingdom. Since a fixed border between Dali and Đại Việt could not be delineated, and numerous upland river communities of the Dong World occupied the boundary between the two states, this frontier ambiguity led to numerous border disputes. Yet the Dali kingdom maintained enough military power, due in part to the trade in war horses between the two states, to prevent the Đại Việt from launching a large-scale war similar to the Song's military build-up that led to the Song–Đại Việt border conflict (1075–1076). On the other side of this triangular relationship, the Đại Việt maintained authority in the borderlands region it shared with the Song. The Đại Việt leadership, unlike the Song, did not follow a center-periphery zonal arrangement, but instead maintained personalized "patron-client" relationships with each of its "satellite" partners along the frontier region. Vietnamese leaders were dependent on controlling the resources of the frontier, both material and human, for economic and political ends.[18] To achieve this control, Vietnamese leaders employed a combination of marriage alliances and military excursions to ensure their supremacy in the region.

In the lowland regimes' relations with local leaders within or on the periphery of the Dong World, trade, migrations, and social issues are intrinsically interrelated. Both Song and Đại Việt court officials ignored at their own peril the Dong World hierarchies of power and sources of regional tensions when they sought to keep the peace and maintain the flow of regional commerce. In various descriptions of encounters with local elites, Chinese authorities carried mental impressions formed by long-held stereotypes and conventions passed down by central courts through preimperial texts, the applicability of which to contemporary situations varied considerably. Details in various accounts show that these preconceived notions were rarely reinforced and often were questioned by Chinese officials posted to the empire's borderlands. Collaborating closely with local elites, using trade routes for the gathering of military intelligence, and depending on upland polities to further the aims of the distant Song court became an all-encompassing responsibility for local officials posted by Kaifeng and later Lin'an to the edges of the Dong World before the arrival of Mongol forces in the 1250s.

Differing borderlands policies on the eve of the Mongol conquest contributed to the survival of an intact Vietnamese polity and the dissolution of the Dali kingdom. The Dali court's treatment of peoples on its southeastern frontier areas differed from the Đại Việt court's relations during the Trần dynasty (1225–1400) with the inhabitants of its northern borderlands. While the Dali kingdom remained a state following the looser Southeast Asian political model, described by the historian O. W. Wolters as the mandala model, the neighboring Đại Việt kingdom was administered on the Chinese model after gaining its autonomy in the tenth century.[19] Under such conditions, local clan leaders received titles and ritual responsibilities within the political order prescribed by the court at Thăng Long. Eventually, borderlands peoples were granted strong enough positions within the general administration of the kingdom that these leaders remained loyal to the Trần court when it faced the series of invasions from combined Mongol and Chinese forces. The survival of the Trần in this period owes a great deal to the participation of its frontier allies. The fortunes of the elite Huang (Hoàng) clan, who were among the indigenous inhabitants of the Upper Tongking Gulf region straddling the regions claimed by both Vietnamese and Chinese authorities, improved with the emergence of Mongol military aggression along the Sino-Vietnamese frontier, as military service and local reconnaissance on behalf of the Song and Trần courts offered a new opportunity for heightened status.

Collectively, these components of the Dong World gave a coherence to the region, socially as well as politically, that persisted through Ming imperial expansion and Han Chinese settlement of the sixteenth and seventeenth centuries and the Qing abolishment of the *tusi* (local rule) system under the Yongzheng emperor in the eighteenth century. This region that intersected both East and Southeast Asia was not an anarchic zone of political escape, although the high mountain ranges separated one riverine valley settlement from another, and at higher elevations it provided space for communities who didn't wish to participate in the political arrangements of valley chieftains. This unified area of Eurasia survived its encounters with both northern and southern lowland regimes through trade and political negotiation, and a common pattern of engagement became a defining feature of the Dong World.

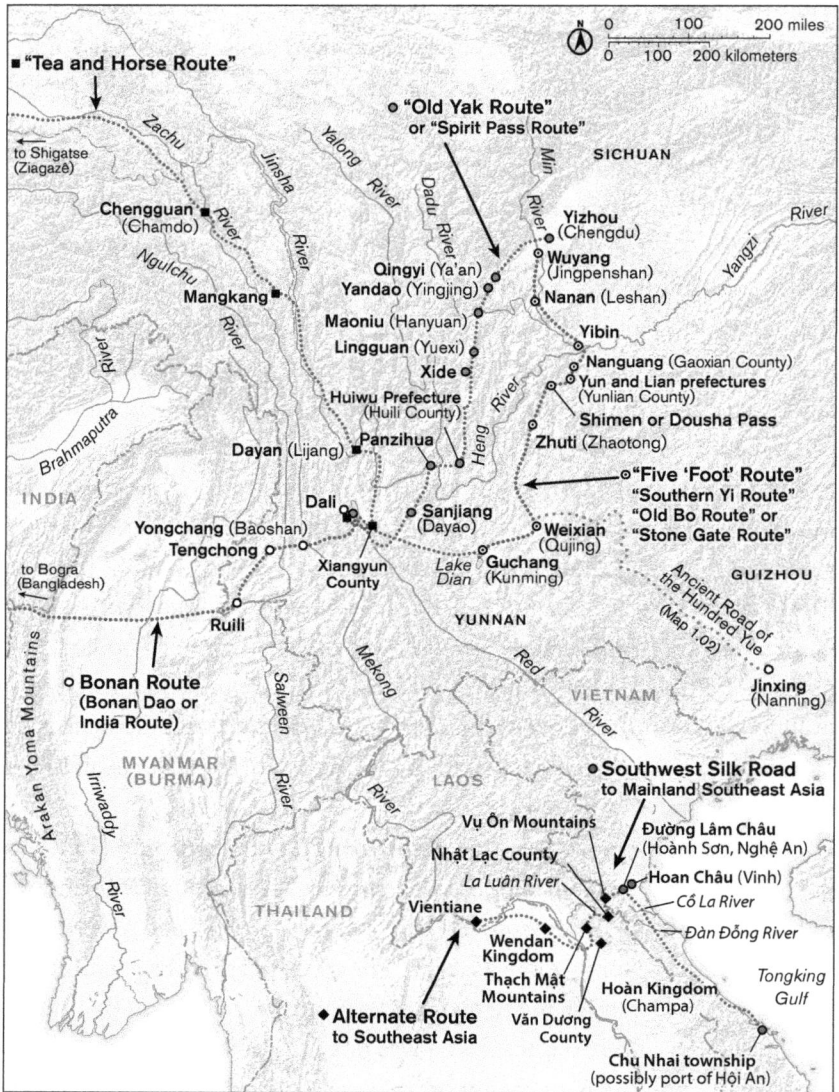

The Southwest Silk Road Region

ONE

THE SOUTHWEST SILK ROAD AND THE DONG WORLD

The Southwest Silk Road has a long ancestry and has played a key role in knitting the world together. Marco Polo wrote of his travels along the spur of this route into Tibet following the Mongol conquest of the Dali kingdom of Yunnan in the mid-thirteenth century.[1] The Southwest Silk Road also served as the site for numerous states located within the Dong World at the divide between modern-day East and South Asia. Some of these polities shared common characteristics. The roots of interaction between several regional centers of settlement and agricultural production, as well as trade flow, extend back into prehistory.

From earliest times, the riverine network of the Dong World shaped the movement of peoples through the region. Archaeological evidence in tombs along routes of communication documents the spread of elite Qiang culture.[2] Sites containing sarcophagi from the Qin-Han period extend from the eastern Tibet region to the plateau region of western Sichuan and the plateau of northwestern Yunnan in a north-south direction, following the Lancang River, the Jinsha River, the Dadu River, the Yalong River, and the Qingyi River.[3] It appears from these archaeological findings that in this period the frontier was expanding more rapidly from west to east and from the plateau to the lowlands, by way of certain river valleys, than it was receiving settlers from the east. However, the next stage in completing the east-west connections intersecting with the Yunnan region was not far in the future.

The Southwest Silk Road was also a critical point of contact between the two great civilizations of China and India, as well as a major conduit for the passage of east-west trade. Historian Bin Yang concluded that the southwestern route supported regional trade between China and India since at least the third century BCE, but that current archaeological evidence does not provide enough detail to confirm either the volume or specific nature of trade in this earlier period.[4] There is the oft-cited account from Sima Qian's (ca. 145–ca. 86 BCE) *Records of the Historian* (Shiji), in which Zhang Qian (d. 133 BCE), chief envoy of the Han emperor Wudi (r. 141–87 BCE), visited the region of Afghanistan—then known as Bactria (Daxia)—in 122 BCE. In Bactria, Zhang saw merchants from northern India (Shendu) peddling two trade articles from the Shu region (modern-day Sichuan): "Qiong bamboo poles" (*Qiongzhu zhang*) and "Shu brocade" (*Shujin*).[5] Zhang Qian concluded that there must be a direct trade route from Sichuan to India to the south, because northern routes were then in the hands of rival Qiang and Xiongnu forces.[6] Zhang's account is the first documented claim for such a route in the Chinese historical record.

Early efforts at the eastward expansion of the northern courts came in the form of military excursions, although the lasting impact of these military occupiers is now debated. The early third-century BCE arrival of the Chu kingdom (ca. 1030–223 BCE) general Zhuang Qiao (ca. 325–270 BCE) and his army is described in the court chronicles as having a major influence on the political and cultural developments in the Yunnan region of the southwest, although many scholars have questioned the existence of this historical figure, attributing his achievements to multiple local actors.[7] Zhuang Qiao allegedly led an army into the western Chu commandary of Ba (modern-day Sichuan) and then south to the area around Lake Dian (Dian Chi) in central Yunnan, where he established himself as the ruler of the Dian kingdom. The first recorded contact between authorities from central China and the Dong World elite, in this case the leadership of the Yelang kingdom, occurred when the state of Chu ordered Zhuang Qiao to lead his military expedition into this region.[8] Historian John Herman argues that the "purpose of this expedition was to prevent the kingdom of Qin, Chu's main rival to the north, from annexing the Ba and Yelang kingdoms for itself."[9] Chu legends credit Zhuang Qiao with creating the conditions for dynastic power to emerge in later centuries by encouraging outside migration into the area and by introducing Chu practices to the local people. By the eleventh century in the Song period, Chinese scholars would go as far as to claim that all native inhabitants residing west of Lake Dian were descendants of Zhuang Qiao. Zhuang, or those persons associated with his legend, may have had some involvement in shaping the culture and society of the settlements around Lake Dian, but the actual extent of his influence remains unknown. More recent scholarship argues a quite different pattern of engagement. Herman writes that "despite repeated attempts by Chinese historians to portray the military campaigns launched by the Qin (221–206 BCE) and Han (206 BCE–220 CE) dynasties into the southwest as proof that the region had come under China's geopolitical control by the beginning of the third century CE, it now appears that the indigenous peoples were able to withstand the various Qin and Han military campaigns and remained largely independent of Chinese political control until at least the eighth century."[10] Rather than filling a political void with an established kingdom, Zhuang Qiao likely stepped into an existing political order, which made room for his participation without being wholly transformed by his presence.

Court chronicles claim that during the rule of Emperor Han Wudi (Liu Che; 156 BCE–87 BCE) the Dali area was opened, along with Sichuan, to direct administration by the northern court. In 120 BCE, the Han court established settlements around Kunming Lake (Kunming Chi) and extended its influence over the region along the Dian River (Dian He). The Han military attempted to wield influence over the region from modern-day Chengdu through today's Yunnan by building up and maintaining two official routes. The first was from Chengdu across Hanyuan, Xichang, Yao'an, Dali, and on to modern-day Myanmar. This route was called the Spirit Pass Route (Lingguan Dao). The other route extended from Chengdu through Yibin and Qujing to Kunming and then continued south to northern Vietnam (Giao Chỉ). This route was called the Five "Foot" Route (Wuchi Dao). Han interest in the trade routes crossing southwest China increased after Han Wudi's successful invasion of the Nam Việt kingdom, a territory that extended from modern-day Guangzhou to the Red River Delta in Vietnam, in 111 BCE. After taking control of and reorganizing the Nam Việt territory into commandaries, the Han court did the same for the region to the northwest of the former Dian kingdom, forming the Zangke, Yueqiong, Yizhou, Shenli, and Wenshan commandaries.[11] These territories were reorganized, according to Han historian Ban Gu, in part to regain access to trade routes to Bactria. Shortly after the establishment of these five commandaries, a local rebellion cut off Han contact with the area until the court launched a military expedition to quell the rebels. The attack resulted in the slaughter of thousands of local inhabitants, but Han territorial administration remained spotty and uncertain.

Some local leaders continued to cooperate with Han representatives and began to adapt to the political norms of the outside authorities. In this period under Han influence, Kunming (actually referring to the Dali area at this time) was an important local administrative center.[12] Initial influence over the area remained in the hands of local families, and distant Han chroniclers even referred to the region as a separate kingdom, Kunmi, administered by the Kunming indigenes. As historian Charles Patterson Giersch writes, local chiefs eventually accepted the notion that "indigenous rulers might be recognized as imperial officials (an idea that was crucial over the long term)."[13] After reexerting influence in the region, the Han court also opened relations with neighboring kingdoms. In 94 CE the court of Emperor Han Hedi (r. 88–105) received a tribute mission from "beyond Yongchang" (modern-day Baoshan) that offered rhinos and elephants as their gifts.[14] Yongchang, once part of the Ailao kingdom (69–478 CE), had been established as a Han commandary in 69 CE, marking the outer limits of Han influence over the southwest. During the Eastern Han in 43 CE a rebellion broke out among local peoples including the Dongcan of Yizhou (modern-day Jinning County, Yunnan). The Han court responded by sending General Liu Shang (d. 47 BCE) to quell the revolt.[15]

The regional market for Dong World trade items continued to grow. Qiong bamboo (*Qiongzhuea tumidissinoda*) was first grown in Qiongdu, which is today part of Xichang, a town in Sichuan that is now better known for satellite launches than it is for bamboo. Shu brocade was a variety of woven silk cloth, or, as other scholars argue, a type of linen that had been produced in Sichuan since the Warring States period (475–221 BCE), at which time it was already widely imitated.[16] Following Zhang Qian's discovery of its trade in Bactria, domestic trade in Shu brocade continued to grow. The Han emperor Chengdi (r. 32–7 BCE) ordered that Yizhou (near modern Chengdu) officials collect and transport three years' worth of taxes in local Shu brocade to produce seven fully finished brocade robes.[17] From the fall of the Han through the establishment of the Sui (581–618 CE), most of China suffered from periodic turmoil that affected local economic production. However, the Xichuan region was largely unaffected by the interregional fighting, and brocade production continued mostly unabated. During the Tang, the central court continued to accept cloth brocade as tribute (*gongjin*) from Sichuan, and a market for Shu brocade could still be found in the "Western Regions" (Xiyu), including modern-day Xinjiang and other parts of Central Asia.

Along with Qiong bamboo and Sichuan brocade, other local products such as Shu ironware and cinnabar could be found along the Southwest Silk Road routes as far west as India and Afghanistan. West Asian, Indian, and Burmese glassware, gemstones, and pearls were the primary products that made their way into China as imports. The specific trade articles of the Southwest Silk Road contributed to the definition of the network itself, emphasizing certain trade routes over others. Yunnan shared the mineral wealth of northern Myanmar (Burma) as a location rich in gold, silver, tin, lead, and copper deposits, among other minerals.[18] However, interregional exchanges were not limited to luxury commodities. Guanghan, located to the south of Chengdu, is the site of the ancient Sanxingdui bronze culture that flourished as it borrowed from southern China to the east and the various non-Han kingdoms to the south, while remaining distinct from the Anyang bronze culture of the North China Plain.[19]

In addition to trade, official corruption went hand in hand with other exchanges along the Southwest Silk Road. After the Guizhou (modern-day Guilin) governor (*dudu*) Li Hongjie's death in 634, his family started to sell pearls from their private collection. When the Tang ruler Taizong heard about this, he issued a declaration from his court, saying: "During the life of this person, the high officials all maintained that he was a pure and honest official. His family members today are already selling pearls.

Are those officials involved indeed innocent of any crime? We must investigate this matter completely!"[20] The Tang court defended the actions of this scholar's dependents, but Taizong was not completely mollified. As a contemporary court scholar Wu Jing (670–749) noted about this episode, temptation proved to be too strong for Li's clan when "the storm put strong grass to the test and tarnished the record of an honest official."[21] Local abuse of positions of power would confound both Chinese and Vietnamese authorities throughout the period under study in this book. Such excesses were treated as a cost of administering a state.

Traveling the Road

The route that travelers have taken through history is a complex web of mountain footpaths and riverside trails, but the general layout of the main arteries have been recorded in the historical sources. The Southwest Silk Road in the east began in Sichuan's modern capital of Chengdu. This route, known as the India Route (Shendu Guo Dao) or the Old Sichuan-Yunnan-Myanmar-India Route (Chuan-Dian-Mian-Yin Gudao), split into two main branches as it passed through Sichuan into Yunnan (see appendix 1). Ya'an, located beside the Min River, also linked Southwest Silk Road merchants with the Tea and Horse Route (Chama Dao) to Tibet, an important offshoot of the Southwest Silk Road. The tea and horse trade was important, signifying a strong reciprocal relationship between China and its neighbors; Tibetans desired tea for use in meditation and for nutrition, while war horses were vital to the Chinese dealing with aggressive nomadic cavalries to the north.[22] The shortest route between India and China by the Song period (960–1279) was through Tibet.[23] Along these routes travelers carried on trade in Buddhist religious articles through the eleventh century before regional unrest with neighboring seminomadic states caused periodic disruptions.[24] For travelers engaged in trade with Southeast Asian and South Asian centers, the route proceeded southward away from these Tibetan linkages. From Ya'an merchants and pilgrims traveled upstream along the Jinsha River, winding in a southerly direction through a system of river valleys to Qiongdu, the ancient site of Shu brocade, and finally southwest to Dali on Lake Erhai, the seat of political power for the Dali kingdom.

From Dali, one took one of three routes to cross through modern-day Myanmar on the way to present-day India. These routes were collectively known as the Bonan Route (Bonan Dao) or the Yongchang Route (Yongchang Dao) in the Han period, and the Western Dian–Tianzhu Route (Xidian-Tianzhu Dao) in the Tang. The most traveled of these routes left Dali and proceeded south past the former garrison town of Baoshan, through the rolling hills around Ruili, and across the modern Myanmar border. Ruili remains one of the most trafficked border-crossing towns. From this point the route passed by Mogok, a town known for its gemstones, and the ancient temple-filled capitals of Bagan and Pyè, across the Arakan Yoma mountain range in western Myanmar, through modern India's easternmost state of Assam, to Bogra in Bangladesh, and finally to the river plains of the Ganges.

Another spur of the Southwest Silk Road connected China's southwest to Mainland Southeast Asia and southward along the Malay Peninsula. The Northern Song scholar Ouyang Xiu's (1007–1072) account in his *New Tang History* (Xin Tang shu) describes several general routes along the peninsula. On one route traders traveled two days east from Hoan Châu (modern-day Nghệ An Province in Vietnam) to Đường Lâm Prefecture's An Viễn County, heading south and crossing the Cồ La River; another two days brought traders to the banks of the Đàn Đồng River, which marked the frontier of the Cham-led Hoàn kingdom (located in modern-day south-central Vietnam). Travelers reached Chu Nhai and Đơn Bồ townships (which is possibly the modern port of Hội An) after four more days, and then arrived at the capital of the Hoàn kingdom two days after that.[25] An alternate route southwest from the lower Red River Delta passed over the Vụ Ôn Mountains to Nhật Lạc County in Đường Prefecture, across La Luân River, the Thạch Mật Mountains, and Văn Dương County before reaching the Wendan kingdom, located in the region between the modern-day Laotian capital of Vientiane and the Thai border province of Nong Khai.[26] From the Wendan kingdom one could travel south overland to a number of port city-states located on the southern Malay Peninsula as far as the Kunlun kingdom, as it was called in Tang sources, a collection of trading ports, which would later be incorporated into the maritime empire of Sri Vijaya (fl. eighth to twelfth centuries).[27]

Ouyang Xiu's account in *New Tang History* described the most important spur of the Southwest Silk Road as a product of the Three Kingdoms military commander Zhuge Liang's (181–234) entry into the region. According to this account,

> one route begins at the Zhuge Liang garrison and extends to the Teng-chong garrison two hundred *li* to the west, and then further west one hundred *li* to the Mi garrison. Proceeding east across the mountains another two hundred *li* to the Lishui garrison. Subsequently crossing the Lishui and Longquanshui rivers, in two hundred *li* one reaches the Anxi garrison. Continuing further west one crosses the Ninuojiang-shui River in one thousand *li* and reaches the Daqin Poluomen kingdom. Further west one crosses the Dudaling mountains and in three hundred *li* one reaches the Gemeilu kingdom on the northern periphery of "Eastern India" [Dong Tianzhu]. Proceeding southwest for another 1,200 *li*, one arrives at the Pundravardhara [Benna Fatanna] kingdom on the northwest periphery of "Central India" [Zhong Tiandu], which connects to the Pyu kingdom and the Brahmin Route [Puluomen Lu].[28]

Ouyang Xiu regarded this route to be product of the expansion of empire into the western frontier areas through its military representatives in a series of garrisons. Two-way exchanges were not highlighted in this picture of the Tang empire's periphery.

Trade relations had long been active in the Dong World region that extended from Southwest China and Mainland Southeast Asia to the shores of the Indian Ocean, and economic exchange often included political interaction between the polities that emerged along these trade routes. The Shan kingdom was an important Dong World state along the Southwest Silk Road during the Han dynasty.[29] Located on the edges of Yongchang commandary, the kingdom covered an area that bridges modern-day western Yunnan, northern Thailand, and northeastern Myanmar. The kingdom's rulers sent tribute on numerous occasions throughout the Han period. The Shan ruler Yong Youdiao (?–?) sent envoys on three occasions to the Eastern Han court in 97 CE, in 120, and again in 131, to establish and maintain good relations with the Han leadership.[30] For the next 120 years, the Shan and Han courts maintained this relationship, which involved numerous contacts both commercial and diplomatic. The Shan kingdom further connected Han rulers to the kingdoms of South Asia. These states included the Shan-dominated Dalhi (Dunrenyi) kingdom, located in the western region of modern-day Myanmar. This kingdom provided an important economic link with markets that would by the Song period become part of the powerful Pagan kingdom. In 94 CE the ruler, known in *The History of the Later Han Dynasty* (Hou Han shu) as Mo Tingmo, sent a tribute mission to the Eastern Han court, including a rhinoceros and an elephant.[31] Farther west was the Panyue kingdom, located in the modern-day Indian province of Assam. The first of the major Assam kingdoms, Panyue lasted from 350 CE to 1140. The Northern Song scholar Li Fang (925–996) noted that from the Han through the Jin of the Six Dynasties period the Panyue kingdom provided an important conduit for trade passing from South Asia to markets within central China.[32] Panyue's closest neighbor was the South Asian kingdom identified by the famous Tang monk Xuan Zang as Kāmarūpa (Jiamolǔbo) in modern-day Bangladesh.[33] Kāmarūpa, located in western Assam, developed early cultural exchanges with Chinese courts. The Kāmarūpa elite were formally Brahmans, but Buddhism and Hinduism mixed into their religious practices, as was the case for other communities in this region.[34] Ouyang Xiu in *New Tang History* described the landscape beyond this point as "rugged" (*ban xian*), and trade routes turned south here to link with the Indian Ocean network through the region of modern-day Myanmar.[35]

Cultural Exchanges

Religious teachings traveled the Southwest Silk Road routes as well. Chinese Daoism may have exerted an early influence on communities as far west as Kāmarūpa. Some scholars have even argued that Daoist principles had an influence on the development of Indian esoteric teachings.[36] However, this notion that elements of Indian Tantrism originated outside of South Asia has its critics.[37] Historians David Gray and Ryan Overby argue that Indian Tantric practices emerged in north Indian society before they were transmitted rapidly to Southeast, East, and Central Asia.[38] In a related point of cross-cultural exchange, the French Orientalist Paul Pelliot once claimed that the Chinese court during the reign of Tang Taizong (599–649) ordered that the central Daoist text *Daode Jing* be translated into Sanskrit at the request of Kāmarūpa's ruler.[39] The Tang envoy Wang Xuance (?–?) in early 648 purportedly presented this Daoist text in translation to the Kāmarūpa royal court, although the accuracy of this account has recently been questioned.[40] The monk Xuan Zang may have participated, quite unwillingly, in this translation project.[41]

There is much controversy surrounding the earliest arrival of Buddhism on the Southwest Silk Road. Several prominent Chinese scholars concluded in the 1980s that the arrival of Buddhism along the overland route through southwest China predated its spread into the Central China Plain.[42] This bit of historical revisionism now seems premature, as archaeological evidence indicates that the overland Southwest Silk Road was only connected by the Eastern Han period, after Buddhist pilgrims had already crossed into the Han empire to the north. Nonetheless, in areas of Sichuan and Yunnan one can see evidence of Buddhist statuary produced by pilgrims who arrived early in the Common Era.[43] Almost all scholars agree that after the third century CE Buddhist pilgrims traveling along southwestern routes to and from South Asian centers of Buddhist learning increased, thereby creating cultural overlaps of historical significance.[44]

Buddhism entered southwest China by several different routes, and the three leading schools of Buddhist thought—Theravada, Mahayana, and Tibetan—all made their presence felt along different spurs of the Southwest Silk Road. The kingdoms of Nanzhao and Dali in turn absorbed elements of all three traditions. As mentioned earlier, the northeastern region of South Asia around Assam produced the original Tantric Buddhist teachings that spread to Tibet by way of the tea and horse trade routes into northwestern Yunnan.[45] Theravada teachings spread along maritime routes and through northern Mainland Southeast Asia into southern and central Yunnan. The southwest border region of Sipsongpannā has long practiced Theravada Buddhism, although this particular school may not predate the early Ming dynasty.[46] Mahayana teachings came into eastern Yunnan from China and northern Vietnam. Buddhism had a profound effect on the political states that emerged along the Southwest Silk Road before the period of Mongol conquest. Both the Nanzhao and the later Dali rulers of Yunnan enhanced their authority and political control with notions of Buddhist kingship.

Religious affairs could also cloak political intentions among states in this region. According to Burmese historical records, there was a tale of how the Pagan (1044–1287) ruler Anawrahta (1014–1077) led his armies north to the Dali kingdom. In response Dali troops assembled on the city wall to defend the Dali citadel and the ruling family. Anawrahta was unable to attack the city and achieve his goal of seizing from the Dali court the holy relic of a tooth of the Buddha (*foya*). One account stated that he instead received a replica of the relic and withdrew his troops. Another account stated that Anawrahta received only a jade Buddha statue before he returned to Pagan.[47] Anawrahta commanded a large military force, and his approach to Dali followed two routes, one over land and the other by water. He had previously appeared before the Dali ruler in the same manner seeking Buddhist scriptures, when this was actually an attempt to request tribute from Dali.[48] Historian Li Xiaomei argues that Anawrahta did so, on the one hand, to seek revenge on behalf of Pagan for past humiliations the kingdom had faced.[49] On the other hand, the primary reason for this approach was to prevent Dali interference when he sought to conquer the Tai-speaking Shan kingdom (actually, a confederation of chiefdoms) east of Pagan. Anawrahta planned on taking a route back to Pagan to cross through the Shan kingdom, and to accept the allegiances of the Shan chiefs. As noted earlier in this chapter, the territory of the Shan kingdom spanned what is now Myanmar, as well as parts of China, and the territory controlled by the Gold Teeth (Jinchi) Shan included Baoshan, Dehong, Gengma, Menglian, and Banna, which is today the home region of China's Dai national minority. In this sense, Anawrahta's strategic military objective is similar to the approach used by the earlier Nanzhao court when it divided these small Shan polities into spheres of influence.[50] Anawrahta successfully achieved this objective, demonstrated by the fact that the Pagan dynasty was subsequently unified and began to grow, while the Dali influence in the region was gradually fading.

Ethnic Dimensions of the Southwest Silk Road

Meng Gong (1195–1246), a military commander in the late Southern Song who played a significant role in the First Song-Mongol War (1235–1241), submitted a short policy suggestion to the court to address conditions the Song empire faced in managing open communication with the Dali kingdom. The single most important factor was human. As Meng reported to the throne,

> When envoys arrive at Yongzhou from the Dali kingdom, these envoys have traveled through several thousand *li* occupied by various separate [*gejue*] tribes [*buluo*].[51] Today we must select local representatives across several regions, in order to rule over the "raw" indigenes [*shengyi*], creating a strategically precarious situation. To oversee this situation properly, it is important to establish mountain pass garrisons staffed by local militia, where we store grain and gather hay. Thereby the fame and power of the empire is spread, and the prestige of the state resonates through the region. If we of the court do not plan to act in this manner, the word will get out and there will be no way for us to receive anything from taxes or grain tribute.[52]

Communications with the Dali kingdom, which was a vital source of the horses the Song cavalry needed to defend against the relentless expansion of Mongol forces around the empire, were conducted through a series of negotiations with intermediaries. Meng Gong understood the uncertain nature of these negotiations with local chiefs, where humanitarian and military means were all employed to gain the participation of local power-brokers with imperial authorities. Interaction with these local communities was the only gateway on the road to Dali for the Song court.

Although the specific terms of authority and power in premodern times varied from community to community in the Dong World, there existed some common notions that extended across the region. The basic unit of social and political organization was the clan. Anthropologists of other regions of the world have defined clan as "an exclusive, boundary-maintaining group which allows no cross-cutting relations."[53] However, clans in this region of Asia pursued many strategies for expanding their ranks, including marriage alliances and "voting with one's feet" through regional migration. Much of the population of the Dong World lived in clan-based villages, the activities of which were structured by the environment and material resources of their location. The rugged nature of the southwest dictated that many villages were given poor conditions for subsistence solely on agriculture. James Scott has recently argued that the infertile nature of the upland region had a political impact, and this area he refers to as "Zomia" became a place of refuge from the dominant political centers of the riverine valleys and lowlands.[54] However, this blanket description of the region misses the particularly strong political traditions in place for generations. These villages supplemented farming with trade, or existed as trading nodes along the different spurs of the Southwest Silk Road. Precisely because of this reliance on trade, cross-regional and interregional political affiliations were quite common, as I will describe here.

The clan system depended on chiefs, the "great man" (*da renwu*) positions of authority that prevailed as markers of leadership into the modern era. From afar, court observers of the Dong World communities knew little about these individual leaders. What was known was attributed to the region as a whole. Separating borderlands peoples into "raw" (*sheng*) and "cooked" (*shu*)—depending on each community's willingness to submit to court authority—distant Chinese courts often engaged these designated chiefs when negotiating matters of local administration without attempting to understand the basis for their power. The personal name of an early chief was often used by Chinese chroniclers to refer to the entire community of indigenous people under his control.[55] Heads of households held sway over their families, but chiefs (*touren*) from a ruling clan had power over the whole community in matters of locating settlements, collective production activities for sustaining the community, the cultivation and collection of food, the patrolling of the settlement and the guarding of outlying territories maintained by the village, the production of clothing, the caring for the elderly, the education of the young, and so on.[56] Chiefs served as mediators of family and community disputes and as shamans that intervened in times of illness or personal distress. The Chinese legal scholar Shi Di notes that the Tai-speaking Bouyei people of southern Guizhou at times organized clan meetings, the purpose of which was to settle family disputes or to assist with divisions of inheritance among the deceased sons and daughters.[57]

The nature of power in the community varied, but overall, for those persons within the ruling clan, authority was accrued through one's age and experience. The strength of collective leadership varied by ethnic group in the region; some communities identified leaders with actual influence over several villages, while others granted active authority only to village heads. The headsmen appear to have ruled effectively over an ethnically diverse population, but the nature of the actual "grassroots" village leadership is not obvious from the existing sources. One cannot easily apply a single model of state formation to the region covered by the Dong World. The process of self-definition and cultural formation among these communities depended as well on forces originating well beyond this region. The spiritual dimension of authority also requires examination. As Shi Di has argued, many of these chiefs, whether men or women, became "half human, half deity" (ban ren ban shen) in the eyes of their community.[58] In a long-standing and still-present practice in the early 2000s, shamans held leadership roles among the Hmong (Miao) of Sichuan and also acted as the guardians of the community's cultural heritage.[59]

From outside of the Dong World, Song court descriptions of its indigenous communities were often moralizing and based in interpretations of ritual behavior. The "Five Barbarian clans" (Wu Xing Fan) was the collective name given to the five local elite communities in the territory of modern-day Guizhou. Describing the invited guests at a New Year's banquet at court, Meng Yuanlao (fl. 1120s) noted that "there were Five Barbarian clans, and they all wore top-knots bound with black felt as monks do."[60] The *Song State Compendium* (Song huiyao) recorded that on the eleventh day of the seventh month of the seventh year of the Shenzong emperor's

Yuanfeng reign period (1085), the Ministry of Ritual issued a decree, stating, "For the Southwest barbarians arriving at court with tribute, the old protocol need not be observed. If we allow the delegation to present their tribute, we ask that the court allow for this precedent of the Five Barbarian clans."[61] Shenzong's court allowed for this exception, as his court had for other tribute emissaries who introduced unorthodox ritual practices as an example of venerable traditions from their own rulers.[62] Acceptance of these unorthodox practices by the Song leadership was in part due to the Song court's need to maintain smooth trade relations that passed through this economically strategic region of the Dong World.

Routes Radiating Out from the Ancient Road of the One Hundred Yue/Việt

An important section of the Southwest Silk Road linked the settlements of China's southwest with the maritime trade of Island Southeast Asia and the Indian Ocean network beyond. In Song sources this spur is known as the Ancient Road of the One Hundred Yue/Việt (Bai Yue Gudao). Here, the link with rulers and frontier subjects of the Đại Việt kingdom became increasingly important by the end of the Song period. Along the main travel routes from Guangxi to Yunnan, there were numerous local chiefs who either facilitated or hindered trade activity. Taking a closer look at the main routes between the markets of the south China coastline and the horse traders of the Ziqi kingdom (1100–1260), we can better understand the complex network of relationships that lay at the heart of this region. As Zhou Qufei notes in the twelfth-century text *Notes from the Land beyond the Passes* (Lingwai daida), to make contact between the Middle Kingdom (Zhongguo) and the Southern Indigenes (Nanman) one had to begin the journey at the Song empire's westernmost projection of authority, the Hengshan garrison (Hengshan zhai) of Yongzhou Prefecture, now located off the modern-day Route 324 in Pingma Township, Baise City, Tiandong County.[63] From the Hengshan garrison, one followed the path of the Right River upstream for one day's travel to several indigenously administered "loose rein" (*jimi*) prefectures in succession, each of which maintained

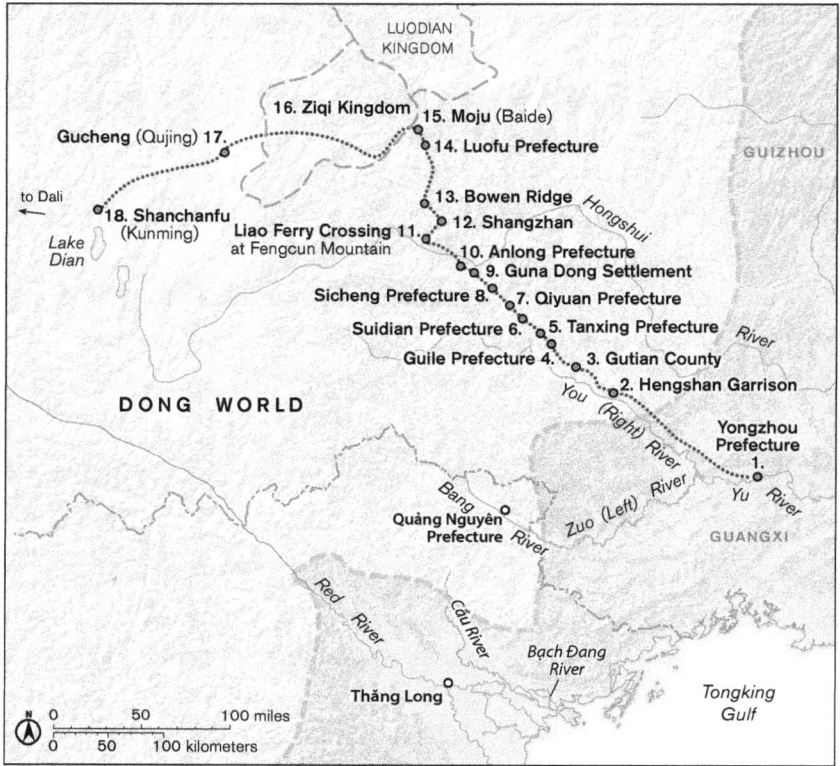

LUODIAN KINGDOM

16. Ziqi Kingdom 15. Moju (Baide)

Gucheng (Qujing) 17. 14. Luofu Prefecture

GUIZHOU

to Dali

18. Shanchanfu (Kunming) 13. Bowen Ridge *Hongshui*

Liao Ferry Crossing 11. 12. Shangzhan

Lake Dian at Fengcun Mountain 10. Anlong Prefecture

9. Guna Dong Settlement

Sicheng Prefecture 8. 7. Qiyuan Prefecture

Suidian Prefecture 6. 5. Tanxing Prefecture *River*

Guile Prefecture 4. 3. Gutian County

DONG WORLD *You (Right) River* 2. Hengshan Garrison

Yongzhou Prefecture 1.

Bang Yu *River* GUANGXI

Quảng Nguyên Prefecture *Zuo (Left) River*

Red River *Cầu River*

Bạch Đang River

Thăng Long Tongking Gulf

N 0   50   100 miles

0   50   100 kilometers

The Ancient Road of the One Hundred Yue Region

some influence over the flow of trade. According to Zhou Qufei, the caravan from Dali to the market at Tiandong followed two routes, one to the northwest and the other in a southwest direction (see appendix 1).

■

Another important but underexamined aspect of trade throughout greater Asia is the connection between maritime and overland trade. Overland trade routes were often complemented by sea routes; the two types of networks worked in tandem. Between 750 CE and 1000 CE, Arab traders from the Caliphate in Baghdad could travel by sea from the Persian Gulf through the Indian Ocean to the South China Sea or cross by land through former Sogdian territory into China's western region. The settlements of Arab traders in Sri Lanka in this period resulted in the connection of long-distance trade between the Persian Gulf region and China's southern seaport of Nanhai (Guangzhou).[64] Farther west along the south China coast was Hepu, often described as the maritime gateway for merchants traveling to or from the easternmost sections of the overland Southwest Silk Road.[65] Along the way several seaports acted as starting points for northerly connections to the prevailing East-West overland routes that flourished when inland empires were at peace; in turn, these gave way to sea routes when the peace was lost. One such hybrid maritime-overland route involved Indian Ocean traders crossing the Bay of Bengal to land at the mouth of the Irrawaddy River and load or unload cargo that traveled the river valleys north to the southern spur of the Southwest Silk Road mentioned earlier.[66]

Such trade links fit well into the general trend of "Southernization" described by Lynda Shaffer in world historical terms, as Indian Ocean trade by Arab, South Asian, and Southeast Asian seafarers created alternate routes for the twelfth-century East-West circulation of goods between south China and the Mediterranean region.[67] The important role maritime links played in sustaining overland routes through northern Southeast Asia into China's southern borderlands until the end of the Song dynasty should not be ignored, just as we must keep in mind the complementary role played by the Southwest Silk Road in global connections.

As we continue to examine the relationship between the two (albeit constructed) entities, the "Southwest Silk Road" and the "Dong World," we see how the circulation of commodities and ideas flowing through the region in turn provided shape to this space, not as an "anarchistic" zone of individual refuge, but as a patchwork of smaller communities and polities interacting and competing within a rugged landscape set between the lowlands centers of power on its periphery.

TWO
THE NANZHAO AND DALI KINGDOMS AS MULTIETHNIC STATES

In a steep mountain valley in the northeast corner of Dali Prefecture, modern-day Yunnan, lies Stone Gate Pass (Shimen Guan). This former landmark on the Southwest Silk Road was renamed in the Qing era as Dousha Pass (Dousha Guan).[1] A historical marker can still be found in modern-day Yanjin County, in the southern foothills of Dali Mountain (Dali Shan), alongside an elevated stretch of highway that parallels the ancient trade route along the western bank of the Guan River (Guan He). This particular passage was known in the Qin era as the Five "Foot" Route, and was later called the Ancient Dian and Bo (Peoples) Route (Dianbo Gudao) during the Han dynasty. It passed through a volatile region, and was the site of imperial expansion and local resistance up through the era of Mongol conquest. Both the first Qin emperor (Qinshihuang; 259–210 BCE) and the Han emperor Wudi (r. 141–87 BCE) fought in vain to conquer the pass and gain influence over their southwestern frontiers. In 794 CE Tang authorities marked their reentry into the region through an alliance with the Nanzhao kingdom, leaving a cliff-face inscription at Stone Gate Pass. Following the fall of the Dali kingdom, Marco Polo reportedly traveled through the pass with his Mongol escorts during his excursion into southwest China. Trade in pu'er tea through Stone Gate Pass may date back to the Tang period, but stronger evidence for this trade begins with the period of Ming conquests in the southwest.[2] Stone Gate Pass was important locally as the primary point of trade contact between the indigenous peoples of the Guizhou and Yunnan regions. It was also a vital entry point into the northeastern region of the Dong World.

The Tang dynasty is well-known as one of the most cosmopolitan and outward-looking eras in Chinese history. Particularly in its earliest decades, the confident and secure central court attracted the attention of political and cultural forces across Eurasia. Only after the near collapse of the dynasty during the An Lushan (the Chinese reading of the Sogdian name Roχšan) Uprising in 755 did the Tang leadership begin to withdraw inward and break many of the ties forged with societies beyond the Sinitic cultural core. In addition to political and cultural connections forged along the northern overland Silk Road routes, the Tang court had contact with the kingdoms on the empire's southwestern frontier, including the Nanzhao kingdom (653–903), located in modern-day Yunnan.

Modern scholars have often suggested that the Nanzhao kingdom was unable to sustain itself as an independent state, and therefore this region had always been in some sense an extension of the Chinese empire.[3] I don't fully accept this conventional view of Sino-Nanzhao relations, but I agree that the accepted interpretation has merit. This vision of a dependent Nanzhao, however, must be tempered with the "border-crossing" way that other local leaders in the region of modern-day Yunnan negotiated their political positions along the frontier routes of commerce and pilgrimage (primarily Buddhist) during the Tang and Song periods. The Nanzhao court benefited from its peripheral location as a political tributary of the Tang empire, while at the same time occupying a space just beyond the direct reach of the Tang state. Through tribute and trade with the Tang, the Nanzhao leaders supported efforts to expand territorial authority in the face of local competition with its powerful Tibetan neighbor. These efforts also involved negotiations with Dong World frontier communities during a crucial period of change in the history of China's southwestern frontier.

The diverse ethnic composition of the Dong World region through which the Southwest Silk Road passed defies easy characterization. Chinese ethnographers have divided the upland peoples of the region into the following eight groups: Achang, Bulang (Palaung), Hani (Akha), Jinuo, Jingpo (Kachin), Lahu, Lisu, and Wa.[4] These groups self-identified in many different ways, and were often in communities ruled by Tai-speaking lowland

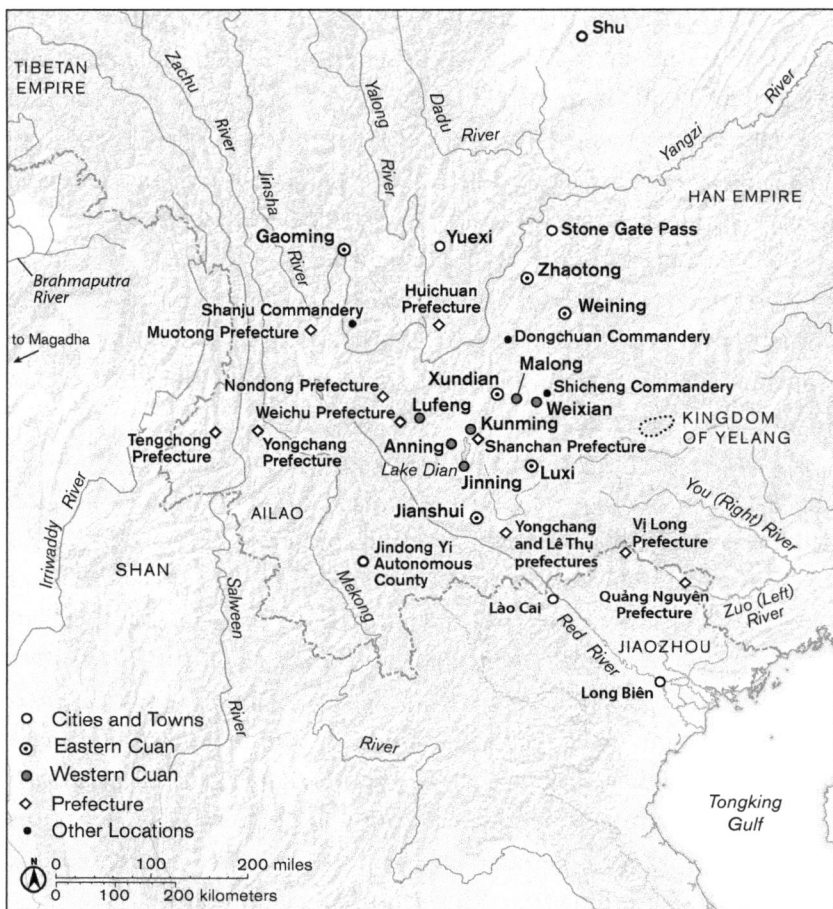

TIBETAN EMPIRE

Zachu River

Yalong River

Jinsha River

Dadu River

Brahmaputra River

to Magadha

HAN EMPIRE

Yangzi River

Shu

Stone Gate Pass

Gaoming

Yuexi

Zhaotong

Weining

Shanju Commandery

Huichuan Prefecture

Muotong Prefecture

Dongchuan Commandery

Malong

Nondong Prefecture

Xundian

Shicheng Commandery

Weichu Prefecture

Lufeng

Weixian

Tengchong Prefecture

Yongchang Prefecture

Kunming

Anning

Shanchan Prefecture

KINGDOM OF YELANG

Lake Dian

Jinning

Luxi

AILAO

Jianshui

Yongchang and Lê Thụ prefectures

Vị Long Prefecture

You (Right) River

SHAN

Jindong Yi Autonomous County

Lào Cai

Quảng Nguyên Prefecture

Zuo (Left) River

Red River

JIAOZHOU

Long Biên

Irriwaddy River

Salween River

Mekong River

River

Tongking Gulf

○ Cities and Towns
◎ Eastern Cuan
● Western Cuan
◇ Prefecture
• Other Locations

0   100   200 miles
0   100   200 kilometers

The Early Dong World Era (to the tenth century)

elite. Tai-speakers from Yunnan and farther east into modern-day Guizhou and Guangxi played important roles in both trade and political activity in this region in the Tang and Song periods.[5] These Tai groups formed the local elite of the Southwest Silk Road in cooperation with communities of Han settlers who relocated to the region through military campaigns beginning in the Qin-Han period and later with Zhuge Liang (181–234) in the Three Kingdoms (San Guo) period (220–280). Eventually, the Mongols and later the Ming-appointed frontier authorities would weaken, but not eliminate, the collective influence of these Tai elite.

Rulers and high officials at Chinese courts, including the Tang, preferred trade in the Southwest Silk Road region, where vassal kingdoms displayed much less aggression than did their northern counterparts, and rare commodities could be obtained while observing tributary protocol. By the late Tang period, travel from the Pyu city states (ca. second century BCE–ca. 1050) of Upper Burma to the Dali marketplace took approximately seventy-one days; travel from Dali to Chengdu took seventy-five days.[6] Merchants traveled mostly on foot while goods were transported by mules, oxen, or horses.[7] Traders likely did not travel the entire length of these routes, as evidence from later periods demonstrates, but instead focused their trading activity on particular circuits, selling their goods in prominent market towns to others who transported these goods forward along other set routes.[8] Tansen Sen writes that the Nanzhao kingdom had kept the region at peace and its interregional trade flourished through the mid-ninth century.[9] After the collapse of the Nanzhao kingdom in 903, the Yunnan-Guizhou Plateau experienced rapid political change. Following the reign of three short-lived regimes, Duan Siping (893–944) rose from the ethnic Bai elite to establish in 937 a multiethnic kingdom with the Bai ethnic group as its main supporters. The Dali kingdom lasted for 317 years, with the exception of the interim period of the Dazhong kingdom (1094–1096) under the usurper Gao Shengtai (d. 1096). The Dali kingdom finally fell in 1254 when Mongol forces destroyed it.

Polities and Peoples along the Southwestern Silk Road

Prior to the rise of the Nanzhao kingdom, connections between polities from the western region of the Dong World and Tai-speaking communities were evident on both sides of the Sino-Vietnamese frontier. In the Western Han dynasty (206 BCE–9 CE) Tai-speaking communities in southwest China formed political alliances with the Dianyue kingdom (or Dianyue Chengxiang kingdom; ca. fourth century BCE–109 BCE). In *Records of the*

Historian, Sima Qian describes the Han envoy Zhang Qian's (?–ca. 114 BCE) encounters with local elite at the center of the Dong World:

> [The Han emperor] heard that more than a thousand miles west of the Han court there is the Chengxiang kingdom, which is called the Dianyue kingdom, and that Shu [Sichuan] merchants have informally traded with this kingdom until the present day. Consequently, the Han court sought to find a route from China to the Dian kingdom. First, the Han authorities sought a route to make contact with the Southwestern Yi Indigenes [Xinan Yi], but the cost was great and the route was never completed, so the court abandoned the effort. Later, Zhang Qian announced that he could find a route to connect China with this region, and he returned to seek ties with the Southwestern Yi.[10]

Zhang Qian made contact with Dian but failed to ally with the Dong World elite he sought. These local leaders ruled the Kunming kingdom, which during the Western Han period extended to modern-day Dali and included an elephant-breeding ground.[11] Sima Qian offered an anarchic picture of Kunming, noting that it "lacked a tribal leadership, and its people were prone to engage in robbery and pillaging. There were occasions when they would rob and murder Han officials. Since then, no Han representatives have made contact with these people."[12] The *Records of the Historian* account of the kingdom of Yelang (located in modern-day central Guizhou) notes that only Yelang and the Dian kingdom received enfeoffments from the Western Han court, because the surrounding smaller polities of the Dong World region refused to engage directly with the distant Han authorities.[13]

Within the Dong World certain local clan elites would over time have a significant impact on political and economic norms in this mountainous region. The rise of the Cuan clan in the Dong World coincided with a significant transformation of local authority along the Southwest Silk Road, following the chaotic end of the Eastern Han dynasty. This period marked the emergence of powerful families collectively called the Great Clans of Nanzhong (Nanzhong Daxing), in an area comprised of China's modern-day southern Sichuan, Guizhou, and Yunnan, which corresponds with the eastern half of the Dong World. Both traditional and contemporary Chinese sources contend that these families arrived from various parts of the crumbling Han empire, and that their local status shifted over generations as their members developed increasingly complex ties with locally influential indigenous clans. Frequently, the Great Clans of Nazhong leaders or their descendants would acquire the status of "native leader" (*yishuai*) or "elder leader" (*soushuai*) after years of living in the southwestern frontier region. Into this group we may also introduce from Chinese court chronicles the Tai-speaking communities of the Sino-Vietnamese frontier, known as the Li and Lao.[14] These communities and their forbearers had dominated the local political landscape even before the emergence of city-kingdoms on the North China Plain.[15] Therefore, the network of trade and kinship that bound all these groups together requires closer examination to understand more fully the region's true dynamics.

Although these Dong World leaders became chiefs of various non-Han ethnic communities, they would surely fit the criteria of anthropologist James Clifford's "ex-centric natives" engaged in, as Clifford describes for the modern era, a "search for somewhere to belong that is outside the imagined community of the dominant nation-state."[16] They were figures whose localized power resulted from positioning themselves simultaneously in two spheres of authority: the imperial political tradition linked to their "foreign" family origins and the political practices drawn from the wellspring of "local" knowledge. However, the Great Clans remained subject to the influence of political powers from outside the region. External forces of regional politics and interregional trade led to the eventual transformation of "Cuan" from a surname to a title of political administration to an ethnonym.

The Cuan's fortunes depended heavily on the Southwest Silk Road trade network, which provided significance to the clan's home region at the center of several important trade routes. On the Chinese side, the Sichuan provincial capital Chengdu is usually designated as the starting point for the primary Southwest Silk Road routes, which passed through Yunnan, Myanmar (Burma), and finally into South Asia. The network of trade and exchange at the heart of the Cuan's home region was the Five "Foot" Route in the Qin, the Old Bo Route or the Southern Yi Route (Nanyi Dao) in the Han period, and the Stone Gate Route (Shimen Dao) or the Zangke People's Route (Zangke Dao) by the Sui period.[17] This route passed through Weixian (modern-day Qujing, Yunnan) and Guchang (modern-day Kunming) and finally on to Dali. The region around Weixian was central to the Cuan clan's local authority. From Dali one could take three different routes through modern Myanmar on the way to present-day India, collectively known in the Han period as the Bonan Route (Bonan Dao) or the Yongchang Route (Yongchang Dao) and in the Tang period as the Western Dian Region-India Route (Xidian-Tianzhu Dao).

Another significant lane of communication and trade was the Zangke River. As described in the *Records of the Historian* account of Tang Meng, the Western Han magistrate of Poyang, in his audience with the Nam Việt ruler in ca. 135 BCE, Tang Meng asked a Shu merchant about the origins of the Ju berry sauce, which according to a modern scholar was the fruit of a species of poisonous nightshade and was a particularly desired food commodity.[18] He was told that the Zangke River flowed from the northwest directly into the Nam Việt capital Panyu (modern-day Guangzhou). Tang was also told that no matter how hard the Nam Việt attempted to take control of the Yelang kingdom, the source of this trade, these efforts all ended in failure. The unwillingness of the Dong World elite to be controlled by distant coastal and Central Plains authorities would reemerge in many interactions between these powers.

A significant transformation of local authority in the southwestern China and northern Southeast Asia region occurred during the period between the Yellow Turban Uprising (Huangjin Zhi Luan) in 184 and the rise of the Jin dynasty (265–420). This period saw the rise of the Great Clans of Nanzhong, which were comprised of Han elite that made their way into the area either as refugees or as members of the military units sent south to pursue fleeing rebels. Descendants of these families would have a lasting influence on the development of political and trade centers along the Southwest Silk Road, which carried trade from the westernmost Han settlements of modern-day Chengdu to the South Asian kingdom of Kāmāpura and the northern India principalities along the Ganges. According to the important local history *Chronicles of the Lands below Mt. Hua* (Huayang guozhi), the Cuan, Meng, Li, and Cui families were considered to be the "Four Great Clans" (Si Xing) of the region.[19] These families had arrived in the Southwest from other Han-populated areas of China, but their local status shifted over generations as their members developed ever increasing and complex ties with locally influential non-Han families.

The prevailing narrative from the imperial Chinese record maintains that the Cuan clan's ascent began with Cuan Xi (?–?), who left Chengdu for Yunnan with his military command to assist the Shu Han (221–263) emperor Liu Bei (161–223) in wielding influence over Nanzhong.[20] Anthropologist Margaret Swain contends that the Cuan leadership came from the local Luomengbu clan, and that Zhuge Liang (181–234) chose local officials to serve under him after sweeping through the region.[21] Historian Giersch maintains that Zhuge Liang believed that he didn't have the personnel to spare for local administration, and so instead turned to local elites for the task.[22] During the Eastern Jin, the local clan leader Cuan Shen (?–?) was given the title of native prefect (*cishi*) of Nanning Zhou.[23] Material evidence of Cuan Shen and Cuan Xi's local appointments may be found on the steles located in the Colored Sand Forest (Caise Shalin) ruins of Luliang County (Qujing): one Eastern Jin period stele is dated Yixi 1 (405 CE) and titled "Treasures of the Cuan Clan Stele" (Cuan Baozi Bei); the second Liu Song dynasty stele is dated Daming 2 (458 CE) and titled "Stele of the Great Cuan Clan" (Cuan Da Bei). Both steles describe the importance and scope of the political role that the Cuan clan played in this region. The text notes that Cuan Xi was a military commander serving the kingdom of Shu Han (221–263) and a native of Jianning in Yuyuan.[24] Therefore, the possibility that he was linked to the incoming army of Zhuge Liang seems more remote. In other sources during the rule of Liu Zhang (?–?), a time when the Cuan was already one of the area's major clans, Cuan Xi received a posting as a local militia commander (*lingzhang*). After Liu Bei (?–?) entered Shu Han and made himself emperor, Cuan Xi was given command on the Xing Can Army, and he took the title of general (*jiangjun*).

Once Cuan Xi had settled with his family in their new frontier home, or, more likely, made his presence known to powerful outsiders, the self-identity of the family and the group identification of the Cuan by outsiders diverged dramatically. Soon the Cuan were no longer a static group of individuals bonded by blood relations. Instead, the group became a synecdoche for Dong World peoples, who alternately competed with or competed against representatives of Chinese imperial interests. The Cuan's ability to attract loyalty at the local level and to dominate trade activity to firm up political and military strengths led the family to grow steadily in importance in the eyes of distant court observers. With a specter-like quality, the Cuan dominated the frontier imaginings of generations of scholar-elites engaged in frontier administration. The family's political fortunes declined when its leadership was caught between contesting spheres of authority; however, the local identity of the Cuan remained ingrained and persistent down to today, when its descendants with only weak biological ties to the earliest settlers still revere the founding members of this influential clan-turned-ethnicity.

From this period, the Cuan clan would retain the *cishi* title generation after generation, maintaining de facto control of the eight commandaries (*jun*) that comprised the southwest administrative region of various kingdoms through the Sui-Tang period.[25] Later generations of the Cuan family settled in Weixian (modern-day Qujing), serving as military leaders to larger authorities and eventually becoming regional authorities themselves in times of upheaval. A modern government account of Qujing's rise as a center of trade places the ancient market town in a pivotal location between the southwestern-most reach of the Qin and later Han empires and the non-Han peoples who sought to make commercial contact. As the report notes, "The immigration of Han people into Qujing caused . . . Qujing itself to undergo major changes during this period. This change is manifested in the contradiction between the borderland and the hinterland, between the county administration system and the indigenous tribes, the Han and other ethnic groups, the central government and local people, the clans and the (Dong World) chiefs, etc."[26] This modern notion of Marxian "contradiction" could be an interpretation of the social unrest that in-migration of outsiders had created for the Dong World residents. Qujing received a great deal of in-migration of Han settlers after the southern advance of Zhuge Liang in 225 CE brought troops and later settlers into the region. Weixian was already populated indigenously with well-maintained agricultural communities from prehistoric times. After this influx of outsiders, indigenous and settler groups interacted on numerous levels, although tensions remained. Several great clans made their names after this wave of settlement. The establishment and flourishing of the Cuan clan at Weixian took place at this time. In 320 Cuan Shen would take the title of king of Kunchuan, which encompassed most of the Lake Dian region. The Cuan clan would then rule this area as a single kingdom for the next few centuries until the rise of the Nanzhao kingdom under the Meng clan and Pi Luoge (?–?).

Although the Cuan surname originally described a particular clan, the term was eventually used in official sources as a title of local leadership, describing to representatives of distant courts the people that ruled the Southwest in areas beyond imperial control. Some scholars have argued that through reliance on local non-Han families and intermarriage, the Cuan lost their original cultural distinctiveness to "barbarize" (*yihua*) themselves and blend thoroughly with the indigenous peoples of the southwest region.[27] Sources would eventually stop referring to the Cuan as a locally powerful Han clan, and instead indicate its members as "Cuan people" (*Cuan ren*) and "Cuan indigenes" (*Cuan man*).[28]

In the early Jin period, Cuan clan members at Jinning (the Lake Dian region) and Jianning (modern-day Qujing) had already divided their communities into eastern and western regions. By the Sui-Tang period, sources referred to two separate Cuan ethnic groups. The Eastern Cuan inhabited areas near the modern-day Yunnan cities of Zhaotong (northeastern Yunnan) and Luxi, Xundian, Gaoming, and Jianshui (southern Yunnan), as well as the Guizhou city of Weining. The center for the Eastern Cuan was the area around Zhaotong. The Western Cuan inhabited central Yunnan at the Lake Dian region, including Qujing, Kunming, Malong, Jinning, Dengjiang, Anning, and Lufeng, with its center at Jinning.[29] In his ethnographic treatise on the region, *Treatise on the Southern Indigene* (Manshu), Fan Zhuo (fl. 860–873) referred to the surname Cuan as a customary name (*fengsu ming*); however, the Cuan certainly had not yet become a separate ethnicity.[30] The principal ethnic group inhabiting the Western Cuan region was the Bai Indigenes (Baiman), a group referred to in official sources as the Bo. Since the Qin-Han period, the Bo had settled in this region and developed a culturally sophisticated community.[31] According to these accounts, the Bo eventually intermixed with other local peoples to grow in size and became the Baiman Cuan ethnicity. The Eastern Cuan primarily came from the Wuman ethnic group, which arrived in the Kunming region during the Qin-Han period. In the Wei-Jin period they mixed with the Sou ethnic group to form the Wuman.[32] The matter of the Wuman as a distinct historical ethnonym requires some explanation. While the exonym Wuman appears throughout premodern Chinese sources as an ethnic category, one cannot determine with certainty which specific people in particular historical periods are labeled in this manner. The collective category for Dong World indigenes labeled as Wuman in these court chronicles include the plethora of historical ethnic groups described here; after the Mongol advance into the Dong World heartland in the thirteenth century, reference to Wuman communities disappear.

Many Chinese scholars argue that the Wuman-related exonyms Eastern and Western Cuan should be considered two distinct ethnicities, and that the groups mixed with other ethnicities before achieving regional status as great clans. Moreover, these regions were never "monoethnic" in early times, but the mixing of peoples to create the Eastern and Western Cuan was a long-term process internal to the Nanzhong region. Both the Baiman and the Wuman communities would comprise a substantial portion of the military assembled by the Nanzhao leadership when that kingdom came to dominate the region.[33]

During the Nanzhao period, the main Wuman communities were distributed within the territory of Nanzhao kingdom and only a few Wuman clans resided within the territory of the Tang empire. Mentions of the Wuman in court chronicles are first found in the late Northern and Southern dynasties materials, but these records referred only vaguely to the actual conditions of Wuman society. By the Tang period, court descriptions of the Wuman became more nuanced. As *History of the Song Dynasty* (Songshi) notes, the Wudeng territory extends for a thousand *li*, and there are six clans of the Qiongbu, and all these people are Wuman. . . . There are two clans of the Yaoman, three clans of the Leiman, three clans of the Mengman, and the indigenous peoples of Li, Gui, and Rongshuzhou all fell within Wudeng territory. . . . Seventy *li* to the south of the Wudeng lands we find the two tribes of the Lin, the three clans of the Shidi, the three clans of the Atun, and the three clans of the Kuiwang. To the south of this territory was the Fengbi tribe, consisting of the two clans of the Anuo.[34]

These tribes were distributed on both sides of the middle and lower reaches of the Jinsha River around a core part of the Wuman people. Their most basic social structure was the clan, and the Wuman people's internal relationships were also more loosely based on surnames as a kinship link with ethnic groups.

In 581 the Sui dynasty was founded at Chang'an, and almost immediately the court turned its attentions to addressing the local presence of the Cuan clan in the new empire's southwestern region. The court twice dispatched its armies to push the Cuan from various territories under the clan's authority into the Jianning and Jinning commandaries. The Sui managed to kill the Western Cuan ruler in an attempt to take over the territory, but soon realized that they were already overextended with other projects and unable to complete this venture.[35] With the founding of the Tang came another court-led attempt to control the Cuan's local influence, this time through collaboration with the local leaders, culminating in the "opening of the southwest" (*kai nanzhong*), which actually marked the limited acceptance of the Cuan clans of Tang authority.[36] Historian Martin Stuart-Fox contends that the Tang court actively encouraged the consolidation of indigenous kingdoms by fostering relations with powerful chieftains, but it seems doubtful that the Tang planned to establish resilient regional rivals by adopting this frontier policy.[37] In any case, the Cuan initially benefited from ties with the Tang. In 621 the Tang court appointed Cuan Hongda, the native prefect of Kunming prefecture, replacing the early Sui administrative region of Nanning zhou (near modern-day Qujing). In this period of time Qujing was one of the political, economic, and cultural foci of the region with its administrative center located at Ningzhou. With the rise of the Nanzhao kingdom, these foci would all shift westward and transform the landscape as a result.

Through the 670s, the Tang attempted to exert influence over Cuan territory through a series of military campaigns.[38] However, these local authorities were not easily dislodged. Around 664, the Cuan clan members of the Eastern Cuan region and the western Er River region established a large number of "bridled and haltered" (*jimi*) prefectures to confirm local authority and link up politically with the Tang court under Tang Gaozong (Li Zhi; 628–683). In fact, these *jimi* regions remained autonomous through the rise of the Nanzhao court to their west, and not even the efforts of Cuan Hongda, and later his son and grandson, were able to bring these self-ruling areas under a single authority.[39] The Cuan were not the only major power with designs on the region. By 717 the Tang court had set up a frontier township (*fanzhen*) in the region of modern-day Sichuan, and this administrative region would grow in importance for the Tang empire.[40] However, the military commissioners (*jiedushi*) that the Tang court appointed to Sichuan focused their attention on thwarting Tibetan expansion to the west while allowing the Cuan to govern locally without intervention. Political change would come from other indigenous forces from the southwest, the Nanzhao. The regional center of power shifted with the founding of the Nanzhao kingdom. The Song scholar Ouyang Xiu offered a succinct description of the Nanzhao kingdom's territory, which maps quite easily on the contours of the Dong World.[41]

The Nanzhao founder had, in fact, used turmoil caused by the Tang's difficulty in dealing with the Cuan-held territories to establish a power base.[42] Once the Nanzhao had gained enough strength, its court turned to curbing the Cuan's power and influence within the Dong World. When the Nanzhao founders first set up their court in 737, the kingdom was surrounded by significant population centers and established kingdoms, including the Cuan territory to the east, the Tang Protectorate of An Nam (or northern Vietnam) to the southeast, Magadha (Mojiatuo) or modern-day Patna and Gayā to the west, the Tibetan empire to the northwest, the Pyu kingdom to the southwest and the Tang empire beyond the Cuan to the east.[43] The Nanzhao leadership was largely Tibeto-Burman, but included Yi (or Lolo) communities, similar ethnically to the Cuan, and related Bai, Lolo-Burmese, and Tai speakers were among the subjects of this kingdom.[44] The variety of ethnicities under Nanzhao authority and the new kingdom's location along the same trade routes that had once passed unobstructed into Cuan territory drew the strength away from the Cuan kingdom. In 748 the Cuan's influence was decisively undermined when the Nanzhao court forcibly relocated more than two hundred thousand Cuan clansmen to Yongchang.[45] This move effectively divided Cuan regional influence and ended Qujing's local economic and political dominance.

Farther south in the Dong World, beginning in the seventh century, numerous polities formed in the area between the western region of the Lancang River and the banks of the Irrawaddy River in southwestern Yunnan at the Kainan, Yongchang, and Lê Thụ prefectures (around modern-day Honghe Hani and Yi Autonomous Prefecture). According to Fan Zhuo's *Treatise on the Southern Indigene* (Manshu), many different indigenous groups resided in this region: the Black Teeth Man (Hei Chi Man), Gold Teeth Man (Jin Chi Man), Silver Teeth Man (Yin Chi Man), Tattooed Feet Man (Xiu Jiao Man), Tattooed Face Man (Xiu Mian Man) in Yongchang and Kainan.[46] The description of these different groups was quite detailed. As Fan Zhuo writes,

The Black Teeth Man used lacquer to paint their teeth, the Gold Teeth Man used gold lamina to wrap their teeth. The purpose for these practices were to be seen by other people as a form of decoration. When they ate, they would remove these decorations. On the tops of their heads, they made a bun [*ji*], and use blue cloth to wrap themselves for pants, and draped over their shoulders a long strip of blue cloth. The Tattooed Feet Man tattooed the leg under the calf and on the ankle with many colors, wearing red cloth and green jewelry. The Tattooed Face Man took a needle to the faces of newborn children after their first month and applied the needle to their skin like embroidering pictures.[47]

Fan Zhuo also noted that all these people served the Nanzhao court and that they could be called upon to serve in military expeditions.[48] Fan Zhuo was reflecting on obvious examples that included the ninth-century Nanzhao invasion of the Tang empire and the later invasion of An Nam to demonstrate how effective this fighting force from the Dong World could be against its neighbors.

The Nanzhao kingdom was initially formed from a confederation of locally powerful clans under the central guidance of the Tibeto-Burman Mengshe ruling family. Historian Megan Bryson notes that when Tang officials first made contact with the Lake Erhai region in the 650s they found six kingdoms (*zhao*) ruling the region.[49] The six clans leading these kingdoms were the Mengshe, the Mengsui, the Langqiong, the Dengtan, the Shilang, and the Yuexi. In 649, Xinuluo (r. 649–674), a chieftain of the Mengshe clan, founded the Dameng kingdom in the region surrounding Lake Erhai. Xinuluo ruled his people as the "rare and excellent king" (*qijiawang*) but he acknowledged the overlordship of the Tang court in the region.[50] In 737 the kingdom's ruler Pi Luoge gave his realm the name Nanzhao, and in 738 the Tang court bestowed on Pi Luoge the title "King of Yunnan." This was the same year in which the Tang launched a major attack on Tibetan forces, so the desire to create a helpful ally on the western frontier seems obvious.[51] Historian Mark Edward Lewis refers to the Nanzhao as a "secondary kingdom," stating that its development depended on "the intrusion of an existing kingdom that serves both as provocation and model"; that is, the Tang empire.[52] Through tributary relations and titles granted to the Nanzhao leaders and their high officials, the Tang bestowed a legitimacy that sustained the Nanzhao's political leadership at a local level. The Nanzhao court borrowed its bureaucratic institutions and its official titles from the Tang, and even implemented a palace examination system. However, as Lewis notes, the Nanzhao leaders also borrowed from Tibetan political practices.[53] The Tang's primary contributions to the political and cultural development of the Nanzhao kingdom, including "the belief in ritual as a model for social behavior, the centrality of the family, the emphasis on hierarchy, the clear separation of genders, and the importance of text-based learning" were shared with other kingdoms throughout East Asia, including Korea, Japan, and the northern half of modern-day Vietnam.[54]

Population migration from the Han heartland of the Central Plains brought the cultural bridges between southwest China and settlements. According to historian Zhang Yunxia, the influx of Central Plains settlers to the interior of the Nanzhao kingdom had an inestimable effect on the spread of Confucianism in Nanzhao society.[55] These settlers included soldiers, merchants, and exiled officials, among others. The Confucian ideas they brought with them had varying degrees of influence on the local culture and values, but the original society was necessarily changed. In the early Tang dynasty, the Lake Erhai region was already home to a few hundred clans with Yang, Li, Zhao, and Dong as the leading surnames, who claimed to descend from Han lineages.[56] One can see that the Han settlers entering the Erhai area had themselves changed and, at the same time, had an impact on the area. As noted in the *Treatise on the Southern Indigene*, "the inhabitants of Qulizhao [the modern-day Erhai region] were originally natives of Hedong, while the four leading clans Wang, Yang, Li, and Zhao were all from the Baiman ethnic group. They originally were from Puzhou, and they had emigrated to this area. In the Tang dynasty several hundred thousand people moved to Yunnan by various means."[57] According to historian Zhang Yunxia, when Nanzhao on four occasions attacked Xichuan (modern-day Chengdu), the attackers seized a large number of Confucian texts, as well as taking by force many Confucian literati and architectural artisans and other craftsmen from a population of one hundred thousand people. Zhang argues that when these people were moved to Nanzhao, they undoubtedly played a vital role in the spread and influence of Confucianism.[58] Additional textual evidence is still required to corroborate Zhang's contention, but examples of the cultural impact on political centers that raided neighboring states may be found in Đại Việt, Cham, and other Southeast Asian polities.

Tang officials serving in the southern and southwestern frontier regions became increasingly important to the empire's overall strategy for maintaining regional stability, and these officials could profit handsomely from their involvement in local commerce passing along the Southwest Silk Road trade routes. However, there were also other individuals who wished to secure their own local authority by balancing personal alliances with both the Nanzhao and distant Tang courts.[59] Such officials from Dali Prefecture include the captured Tang official Zheng Hui.[60] A native of Xiangzhou (in modern-day Anyang, Henan), Zheng passed the civil service exams during the Tianbao reign period (742–756) of Emperor Tang Xuanzong, and received the title "Worthy Talent, Proven by Examination" (Zhuming Jing).[61] Zheng was posted to Xihu County in Xizhou (modern-day Dechang, Sichuan). An attack on Nanzhao by the Tang frontier commander Xianyu Zhongtong (b. 693) in 751 led the Nanzhao to throw its support once again behind Tibet. During the An Lushan Uprising (755–763), Nanzhao forces entered and occupied Xizhou, taking Zheng Hui prisoner.[62] The Nanzhao ruler Ge Luofeng (712–779) valued the former Tang official's expertise, and sought Zheng Hui's guidance in many matters, including Confucian teachings. The ruler eventually granted Zheng the honorific title "Benefactor of the Man" (Manli) and made Zheng the tutor to his son Ge Luojia.[63]

The Dong World after the An Lushan Uprising

In the chaos that followed the An Lushan Uprising, the greatest threat to the Tang in the western region was Tibet, under the leadership of King Trisong Detsen (r. 755–797?). In 763 King Trisong Detsen invaded the Tang with an army of two hundred thousand men, seizing the capital Chang'an. Political in-fighting involving the palace eunuchs prevented a decisive military response from the Tang imperial forces.[64] At this time, there were other tribes to the west and southeast of Nanzhao that had not yet entered into an alliance with the Nanzhao leadership, such as the Xunchuan Man and the Luoxing ("naked-looking") Man. According to the Nanzhao Dehua Stele, in 762 the Nanzhao kingdom forcibly annexed the territory inhabited by the Xunchuan Man. In the winter of the fourteenth and final year of the Nanzhao ruler Ge Luofeng's Zanpuzhong reign period (768), the Nanzhao ruling family built river boats to reach Liang Yao "for greater control and to reassure the settlers in this area."[65] Facing this aggressive expansion, the Luoxing Man and the Qixian Man communities soon acquiesced to Nanzhao authority. The Burmese Pyu kingdom (Biaoguo), at an even greater distance from Nanzhao, also submitted to Nanzhao tributary authority.

In order to further strengthen influence over the Dong World of the eastern Yunnan region, the Nanzhao kingdom established the Tuodong citadel in Kunchuan, located near modern-day Kunming. Soon after, the Nanzhao court ordered the son of Ge Luofeng, Feng Jiayi, to travel to the Tuodong citadel to serve as the left-hand military commissioner (*zuo zhenfu*). The Feng family would hold the position for six generations, at which point the place name would be changed to Shanchan, the name it would retain through the Song period.[66]

Regarding this strategic territory, Fan Zhuo's *Treatise on the Southern Indigene* commented: "the Qujing area was originally part of two flanks in our conflict, but our rapid expansion of the two flanks in the region from Qujing, Shicheng, Shengmachuan, and Kunchuan south to the Longhe citadel was taken by Nanzhao forces. Soon thereafter, the area of An Nam became an important military stronghold that was also annexed by Nanzhao."[67] Thus, Nanzhao took advantage of the An Lushan Uprising to help the Tibetan military seize the area west of Jiaozhou, while the Luoxing Man peoples wielded influence over the eastern territories of the Pyu kingdom to establish the Tuodong citadel, after which the Tang-Tibetan rivalry caused enough chaos in the region to allow room for the Nanzhao to take control of the entire territory.[68]

The sixth Nanzhao ruler Yimouxun (754–808) put pressure on the Tang frontier, but he also broke off close relations with the Tibetan empire. The grandson of the fifth ruler, Yimouxun took the throne in 779 at an early age and sought out Zheng Hui for support. When Yimouxun succeeded in retaining power, Zheng Hui continued to serve the Nanzhao court.[69] In 779 Tibetan armies launched a widespread invasion of Sichuan, but the alliance between the Tibetans and the Nanzhao had soured, and the Nanzhao resisted the Tibetan military expansion. With this intervention, the Tang forces were able to drive back the invaders.[70] The Tang military decisively repulsed another Tibetan invasion in 802.[71] Chinese court chroniclers contend that Zheng Hui encouraged the Nanzhao ruler to resist Tibetan encroachment by uniting again with the Tang as allies.[72] In fact, it appears more likely that Zheng Hui had negotiated both the withdrawal of official relations with the Tang and the resumption of those relations as part of an overall strategy in the three-way balance of power between the Tibetan, Nanzhao, and Tang courts. The Nanzhao court appointed Zheng Hui as tranquility official (*qingping guan*), the equivalent of the Tang position of prime minister (*caixiang*), as a reward for his diplomatic efforts. There is an extant Nanzhao period stele near Dali in the Taihe citadel (*Taihe cheng*), located in the village of Taihe, extolling Ge Luofeng's achievements, titled "Nanzhao Stele of Virtue and Education" (Nanzhao Dehua Bei). This stele was long thought to have been composed by Zheng Hui. Presently, most scholars believe that the stele was created by another Chinese official at the Nanzhao court, Wang Mansheng, who also had been appointed tranquility official.[73]

Throughout the mid-Tang period, the Sino-Tibetan frontier was in a state of war. The Tibetans invaded the Tarim Basin and seized four garrisons. In 794 the Sichuan governor Wei Gao (d. 805), promoted from within the Nanzhao court by Zheng Hui, entered into the Tang-Nanzhao negotiations and managed to convince the Nanzhao leadership to profess its loyalty to Chang'an. In 801 the combined Tang-Nanzhao armies launched an attack on Tibet, scoring a major military victory that halted further Tibetan expansion along the Tang's western frontier.[74] Various chieftains from upland communities in the southwest sent troops to support the Tang and Nanzhao in their military expedition.[75] In 805 regional instability would eventually provide a pretext on the part of the Nanzhao leadership to extend its own authority toward the southeast. By the 820s local leaders in the southwest also began to exercise their power again, sensing a drain on Tang resolve to maintain its influence in the region. When an ill-prepared Tang army failed to pacify a local uprising from 823 to 826 by the Nùng-led Yellow Grotto (Huangdong) militia, other acts of political unrest destabilized the frontier region.[76] Tang efforts to regain local control were incomplete, and the regional unrest fed into wider conflicts among local chiefs. In 820, when Tibetan armies attacked the Tang southwestern frontier, the Nanzhao court offered to send military assistance to the Tang defenders.[77] Soon after, Tibet entered negotiations with the Tang that resulted in a peace treaty in 821, granting Tibet all territory from modern-day Gansu to western Sichuan.

However, when Trisong Detsen died, the Tibetan court got caught up in a succession crisis. In 842, due to the internal political struggles, the court broke apart. In 851 the region around modern-day Ningxia and Gansu was returned to Tang control when the Tibetan military crumbled.[78] Tibet would never again function as an expansionist power in Central Asia, and direct contact with Chinese authorities would remain limited until the Mongol expansion into Eurasia. Although negotiations between the Tang and the Tibetan empire had brought peace, the Nanzhao kingdom, also on good terms with the Tang, now viewed the Chinese empire as less willing to become embroiled in affairs on its western frontier.

Despite the earlier alliance against the Tibetan armies, the mood in Tang-Nanzhao relations soon changed once again. Shortly after the Tang-Tibet peace treaty had been signed, Nanzhao armies in 829 pushed eastward into Sichuan, where they briefly occupied Chengdu. Although these tensions were ameliorated with further negotiations, Nanzhao armies were advancing into Tang territory again by the 850s. One reason for renewed tensions could be the request by Xichuan's military commissioner Li Deyu (787–849) that fewer Nanzhao students be permitted to travel to Chengdu and that Nanzhao tribute missions should be significantly curtailed.[79] The Nanzhao court reacted strongly to these limitations, and when the new Nanzhao ruler Shilong (r. 859–877) took the throne, plans for a punitive expedition against the Tang were put into place. This time Nanzhao forces attacked (or co-opted) upland communities near modern-day Guizhou, and then moved farther south against An Nam. Local communities had experienced mismanagement under the Tang-appointed local officials in the upland areas around Guangxi and An Nam, and local leaders were more than willing to collaborate with the invading Nanzhao.[80]

In this same period the Tang court under Emperor Yizong (Li Cui; r. 859–873) realized that it had very little knowledge of Nanzhao's domestic situation, and its lack of direct knowledge hampered efforts to establish effective policies for dealing with Nanzhao. For this reason, the court reached out to officials posted to the frontiers of the Dong World for actionable information. In 862 Fan Zhuo was appointed by Yizong to the staff (*shuli*) of the An Nam fiscal commissioner (*Annan jinglüeshi*) Cai Xi, who served as the de facto administrator of the An Nam Protectorate (Annan Duhufu) at the citadel located in modern-day Hanoi. Fan Zhuo was immediately tasked with gathering this information, and he compiled what he could obtain about Nanzhao from such sources as Yuan Zi's (739–818) *Yunnan ji* (Record of Yunnan), Wei Qixiu's *Yunnan xingji* (Travels in Yunnan), Dai Fu's (*jinshi* 757) *Guangyiji* (A record of strange things in the Guangnan region), and the anonymously authored *Kuicheng tujing* (Maps of Kuicheng).[81] Fan Zhuo completed his book, but its usefulness would be limited.[82] Before the Tang court could act on any information gathered by Fan, relations with Nanzhao reached a breaking point.

Nanzhao's invasion of Guizhou had ignited the Nanzhao War (862–866), through which the Nanzhao initially conquered the region from Yunnan's Erhai plain to the Tongking Gulf, consolidating political influence over, if only briefly, the eastern half of the Dong World. During the initial stages of fighting, Nanzhao forces repeatedly launched raids on the An Nam capital.[83] In early February of 863, Nanzhao forces captured the capital, and Cai Xi's entire family, along with an entourage of more than seventy people, died in the fighting. Fan Zhuo's eldest son Fan Tao banded together with fourteen enslaved servants and their families and fled the fighting. Fan Zhuo himself gathered the official seals of the fiscal commissioner's office and fled to nearby Junzhou (modern-day Wuchang County) to await orders. The Tang court soon ordered a military response to be organized in Chang'an, and ordered the Kuizhou Protectorate commissioner (*Kuizhou duhufu changshi*) to act.[84] In the midst of this fighting the Nanzhao ruler changed the title of his kingdom to Dali, and adopted a new calendar based on his own reign date, abandoning the practice of following the Tang. The Tang general Gao Pian (ca. 821–887), famous for fighting rebellious Turkic forces, was sent to stop the fighting. After his forces successfully drove back the Nanzhao army, Gao Pian arranged for repairs to be made to the An Nam Protectorate's Đại La citadel to provide additional defense for the late Tang empire's southwestern frontier areas.

Political fortunes would soon shift at the center of the Dong World. The Nanzhao kingdom's ruling family was overthrown in 902. During the subsequent thirty-five years, the region was governed by the three short-lived regimes of Dachanghe (902–927), Datianxing (928–929), and Dayining (929–937), at which point the powerful Nanzhao military commissioner Duan Siping rose among the ethnic ruling elite, conscripted troops for his army from upland areas on the outskirts of his command, and led this army to victory to establish the multiethnic Dali kingdom (937–1253) with the Bai ethnic group as its main supporters. With the fall of the Nanzhao and the rise of the Dali, the remaining Cuan leadership received another opportunity for growth. The Dali kingdom left local elite such as the remaining Cuan clan leaders in place to secure their loyalty, and the local elites of Qujing (or Shicheng Commandary under the Dali court) received new political responsibilities, albeit at a lesser degree of influence than was the case before the Tang. With the rise of the Yongzhou Dao trade route into modern-day southern Guangxi, local elites from the thirty-seven tribes of Wuman (*Wuman sanshiqi buluo*) of the Qujing area once again took part in trading activities.[85] In 971, the Dali founders, the Duan clan leadership, and representatives of the thirty-seven tribes met at Shicheng (Qujing) to form an alliance, which benefited this group until the fall of the Dali kingdom during the Mongol invasion.

The Dali kingdom began at a disadvantage for a newly established state. Although its territory was large, the plains and arable land only accounted for about 5 percent of its land. If the Dali kingdom's territory covered 800,000 square kilometers, the arable region would only be about 40,000. The rest of the kingdom was mountains and plateaus, as is the case for much of the Dong World.[86] Dependence on trade commodities became increasingly significant. As noted earlier, the Bai ethnic group were the ruling elite of Dali, and under their authority were Baiman, Wuman, the Golden Teeth Baiyi, and other ethnic groups. The Dali kingdom's remote hinterlands and frontiers were home to local ethnic groups, such as the thirty-seven Wuman tribes, as well as the neighboring polities of the Ziqi kingdom, the Luodian kingdom, the Dong World Tai-speaking chiefs of the Temo Circuit in modern-day western Guangxi, and the various chiefs of the Qiongbu region, among others, with whom the Dali maintained close contact in a mutually beneficial arrangement similar to the "bridled and haltered" policy practiced by the Tang and its successor the Song dynasty.[87]

Rather than resembling a territory of political refuge in Zomian terms, the Dong World region consisted of "galactic polities" that had adopted Sinitic-style political arrangements for the smaller polities arrayed around larger states at its center.[88]

As the Dali kingdom's largest neighbor, the most detailed description of the ruling elite of the Luodian kingdom during the Song is found in the *History of the Song Dynasty*:

> Just beyond the prefectures of Qianzhou and Fuzhou is the territory of the Southwestern Yi Barbarians. In the Han dynasty it was the Zangke Commandary. In the Tang period was the native prefectures of Nanning, Zangke, Kunming, Dongxie, Nanxie, Xizhao, and Chuzhou. From this territory one would travel northeast to Qian [modern-day Guizhou] and Fuzhou, then one traveled northwest to reach Jiazhou [modern-day Leshan in Sichuan] and Xuzhou [northeast of modern-day Yibin City]. Traveling east one reaches Jingchu [modern-day Hunan and Hubei], and traveling south one comes to Yizhou [modern-day Yizhou District, Hechi City, Guangxi] and Guizhou. These people all practice such vulgar customs as wearing buns, fastening gussets on the left side of their tunics, or braiding their hair. Following local practices, they engage in animal husbandry and often move with their herds; they enjoy dangerous work, and they are good at fighting. Members of the tribes all have the same surname, although each has a monarch, and the customs are slightly different. Since the beginning of the Song dynasty, the clans Longfan, Fangfan, Zhangfan, Shifan, Luofan were nicknamed the "Five Fan Clans" [Wuxingfan], and they often pay tribute in service to the Song court and so were presented noble rank [*jueming*].[89]

The Dong World social and political order in this period extended south into upland areas of modern-day Mainland Southeast Asia. According to *The New Tang History*, the area between the Red River Delta and Yunnan, extending from modern-day Phong Châu in Vietnam to Lào Cai in the northwest and downstream along the Red River, was a settlement region of the Sinh Lão ethnic group.[90] These ancestors of the Thai and Zhuang in Yunnan were formerly known as the Sa and the Nùng, and this region was also the home of the Yi, an ethnonym that first appeared in descriptions of borderlands events from the Tang dynasty.[91] *The New Tang History* author, the Song official Ouyang Xiu, wrote: "During the Dazhong reign period [847–860], Li Zhuo served as military commissioner [*jinglueshi*] in An Nam, significantly benefiting himself economically, offering one *dou* of salt in exchange for a buffalo. The Yi people had many grievances regarding Li's greedy behavior, and they colluded with the Nanzhao leader Duan Qiuqian to attack the An Nam frontier protectorate [*duhufu*]. As a result, they took the nickname 'Baiyi Army without a Mandate.'"[92] Southern Song scholar Zhao Rukuo's text *A Description of Barbarian Nations* (*Zhu fan zhi*) notes that the Vietnamese kingdom of "Jiaozhi was Jiaozhou, [and its territory] to the east extends all the way to the sea, while the kingdom is adjacent to Champa [Zhancheng] [to the south] and to the west bordered the territory held by the Baiyi Man people."[93]

The Southern Song scholar Fan Chengda (1126–1193) wrote in his book *Well-Balanced Records of the Cassia Sea* (Guihai yuheng zhi): "South and slightly beyond [Yongzhou] and the South River there were the Luodian and Ziqi people, which [took] their names from kingdoms. The Luokong, Temo Baiyi, and Juidao, and so on [took] their names from their circuits. All these tribes and their territories are close to Nanzhao."[94] According to the collection of local legends *Storytelling of the Mường* (Quẳm tố mường), these Tai-speaking communities came from the *mường* their ancestors had settled as Mường Ôm, Mường Ai, Mường Lò, Mường Hồ, Mường Bo Tè, Mường Óc, Mường Ác, Mường Tum Hoàng, and Mường Thanh, extending from modern-day Điện Biên Phủ to Laos and north into Yunnan.[95]

In the period between the sixth and tenth centuries, the Tai-speaking elite were also dominant in the riverine valleys of the western and southwestern areas of the Nguyên Giang (Red River), as well as southern and western Bắc Sơn. During the period from the eighth century to the tenth century under the authority of the Nanzhao kingdom, the Tai-speaking communities extended from the modern-day Jingdong Yi Autonomous County (Jingdong Yizuzizhhixian; Pu'er, Yunnan) southward. There also emerged in this region a Thai group with special cultural characteristics and living arrangements common to the area, collectively known as the Wuman. Nguyễn Chí Buyên found references in the collection of Black Tai poetry *Tày Pú Xấc* to Mường Ôm and Mường Ai as places of origin, from which the Wuman's ancestors came to Vietnam, by way of the Red River to Mường Lò in Nghĩa Lộ and Mường Thanh in Điện Biên.[96]

The Wuman people were the major ethnic group of the Dali kingdom in terms of population and distribution. In the early period of Dali rule, its social order experienced a transition from a society based on the clan (surname) group to one based on a confederation of smaller polities. Around the end of the ninth century until the beginning of the tenth century, the Thai population in Jingdong boomed, which led to a need to expand the "mường bản" in search of new arable land.[97] The new region was located north of Jingdong and formally belonged to the Nanzhao kingdom's Yinsheng Prefecture. When Jingdong Tai-speaking settlers usurped this land, they forced Nanzhao authorities to return to Nanzhao's Weichu Circuit (modern-day Chuxiong Yi Autonomous Prefecture [Chuxiong Yizu Zizhizhou]) and Yinsheng became the northernmost settlement of the Jingdong natives at the end of the Nanzhao period. In the tumult of this large-scale migration, part of the Black Thai (Thái Đen) from the eastern region of the Nguyên Giang River entered northwestern Vietnam.[98] During the course of these migrations, the Dali kingdom was founded and began to flourish in the area to the north of these Dong World communities.

The Dali Kingdom's Engagement with the Song Empire and the Đại Việt Kingdom

The Dong World political situation gradually stabilized after the establishment of the Dali kingdom in 937.[99] For regimes ruling from the Central Plains, the fall of the Tang and the subsequent regional chaos of the Five Dynasties period marked a general withdrawal of imperial authority from the borderlands adjacent to the Dong World, and the founding of the Song empire would not completely reestablish this territorial influence. In 965, the Song general Wang Quanbin (908–976) produced an invasion map of

Sichuan at court and recommended that the Song army push into Yunnan. Emperor Song Taizu (Zhao Kuangyin; 927–976) referred to the Nanzhao War as grounds for concern. He then allegedly took a jade axe to draw a boundary at the Dadu River, saying: "beyond this is not ours [*ci wai fei you ye*]!"[100] The court decided that the boundary with the Dali kingdom would be set at the Dadu River, even though the Dali kingdom was in no position to push back against the Song expansion.

The Dali leadership had already adjusted the Nanzhao policy of aggressive territorial expansion to a policy of "good-neighborly friendship."[101] According to the Ming scholar Zhuge Yuansheng's (fl. 1581) *History of the Dian* (Dianshi), "In the first year of Song Taizu's Jianlong reign period [960], the ruler of the Latter Shu kingdom [934–965], Meng Zhixiang [874–934] [or Emperor Gaozu] died [in the first year of his reign].[102] Meng Chang [r. 934–965] succeeded him on the throne, ignoring affairs of state, engaging in extravagant daily recreation, and appointing unqualified personnel."[103]

From across the Latter Shu kingdom's border to the south, the Dali court observed Meng Zhixiang's behavior and their discussion turned to a dispute over whether or not to attack Shu. A single Dali official argued against the invasion, saying to his fellow officials,

> When the Meng leadership was strong and united militarily with the Tubo [i.e., Tibetan] forces, they still could not invade Ba and Shu. Troops were deployed in an indiscriminate manner, which led to internal uprising, and the society of [Meng Zhixiang's] ancestors could not be preserved. Today I hear that . . . the Latter Shu kingdom should be incorporated into the Dali kingdom. In our kingdom of Dali, while we repair our citadels, train our soldiers, and support the people, why bother organizing military expeditions to far-flung regions and provoke controversy?[104]

The Dali ruler Duan Sizong followed this dissenting official's words, and chose not to invade the Latter Shu. As historians Li Weiwei and Wan Xuebo contend, at the establishment of the Dali kingdom its leaders soon learned the profound historical lessons of the Nanzhao kingdom's militarism that led to civil unrest. Consequently, the Dali abandoned the policy of aggression and expansion, and adopted a policy of internal defense and self-protection.[105]

However, the Dali leadership was unable to use their policy of nonaggression as an enticement to establish routine tributary relations with the Song court. A comparison of Song-Dali and Song–Đại Việt relations bears out this failure. After several decades of borderlands conflict, the Đại Cồ Việt kingdom would successfully establish a formal relationship with the Song court in 1009, following the establishment of the Lý dynasty. However, due to an official Song court prohibition on official interactions with Dali, Kaifeng rejected eleven requests for the establishment of formal relations by the Dali kingdom between 965 and 1116, and the Dali kingdom remained marginalized at the bottom of the Song-led regional system of interkingdom relations.[106] Historian Li Weizhen argued that the Song considered two factors in the decision to disengage from the Dali kingdom. First, concerned that contact with Dali's predecessor the Nanzhao kingdom caused the demise of the Tang dynasty, the Song court chose to regard the Dali kingdom as "beyond the pale of civilization" and its leadership as "barbarians," with whom one needed to develop specific diplomatic policies. Second, in comparison with the neighboring Liao (Khitan) and Xixia (Tangut) kingdoms, both the Dali and Đại Cồ Việt kingdoms posed much less of a direct military threat. The realistic geopolitical considerations of stronger northern neighbors led to a primary policy of shielding the Song frontier from the Dali and the other southwestern peoples of the Dong World, so as to concentrate on dealing with the enemy to the north.[107]

Regarding Dali–Đại Việt relations, prior to the tenth century there had been regular and fluid movement of people across the frontier areas, but after the establishment of the Dali and Đại Việt states, border issues emerged. The frontier management agendas of the two kingdoms became intertwined, fostering opportunities for both conflict and cooperation. During the early period of the Dali kingdom and shortly after the establishment of the Vietnamese Lý dynasty, people in Dali entered Đại Cồ Việt to trade through the "bridled and haltered" (*jimi*) prefecture Vị Long (modern-day Tuyên Quang Region, Vietnam).[108] Because the Đại Cồ Việt kingdom was a new polity, the border between the two states was unclear. In the borderlands of the Dali kingdom resided the Golden Teeth Baiyi (Jinchi Baiyi), Lao, Wuman, Heman and other indigenous communities.[109] These peoples would circulate freely between Dali and Đại Cồ Việt. Li Weizhen notes that these frontier communities maintained good relations with the Dong World Vị Long prefect Hà Trắc Tuấn.[110]

In late 1013, Hà Trắc Tuấn led an uprising to gain independence from both Dali and Đại Cồ Việt.[111] The Hà clan had long been among the local ruling elite in this region of the Dong World. The Dali kingdom exported to Đại Cồ Việt a number of trade items, including horses, knives, copper, tin, gold, silver, amber, jade, and medicinal herbs. The Đại Cồ Việt kingdom exported to Dali specialized trade items, such as medicinal materials, Chinese books, and silk obtained from the Song court.[112] In addition to official trade, private trade, including smuggling, also flourished. Vị Long Prefecture, between Dali and Đại Cồ Việt, was similar to Quảng Nguyên Prefecture (in modern-day Cao Bằng Province), between Đại Cồ Việt and the Song, in that they both were *jimi* administrative zones and had a certain amount of autonomy. For this reason, the two courts did not seek to profit from their borderlands trade but instead to strengthen their influence in these areas in order to prevent local elite from becoming too powerful, and, in the case of Đại Cồ Việt authorities, to check the local influence of an increasingly powerful Dali kingdom.[113] For this reason the Lý court decided to attack Vị Long Prefecture with a military expedition.

The *DVSKTT* (Complete book of the history of the Great Việt) account notes that "this year [1014], groups of [Dong World] residents passed the bronze pillars [of Ma Yuan] to enter Kim Hoa Bộ and Vị Long to trade.[114] When the emperor sent men to capture the indigenes and more than ten thousand of their horses, the Vị Long prefect and his men rebelled. The emperor sent a military expedition to suppress the uprising."[115] The account also notes that the emperor sent envoys to obtain more than ten thousand horses. This passage indicates that the volume of trade through Vị Long Prefecture's border market was quite large, especially regarding the trade in Dali horses. Horses were not considered commercial commodities at this time, but instead were important strategic military purchases for both Song and Đại Cồ Việt authorities. The alpine regions of the Yunnan Plateau at the center of the Dong World were abundant with good horses, while lowland areas of the Đại Cồ Việt only produced small ponies. Only on the Yunnan Plateau were people able to raise the high-quality war horses in this southern region of East Asia.

Vị Long prefect Hà Trắc Tuấn and his followers were captured by Lý forces and suffered heavy losses. After he withdrew into Dali territory, Hà Trắc Tuấn received the support of the Dali court. This assistance from Dali for Dong World local elite would explain Nùng Trí Cao's father Nùng Tồn Phúc's efforts to curry favor with the Dali leadership in the naming of his erstwhile independent kingdom on the periphery of the Đại Cồ Việt kingdom twenty years later. In order to counterbalance the rapidly rising Đại Cồ Việt, the Dali leadership dispatched Yang Changhui and Duan Jingzhi to lead two hundred thousand troops in a large-scale attack on Đại Cồ Việt.[116] It was the largest foreign military force assembled since the establishment of the Dali kingdom, demonstrating the foremost importance that Dali leaders attached to the frontier market with Đại Cồ Việt, and the frustration the Dali leaders felt regarding the provocative behavior by the Lý court.[117]

Li Weizhen notes that the Dali followed the military strategy of its predecessor the Nanzhao kingdom by advancing toward the sea in an attempt to box in the Lý forces. After entering northern Đại Cồ Việt territory, however, the Dali force was defeated by the Đại Cồ Việt army at Kim Hoa Bộ (near modern-day Cao Bằng). The *DVSKTT* account describes the battle this way: "in the fifth year of Jiayin [Song Dazhong Xiangfu seventh year; 1014] in the first month of the year, the [Dali] generals Yang Changhui and Duan Jingzhi led a force of two hundred thousand invaders in an attack on the garrison at Kim Hoa Bộ and the Bồu Trí military barracks [*junying*] at the Ngũ Hoa Trại garrison. The Bình Lâm Châu indigenous prefect Hoàng Tư Vinh heard of the attack. The emperor ordered his younger son the Dực Thánh Prince (?–?) to attack the Dali general Yang Changhui's army, and the Lý forces succeeded in beheading ten thousand of the enemy and capturing an innumerable number of soldiers."[118] The *Khâm định Việt sử Thông giám cương mục* (The imperially ordered annotated text completely reflecting the history of Viet) account notes, "In the first month of 1014, barbarian troops attacked and pillaged our lands. The [Đại Cồ Việt] emperor ordered the Dực

Thánh Prince to confront the invaders."[119] This was an important military victory for the Dực Thánh Prince and the new dynasty he represented, but the Vietnamese leadership were concerned that such a formable force could be assembled from within the Dong World, making use of Dong World militia that could be summoned to do the bidding of the Dali court. Li Weizhen concludes that after this incident, the Lý court was overwhelmed by the size of the conflict, fearing that it may someday be overthrown by Dali forces and its upland allies. As Li phrases it, not only did the Song court have a "Nanzhao/Dali phobia," the same was true for Đại Cồ Việt.[120]

In order to preserve the victory of the Kim Hoa Bộ campaign and to avoid further retaliation by the Dali kingdom, the Vietnamese ruler Lý Thái Tổ urgently dispatched a team of envoys to Kaifeng, led by the foreign minister Phùng Chân, to report victory to the Song emperor Zhenzong, presenting the Song ruler with a gift of the horses the Lý army had seized. *Song Essential Documents* (Song hui yao ji gao) contains this account of Lý Thái Tổ's triumphant report: "The hordes of Hetuo Man [i.e., Dali] established a garrison on the border of this prefecture, and they had designs on controlling this circuit. I sent cavalry and troops to fight in Fanglin Prefecture. Bandit hordes were defeated, and its leadership was beheaded or captured alive, along with the main army of Yang Changhui and the [Dali] barbarians. They [Đại Cồ Việt] sent Phùng Chân and Left-Hand Chief Lackey [Zuodouyaya] Lý Nghiệt to report to the throne. Sixty horses were offered in tribute."[121] Emperor Zhenzong replied, "please direct these envoys to the city watchtower [*que*] where a banquet has been prepared. Once all have been notified of this gathering, we will be ready to share in the abundance [of the emperor's feast]."[122] The envoy mission was summoned to the Chongde Hall (Chongde Dian), where "they were bestowed with gifts of caps, belts and coins, although the offered horses were of poor quality."[123] Li Weizhen contends that the Song court's willingness to offer a full reception for less-than-stellar tributary offerings demonstrates that the Song dynasty was clearly a strong political supporter of Đại Cồ Việt in the conflict between Dali and Đại Cồ Việt, staying close to the strictures of the "tributary system," of which the Song assumed that it was the pivot. Since a formal tributary relationship between the Dali kingdom and the

Song empire had not been established, the Song court had only the responsibility to protect the vassal states such as Đại Cồ Việt, not to protect Dali. Therefore, it is not surprising that Song favoritism was evident in the political and military conflict between Dali and Đại Cồ Việt.

Due to the diplomatic intervention of the Song court, the Dali leadership elected not to send troops to retaliate after their initial defeat by the Đại Cồ Việt forces. The Vị Long prefect Hà Trắc Tuấn, who remained in place in his usurped territory, was suddenly vulnerable. The following year (1015), the Lý court seized on this opportunity to act. According to the *DVSKTT* account, "in early 1015, the Lý emperor ordered the Dực Thánh Prince and the Vũ Đức Prince to attack the Dong World prefectures of Đô Kim, Vị Long, Thường Tân, and Bình Nguyên, capturing the Dong World chief Hà Trắc Tuấn. When the troops returned to the capital, the Dong World chief was executed in the East City."[124] After Hà Trắc Tuấn was killed, the Lý dynasty eventually occupied the "Lao" area in northern Đại Cồ Việt.

Lý's victory and the submission of the Hà clan would later pay off for the Lý court. Referring to the Dong World chiefs of the region of modern-day Yên Nguyên, Chiêm Hoá, and Tuyên Quang communes in a stele in Vị Long Prefecture (Chiêm Hoá–Tuyên Quang), the Vietnamese court described a chieftain with the Hà clan, who responded to the court mandate for the forty-nine *dong* under his influence to hold the line in defending against the Song army during the Song-Lý war (1075–1076). After achieving victory in the conflict, the local chief was awarded with the honorary title "Hữu đại liên ban," normally granted to high officials in the Lý period. In 1077 his son Hà Dị Khánh was married to the Khâm Thánh princess. The defense contributions of chiefs such as the loyal Hà played a strategic role in thwarting Song military aggression in this later period.

The battle for the Vị Long Prefecture at Kim Hoa Bộ could be seen as a conflict triggered by border trade. The Dali and Lý courts were also competing for influence over Vị Long Prefecture and all the other *jimi* Dong World prefectures, inhabited by the Lao and Bai communities in the borderlands between the two kingdoms, while these Dong World communities were also fighting for dominance over each other. As part of the Dong World, the northern part of the Đại Cồ Việt kingdom was a mountainous region with steep terrain, and it shared its topography with the southeast corner of the Dali kingdom. The frontier communities of this region were inextricably linked with the Nanzhao's local governance by the end of that kingdom's reign.[125] The Dali was founded in confederation with the Dong World elite that inhabited its southern territory and provided the new state with the military force to project its influence into the southern borderlands. Li Weizhen argues that a lack of adherence to the traditional Sinitic concept of "Hua-Yi order" (*Hua Yi zhixu*), an imagined fixed division between the cultured center and the barbarian periphery, explains why the Dong World communities were more receptive to Dali leadership. It appears that the Dong World elite would more easily abandon their support for Dali rule when faced with the arrival of Mongol forces.

The Dali kingdom may have been unable to foster regular tributary relations with Kaifeng, but because its center of power was located at the crossroads of commercial and transportation routes through the heartland of the Dong World, Dali was at the center of regional trade in the tenth and eleventh centuries.[126] In this period Dali maintained trade ties with its southern neighbors such as Pagan, which offered gold and cowries to continue trade links. Dali, in turn, supplied horses through Guangxi to the Song court, with which the Yunnan kingdom also engaged in salt trade.[127] This trend toward trade-centered ties would have a dramatic impact on imperial Chinese relations with these emerging frontier kingdoms. The commodity that drew the Song court to Dali was horses, and at its height, this trade supplied around 1,500 head annually to Kaifeng from Yunnan.[128] The Song court's move south following the Jin conquest had a significant impact on the horse trade with the Dali kingdom and other southwestern local communities, moving the central contact point of trade from southern Sichuan to Guangxi.

The Dali court didn't establish regular tributary ties with the Song, but there were some efforts at contact that paralleled the commercial exchanges or marked major events at the Song court. In 1076, during a year in which the Song would engage in a bloody borderlands conflict with the Đại Việt kingdom, the Dali ruler sent envoys to the Song court on a formal tribute mission, which included golden adornments (*jin zhuang*), a mountain statue fashioned from jade and gemstones (*bigan shan*), a felt carpet (*zhan ji*), swords, shields, and a rhinoceros skin saddle and reins (*xipi jia'anpei*). After this tribute mission, Dali envoys did not come to the Song court often, nor were these subsequent missions hosted by Song officials in the Honglu Pavilion.[129] Soon, the primary point of contact between the two states would be the horse trade, which was facilitated by the indigenous inhabitants of the Dong World.

The Song–Đại Việt borderlands conflict (1075–1076), which will be discussed in chapter 3, also spread to the Dali kingdom. Song military forces had occupied the Temo Circuit following Nùng Trí Cao's third uprising (1052–1053), and a portion of the Temo Circuit located in the southeastern region of the Dali kingdom (eastern modern-day Wenshan Prefecture) was taken over by the Dali forces after Nùng Trí Cao's defeat. The inhabitants of the Yanzhong garrison township, an aboriginal prefecture within Temo Circuit, were then under the authority of Yongzhou Prefecture in the Song's Guangnan West Circuit.[130] Two decades later, fighting and regional instability from the Song–Đại Việt conflict spread to the Song frontier *jimi* region, which included the Temo Circuit.[131]

Several decades after the Song–Đại Việt conflict, the Dali ruling elite was caught up in an interclan power struggle that offered an opportunity for Lý expansion. In 1094 Gao Shengtai, a leading court official, usurped the throne from the Duan clan leadership, subverting the Dali kingdom's authority and allowing Gao an opening to establish his own "Da Zhongguo" (Great Central Kingdom).[132] After Gao Shengtai died of illness in 1096, the Gao clan maintained peace with the Duan clan, and the Dali kingdom was reestablished. The two courts peacefully coexisted without bloodshed. This was a unique political situation, in which the Dali kingdom created a political arrangement with the Duan clan occupying a nominal position in government and the Gao clan retaining administrative power. Given the turmoil at court and the relative lack of attention to guarding the borderlands region, the Đại Việt leadership saw an opportunity to continue its aggressive expansion into territory once controlled by Dali.

The opposite situation would occur when Đại Việt was itself facing political turmoil. Such an event occurred when Ông Thân Lợi, son of Emperor

Lý Can Đức (Lý Nhân Tông; r. 1072–1128) and his concubine, fled to the Dali kingdom. *Song Essential Documents* gives an account of the episode:

> In the summer of 1139, the Guangxi military commissioner [*jinglue anfuci*] reported, "I have discovered that Lý Can Đức had a child with a concubine, and they have fled to Dali for support. The child has changed his surname to Triệu, his given name was Trí Chi, and he has taken the title Bình Vương.[133] I know that Lý Dương Hoán [Lý Thần Tông; r. 1128–1138 and nephew of Lý Can Đức] has died, and Lý Thiên Tộ [Lý Anh Tông, r. 1138–1175 and son of Lý Dương Hoán] is now the king. The Dali kingdom has repatriated [Thân Lợi]. Now [Thân Lợi] has garrisoned his forces at the Lý military garrison [*zhuza*] at Tuohe River [or Tuoluhe River near Daxin] in Longjin Prefecture, and from here [Thân Lợi] wants to take the throne from Lý Anh Tông. Lý Anh Tông has subsequently led an army to fight his enemy. I also found that Thân Lợi wishes to pay fifty-two *liang* of gold and one elephant in tribute [to the Song], saying that he wants to borrow militia soldiers from this garrison. Afterward he made a secret agreement with the borderlands chiefs. If I receive an official order from the Song throne, I will send word to Kaifeng as to how best to understand the situation along this region of An Nam and how to gain their surrender."[134]

The Dali court took advantage of Lý Thần Tông's death and Lý Anh Tông's effort to establish a new position, assisting Thân Lợi in his return to Đại Việt to fight for the throne. One source noted that Dali sent three thousand soldiers to assist Ông Thân Lợi in winning the battle with the first cohort of Lý forces and with occupying a vast area in the north of Đại Việt.[135] Ông Thân Lợi occupied this region until he and his forces were defeated by the high-ranking Lý official Tô Hiến Thành (d. 1179). After his defeat he was captured and brought to Thăng Long, where he was executed. The *DVSKTT* account notes instead that the Song grand mentor (*taifu*) Su Xian captured Ông Thân Lợi and twenty of his chief followers, all of whom were beheaded.[136] As we can see in the official dispatch to Kaifeng, Song officials were also aware of the tensions, and local officials wished to capitalize on any opportunities presented by the chaos.

It was around 1139 when the East Asian geopolitical system changed dramatically with the rise of the Jin under the Jurchens and the demise of the Khitan-led Liao and the Northern Song.[137] The Jin and the Southern Song dynasty would go on to shape the East Asian interstate relations, and this new configuration of power had an impact on the Dong World. Some of the borderlands communities between the Dali kingdom and the Southern Song offered their allegiances to both the Dali and the Southern Song courts. They were separated between these two powers and resorted to a "double vassal" (*shuangchong chenshu*) manner of interacting with both Dali and Song authorities.[138] Moreover, Dali and Đại Việt established tributary relations with their own neighbors, emulating the type of relations states had with the Song. Some neighboring polities, however, resisted tributary arrangements all together. The Ziqi kingdom, the Luodian kingdom, and the Tai-speaking Temo Circuit within the Dong World region remained outside the bounds of tributary ties and instead operated as independent political entities.

During the Southern Song dynasty, on the southern borderlands of the Southwest Tongchuan Circuit (Xinan Tongchuan Fulu) in today's Santai County, a group of Wuman Dong World elite, who ruled large parts of western and southern Sichuan and sections of Guizhou Province, established an independent local ethnic polity, known as the "Luoshi Ghost Kingdom" (Luoshi Guiguo), or alternately written as "Luo Clan Ghost Kingdom."[139] It appears that the Luodian elite managed their realm independent from Song influence. In 1045 the Longfan elite sent a special envoy mission of 719 persons to Kaifeng to offer tribute.[140] At the end of 1067, the Luodian ruler Long Yige, identifying himself to the Song court as leader of the "Man Calming Army" (Jingman jun), Tribal Envoy (Fanluoshi), and "Great Sage King Defending Heaven" (Shoutian Sheng Dawang), had an audience with the emperor Song Yingzong (Zhao Shu; r. 1063–1067). Yingzong ordered that Long Yige be granted the title "Martial Serenity General" (Wuning Dajun). The entourage accompanying Long Yige included 240 persons, who each received titles from the Song court.[141]

Official engagements with Kaifeng continued on a periodic basis. In 1067 the Luofan clan leader Fang Yi and Zhang Hanxing each traveled from the Luodian kingdom to present tribute gifts to the Song court. The new emperor Song Shenzong (r. 1067–1085) gave Fang Yi the title "Man Pacifying General" (Jingman Jun) and gave Zhang Hanxing the titles "Man Withstanding General" (Hanman Jun) and Military Governor (Jiedushi). The *History of the Song Dynasty* account notes that in 1073, 890 people from the Dong World clans Longfan, Luofan, Fangfan, and Shifan entered the court for an audience with the emperor, and the mission leaders presented to the throne tributary gifts of cinnabar (*dansha*), felt (*zhan*), and horses. The Song emperor bestowed to the mission gifts of belted robes (*paodai*), coins (*qian*), and silk brocade (*jin*).[142] Several years later a group of four hundred followers of the Longfan clan made their way to the Song court, traveling many thousands of *li* to their destination. Emperor Shenzong showed compassion for their group, given their diligence in observing ritual protocol, but he ordered that the Five Clans should only send tribute once every five years in the future. Moreover, as the *History of the Song Dynasty* account notes, there should be a fixed number of people with each mission, and that number should not increase. The court would also determine the identity of the chieftain from each clan represented, to avoid any confusion of public and private interests in these tribute missions. The emperor ordered the court official Song Min to compile the tribute items offered by each clan. Protocol would be established for each visiting tributary clan and its delegates would be met at the Sifang Pavilion (Sifang Guan).[143]

By the Southern Song period, the Luofan clan elite had established the independent Luodian kingdom.[144] The Ming period *New Gazetteer of Guizhou* (Guizhou tujing xinzhi) contains this account:

In the Han dynasty this polity was the Southwest Yi territory [Yidi], in the third year of the Tang Wude reign the name was changed to Zangzhou, in the fourth year the name changed again to Kezhou, and it was the home to seven tribes. These tribes were known as the Lulu Man, who are now referred to as the Luoluo. The chieftain who was popularly known as a "ghost" for presiding over funerary rites for the benefit of spirits, resided in Puri, Guizhou [today known as Anshun City], and a number of times sent troops to invade Zang territory, which soon joined the Luodian kingdom. In the eighth year of Yuanhe [813 CE], the emperor ordered that the territory be returned to the Zangke Circuit. In the first year of Kaibao [836 CE] the ghost master [*guizhu*] A Pei was ordered to submit as ruler of an inner dependency *neishu*. During the Huichang reign period [840–846 CE], he was granted the title "Luodian king," and his realm became the Luodian kingdom. Later in the second year of the Latter Tang's Tiancheng reign era [927 CE], the Luodian king Pu Lu with members of the nine tribal peoples under his influence presented their tribute at the Latter Tang court. In the fifth year of the Latter Jin's Tianfu reign period [940 CE], the kingdom attached itself to Chu. During the Song it again became known as the Luodian kingdom. . . . In the beginning of the Yuan dynasty it was named the Luo Clan Ghost Kingdom.[145]

From the original thirty-seven tribes, the Yushibu tribe unified with the people of southern Guizhou to be known as the Luodian kingdom. The Song court depended on these neighboring kingdoms for regional information, particularly when the dynasty faced its biggest challenge from the invading Mongols. In 1256 envoys from the Luodian kingdom reported to the Song court that Mongol-led troops had seized the Dali kingdom and subsequently sought entry along the Song's southwestern frontier. The Song emperor Lizong (Zhao Yun) offered the envoys ten thousand *liang* in silver for this worrisome information.[146] In 1279 the Luodian leadership would pay allegiance to the newly established Yuan, and they would claim to control 1,600 *dong* with more than 101,000 households.[147]

Other small polities within the Dong World acted independently in the region west of the Song empire. Various clans of the region south of modern-day Kunming expanded east toward the western border of modern-day Guangxi, culminating in the establishment of the Ziqi (1100–1260) kingdom.[148] The Ziqi kingdom was founded between the Song's Guangnan West Circuit and the Dali kingdom, and occupied a vast territory: at its height the Ziqi's territory bordered Qujing to the north, the Red River to the south, the Kunming region to the west, and the Hongshui River in Guangxi to the east. The Ziqi's sudden emergence during the early Southern

Song dynasty added a new factor in the regional situation, due to the kingdom's influence on the Southern Song through its activities associated with extensive horse trading. The Ziqi used the horse trade to become wealthy, which formed the foundation for its entire economy.[149] In the short span of over a hundred years, thanks to horse trading, the Ziqi kingdom's influence outshone Luodian's, and it jumped into second place behind only the Dali kingdom as the Dong World's most important regime. Fan Chengda, the well-known Southern Song official posted to this region, wrote in 1173: "The Ziqi kingdom was originally a petty indigenous state, especially fierce and cunning, and addicted to profits, whose merchants sell horses at Hengshan. When their young men perceive a personal slight, they're keen to draw knives to confront each other, and some have developed a taste for bloodshed. The Yongzhou prefect ordered the execution of several of these indigenes, after which the fighting stopped."[150] As the horse trade caused the Ziqi kingdom to grow stronger, it led to greater competition between the Ziqi and the Luodian, and even to challenge Song authority at the Hengshan garrison. In 1177, a chieftain by the name Bi Chengzhe "bearing his kingdom's credentials" arrived at Yongzhou to negotiate with the local officials. At the same time he asked that he "might use *qianzhen*" as his reign period, which, in fact, was the same as asking the Southern Song court to recognize his independence.[151]

While the horse trade had increased interaction, however tense, between the Southern Song court and Dong World polities, after Ông Thân Lợi's capture, the contact between Dali and Đại Việt diminished greatly. According to the *Việt sử lược*, in 1189 two Dali monks named Huệ Minh and Giới Nhật were recorded as traveling to Đại Việt for Buddhist activities.[152] The Dali and Đại Việt states circulated Sinitic texts, including esoteric Buddhist teachings, and both states were located along the Red River as a main transportation route. Therefore, religious and cultural exchanges were likely frequent.[153] While it is possible that these conditions would support a transformation of the tense relationship between Dali and Đại Việt, eased into a generally pacific friendship through Buddhist diplomacy, more evidence is necessary to confirm this claim.

The Dali court continued to maintain sporadic relations with the Song court. In 1115, Guangzhou Inspection Commissioner (Guangcaishi) Huang Lin memorialized the court that an official from the "Nanzhao-Dali kingdom," Muyi Huailai, wished to approach the Song court with tribute. The Huizong emperor ordered Huang Lin to establish an official site for receiving this tribute at Binzhou (modern-day Guangxi). At this location the Song could monitor all requests to memorialize the court and host banquets for visiting envoys, accepting and rejecting all requests on a case-by-case basis.[154] In 1116 Huang sent his tribute envoys (*fengshi*) Tian Sishuang, Yan Ben, Li Zichong, as well as the deputy envoys (*fushi*) Tan Chuo and Li Boxiang, and the emperor ordered Huang Lin and Guangdong Deputy Transportation Commissioner (Zhuanyu Fushi) Xu Tixie to approach the palace for an audience with the emperor (*yi que*). At the appointed site, the envoys passed through the ranks of the court, and Huizong ordered the supervisor (*jiansi*) to act as the main host of this party. In early 1117, Dali envoys came to the capital and presented 380 tribute horses (*gongma*), musk (*shexiang*), bezoar (*niuhuang*), fine mats (*xizhan*), and jade and gemstone mountain sculptures (*bigan shan*), among other items. The court ordered that their ruler Duan Heyu (Duan Yu; r. 1108–1147) be granted the official titles Glorious Grandmaster of the Gold and Purple (Jin Ziguang Lu Dafu), Acting Minister of Works (Jianjiao Sikong), Yunnan Military Governor (Yunnan Jiedushi), Pillar of the Kingdom (Shangzhuguo), and King of the Dali Kingdom (Dali Guowang). The Song court then rewarded the ruler's service by honoring his son Duan Hui; before all assembled officials, the ruler's youngest child Duan Geng was given the illustrious title Tutor of Imperial Audiences (Ge Men Xuan Zan She Ren). Afterward, the prefect of Guizhou Tong impeached Inspection Commissioner Huang Lin for falsely claiming ownership of stolen goods and Lin was punished for this crime. At this point Dali envoys were temporarily prevented from entering the Song empire, but instead proceeded directly to a borderlands marketplace established at Lizhou.[155]

The Southern Song leadership revived relations with Dali shortly after the fall of Kaifeng and the establishment of the new capital at Hangzhou. In 1133 the Southern Song court established at Yongzhou the new government office of Department for the Supervision of Horse Trade (Matijusi), and set up a large stable for cavalry horses at the Hengshan garrison. The new Song emperor Gaozong also appointed Guangnan West Circuit (Guangnan Xilu) as the primary authority for supervising the horse trade in Yongzhou.[156] However, the Southern Song would adopt a more conservative diplomatic policy toward the Dali kingdom. Although the court explicitly allowed the trade in horses, it would not accept tribute from Dali envoys.[157] In the eyes of the Song officialdom, it was not an open frontier. As noted in Zhou Qufei's *Notes from the Land Beyond the Passes* (Lingwai daida), the Southern Song court "has contact with the southern Man, but one must pass through Yongzhou and Hengshan Garrison."[158] Even while engaged in fighting with the invading Mongols, the Southern Song commander Meng Gong (1195–1246) refused to reopen the Clear Stream Pass.

In the autumn of 1133, the Guangnan West Circuit through the Yongzhou defense official (*shou chen*) memorialized that Dali envoys petitioned to submit tribute and to engage in the horse trade. The imperial court had ordered Song officials to prohibit the purchase of horses.[159] Therefore, the court prohibited this exchange, because the emperor didn't wish to allow Dali to trouble the local people with a tribute mission conducted on false pretenses (*xuming*).[160] Zhu Shengfei memorialized the court, saying "in previous years Dali envoys presented tribute, but their attitude was deeply presumptuous. Huang Lin thereby was convicted of his crimes." The emperor replied, "as for these exotic distant lands, how do we ascertain their true sentiments? How do we calculate the proper price of their horses, so that they might bring us horses for use in our cavalry and not waste our efforts in doing so?"[161] The Song court responded by moving the Guangnan West Circuit Horse Trade Command (Maimaci) to the Yongzhou Prefecture. Each year Dali envoys brought gold brocade (*jinbo*) to the market and received several times as much in the value of their trade in horses. Due to the language barrier, translators would negotiate the quality of the commodities with their hands, and minor officials found in this system opportunities for official abuse.

In the summer of 1136, the Guangxi fiscal commissioner (*jinglue anfusi*) memorialized the throne, reporting that the Dali court had again dispatched envoys with a herd of tribute elephants and five hundred horses.[162]

Emperor Gaozong ordered the fiscal commissioner to greet these envoys and the tribute mission was offered proper courtesy. The emperor also ordered local officials to pay for these horses directly, and even though the elephants were not accepted, the court envoys duly recorded the offer of these animals to "console" the Dali delegation.[163] In the fall of the same year, the Imperial Hanlin Academy (Hanlin Xue) academician Zhu Zhen addressed the court, urging the throne to order Guangxi officials in all ordinary market transactions for horses to choose their steeds carefully and to take responsibility for these purchases, because no one had been dispatched for this important task. Lines of communication between north and south were unobstructed, the Song official argued, but the horse trade had begun to decline. Zhu maintained that taking these preventive measures would prevent the potential elimination of this important trade. An imperial edict was issued in support of this measure.

Even with some officials arguing for the maintenance of trade links with Dong World contacts, the Song court was beginning to withdraw inward and to seal itself off from cross-border economic exchanges. In 1149 the court banned all border markets run by diplomatic personnel. In 1156 the emperor banned the acceptance of tribute pearls from coastal Lianzhou, and he ordered the scattering of the ethnic Tanka residents of Lianzhou.[164] The Tanka or Danjia community, a term for marginalized trading communities living in boats along the south China coast from at least the late Tang period, were pearl-fishers and primary collectors of the valuable local products from the coastal trade along the Tongking Gulf.[165] There existed more than ten pools established for pearl farming in Lianzhou, and according to visitors from Đại Việt, the pools were one hundred *chi* in depth, and it was at this depth that large pearls were cultivated. The Tanka divers selected them, providing a considerable number for the Đại Việt market. Abruptly, the Song court banned their sale. In 1159, while the court decided to maintain the Xuyi army-managed market along the northern border with the hostile Jin kingdom, all remaining border markets were closed.[166]

In the late autumn of 1176, the magistrate of Jingjiang Protectorate (Jingjiang Fu) Zhang Shi ordered the cessation of the "strict protection of imperial forces" (*shenyan baowu*) policy, reporting that the Yongzhou garrison had no more than a thousand troops, while the Left and Right River *dong* militia (*ding*) numbered more than one hundred thousand troops. Zhang argued that each Dong World militia soldier was a "barbarian shield" (*fan bi*) for the empire, relying on Yongzhou for directions to act. A patrol officer (*xun jian guan yi*) managed their selection to provide support for these Dong World militia soldiers. The Song court desired to regulate the Dali kingdom, which would only be conducted from Yongzhou. However, there is no indication that Kaifeng was ever able to exercise such coordinated military mobilizations of Dali or any other potential Dong World allies in this period. Instead, as we'll see in the last chapters of this book, the Dali would fall to Mongol aggression and provide, unwillingly perhaps, a springboard for the Song's enemies to launch attacks on its vulnerable flank through a shattered Dong World landscape.

■

The phrase "the Song wields the jade axe" (*Song hui yufu*) refers to the relationship between the Song dynasty and the Dali kingdom. Yet the Dali kingdom lay at the center of regional Song trade. In the Song, the Dali maintained trade ties with its southern neighbors such as Pagan, which offered gold and cowries to continue trade links. Dali, in turn, supplied horses through Guangxi to the Song court, with which the Yunnanese kingdom also engaged in salt trade.[167] This trend toward trade-centered ties would have a dramatic impact on imperial Chinese relations with these emerging frontier kingdoms. The Chinese leadership revived relations with Dali shortly after the fall of Kaifeng to the invading Jurchen and the establishment of the Southern Song capital at Hangzhou. The commodity that drew the Song court to Dali was horses, as already mentioned.[168] In sharp contrast to the once prevailing view that the Chinese court pursued relations with its neighbors through a "one size fits all" tributary system of ritual ties, it is important to note that trade shaped the Chinese empire's relations with the emerging kingdoms of Southeast Asia at the same time when debates about border security informed the court's policy toward its northern neighbors. When we take into account the Song's relations with kingdoms and smaller polities along the Southwest Silk Road, the Chinese empire in this period appears flexible and adaptable in its relations with its neighbors, contrary to the inwardly focused depiction of the Song in early Chinese historical literature.

During the Northern Song period, scholars had concluded that the Nanzhao kingdom prior to the Nanzhao War had successfully manipulated surrounding upland communities into serving their cause, including communities that rightfully owed their allegiances to the Tang court. As Ouyang Xiu wrote, "early in the Tianbao period [ca. 754], when the [Tai-speaking] Huang clan was strong, Nanzhao joined forces with the Wei, Zhou, and Nong clans to invade, pillage, and annex ten neighboring prefectures. When shame caused the Wei and Zhou clans to be unwilling to attach themselves to the Nanzhao, the Huang clan attacked them and drove them to the shores of the South China Sea."[169] Even after the collapse of the Nanzhao court in the late ninth century, the Tang would not regain a strong influence over political affairs in the southwest.[170] The Song would attempt to intervene at times, but the central court would focus eventually on trade relations when political sway proved difficult to exercise. Only after Khubilai Khan's invasion of the region in 1254 would a direct connection between a northern empire and the southwest be revived. Until then, local cultural practices prevailed at the former heart of Nanzhao power in this distant corner of the Dong World.

THREE
THE ĐẠI VIỆT KINGDOM'S ENGAGEMENT WITH THE DONG WORLD

The modern Vietnamese state has placed a great premium on a sense of political unity across its territory that transcends ethnic divisions. The modern-day official sentiment is one of absolute unity, often referencing Hồ Chí Minh's exhortation, "Vietnam is one. Vietnamese people are one. Rivers can run dry, mountains can wear away, but that truth never changes."[1] Modern Vietnamese historiography emphasizes that a guiding policy of national unity led to revolutionary success in the August Revolution in 1945, including the Điện Biên Phủ campaign and other major military campaigns against the French and American forces. However, this picture of ethnic unity has been complicated by recent research on the history of modern Vietnam that touch on the Dong World. Christian Lentz's 2019 study of the Điện Biên Phủ campaign demonstrates how the DRV administration of the Black River region after 1954 offered mixed results for local communities of swidden agriculturalists. The Thài-Mèo Autonomous Zone, established in 1956, gave Tai elite more power and undermined the existing social and economic practices of the region's non-Tai communities, contrary to the popular political rhetoric decrying a legacy of local Tai hegemony.[2] The same frontier area one thousand years earlier must be judged on its own terms, but there was some similarity in the ways that lowland *dong* were able to control access to trade and political power as the early leaders of the developing Đại Cồ Việt state attempted to expand into its northern frontier.

The Dong World before the Đại Việt Kingdom

Features of the Dong World are clear in the Sino-Vietnamese borderlands, with each locality along the frontier distinguished by distinctive characteristics. Dong World inhabitants have long farmed the valleys in the northwest. The Việt Bắc is about three hundred meters (984 feet) above sea level, and villages crowd the valleys in the Tai areas of Cao Bằng and Lai Châu. There are also other ethnic groups, including Hmong, Dao, and Tibetan-Burmese peoples, who migrated to Vietnam later than these Tai-speaking communities, and, due to a lack of arable land, reside in the middle of or on the summit of neighboring mountain ranges at an altitude of five hundred to one thousand meters above sea level.[3] The non-Tai local inhabitants depended on shifting cultivation and the maintenance of small terraced fields at the foot of the mountains. Interaction between upland and lowland communities in the Dong World region was an important dynamic in state formation from early times. At the end of the third century BCE, according to Chinese and Vietnamese court chronicles, an alleged northern emigrant Thục Phán (257 BCE–179 BCE), known to history by his posthumous title An Dương Vương (r. 208 BCE–179 BCE), joined the frontier area *dong*, collectively ruled as the Nam Cương kingdom; remaining subjects of the disputed Văn Lang kingdom (ca. 2879 BCE–?), meanwhile, founded the Âu Lạc kingdom (208 BCE–179 BCE).[4]

According to Lã Văn Lô's Vietnamese translation of the disputed Tai local legend "Nine Lords Compete to Become King" (Cẩu chủa chenh vùa), the Tai-speaking inhabitants of northern sections of the Văn Lang kingdom formed a tribal union that was named "Nam Cương" and headed by a member of the local elite Thục Chế, who was based in Nam Binh (modern-day Hòa An, Cao Bằng).[5] This federation was comprised of Nam Binh and nine other *mường* (a traditional sociopolitical unit administered by Tai elite in uplands areas): Thạch Lâm, Hà Quảng, Bảo Lạc, Thạch An, Phục Hoà, Thượng Lang, Quảng Nguyên (Cao Bằng), and Thái Ninh and Quy Sơn (in Guangxi). Thục Chế allegedly ruled for sixty years and was ninety-five years old when he died. After Thục Chế died, his son Thục Phán went on to succeed his father, eventually strengthening his hold on Nam

Cương's territory and defeating his lowland neighbors to create a unified kingdom across modern-day northern Vietnam. Liam Kelly has argued for a different understanding of this legend, contending that although Thục Phán appears to have been a historical figure, little evidence prior to the late fifteenth-century account in Ngô, Sĩ Liên's *Complete Book of the History of the Great Việt* (Đại Việt sử ký toàn thư), provides any support for the earlier founding of Nam Cương as a Dong World Tai federation and the later rule of An Dương Vương from Cổ Loa in the Red River Delta.[6] This shared history between the Việt and Tai peoples would need to wait for a later period to emerge.

In any case, the native inhabitants of the Dong World remained at the center of the network of routes connecting this area to the trade and technology that defined Đông Sơn bronze culture in the premodern period throughout south China and Mainland Southeast Asia. The continuing importance of bronze-casting for the dominant Li and Lao people that separated the Red River region from the northern regimes of central China provided a distinguishing feature of these Dong World occupants of this region.[7] Migrations from elsewhere in the Dong World also brought others for various reasons to the Sino-Vietnamese frontier area, where they divided into many different communities in the high mountains of Hà Giang, Cao Bằng, and Lào Cai.[8] The mountain ranges in these areas consist of weathered limestone peaks that are full of caves. In some places the mountains are quite high, such as the tallest peak in Mainland Southeast Asia: Phan Xi Păng (3,142 meters/10,312 feet) in the Hoàng Liên Mountains. Interspersed between these mountains are the plateaus, such as the Cao Bằng plateau, the Đồng Văn plateau, the Lào Cai plateau, Sơn La, Mộc Châu, Plâyku, Đắc Lắc, Lang Biăng, Di Linh, which throughout history have hosted settlements beside their terraced valleys and fertile mountain fields in such *dong* as Thất Khê (Lạng Sơn), Hoà An (Cao Bằng), Than Uyên (Lào Cai), Quang Huy (Sơn La), Mường Thanh (Lai Châu), and Mường Lò-Nghĩa Lộ (Yên Bái).[9]

Once settled in the region, the Tai-speaking communities of the borderlands lived in low-lying valleys that were interspersed with fields, streams, and rivers, which together created the conditions for developing a multisector agriculture. In the fields, people grew upland rice, maize, potatoes, cassava, and fruit trees (plums, pears, oranges, tangerines, persimmons), as well as cultivating bamboo, palms, and other trees. Farmers used a variety of techniques, including plowing, weeding, and fertilization, and had particular experience in building dams for treadle systems for crop irrigation, especially on the terraced fields on the mountain slopes. Many families raised buffaloes, cows, pigs, chickens, fish (in ponds), and silkworms.[10]

The region's mountainous forests were home to many kinds of animals, including elephants, rhinos, tigers, leopards, deer, forest buffalo, and gaur cattle (*bò tót*). The streams and grassy hills in the southwest central region of the frontier area provided ideal conditions for raising cattle.[11] Residents of low-lying valleys had little need for domesticated horses, because lowland transportation was easier than travel in the remote mountain areas occupied by Hmong, Dao, and other upland groups, where horses were more commonly raised. Between the mountains and the plains there was also a complex river system that flowed from the mountains down to the plains, bringing fertile silt. The main waterways include the Cầu River, Thương River, Lục Nam River, Đà River, Hồng (Red) River, and the Lô River, which functioned as the arterial routes between the mountains and the plains.[12] The mountainous areas of Vietnam not only had economic advantages, but also played a strategic role in borderlands defense. Lạng Sơn has two strategic passes—Ải Chi Quan and Quỷ Môn Quan, in the southern section of modern-day Chi Lăng Commune—which have been sites of conflict with numerous northern powers throughout history.[13] The role indigenous communities played in defending this strategic territory within the Dong World will be examined later in this chapter.

The Tai-speaking peoples of this region of the Dong World usually lived in villages of thirty to fifty households, although villages in the eastern section of the Sino-Vietnamese frontier area may have had up to one hundred households. The largest village at the center of this configuration was called a *chiềng*.[14] Dong World village and prefectural chiefs through history appear to have wielded great authority and power. The local elite had full rights to use or seize the lands of any resident under their authority.[15] The leading Dong World Tai-speaking clan families of this region, such as the surnames Đinh, Quách, Hoàng, Bạch, and Xa, passed on their ancestral authority from generation to generation. Governance of the Tai-speaking regions of the frontier area was similar to the style of local administration practiced in the elevated regions occupied by non-Tai communities, adding that the circulation of local elite between the non-Tai and Tai areas would lead at times to the establishment of integrated chiefdoms. It was also the case that some Tai-speaking local elite were the descendants of lowland court officials, whose families originated in the delta region and were sent by the court to the borderlands mountain areas.[16] The leading clans were noted in the Vietnamese court chronicles pejoratively as the "Seven Barbarian Vassals" (Thất Tộc Phiên Thần), and their active administration of the region persisted through the mid-twentieth century.[17]

The northern frontier was home to ethnic groups described in conventional Vietnamese scholarship as the Thổ, Nùng, and Mán (a reference in this case to the upland Yao/Dao), who occupied the wide mountain area located between two large river plains. These were the plains between the Lô River (Nhị Hà) on the Đại Việt frontier and the banks of the Yu (Uất) River, which flowed to the Yongzhou (Nanning) administrative center in Song territory. Historian Hoàng Xuân Hãn has argued that from the Cao Bằng region to the east, the Đại Việt border was pretty clear, located near Qinzhou Bay (China), but that "to the west of Cao Bằng, the Southern Man people lived in *dong* that didn't belong to any state authority, so the (Đại Việt) border, so to speak, did not exist."[18] The settlements of these Tai-speaking communities, often known by the surname of their chiefs, paid little attention to shifting political boundaries of distant lowland states. Members of the Hoàng clan resided on the two sides of the frontier at Như Tích *dong* and Vĩnh An Prefecture (châu Vĩnh An). The Vi clan occupied the areas of Siling, Lüping, and Xiping in Song territory and Tô Mậu Prefecture in the Đại Việt.[19] As noted in court chronicles, clans with the surnames Nùng, Hoàng, and Chu lived on the banks of the Left River (Tả Giang) and Right River (Hữu Giang). The Nùng clan administered four Dong World prefectures: An Bình, Vũ Lặc, Tư Lăng, and Thất Nguyên, which belonged to the Left River region, and Quảng Nguyên, which today is east of Cao Bằng.[20] The Hoàng clan resided in the western region of the

Right River region. The largest four *dong*, An Đức, Quy Lạc, Lộ Thanh, and Điền Châu, were located in northern and northwestern Cao Bằng, western and southwestern Guangxi, and southeastern Yunnan. The paths of both the Left and Right Rivers include fifty to sixty *dong*, and the *dong* chiefs governed only the inhabitants from their own community.

Beginning with the Tang in the late seventh century, northern dynasties tried vigorously to win the loyalty of these frontier area clans. In the Right River region the Tang court established thirty-six *jimi* prefectures for indirect control, but these Dong World prefectures would eventually escape the grip of Chang'an when local elite grew strong enough to recruit local militia and rebel against the Tang dynasty. The aftermath of the An Lushan Uprising presented the setting for these local challenges. At the beginning of the Zhide reign period (756–758) of the embattled emperor Tang Xiaozong (711–762), the widespread Xiyuan Uprising was launched by Huang Qianyao and Zhen Congyu, whose leadership had attracted support from the Dong World elite of Luzhou (west of modern-day Hepu), Wuyang (north of modern-day Luocheng), and Zhulan (in modern-day Guangxi) *dong*.[21] The rebel leadership promoted Wu Chengfei and Wei Jinglan to the position of general (*shuai*), while taking the additional title "King of the Central Yue/Việt" (Zhongyue Wang). Close supporters adopted additional titles of authority; Liao Dian took the title "King of Southern Gui" (Guinan Wang), Mo Chun took the title "King of the Expanding South" (Tanan Wang), Xiang Zhi became "King of the Southern Yue/Việt" (Nanyue Wang), Liang Feng became "King of Zhennan" (Zhennan Wang), Luo Cheng became "King of Military Achievement" (Rongcheng Wang), and Mo Xun took the title "King of the Southern Sea" (Nanhai Wang).[22] All of these clan leaders pledged their militia and subjects to the concerted effort to carve out an autonomous region of the Dong World in the face of Tang weakness and uncertainty. The *New Tang History* (Xin Tang shu) account contends that the area captured by the rebels was comprised of more than two hundred thousand persons, and it occupied "a territory of thousands of miles" (*mian de shu qian li*). The region would remain beyond Tang control for four years, but Dong World local authority would not go unchallenged. The Tang court sent a large force to suppress the uprising and in 760 the local defenders were defeated. Huang Qianyao and his elite supporters were captured and beheaded along with two hundred followers.

In 794 frontier leader Huang Shaoqing led an attack on the Tang forces at Yongguan, laying siege to the force led by the transit minister (*jinglueshi*) Sun Gongqi, who petitioned the Tang court to allow a counterattack by all available local militia in the Lingnan region. The Tang emperor Dezong declined the request.[23] Shortly thereafter, the four Dong World prefectures of Qinzhou, Hengzhou, Xunzhou, and Guizhou fell into the hands of Dong World authorities. Huang Shaoqing and his son Huang Changmian seized a total of thirteen frontier area prefectures.[24] The *XTS* account notes that the Tang court was angered by these developments and the emperor ordered the Tangzhou prefect Yang An to form a joint military expedition with transit minister Sun and, in the emperor's words, to "spring a surprise attack on the traitors" (*yinshi yanzei*).[25] The Tang force successfully defeated Huang's forces, capturing the leaders and regaining control of seized territory.

The trouble the Tang court faced with the Dong World elite hadn't yet abated. In the first year of Emperor Xianzong's (778–820) reign in 806, Yongzhou militia captured another chief from the Huang clan, Huang Chengqing. In the following year the Tang court switched tactics and released Huang Shaoqing, giving him the title of native prefect (*cishi*) of Xunzhou Prefecture. The Tang court gave his younger brother Huang Shaogao the position of prefect in Youzhou, and the *XTS* account notes that no other attempts at an uprising came from this specific family.[26] Official accommodation was now the most effective strategy. However, this arrangement with the Tang court did not mark the end of trouble from the Huang clan. Shortly thereafter, clan members Huang Shaodu and Huang Changguan also rebelled against Tang rule, attacking the Dong World prefectures of Binzhou and Luanzhou and seizing these territories. In 816 these two Huang chiefs and their followers attacked the coastal prefectures of Qinzhou and Hengzhou. The regional defense forces of the Yongguan prefect Wei Yue were defeated, and the official was driven from his residence. Several years later the Huang rebels returned to the area and massacred the inhabitants of the Yanzhou Prefecture. The Guiguan inspection commissioner (*guanchashi*) Pei Hangli memorialized the throne to complain about the relative weakness of his local military force and asked that imperial troops be dispatched to round up the Dong World chiefs and their followers.[27] Tang Xianzong allowed for this court request to be honored. Pei Hangli led his troops in a series of counterattacks on the Huang forces, which took two years. During this period he falsely memorialized the Tang court that he had beheaded twenty thousand rebels.[28] At this time, some type of sickness spread through the local inhabitants of Yongguan and Rongguan and caused more than eighteen deaths. Soon thereafter, troops from the Vietnamese side of the borderlands attacked the site of the Tang frontier administration, killing Governor-General (Duhu) Li Xianggu. In response, the Tang court gave the Tangzhou prefect Gui Zhongwu the position of governor-general. Gui took the position but refused to engage the attackers, so the court demoted him and sent the Anzhou prefect to replace him; Gui died before he could be recalled.[29]

In the early ninth century, the Nùng/Nong leaders also rebelled against the domination of the Tang dynasty. The Huang and Nùng clans were in control of eighteen of the Tang's frontier prefectures, and when a new military commissioner (*jinglueshi*) took up his post, he dispatched one envoy to meet with the two clans.[30] In response, the two Dong World leaders offered a show of combined force by plundering the surrounding prefectures. The military commissioner had five hundred Dong World militia soldiers at his disposal, but he was unable to command them to defend their position. Soon thereafter, during the Dahe reign period (827–835), the new military commissioner Dong Changling sent his son Dong Lan to attack these *dong* and wipe out their local network of allies. All those persons who were unwilling to submit to the Tang authorities would be considered violators of the Mandate of Heaven (*You Weiminzhe*) and severely punished. The surrounding eighteen prefectures soon submitted tribute, and the major routes between the court and the borderlands region were cleared and pacified.

After that, however, the Nùng settlements continued to maintain strong ties with the Nanzhao kingdom. Although the Tang emperor Yizong had signed a peace agreement with the Nanzhao, the two indigenous communities (Huang and Nùng) repeatedly broke the agreement. The Yongguan military commissioner Xin Jian was then charged by the Tang court with establishing peace with the Nanzhao and these local leaders. Xin presented beautiful gifts to the leaders of the two river communities, which included the Taizhou native prefect Huang Boyun, Tundong chief Nong Jinyi, and the Yuanzhou chief Nong Jinle. However, shortly thereafter in Yuanzhou, the chiefs Nong Jincheng, Nong Zhongwu, and Nong Jinle attempted to attack the Huang community leader Huang Boshan, but Huang Boshan ambushed their troops by the Dewy Waters (Rangshui) River. Nong Jincheng and Nong Zhongwu were killed; only Nong Jinle managed to escape. Wanting to avoid an act of revenge, Xin Jian sent the chiefs cattle and wine in an effort to seek reconciliation between the attackers, making an emotional speech in which he offered himself as a prisoner if the feuding clans would reconcile. The *XTS* account notes that Nong Jinle was moved by this speech, and he chose to call off his militia forces.[31]

The court chronicle example of the late Tang frontier administrator Li Zhuo offers another less cooperative picture of the interaction between appointed and indigenous leaders in this region. Đỗ Thành Tôn served as the indigenous governor-general of Ai Prefecture as a member of a clan that had benefitted politically in an earlier period of Tang rule on the borderlands. When Li Zhuo came into conflict with Đỗ Thành Tôn, who formed an alliance with neighboring chiefs to exercise their local authority, the Tang official had the Dong World leaders and their followers arrested and executed. Keith Taylor has noted that Li Zhuo, as a frontier area administrator, took advantage of the frontier communities and that his harsh rule led to additional revolts among the upland chiefs. His harsh administration also caused these local leaders to lend their support to the Nanzhao forces when they swept into the region in 858.[32] The Dong World elite would return to enduring political alliances within their sphere when cooperation with representatives of lowland regimes became untenable.

When the Song empire was established, local Song officials planned from their center of power at Yongzhou (modern-day Nanning) how to win over the loyalty of the residents in the surrounding *dong*. In fact, Song dynasty officials only maintained a relationship with a number of *dong* near the Yongzhou garrison, while those communities at a distance only paid tribute to the Song or instead served the Lý dynasty. The *dong* of Vạn Nhai (modern-day Thái Nguyên), Vũ Lặc (modern-day Cao Bằng), and Quảng Nguyên (modern-day Cao Bằng) all paid tribute to the Lý court.[33] Hoàng Xuân Hãn argued that Song officials believed that this territory already belonged to the Song empire, so that when local people of these communities harassed others tending the fields along the Right and Left Rivers, Song officials were not required to make inquiries.[34] There were occasions when local elite grew disgruntled over every disturbance from one territory to another, but there was little that the distant Song officials could do to sway events, despite claims to hold the authority to do so.

On the other side of the Dong World frontier, the Lý court abandoned the Tang-style administrative units employed by the Đinh and Lê courts to adopt a Song-style administration, dividing the provinces (*đạo*) into smaller military districts (*lộ*). As will be discussed, this militarization of the frontier administration had the effect of rewarding loyalty to the lowland court in times of unrest and of limiting local disturbances in times of peace. As the basic administrative unit, Lý and later Trần administrative authorities had applied the term *châu* for both lowland and upland administrative units, although the upland elites likely accepted the administrative titles *thứ sử* and *tri châu* for their honorific value as status enhancers. In the Lý and Trần administrative orders, a *châu* could describe three different kinds of boundaries: (1) an upland district, usually governed by hereditary chieftains (Tai or Mường), who, following the customs of the Tang-style "bridled and haltered" (*jimi*) system, accepted the titles *mục* and *thủ lịnh* (designating slightly lesser status) from the Vietnamese court, but were ruled largely autonomously; (2) an upland district, similar to the first, but, due to the political fragmentation of the territory or the weakness of the surrounding clan leaders, was administered by a court-appointed lowland official (*tri châu*), who had under his direct command a group of hereditary chiefs as his *thủ lịnh;* and (3) a lowland district, ranked similarly to a county (*huyện*) and led by a prefect (*tri châu*).[35]

The Đại Việt leadership, unlike the Song, did not follow a center-periphery zonal arrangement, but instead maintained personalized patron-client relationships with each of its satellite partners along the frontier region.

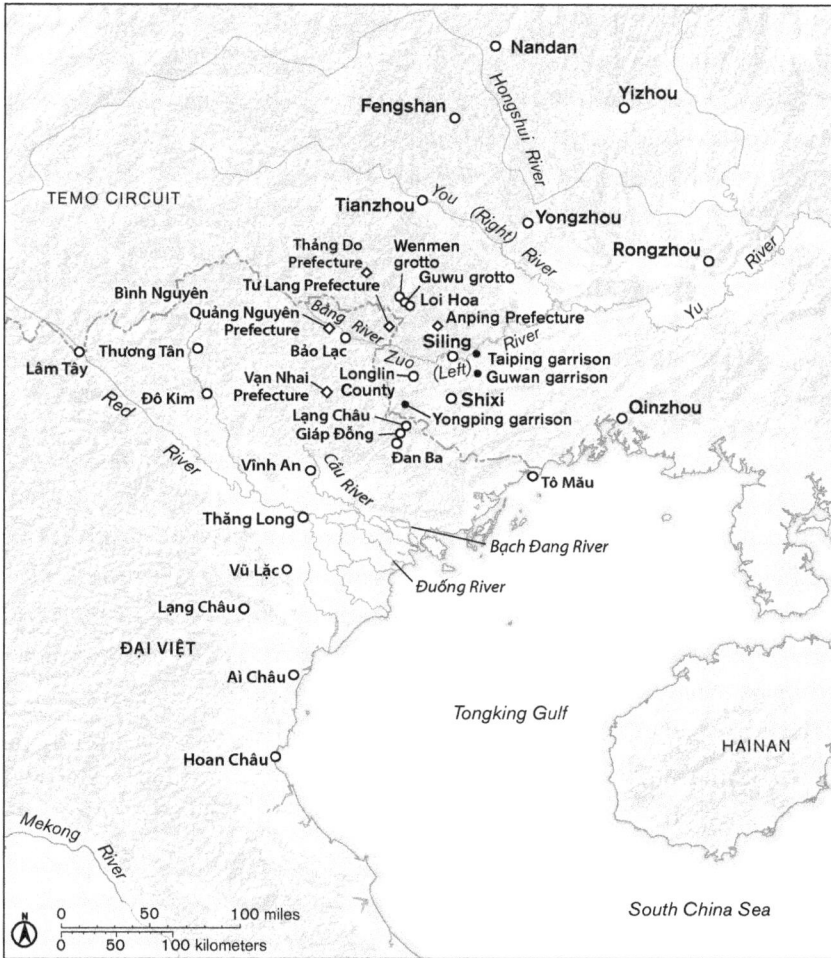

The Middle Dong World Era (tenth–twelfth centuries)

Moreover, Vietnamese leaders were dependent on controlling the resources of the frontier, both material and human, for economic and political ends. To achieve this control, Vietnamese leaders employed a combination of marriage alliances and military excursions to ensure their supremacy in the region. Moreover, several different Vietnamese courts based their efficacy along the frontier on the projection of influence, measured in resources extracted, and not primarily on the "centering" of loyalty among frontier vassals. The Lý rulers soon realized that the distance between Thăng Long and the *dong* in the northeast was not that great, and that Đại Việt influence over borderlands territory west of the Left River was easier to maintain than it was for the Song court.[36] Hoàng Xuân Hãn argued that this effort was also predicated on gaining the allegiance of the frontier elite before the Song officials were aware of the effort, at which point it would be too late to object, and the Song court would need to accept the new frontier arrangement.[37]

Early Đại Việt Power Consolidation

With the rule of Đinh Bộ Lĩnh, Vietnamese rulers used the evolving relationship with China to set the foundation for their own indigenous base of power.[38] The emerging Vietnamese political order was shaped by interplay between Chinese signs of authority expressed through the tribute system and local Vietnamese responses to and adaptations of these signs. Three successive Vietnamese ruling families, the Đinh (968–980), the Lê (980–1009) and the Lý (1009–1225) expanded their regional influence within this tributary framework while the leaders of these clans competed with others, even their own kinsmen, for local dominance. Cooperation with frontier elite was a part of this consolidation of power.[39] According to a Tai legend, during the borderlands conflict with Song forces in 980 and 981, Lê Hoàn (r. 980–1005) stayed up one night with his military commanders assembled in Thái Đức village, discussing with the local elders and village chiefs how to fortify the Chi Lăng frontier pass (in modern-day Lạng Sơn) to defend against the Song attack.[40] Lê Hoàn would call for a strategic ambush near this site, which would wipe out the Song forces led by Hou Renbao (d. 981) and effectively end the northern invasion. Local inhabitants of this borderlands region in northern Vietnam commemorated Lê Hoàn's deeds with this folk song:

> Poetry to the spirit of Mount Hàm Quỷ's stone cliffs [of Chi Lăng
> Pass] still remains.
> Its greenery reminds us of the nation.
> The famous tale of Lê Hoàn beating the Song is widespread.[41]

Another important point to consider here is the interclan rivalry that affected the borderlands alliances on both sides. Song forces had granted titles to other Tai-speaking elite from the Left and Right River region, who joined them for this unsuccessful expedition.[42]

Beginning with Lý Thái Tổ (Lý Công Uẩn, r. 1010–1028), the Lý court employed the titles and political associations of the tribute system to establish local institutions of political influence. In 1010, Lý Thái Tổ ascended to the throne and moved the capital from Hoa Lư north to Thăng Long. After completing construction of the capital, Lý Thái Tổ divided the Đại Cồ Việt kingdom into twenty-four circuits (lộ), as well as the subordinate administrative regions of the prefecture (phủ and châu), the district (huyện), village (hương), and the stockade (giáp). For the mountainous frontier areas, the subordinate administrative units under the prefecture (châu) were the dong (động) and the mountain village (sách). The Lý court also established a permanent presence of court authority with the construction of the Vọng Quốc township (trấn) and the courier-stations (trạm) Quy Đức, Bảo Ninh, Tuyên Hoá, Thanh Bình, Vĩnh Thông, Cảm Hoá, and An Dân to establish resting stations for the mountain chiefs, who traveled every year to the court at Thăng Long.[43]

Hoàng Xuân Hãn contended that the Lý court's calm state of internal affairs at that time allowed the leadership to pay close attention to the southern and northern borders.[44] Anthropologist Đàm Thị Uyên wrote that the Lý leadership allowed the frontier area chiefs to govern themselves according to indigenous practices, and that the Thăng Long employed lenient policies of control to entice these communities to ally themselves with the lowlands court. The Lý paid special attention to the communities along their northernmost frontier and to maintain influence west of the Left River dong and along the long frontier from Bảo Lạc Prefecture (modern-day Cao Bằng) to Vĩnh An Prefecture (modern-day Vĩnh Phúc). The Lý court advisers advocated getting close to the leading local clans by bestowing high rank on their leaders.[45]

Responsibility for frontier management, including the maintenance of border militia, was assigned to the Dong World prefects. According to *The Imperially Ordered Annotated Text Completely Reflecting the History* of *Viet* (Khâm định Việt sử Thông giám cương mục), "At that time there was no restraint, the civil and military affairs in the prefectures were governed by the native prefects [*châu mục*]. The uplands were left to the local chiefs."[46] As Đàm Thị Uyên writes, the basic policy of the Lý court was to consolidate and centralize control of the state by enlisting the frontier area chieftains to tighten their own influence over their local populations and by expanding Lý influence in the borderlands, through such practices as marriage alliances and the formal granting of court titles to local chiefs.[47] During the reign of the first Lý ruler, Lý Thái Tổ married his daughter to a local chief named Giáp Thừa Quý (or likely Thân Thừa Quý; 966–1029) in Lạng Châu Prefecture (modern-day Lạng Sơn) south of Chi Lăng Pass. In 1029, Lý Thái Tông (r. 1054–1072) married the Bình Dương princess to Thân Thiệu Thái (996–1066).[48] In 1066 Thân Thiện Thái's son Thân Cảnh Long (Thân Cảnh Phúc; 1030–1077) married Princess Thiên Thành, who was Lý Thánh Tông's daughter.[49] In this manner, close ties with frontier clans were maintained across generations.

Most of the powerful chieftains in the upland borderlands married princesses in the Lý court. In 1033, Lý Thái Tông took in marriage the daughter of Đào Đại Di in Đăng Prefecture (located in Hưng Hoá Province) and brought her to the palace. In 1036, Princess Trường Ninh married the Thượng Oai (Sơn Tây) prefect Hà Thiệu Lãm. During the same year, Princess Kim Thành married the Phong (Sơn Tây) prefect Lê Thuận Tông.[50] In the spring of 1082, Princess Khâm Thánh married the Vị Long prefect Hà Dị Khánh.[51] Lý Thánh Tông married the princess Ngọc Kiều to a Chân Đăng prefect by the surname Lê.[52] In 1144, Princess Thiều Dung traveled to Phú Lương (Thái Nguyên) to marry Dương Tự Minh and the commander-escort (*phò mã*).[53] As Đàm Thị Uyên writes, "With all of these marriage alliances, the Lý dynasty attached the ruler with Dong World chiefs in a 'father and son' relationship, causing local elite to become royal family members or officials of the court."[54]

The northern borderlands of Đại Việt were located in the lower half of the Dong World at the hub of what historian Li Weizhen termed "the Red River Commercial Route" (Honghe Shangdao), which connected trade items from the Dali kingdom along the Tea and Horse Route (Chama Dao) to the littoral trade markets of Mainland Southeast Asia. During the existence of the Dali kingdom, the route from modern-day Kunming through Mengzi to Thăng Long was one of the most important commercial routes for Yunnan to connect with overseas kingdoms. The Lihou monument (*Lihoubei*) preserved at the Yunnan Relay Station, located in Xiangyun County, described this route as the "Yunnan to Jiaozhi Route."[55] The Song official Yang Zuo's text *A Record of Buying Horses in Yunnan* (Yunnan mai ma ji) contains the passage, "the Yunnan Relay Station was located with Rongzhou to its east, India [*Shendu*] to its west, and Đại Việt to its southeast, . . . in all cases, this region is easily accessible."[56] The waterway from the heart of the Dong World to Đại Việt was divided into an eastern route and a western route.

The best port in Southeast Asia from the Dali leadership's perspective was in Đại Việt.[57] Yunnan was much closer to the Đại Việt kingdom than Guangzhou, and there were no large ports in Guangxi, only small ports such as Qinzhou. The late Nanzhao rulers at the center of the Dong World failed in their attempt to control the entire Red River Delta through invasion, but such plans were contemplated by the Nanzhao's Dali successors, considering the possibility that the Dali cavalry could take control of the Red River Delta and even blackmail the Đại Việt court, as the Liao had done with the early Northern Song court by forcing the terms in the 1004 Chanyuan Treaty (Chanyuan Zhi Meng), which included large payments the Song was obligated to give the Liao.[58] If successful, the Dali kingdom could occupy Đại Việt territory and benefit from the maritime access that the Nanzhao leadership failed to acquire. For the Đại Việt leadership, direct control of the northern frontier area of the kingdom was an existential matter. Controlling this area would provide a defensive barrier for the core economic zone of the Red River Delta and Southeast Asia's largest trading port.[59]

For these reasons, the lowlands Đại Việt court fostered relationships with borderlands chiefs to cement in place a political and strategic military influence in this important region. However, the court also sought economic gain from its links to the frontier area. In 1013, Lý Thái Tổ established a domestic taxation system and collected taxes of all kinds.[60] In the *DVSKTT* account, it is noted that the Lý court received taxes from the following sources: land and lakes, holdings in material wealth and paddy fields up to the shoreline, local products from the mountain regions, salt transported across the borderlands, supplies of rhino horns, ivory, and incense in the Man communities, and timber and fruits collected in the uplands region.[61]

The Lý court asserted state control with their tax policy over the exploitation of natural resources. According to the tax code of 1013, mountain communities were required to pay tribute in local products to the state on a regular basis. In 1039, the Vũ Kiến *dong* in Quảng Nguyên Prefecture produced gold in the amount of 112 taels (*lạng*). Local officials in Liên District (Ngân Sơn, Bắc Kạn), Lộng Thạch Prefecture (Thạch An, Cao Bằng), and Định Biên Prefecture (Định Hoá, Thái Nguyên) collected locally mined silver from neighboring pits.[62] In 1067, the Ngưu Hồng state (an independent Dong World polity located northwest of the headwaters of the Black River [Sông Đà] in Sơn La) offered as tribute gold, silver, aloewood (*trầm hương*), rhino horn, ivory, and other local items.[63] In 1117, the local borderlands official (*phò mã*) Dương Cảnh Thông offered white deer (*hươu trắng*) and the Tư Nông Prefecture (Phú Bình, Thái Nguyên) chief Hà Vĩnh Lộc offered red horses (*ngựa hồng*).[64] In 1124, as Quảng Nguyên prefect, Dương Tự Hưng offered white deer. Dương Tuệ, the leader of Tây Nông Prefecture (Thái Nguyên) offered two gold nuggets in the spring of 1127.[65] In 1129, the chief of Tây Nông Prefecture Hà Văn Quảng offered two gold ingots weighing thirty-three taels (*lạng*) and five pounds (*đồng*).[66] The Chân Đăng prefect (*mục châu*) Lê Pháp Quốc in 1132 offered black deer (*huyền lộc*).[67] In 1140 Lê Pháp Viên as the Chân Đăng prefect offered white deer as tribute for the Lý court.[68]

The Lý rulers also employed violent suppression of frontier area elite when doing so allowed the ruler to consolidate power and to draw royal family members closer in support of a particular ruler's reign. In 1010 after ascending to the throne, Lý Thái Tổ changed the administrative order of his realm by reorganizing the ten existing circuits (*đạo*) into twenty-four smaller circuits (*lộ*) and designating Aí Prefecture and Hoan Prefecture as garrisons (*trại*), giving a smaller share of local administration to a larger number of local officials, while further militarizing the landscape beyond the capital.[69] In 1013 Lý Thái Tổ suppressed the Dali prefect Hà Trắc Tuấn at

Kim Hoa Bộ in Vị Long Prefecture, causing the Dong World chief to retreat back into Dali territory.[70] The next year, 1014, the Lý royal family member the Dực Thánh Prince[71] (?–?) led an army to suppress the Dali military commander Dương Trường Huệ[72] and Đoàn Kính Chí, whose force of two hundred thousand troops were stationed at the Ngũ Hoa garrison, located in modern-day Kunming.[73] In 1015 the Dong World prefect Hà Trắc Tuấn seized the prefectures of Đô Kim (modern-day Hàm Yên District, Tuyên Quang Province), Vị Long (modern-day Chiêm Hóa District, Tuyên Quang Province), Thường Tân (modern-day Thường Tân Commune in Bắc Tân Uyên District, Bình Dương Province), and Bình Nguyên (modern-day Vị Xuyên District, Hà Giang Province), which had rebelled. Leading the Lý court's response, the Dực Thánh Prince and the Vũ Đức Prince both fought in this conflict and succeeded in capturing Hà Trắc Tuấn.[74] In 1022, the Dực Thánh Prince defeated Đại Nguyên Lịch and burned the granary treasure at the Song-administered Ruhong garrison, located near modern-day Móng Cái.[75] In 1029, the residents of the Đản Nãi Hamlet (*giáp*) in Ai Prefecture (Thanh Hoá) rebelled and the Lý ruler himself went to fight Đản Nãi, after which he sent envoys to the border to dig a canal to Đản Nãi's territory to bring his community into direct contact with the court.[76] In the same year, Lý Thánh Tông attacked Thất Nguyên Prefecture (Thất Khê, Cao Bằng), and the Đông Chinh Prince attacked Văn Prefecture (Văn Uyên, Lạng Sơn).[77]

In 1028, Lý Thái Tổ died. When the officials of the Lý court came to the Long Đức Palace to welcome the Khai Thiên Crown Prince (Lý Thái Tông [1000–1054] or Lý Phật Mã) to the throne along with the remaining members of the royal family, the Dực Thánh Prince, the Đông Chinh Prince, and the Vũ Đức Prince refused to submit to the new ruler, and turmoil emerged inside the court and along the borderlands. The Đông Chinh Prince relocated his army to the Long Thành citadel, and the Dực Thánh Prince and the Vũ Đức Prince relocated to the Quảng Phúc border pass, waiting for an attack by Crown Prince Khai Thiên.[78] Palace forces loyal to Lý Thái Tông eventually led attacks on the other princes and quelled the court rebellion, but the incident had an impact on frontier area management for the Lý court. In early 1033, the Định Nguyên (Yên Bái) prefect rebelled against Thăng Long and the Lý ruler personally quelled the unrest. When

Trẻ Nguyên Prefecture (near Định Nguyên) also rebelled in the autumn of the same year, Lý Thái Tông completed the suppression of these local elite before bringing troops back.[79] In the summer of 1034 the Hoan Prefecture rebelled against the throne and Lý Thái Tông sent forces to fight the rebels. When the Hoan Prefecture surrendered, the king announced a general pardon of the local leaders and sent envoys to appease the Dong World inhabitants. In 1036 the Khai Hoàng Prince (Lý Nhật Tôn or Lý Thánh Tông; 1023–1072) led an expedition against the Lâm Tây Circuit (Sơn La, Lai Châu), Đà Giang, and the prefectures Đô Kim, Thường Tân, and Bình Nguyên. Lý Nhật Tôn and his forces managed to quell all of the uprisings in Lâm Tây Circuit.[80] The successes achieved by Lý Thái Tông and his loyal family members consolidated Lý Thái Tông's hold on power and demonstrated that his central government was strong enough to keep the edges of his realm in check, including the areas where the Đại Cồ Việt kingdom overlapped with the Dong World. This uneasy balance would be challenged again within a decade by the stirrings of autonomous power nurtured by one of the borderlands most influential clans, the Nùng clan.

Nùng Trí Cao

Nùng Trí Cao (1025–ca. 1055), a native of Quảng Nguyên (modern-day Cao Bằng), was a descendant of a borderlands clan that had settled in the region in the Tang dynasty, occupying the areas around Quảng Nguyên together with the Hoàng and Chu clans. The Nùng became powerful local elite, as the *Cao Bằng thực lục* notes, annexing territory "like silkworms eating" to expand their local control.[81] At the end of the Tang dynasty, Quảng Nguyên Prefecture was established as part of the Lâm Tây Circuit. The activities of Nùng Trí Cao's grandfather Nùng Dân Phú on the Sino-Vietnamese frontier may be found in the early 977 memorial from the Yongzhou prefect, which noted that the local chief of Quảng Nguyên, the "peaceful and generous" (*thần xước/tanchou*) Nùng Dân Phú, was established as chief of ten Dong World prefectures on the Lý side of the frontier during the Southern Han dynasty (917–971).

With the founding of the Song dynasty, the emperor had ordered Nùng

Dân Phú to approach the throne with tribute.[82] The *SHY* account of this encounter noted that the Left River region's ten *dong* of Quảng Nguyên Prefecture, Vũ Lặc Prefecture, Nam Nguyên Prefecture, Tây Nùng Prefecture, Vạn Nhai Prefecture, Phúc Hoà Prefecture, Uẩn Prefecture, Lộng Prefecture, Cổ Phật Prefecture, and Bát Đam Prefecture were all under the administration of Thất Nguyên Prefecture (Thất Khê, Lạng Sơn), which he led.[83] Nùng Dân Phú wanted to establish Thất Nguyên Prefecture as a "an inner vassalage" (*neifu*) of the Song empire, and so be exempt from local taxes collected by the Lý court.[84] The Dong World residents of the Tư Lang Prefecture (modern-day Hạ Lang District, Cao Bằng Province) were protected by their Lý-guided garrison militia and Nùng Dân Phú couldn't get to them.[85] The borderlands chief requested that the Song court send troops to punish residents of Tư Lang Prefecture. After reading this memorial, the Song emperor ordered that Nùng Dân Phú be granted the honorific title acting minister of Works (*jianjiao sikong*), as well as the titles "grandmaster of splendid happiness bearing the golden pocket with purple trimming" (*jinzi guanglu daifu*), censor-in-chief (*yushi daifu*) and pillar of the state (*shangzhu guo*).[86] The Song court ordered Xu Dao, the transport commissioner (*zhuangyunshi*) posted to Guangzhou, to present these titles to the borderlands chief. However, after the failed 980 Song invasion of the border region, Kaifeng may have concluded that it was unable to curry favor with enough of these distant local chiefs to sway the entire region, and so the Song paid little attention to this region for the next few decades, during which the Lý court attempted to exercise their own control.

Trade was at the center of the power struggle that soon divided the Nùng clan and would eventually push Nùng Trí Cao down the path to uprising against both the Lý and Song courts. In 1038 Nùng Trí Cao administered Tư Lăng Prefecture and its taxable populace, which his grandfather had been denied, but Nùng Trí Cao's father Nùng Tồn Phúc, chief of the Thảng Do Prefecture near Cao Bằng, and his younger brother Nung Tồn Lộc, chief of Vạn Nhai Prefecture, located farther downstream in northeastern Thái Nguyên, had inherited from their father the vital trade route that connected the Red River Delta with the lower reaches of the Dong World. Nùng Trí

Cao's mother A Nùng, and her sister-in-law, Nùng Tồn Lộc's wife Dương Đạo, chief of Vũ Lặc Prefecture in the Right River region, both engaged in trade along the ancillary routes of the Southwest Silk Road that passed west to east through the borderlands. Family matters took a turn for the worse when Nùng Tồn Phúc killed his younger brother, Nùng Tồn Lộc, along with Lộc's wife Đương Đạo, and seized their commercially strategic territory.

Assuming that his influence over regional trade would enhance his local authority enough to throw off Lý patronage, Nùng Tồn Phúc created for himself the title Chiêu Thánh emperor, for his wife A Nùng, the title Minh Đức queen, and he appointed his eldest son, Nùng Trí Thông, as the Nam Diễn prince, likely with Dali support.[87] He renamed his territory the Trường Sinh (Longevity) kingdom, providing armor and training for his militia soldiers and preparing to fight.[88] On the New Year's Day of 1039, the leader of Tây Nùng Prefecture, Hà Văn Trinh, joined forces with Nùng Tồn Phúc to establish this Dong World polity. One month later the Lý ruler Thái Tông led the punitive expedition himself against the Nùng rebels. Lý Thái Tông captured Nùng Tồn Phúc and his leadership, including Nùng Trí Thông, all of whom were brought in chains back to the capital and executed. The violent court intervention did not bring lasting peace to the frontier area. A Nùng and her second child, Nùng Trí Cao, fled a short distance north to the Lôi Hỏa *dong*, located near modern-day Xia Lei village, Guangxi, which would become Nùng Trí Cao's main military training camp for his subsequent three attempts to form an independent Dong World polity.[89]

A Nùng married her third husband, Nùng Hạ Khanh, a local chief in control of the large Temo Dong World circuit, which reached from the area of modern-day Jingxi, slightly west of Xia Lei, to Wenshan in eastern Yunnan. This marriage created a powerful political presence of the Nùng in a strategic region of the Dong World between Dali and the lowlands Đại Cồ Việt kingdom. As mentioned earlier in this chapter, the Dali leadership wanted to have access to the trade route that connected their upland region to the maritime links in the Tongking Gulf. The Nùng would then need to be included in any negotiation for access to this trade, or they could serve as a useful ally in forcing the Đại Cồ Việt kingdom to give access to these inland Dong World states. Either way, a powerful Tai-speaking state encroaching on the frontier area, over which the Lý court desired to wield influence, was a clear point of tension between these upland and lowland powers. In 1042 and 1048, Nùng Trí Cao, his mother, and their growing militia of followers occupied strategic borderlands territory, such as the *dong* of Thắng Do, Lôi Hỏa, Bình, An, Bà and Tư Lang, but on both occasions, the Lý were able to defeat them and thwart their territorial ambitions. Nùng Trí Cao's uprising was not the only Dong World revolt that the Lý court had to contend with. In 1042, Lý Nhật Tôn as the Khai Hoàng Prince suppressed an uprising in Văn Prefecture (Văn Uyên, Lạng Sơn).[90]

In 1049 Nùng Trí Cao led the army from Yulin Subprefecture to attack the Hengshan garrison, followed by an attack on the Yongzhou prefectural seat farther downstream. Following this attack Nùng Trí Cao sent envoys to the Song court for negotiations.[91] News of major attacks on Hengshan and Yongzhou was certain to reach Kaifeng, given the importance of Yong-zhou for frontier management and Hengshan as a major trade node on the Southwest Silk Road. Nùng Trí Cao was attempting to grab the Song court's attention and negotiate for "inner vassal" (*neifu*) status with Kaifeng. Nùng Trí Cao didn't receive the response he sought, and although he tried periodically throughout his second and third uprisings, he also continued his effort to carve out an independent Dong World state. In early 1050, Song officials in Yongzhou appealed to the Dong World chiefs Vị Thiệu Tự and Vị Thiệu Khâm in Tô Mậu Prefecture (Đình Lập, Lạng Sơn) to call on three thousand people under their administration to profess loyalty to the Song court. The Vietnamese leadership attempted the same when Lý Thái Tông took military and diplomatic measures to retain the township of Triều Dương and reclaim Tô Mậu Prefecture.[92] After that, one of the leaders of Tô Mậu, Vi Thủ An, demonstrated his loyalty to Thăng Long with his vigorous participation in the anti-Song resistance organized and led by Lý Thường Kiệt in the 1075 borderlands conflict.[93]

In the summer of 1052 Nùng Trí Cao again captured Yongzhou and launched his rapid conquest of the south China coast, culminating in his force's siege of Guangzhou.[94] Although the Song-appointed deputy palace secretary (*shumi fushi*) Di Qing (1008–1057) eventually defeated the Tai-speaking chief and his followers, the Kaifeng court faced decades of regional turmoil even after Nùng Trí Cao's series of revolts had been quelled. According to the *Cao Bằng thực lục* account, Lý Thái Tông commanded his general Vũ Nhĩ to bring ten thousand troops in assistance of Nùng Trí Cao's army, but when he arrived in Yongzhou, he heard that Nùng Trí Cao had lost the battle, so Vũ Nhĩ brought his troops back to the Lý court, causing Nùng Trí Cao's defeat and his flight to Dali. After Nùng Trí Cao was gone, the people in Quảng Nguyên celebrated his achievements by establishing a temple of worship. Even the Lý court eventually commemorated Nùng Trí Cao as the "Great Khâu Sầm King" with a temple in Bán Ngân Village (*thôn*), Tượng Lặc Commune (*xã*) in Thạch Lâm District (*châu*). His mother, A Nùng, was celebrated in the Bà Hoàng đại vương temple in Phù Vạn Village, Kim Pha Commune, Thạch Lâm District.[95]

Lý Thường Kiệt

Despite the pressure placed on fellow clansman Nùng Tông Đản (1046–?) to follow the Song court after Nùng Trí Cao's defeat, Đại Việt authorities managed to retain influence over the Lôi Hỏa *dong*. With the exception of his eldest son Nùng Tông Tăn (fl. 1050–78), Nùng Tông Đán's other children refused to follow Song authorities. As Song emperor Shenzong mentioned in a related edict, "as for the children of Nùng Tông Đán, according to Lưu Kỷ, they're afraid of Nùng Tông Đán, so they will not follow." Hoàng Xuân Hãn noted that the Song emperor also told his generals, "If we can make a contract with local people occupying the gaps in the enemy's land near the border, we should do it. Then we will fight, and arbitrarily execute [disobedient Dong World leaders] . . . [as well as] employ peaceful means by granting titles, gold, silk, land, and rice . . . to lure these people."[96] Although Song officials used many means to attract these communities, the borderlands chiefs were not enticed by the Song. Instead, they remained actively engaged with the Đại Việt court, as was the case for Thân Thừa Quý, Thân Thiện Thái, and Lưu Kỷ.[97] The Lý court quickly suppressed open acts of rebellion, but the leadership was lenient toward those who surrendered to court authorities. In 1064, the Lý ruler sent forces to suppress the leaders of the Ma Sa *dong* (Đà Bắc Prefecture, Hưng Hoá), but after quelling the uprising, the ruler tried to attract the peaceful frontier inhabitants who had not participated in the fighting.[98]

During the eleventh century, political, economic, and demographic factors led to tensions and conflict in Song engagements along the Sino-Vietnamese frontier area, particularly following the suppression of Nùng Trí Cao's uprising. Although many Vietnamese scholars have blamed the Sino-Vietnamese borderlands war on the expansionist Song policies inspired by Wang Anshi (1021–1086) and his reforms, growing tensions at the border were the product of shifting demographics and local disturbances. While Song settlers were streaming south, the Lý rulers expanded the court's influence over the Dong World's frontier region. Political events at Thăng Long seemed to indicate that the Lý leadership was anxious to firm up a physical divide before the Song empire extended any farther south. By 1069, Lý Nhật Tôn (r. 1054–1072) felt confident enough to change the name of the kingdom to Đại Việt and drop all court references to the Song court's reign periods. Events of this period were instrumental in the negotiation of a physical border between China and Vietnam.

Famed Đại Việt military commander Lý Thường Kiệt (1019–1105) took the initiative to recruit local militia from the frontier area to become an integral part of the front line of his 1075 defensive strategy. To draw on local military expertise, he invited fellow royal family member Lý Đạo Thành (d. 1086), earlier demoted to the position of governor-general in Nghệ An Province, to return to the capital to serve as chancellor in the royal court.[99] Lý Thường Kiệt also worked hard to consolidate the Đại Việt military forces, enlisting leaders of ethnic minorities from the northern border region for military service.[100] In this manner the Đại Việt military response to Song aggression would be largely based on mobilizing militias drawn from the region these soldiers would be defending. Lý Thường Kiệt advocated attacking first and using Đại Việt forces at the northern border to cross into Song territory to harass the border area, causing the Song court to conclude that a Đại Việt attack was focused on Yongzhou. As historians Lê Văn Yên and Phạm Thị Hải Châu wrote, if the Song army left Yongzhou to rescue the border garrisons, the abandoned Yongzhou citadel could be lost immediately. If many troops remained in Yongzhou, the advancing

Vietnamese army could easily attack and destroy the surrounding fortifications protecting Yongzhou.[101] In the autumn of 1075, Lý Thường Kiệt launched a coordinated offensive across the Sino-Vietnamese frontier, which was divided into two advancing armies: a sea-faring force led by Lý Thường Kiệt from Vĩnh An (modern Móng Cái) to attack coastal Qinzhou and Lianzhou, as well as a militia force consisting of fifty thousand men that simultaneously attacked the entire Song garrison system of Hengshan, Taiping, Yongping, and Guwan, which protected Yongzhou. These four garrisons had been established under the direction of Di Qing as a means for protecting Yongzhou and the borderlands communities that had elected to ally with the Song.[102] The Lý land army was led by Lưu Kỷ, chief of the Quảng Nguyên area (Cao Bằng); Nùng Tông Đản (1046–?), who was once again a Lý court ally and chief of Lôi Hoả (northwestern Cao Bằng); Hoàng Kim Mãn, chief of Môn Châu (Đông Khê, Cao Bằng); Thân Cảnh Phúc (1030–1077), chief of Lạng Châu area (Bắc Giang); and Vi Thủ An, head of the Tô Mậu area (Lạng Sơn, Quảng Ninh). This militia of uplands chiefs coordinated with the army led by Lý Thường Kiệt to encircle Yongzhou.

The land-based militia army along the border occupied the garrisons of Yongping and Taiping. The troops from Lạng Châu took the areas of Taiping and Luzhou. The troops from Quảng Nguyên and Môn Châu occupied the Hengshan garrison (modern-day Pingma Township, Tiandong County, Guangxi). The Song generals fought back aggressively, but they all failed, and the commander of the Hengshan garrison, Lin Maosheng, the governor of the Yongping garrison, Su Zuo, the administrator of Taiping garrison, Wu Ju and the supervisor of Taiping garrison, Guo Yongyuan, all died.[103] The Song defenders quickly retreated to Yongzhou. The borderlands militia troops pursued the retreating Song troops, and then joined forces to encircle Yongzhou. Su Jian, the Song commander of Yongzhou, urged his soldiers to fight off this first attack, but it was, in fact, only the first stage in Lý Thường Kiệt's larger plan.

The larger naval force led by Lý Thường Kiệt, consisting of six thousand men, departed from Vinh An (modern-day Móng Cái), crossed the sea, and entered Qinzhou and Lianzhou. On the night of December 30, 1075, Lý Thường Kiệt's army invaded Qinzhou.[104] Caught by surprise, the

Song offered little resistance, and Qinzhou was quickly defeated. The Đại Việt forces stationed near the border of Qinzhou rushed in to occupy the Song garrisons, including Ruhong, Ruxi, and Didiao. Wu Huan, commander of the Ruxi garrison, and Zhang Shou, commander of the Didiao garrison, were killed, and the garrisons around Qinzhou were all conquered. On January 2, 1076, Lý Thường Kiệt landed at Lianzhou and sacked the citadel.[105] The Lianzhou prefect Lu Qingsun and the leading officials of Qinzhou and Lianzhou, including the Lianzhou prison jailers (*jianya*) Wen Liang, Zhou Zongshi, and Wu Fu; the Qinzhou military inspector (*xunjian*) Jiang Jin; the Qinzhou commander (*zhishi*) Song Dao; the Qinzhou acting special prefectural tax inspector (*jianshui shezhou*) Ouyang Yan; the Hepu District assistant magistrate (*zhubu*) Liang Chu; and the Lianzhou commander Wu Zongli were all killed.[106] Shortly thereafter, Lý Thường Kiệt directed his army toward the citadels at Baizhou and Yongzhou. In the assault on Yongzhou, the citadel commander Su Jian died alongside his family members and thousands of defenders; later in the same year, the Song court posthumously awarded Su the title "Military Commissioner Charged with Defending the State" (Fengguo Jiedushi).[107] Đại Việt forces also defeated the Dong World leader (*cishi*) of Xiaxi Prefecture Peng Shiyan, and the *jimi* prefecture of Tianci likewise surrendered to the attackers.[108]

The Song court managed to ally with Champa and the Angkor kingdom to launch a counterattack in late 1076.[109] More than three hundred thousand Song troops attempted to invade Đại Việt, but the communities of this region of the Dong World were prepared to drive off the intruders. In early December 1075, Guo Kui (1022–1088) sent Commander Yan Da to bring troops to Quảng Nguyên, but the Song force stumbled into a fierce fight with an army of five thousand local militia under the command of local chief Lưu Kỷ. Wherever the Song army went, they encountered ambushes. When Yan Da ordered his troops to venture into the area around Quảng Nguyên, the Dong World commander Hoàng Lục commanded the militia force that took advantage of the terrain, dividing the enemy into small groups and destroying them.[110]

During the first half of 1076, the Song forces pulled back to the protection of Yongzhou to recover strength and prepare for an advance into the Đại

Việt kingdom. Song military preparations lasted for six months, during which the Dong World militia of Qinzhou and Lianzhou were reconstituted and resupplied, after having been devastated in the first waves of attack.[111] Guo Kui reported to Kaifeng that the invading Vietnamese troops had brought with them disease, a common trope for the "pestilent south," and the court responded by forbidding anyone among the Song troops from eating raw foods or drinking local rice wine. Moreover, the troops assigned to the Maozhou barracks were given a supplemental stipend.[112] By the end of 1076, the Song army led by Guo Kui with Zhao Xie (1026–1090) and Yan Da as his deputy generals directed their troops to enter Đại Việt territory.[113] In planning his defense against the Song advance, Lý Thường Kiệt used both the Dong World landscape and his alliances with the uplands elite to prepare a battle plan. Lý Thường Kiệt ordered troops to block the road from Yongping garrison to Như Nguyệt River (or Cầu River) and to set up garrison camps in Quyết Lý in the north and Giáp Khẩu (or Chi Lăng) and Lang Prefecture in the south.[114] The Như Nguyệt River would be the last line of defense. In order to prevent the Song army from crossing the river, Lý Thường Kiệt built high dikes along the banks of Như Nguyệt, and a series of earthen and bamboo forts connected to the Tam Đảo mountain range, forming a protective wall for the central highlands and Thăng Long citadel.

The Lý's naval battalion, commanded by the Hoằng Chân Prince (?–1077), was stationed at Lục Đầu in the Vạn Xuân region and ready to respond everywhere along the waterways that pass through the Thương River up to the Lục Nam River, with access to the Như Nguyệt River and the Thiên Đức River. These forces were also able to reach the famous Bạch Đằng estuary, where they would reinforce naval forces stationed in the Đông Kênh River. The army of Lý Thường Kiệt was stationed along fabricated bamboo ramparts, blocking the path along the Thiên Đức River to Thăng Long. Lý Thường Kiệt's army consisted of two wings. The left wing was stationed in Quảng Nguyên and led by the Dong World military commander Lưu Kỷ, as well as other local elites such as Lư Báo; the prefect of Hữu Nông *dong*, Nùng Sĩ Trung; and the prefect of Lũng Định *dong*, Hoàng Lục Phẩn, who protected Lũng Định.[115] The children of Nùng Tông Đản, including Nùng Hạ Khanh, Nùng Binh, and Nùng Lượng, guarded the Lôi Hỏa, Vật Ác, and Vật Dương *dong*. These troops were tasked with keeping the territory and threatening the rear and supply lines of the Song army.[116] The right wing had an army stationed at Ngọc Sơn garrison and an extraordinarily strong riverine naval force in Vĩnh An Prefecture, organized by Lý Kế Nguyên. The army here was responsible for preventing supply boats or Song infantry from crossing the river. Meanwhile, the frontline fighting was assigned to the cavalry position Commandant-Escort (phò mã), Thân Cảnh Phúc, who was stationed at Giap *dong* to control the two dangerous fronts of Quyết Lý and Giáp Khẩu. The military commanders on the left side of the front included Sầm Khánh Tân, Nùng Thuận Linh, and Hoàng Kim Mãn, prefect of Môn Châu. The right side was held by Vi Thủ An, who controlled Tô Mậu, as well as the road from Tư Lăng to Lạng Châu.[117]

When the Song army entered the border area, they easily subdued the Lý troops, who were all Dong World Tai-speaking militia, and the vanguard could not hold the Quyết Lý and Giáp Khẩu frontiers.[118] Because of the astute placement of the Như Nguyệt river defense force, however, Lý Thường Kiệt was able to prevent the Song's fierce advance.[119] After crossing the frontier area and passing through the military passes at Quyết Lý and Giáp Khẩu, the Song army proceeded along the northern bank of Như Nguyệt River. As for the Đại Việt army, the troops stationed at Giáp Khẩu retreated to the Giáp *dong* in the Vạn Xuân region. The majority of this force retreated south to the Như Nguyệt River. The Vietnamese defense of Như Nguyệt River was solid, and although the Song army was anxious to cross the river, there were no boats. The two Song commanders charged with bringing the boats for this crossing had been stopped by Lý Kế Nguyên's troops at the Đông Kênh River.[120] The Song court asked Guo Kui to let the army build a bridge across the Như Nguyệt River, and Guo Kui ordered his general Wang Xian to do so. Lý Thường Kiệt's army fiercely retaliated, and Wang Xian, fearing that the Vietnamese army would use the bridge to attack him, quickly destroyed it.[121] When none of the remaining Song forces were able to cross the river, Guo Kui was forced to order a retreat to the north bank. Lý Thường Kiệt's army also organized a river crossing, but this crossing was blocked by the Song army. Prince Hoằng Chân (?–1077) and Prince Chiêu Văn (?–1077) both died fighting on the river.[122] The failure of either army to advance was, in essence, the effective end of the conflict, and it was by default a victory for the Lý, as they had driven back the Song invaders. The battle of the Như Nguyệt River was fierce, and it lasted more than a month. However, general fighting in this region continued for more than a year, and Quảng Nguyên was again seized by Lý forces. During the early winter of 1077, the local inhabitants of Lạng Giang (Bắc Giang, Lạng Sơn), under the command of local chief Thân Cảnh Phúc, ambushed Song forces at the passes Kháo Mẹ, Kháo Con, and Quyết Lý (Lạng Sơn). As Đàm Thị Uyên notes, these militia units relied on the mountains and forests for effective guerrilla tactics, causing the Song troops to fear them as "ghosts" (*thiên thần*).[123]

After the victory on Như Nguyệt River, the Song returned the territory of Quảng Nguyên in 1079. The Đại Việt area was gradually expanded to the Right and Left river region.[124] The nineteenth-century historian Phan Huy Chú remarked: "Much borderlands territory during the Lý dynasty was returned by the Song court. Due to the earlier impressive military victories, it was enough for the Song ruler to submit to the Lý demands, and then the Lý envoy discussed the return of the seized territory with great skill, subduing the Song court's counter-argument."[125] In 1083, with Song court permission, the Lý's envoy Đào Tông Nguyên (?–?) went to Yongping garrison at Qinzhou and discussed the proper territorial authority in the Quang Nguyên area with the Song officials. Historian Sun Tingjin contends that during the talks, Đào Tông Nguyên did not show sincerity and the talks ended without results.[126] Soon after these talks ended, the Lý court sent troops to invade Wuyang, Wu'e, and other places under the authority of the Guangnan West Circuit, but the attacking Vietnamese forces were eventually defeated by Song troops. At this time, the Lý leadership changed tactics and instead dispatched tributary envoys to ask the Song for forgiveness for the Lý "crime" of defeating the Song invasion. The Song emperor responded by "giving the mulberry vines to the barren land of eight *dong*" (*ciyi susang badong bumao zhidi*) as an act of appeasement.[127]

In 1084, the Lý court dispatched Lê Văn Thắng and Nguyễn Bầu back to Yongping garrison in Qinzhou to meet with the Song border officials Cheng Zhuo and Deng Pi to discuss the border issues. Through these negotiations, the boundary was delineated from the southeast section of Shun'an Prefecture in a north-south direction to the southwest section of the Pingxiang *dong* near the modern-day Friendship Gate (Youyi Guan). Modern Chinese scholars confirm that the negotiated boundary here is nearly the same as the current boundary between China and Vietnam.[128] In that same year, the Song court returned six Dong World districts and three *dong* located in northwest Quảng Nguyên (Cao Bằng).[129]

The Song bargaining power along its shared frontier area with the Đại Việt kingdom was diminished after the fall of the Northern Song dynasty. Sun Tingjin argues that by 1174, all that remained of the Southern Song was located between the Jin kingdom to the north and the Đại Việt to the south, and while under the threat of military strikes, the Song court formally recognized the Lý court's autonomous authority.[130] At the same time, the Song court referred to the Đại Việt kingdom as "Annan" in official correspondence and, according to Sun, concealed from other Song officials references to the Đại Việt's ruler as "emperor."[131] None of this mattered to the Lý leadership, which had broken from the Song court's strict tributary protocol by the mid-eleventh century, and was busy consolidating its territorial gains to the north and to the south of the Lý court's center of power in the Red River Delta.

Sino-Vietnamese Borderlands in the Twelfth Century

Even after the borderlands issues with the Song court had been ameliorated, the Lý court's Dong World troubles were not over. In the Thái Nguyên area, there was a person named Thân Lợi (?–1141), calling himself the son of Lý Nhân Tông, who gathered local forces to occupy the Dong World prefectures Thượng Nguyên, Tuyên Hoá, Cảm Hoá, and Vĩnh Thông, while also raiding the Phú Lương Prefecture (Thái Nguyên).[132] Thân Lợi had managed to raise an army of two thousand troops, so this was not an insignificant matter for the Vietnamese court. In April 1140, the Lý court sent Đỗ Anh Vũ with troops to capture Dong World collaborators with Thân Lợi, such as the leader of Vạn Nhai Prefecture (Thái Nguyên) Dương Bối and the Kim Khê *dong* leader Chu Ái.[133] The Lý ruler announced, however, that Chu Ái and Dương Bối were merely followers of Thân Lợi, and so they were spared and offered salt in return for their loyalty, while Thân Lợi was arrested and his twenty closest followers were executed.[134] In 1142 Dương Tự Minh assisted the court and Đỗ Anh Vũ as a loyal upland chief in suppressing attacks by other Tai-speaking militia leaders from the frontier area, until this alliance ended with Dương Tự Minh dying in exile.[135] In 1154 the Lão people in the Chàng Long Mountains (the northwestern region) rebelled and the ruler Lý Anh Tông (Lý Thiên Tộ; 1136–1175) ordered Đỗ Anh Vũ to fight and arrest his relatives.[136]

During the Trần dynasty, interaction between lowland rulers and upland elite continued to be dynamic. Even with the threats coming from the regional advances of Mongol forces into the Dong World, which will be discussed in more detail in the fifth chapter, localized conflicts continued to rise and fall. In 1277, Trần Thánh Tông (Trần Hoảng; 1240–1290), after dealing with the aggressive attacks of Mongol forces, sent troops to punish the rebels at the *dong* Nầm Bà La, Quảng Bình, and the western side of Bố Chính.[137] As the Chiêu Văn Prince, the future ruler Trần Nhật Duật (1255–1330) squashed an uprising by A Lộc. Trần Nhật Duật, who allegedly mastered knowledge of the martial arts and customs of Thái and Mường people, had been appointed by the court to defend the area of Đà Giang (in the northwest), and later he was reassigned to administer Tuyên Quang (Tuyên Quang, Hà Giang, Yên Bái, Lào Cai). When the powerful chief of Đà River region Trịnh Giác Mật rebelled in 1280, Trần Nhật Duật intervened. There is the well-known *DVSKTT* tale of how the Trần ruler sent Trần Nhật Duật to Trịnh Giác Mật's citadel, so that "Trần Nhật Duật climbed on to Trịnh Giác Mật's platform to eat together, drinking through his nose with Trịnh Giác Mật. The Man people were impressed. When Trần Nhật Duật prepared to return to the court, Trịnh Giác Mật called on his clan to surrender the garrison."[138] Finally, Trịnh Giác Mật brought members of his family to Thăng Long to meet the Trần ruler. After that time, the Đà River region remained at peace.

During the Trần period, many royal family members were employed along the northern borderlands. Trần Khánh Dư was assigned to administer the northeast coastal area.[139] The Hưng Nhượng Prince Trần Quốc Tảng

(1252–1313) led expeditions against the Dong World prefecture Sầm Tớ on the modern-day border between Thanh Hoá and Houaphanh Province, Laos.[140] In 1312, Emperor Trần Minh Tông (1300–1357) personally commanded the army to punish the Ngưu Hống state led by a chief Lò Lẹt in Mường Mỗi (Thuận Châu, Sơn La).[141] In 1337, the Hưng Hiếu Prince killed the chief Xa Phần at Trịnh Kỳ garrison, so that the territory was changed to Mường Lễ (Lai Châu) citadel and handed over to the Đèo clan. The pacification of uprisings during the Lý and Trần dynasties were directly conducted by the princes and frequently resolved by violence, but the extended periods of peace by the Trần period contributed to strengthening of the border between the Đại Việt kingdom and the regimes to the north.

■

To the south of Song territory, the Đại Việt leadership was consolidating their control and influence along their northern periphery in the region that comprises modern-day Cao Bằng Province.[142] The Vietnamese court also established religious sites to honor the native leadership engaged in the conflict. The Viên Minh pagoda (Đà Quận Hamlet, Hưng Đạo Commune, Cao Bằng) was allegedly built on a mound with a dragon symbol in the Lý dynasty during the reign of Lý Anh Tông (1138–1175), after the fixed boundary was established between the Song and Đại Việt states.[143] The Quan Triều temple was built to honor the military leader Dương Tự Minh, who was a Tai-speaking native of modern-day Bản Danh (Quan Triều Commune, Phú Lương Prefecture, Cao Bằng) and made great contributions in defending the northern frontier area of Đại Việt. He served the administrations of three Lý rulers, Lý Nhân Tông (1072–1128), Lý Thần Tông (1128–1138), and Lý Anh Tông. In the middle of the twelfth century, he was appointed as Phú Lương prefect. Dương Tự Minh became an essential member of the royal clan when he married the Diên Bình princess under Lý Nhân Tông and the Thiều Dung (Hồng Liên) princess during the reign of Lý Anh Tông. In 1143 Dương Tự Minh received the title "Commandant Attendant" (Fuma Lang) at Lý Anh Tông's court, making him an important figure at the center of power and no longer on the periphery.[144] In this elevated position, however, he came into conflict with Grand Councilor Đỗ Anh Vũ (1114–1159), who had recently amassed great power at court and challenged his detractors. Dương Tự Minh and other top officials organized a public indictment of Đỗ Anh Vũ on the grounds of official corruption. Although the emperor responded by calling for Đỗ Anh Vũ's arrest, the grand councilor had the protection of the empress dowager. As a result, Dương Tự Minh and his supporters were accused in 1148 of treasonous crimes against the court. Although Dương Tự Minh escaped execution, twenty of the defendants were beheaded and others were exiled.[145] Such was the political struggle in this stage of Lý dynastic rule. Figures from the frontier area who were drawn into the inner circle were no less vulnerable to these machinations.

During the Lý dynasty, both military and civilian affairs were assigned to the local chiefs to oversee, but under the Trần dynasty, the court also assigned some members of the royal family and other officials to local garrisons to manage regions along the northern borderlands.[146] The outcome of the closer contact between lowland authorities and upland leadership would be tested when an aggressive Mongol presence in the region would require a total commitment to territorial defense.

FOUR

BORDERLANDS ENGAGEMENT
IN THE SONG PERIOD

It was a spring morning in 1177 and the prefect of Yongzhou, Wu Jing (1125–1183), had his work cut out for him. A chief from the Ziqi kingdom (1100–1260) had led his militia into the prefectural courtyard to confront the Song official in person. In his own account of events, Wu Jing wrote that he severely reprimanded and threatened the Ziqi leader, saying:

> Your kingdom was once a tiny settlement. You've grown only because the Song court has allowed you for years to come sell your horses at our market. Now it has been more than thirty years, and with an annual income of more than two hundred thousand in silver, your kingdom has become rich. If you should forget our court's profound kindness and dare to presumptuously make rash demands, this action would necessitate my presenting a petition to the court, and it would cut short any plans you may have for coming here to sell horses next year.[1]

Several months later, in a subsequent analysis of the general situation on the Guangnan frontier area, Wu Jing reflected on his experience with the Ziqi chief in a memorial to the Song court:

> Beyond Yongzhou lies various kingdoms, such as Dali, Luodian, and the southwestern indigenes. [These polities] are small, remote, and desolate lands, and each is content with receiving nothing from our court. The kingdom of An Nam presents the primary threat to these smaller kingdoms, and this situation angers your servant sufficiently

so that I wish to act.[2] Feuding leaders in this region are like brothers at war, and this has gone on year after year without resolution. Only the Ziqi kingdom is united as a single clan, the influence of which in recent years has grown stronger, so that this kingdom is uniquely powerful among the various Man indigenous communities. . . . If we should face instability along the frontier area, it would necessarily be due to the actions of this kingdom.[3]

Wu Jing understood the independent nature of these Dong World states, but he perceived regional stability as a product of Song intervention, even when he realized that there was little that these states desired from direct engagement with the central Song court.

The horse trade was an important link between the Dong World and the Southern Song heartland, and this trade was conducted on Dong World terms. In his court memorial Wu Jing pointed out that:

Each year the southwestern indigenes come to Hengshan to sell more than four thousand horses, and of this total the Ziqi kingdom sells about three thousand horses.[4] Therefore, this kingdom benefits from the horse trade, and its leadership has expanded its authority across thousands of *li* of territory, forcing the various indigenous tribes beyond our frontier to submit as leaders of "bridled and haltered" subordinate prefectures around the kingdom's periphery. . . . Each year thousands of people come from Ziqi to sell horses at Hengshan. They disregard my authority in this region and have become increasingly arrogant.[5]

Wu Jing was not alone among Song officials in perceiving difficulties in engagement with the Dong World. However, the distant Southern Song court at Lin'an (Hangzhou), more preoccupied with the perilous northern frontier along the Jin kingdom, often overlooked and disregarded political changes and challenges in the southwest.

Wu Jing's experiences were not isolated incidences. In the complex network of relations between the Song court and its southwestern neighbors within or on the periphery of the Dong World, trade, migration, and social competition are intrinsically interrelated. Both Song and Đại Việt court officials ignored at their own peril the local hierarchies of power and the sources of regional tensions when they sought to keep the peace and maintain the flow of area commerce. As various descriptions of encounters with local elites show, Vietnamese and Chinese authorities carried mental impressions formed by long-held stereotypes and conventions passed down by central authorities through court chronicles, the applicability of which to modern situations varied considerably. These preconceived notions were rarely reinforced and often challenged among the officials posted to the frontier area. Collaborating closely with local elites, using trade routes for the gathering of military intelligence, and depending on uplands polities to further the aims of these two more distant lowland states became elements of Chinese and Vietnamese borderlands administration through the arrival of Mongol forces, at which point these local arrangements would be violently upended.

The career backgrounds of those Song period officials posted to the periphery of the Dong World varied, but some specific qualifications stand out. Military prowess was important, even though the early Song saw dramatic changes in the administration of its frontier area. The Tang period military commission (*jiedushi*) frontier system did not survive intact into the Song. By 977 the dynastic founder Zhao Kuangyin's brother Zhao Gui (Taizong, r. 976–997) eliminated the positions of the last eighteen military commissioners and installed civilian officials under the direct authority of the central government in their place.[6] The fact that Taizong was suspected of the 976 poisoning of his brother the emperor and his subsequent usurpation of the throne from his nephew made Taizong's court more vulnerable to independent military power on his southern flank.[7] Only in 997, the last year of Taizong's reign, did the court complete the transition to dominant civilian posts by establishing the fifteen regional circuits and dividing the Lingnan region into the Guangnan East Circuit (Guangdong) and the Guangnan West Circuit (Guangxi). At this point the Song vision of frontier administration privileged civilian authority over military muscle, but the effective frontier officials would all have either experience in military posts or a demonstrated talent for using coercive force to forward the interests of the Song court.

The separation of selection between military (*wu*) and civilian (*wen*) officials appears to have begun at the end of the Tang dynasty and was accelerated by the late Tang with the diversification of bureaucratic responsibilities, a trend reinforced by the specialized training required to take the military and civil service exams early in the Song period.[8] Civil officials and military officials were not only divided into two groups, but they also had their own paths through the bureaucracy. However, following bureaucratic changes during the Northern Song period, there were provisions for the civilian conversion of military posts, and the practice was quite common.[9]

Along the southern borderlands local officials served the Song court, demonstrating great skill in managing the military conflicts in the frontier area. These officials were often rewarded handsomely for their efforts. The seasoned official and later hero of the Early Tangut Wars (1038–1044) Cao Keming took over as Yongzhou prefect from the less successful administrator Yin Huangshang during the Jingde reign period (1004–1008). Cao had earlier served as prefect of Guizhou, where Kaifeng had instructed him to form alliances with local chieftains across this region of the Dong World and to establish a series of indigenous *dong* magistrates (*xidongsi*).[10] Cao's success with the military dimensions of these local alliances was the primary reason Kaifeng called on Cao to serve as Yongzhou prefect. At this time, Lý forces, under orders from the ruler Lý Thái Tổ early in the founding of the dynasty, had attacked Yongzhou during an extended military expedition against restive *dong* along the borderlands. The *History of the Song Dynasty* (Songshi) account contends that Cao dispatched his forces south into Đại Cồ Việt territory and the kingdom's ruler Lý Thái Tổ quickly "begged for forgiveness" for his military's transgressions.[11] Cao was serving in a civilian role, but he would receive posts with primarily military responsibilities. More will be said of Cao's exploits later in this chapter.

Another important characteristic in the behavior of successful frontier officials was the maintenance of useful political associations. Political connections with powerful officials or associations with powerful families distinguished many officials who served the Song frontier on the Dong World's periphery. In the spring of 1076, facing an imminent attack by Đại Việt troops under the coordinated leadership of Thăng Long's most trusted general Lý Thường Kiệt, the Song emperor Shenzong dispatched the well-known and well-connected Tao Bi, prefect of Chenzhou, to coordinate with the administrators of Kangzhou and to organize a local militia for defensive action.[12] The Song court gave Tao Bi the special title capital security commissioner (*huangchengshi*) and shifted his administrative position to Yongzhou prefect.[13] In the turmoil before the invasion, the Dong World residents of Yongzhou had fled to the surrounding mountains and ravines for safety. This group of well-connected officials also included Tan Bi (d. 1076), an ardent advocate of Wang Anshi's New Policies (Xinfa) who died in the defense of Yongzhou's citadel when the Lý forces attacked the city.[14]

Dependence on local militia and allowing local leadership to act autonomously had been the policy of the Song court on the borderlands, particularly during the second half of the dynasty. The Song official Zhang Shi (1133–1180), who reorganized the administration of the southern borderlands following the fall of the Northern Song to Jurchen invaders, maintained vehemently that he would employ local militia as the only effective means for maintaining order in the region.[15] Zhang understood the power of place and the loyalty these local militia had to the larger Song empire depended heavily on the bond first forged with their own commanders, who felt the same desire to defend the frontier area not as a distant imperial periphery but as an important center of their Dong World community.

Finally, expertise in fostering trade relations across the frontier area was another important characteristic of Song officials posted to this region of the Dong World. Trade could result in gaining the loyalty of communities that spanned the frontier between the Song and Đại Việt states, as well as providing a conduit for communication that allowed both commodities and intelligence to flow across the borderlands. The most important commodity traded in this region were horses, and when Deng Xiaolian received his position of deputy prefect of Yongzhou in the early Shaoxing reign period (1131–1163), it was the height of Yongzhou's importance as a horse market for the Southern Song court. Deng faced disruption in the trade following a series of raids on the horse herds by local bandits.[16] In response, Deng spent most of his allotted state revenue on building a new granary for the community and on increasing the salaries of Dong World officials and their staff who had received meager pay from Song administrators in the past.[17] As a result of these expenditures, Deng was able to stabilize the horse trading activity and eliminate much of the banditry. The Song official had ameliorated the economic desperation present before his arrival and thereby allowed the network of trade to continue unhindered, as it had well before the Song attempted to establish its authority in this area of the Dong World.

The Horse Trade

During the Song dynasty, procuring an adequate supply of military-grade horses and maintaining neighborly relations with the producers of these herds became the main preoccupation of many local authorities along the Dong World's periphery. The domestication of horses has been practiced in the southwest since ancient times. The horse breeds of the southwest originated on the Tibetan plateau as early as the second millennium BCE, and a horse-trading network had developed between the Kham region and Qin representatives by the fourth century BCE. There is archaeological evidence that the practice of domestication had entered the Dong World by the sixth century BCE.[18] In the late Spring and Autumn Period (ca. 771–476 BCE), horse breeding in Yunnan had become widespread. The Shizhaishan Tomb Site (Shizhaishan Gumuqun), located in modern-day Jinning County, contains many Western Han period bronzes with horse figures, indicating that Dong World communities were cultivating different breeds of horses.[19] In the first century BCE, Sima Qian wrote in *Records of the Historian* (Shiji) that in the western region close to Qiongye, there were Qiong horses and yaks.[20] Sima Qian noted that "the people of Ba and Shu [modern-day Sichuan] engage in petty trade with their Qiong horses and yaks, and thereby Ba and Shu have become prosperous."[21]

During the Eastern Han's Yuanhe reign period (84–87) of Emperor Han

The Late Dong World Era (eleventh–thirteenth centuries)

Xiaozong (Liu Da; 56–88), the Shu commandary prince (*junwang*) received the position of governor (*taishou*) for this region, and he brought to court as tribute four "divine horses" (*shenma*) from the area around Lake Dian (near modern-day Kunming).[22] The horses in the southwest were already well-known for their small stature, endurance, and foot strength, as well as their ability to climb rugged terrain.[23] The late Tang scholar Fan Zhuo's *Treatise on the Southern Indigene* (Manshu) noted that horses "are produced in a region on the eastern side of Yuedan River Valley [Yuedanchuan], [where the land] possesses natural springs and beautiful grasses, and thus is most suitable for horses . . . [the regions of] Xichong and Shendan also produce horses, though they are second to the outstanding horses of Lake Dian."[24]

In the Tang period the southwest region became well-known for the commercial network today known as the Tea and Horse Trade Route (Chama Dao).[25] During the Song dynasty, when the war horses in the empire's northwest were in short supply, the court turned to horses from the southwest for military needs. From the Song court's perspective, southwestern horses were considered to be inferior to the northwestern horses, but Dali horses were more suited for combat than were other southern breeds.[26] As a passage in *Notes from the Land Beyond the Passes* (Lingwai daida) notes: "All the southern wild horses come out of the Dali region."[27] The *History of the Song Dynasty* (Songshi) account notes: "The native leadership of the Ziqi kingdom originally had no horses, and they have turned to Nanzhao [Dali] as their market. . . . The Dali region is connected to the Western Rong [Xi Rong] region, where in ancient times there were many horses. Although there is a horse market located in Guangnan, these horses are actually from the West."[28] Fan Chengda's *Well-Balanced Records of the Cassia Sea* (Guihai yuheng zhi) notes, "the Dali horse is the most popular among native peoples in the Southwest."[29] The *Miscellaneous Notes on Official and Unofficial Politics Since the Jianyan Reign Period* (1127–1130) (Jianyan yilai chaoye zaji) account notes, "these horses thrive in alpine areas, and they don't benefit from the warm regions. . . . Annan [Đại Cồ Việt] also does not produce horses, so they fight with elephants."[30] The Dali kingdom monopolized the breeding of high-quality war horses.

During the Southern Song, most of the historical records on the Ziqi kingdom were related to the "Guang horses" (Guangma), which the Song court bought in the Guangnan West Circuit.[31] "The earlier horse merchants at the Hengshanzhai Garrison were from the Ziqi kingdom, Luodian kingdom, and the Temo Aboriginal District, among others. . . . For generations, the horses have been known as 'Guang horses,' but this is not true."[32] In order to resist Liao, Xia, Jin, and Mongol invasions, the Song court purchased large numbers of horses from Shaanxi, Sichuan, and Yunnan. When the court moved to the south, access to the western horses was obstructed, and the court had to rely on horses from Yunnan. The *Sea of Jade* account notes that in the spring of 1133, Yongzhou's Tiju District was a market for native merchants from the Luodian, Ziqi, and Dali kingdoms. This is the earliest mention of the Ziqi kingdom in official sources.[33]

During the Song period the Hengshan garrison, located west of Yongzhou in central Guangnan, was the principal site for the official horse trade with the Dali kingdom, Ziqi kingdom, and the Temo Circuit, which were the various regions of the Dong World that produced the Guangnan horses. During the Yuanfeng reign period (1078–1085), a commandant (*shuaici*) was appointed to Yongzhou "for the single purpose of managing the purchase of horses from the Dong World militia [*dongding*] of the Right and Left river regions [i.e., the Tai-speaking communities of the central Sino-Việt borderlands]."[34] In 1113 the Yongzhou prefect established a supervisorate to manage a market for trade with the various southwestern chiefs. After the Jin invasion of the north, the Song court principally relied on three regions: Chuanqin, including sections of modern-day Sichuan and Gansu; Huaibei, located north of Huaihe at the adjoining borders of modern-day Anhui, Jiangsu, and Henan; and Guangxi for the purchase of horses.[35] The distance from the Jingjiang Military Prefecture (modern-day Guilin) to the Southern Song capital Lin'an was much closer than were the other two regions, so the purchase of Guangnan horses became necessary.[36] During the reconstruction of the dynasty's political order in Song Gaozong's first reign period (1127–1130) the Guangnan West Circuit's supervisor of Dong World militia (*tizhu dongding*) Li Yu petitioned to bring horses to market for sale.[37] In the early Shaoxing period, the horse trade along the southern frontier area became the responsibility of the military commissioner (*jingluesi*), demonstrating clearly the primary strategic importance of maintaining access to these herds.

Song officials used currency, gold and silver, textiles, and salt, abundantly available through the state monopoly, for the purchase of horses. Following the official criteria used to determine the price of a horse, a horse standing 12.2 hands high was worth forty *liang* of silver, each additional inch was worth ten *liang* of silver, up to a maximum of seventy *liang*.[38] With the purchase of thousands of horses each year, this could become quite costly. In 1117 when Hu Shunzhi (1083–1143) served as the Yongzhou prefect, the total trade in Guangnan horses that year was 2,400 head.[39] Yongzhou in the late Northern Song spent five *yi* in gold for a year's supply of horses.[40] After the fall of the Northern Song, Yongzhou horse purchases skyrocketed and, at their height, annual purchases of horses reached a total cost of 250 *yi* in gold.[41] In Lianzhou, salt in the amount of two hundred thousand *jin* was required to purchase 1,500 horses.[42] The *Jianwu Gazetteer* (Jianwu zhi) notes that "the Jingjiang Military Prefecture, together with Hunan Consul General [*zongling*], requested from the Imperial Treasury the allocation of 602,800,000 copper cash as the price for additional horses. The court appropriated this amount for the purchase."[43]

The Dong World inhabitants of the frontier area maintained that for superior horses, purchased at the site of their breeding, a fair price should be twenty *liang* in gold. Such horses in one day could ride four hundred *li*. However, due to the set official price, good horses cannot be delivered for this local price.[44] Such a difference in evaluations of the available local breeds led to conflicts between buyers and sellers and dissent in the marketplace. In 1114 the Song court had ordered the Yongxing Army (Yongxing Jun) to establish another frontier market (*boyichang*) for the horse trade near the Dong World prefectures of Weizhou and Maozhou.[45] However, the Sichuan and Shaanxi pacification vice-commissioner (*Chuan Shan xuanfu fushi*) Shao Pu had petitioned the court that he be allowed to avoid the horse trade in this region to lessen the likelihood of "provoking borderlands tensions" (*suo gui buzhi yin re bianshi*).[46] In 1137 Zhu Zhen (1072–1138) reported to the Song court that "the task of managing the *jimi* regions is by no means over, yet the border is now quiet. Once the court has access to the route leading into the northwest, then we can gradually reduce the number of Guangnan horses we purchase and eliminate all the associated suffering [of purchasing inferior horses] in the first place."[47] The Dong World horse trade had its share of corruption, with local Song officials substituting copper for silver, and swapping the standard one hundred-*jin* (110 pounds) basket for baskets holding sixty *jin*. Dong World traders could engage in similar behavior, so that they "refused to offer fine quality horses, and so the markets were filled with old, sick, and worn-out horses, so many one couldn't keep proper records."[48] The Southern Song court continued to purchase Guangnan horses from their Dong World sources, while seeking to increase their acquisition of Sichuanese horses whenever circumstances allowed.

The horse trade was the most significant element in the Song-Dali official relations, as the following passage from the Qing period chronicle *A Continuation of the Comprehensive Mirror on Government* (Xu Zizhi tongjian) illustrates.

In 1134 the Dali kingdom requested permission to approach the Song court to pay tribute and to sell horses. Song Gaozong issued the following order to his high officials, stating "I am permitting the sale of these horses, but the Dali delegation will not be permitted to approach the court with tribute. How could we allow them to benefit from their villainy and still console our people?" Prime Minister [Zaixiang] Zhu Shengfei asked, "How do we distinguish between times when representatives of the Guangnan West Circuit memorialize the throne and when emissaries from the Dali kingdom come to pay tribute?! How might these two events be variants of each other?" The emperor said, "As for distant lands and foreign kingdoms, how can one ascertain what the truth is? There are those who say these delegations should be allowed to enter and present tribute, taking advantage of the merchants coming to peddle their wares. From magistrates, military commanders, and high officials, our border officials call for their cavalry horses, and, if the price is fair, the horses are then delivered. If all the generals receive their horses, would one not say that this is a good thing?"[49]

The desire for horses drove the Song-Dali relationship. While diplomatic exchanges were placed on the back burner, as noted in chapter 3, or taken off the table altogether, there would be a constant connection to the heartland of the Dong World through the desire of Song borderlands officials, particularly after the establishment of the Southern Song, to procure as many horses as possible.

At the same time, the Dali officials could use the Song desire for horses to score diplomatic points, as illustrated in this particular horse trade described in the *History of the Song Dynasty*:

> Since the Ziqi kingdom indigenes presently have no horses, the court trades with the kingdom formerly known as Nanzhao.[50] Nanzhao is the current Dali kingdom. In 1173 the Dali official Li Guanyin, together with twenty-two other envoy personnel, arrived at Hengshan garrison seeking to trade horses. The Yongzhou prefect Yao Kesheng brought out gold brocade to great fanfare. The envoys were happy to see this, and when they recorded their arrival in writing, they wrote "Twelfth Day of Second Year of the Reign of Li Zhen" [Li Zhen er nian shi'er yue], [which was the reign title of their Dali ruler and not the reign title of the Song emperor, an unforgivable departure from diplomatic protocol], and at this point trade missions began to arrive every year with horses. Dali envoys requested in return certain literary works, such as the Five Classics, the *Guoyu*, the *Three Histories* [Sanshi], elementary study guides and medicinal texts, translations [of Buddhist texts?]. The Song authorities respectfully heard these requests, and politely declined to offer the texts, but they did not make these requests known to the central court. Southern China [Lingnan] produced small horses, and there only numbered a few thousand. The regions of Huai and Hu were no different. The Dali kingdom bordered on the lands of the Western Rong [Xirong; i.e., the Tibetans], where since ancient times many horses may be found. Even though the market is in Guangnan, in fact these are the western horses. The best quality horses selected are sent to the Yamen [*Sanya*] and the remaining horses are distributed to the various military commands.[51]

The Dali trader-envoys were certainly aware of the diplomatic kerfuffle their use of the Dali reign date would cause for Song officials. They knew also requests for a variety of texts, some of which were banned or limited in the borderlands trade between Song and Đại Việt officials, would place the local Song officials in an untenable position. However, as the account notes, the Lingnan region had no other reliable sources of horses, and the Dali officials were free to play any diplomatic games they found to be amusing.

Guangnan Gold: Another Dong World Treasure

Due to the complex geological composition of the Dong World, Carlin-type gold, copper, and tin deposits, alongside other precious metals, are still found from southwest Guizhou to the Right River (You Jiang) region along the Sino-Vietnamese border and west to central Yunnan.[52] Local knowledge of these deposits already existed in the eighth century. The borderlands region south of Yongzhou during the Tang dynasty was one of the most important gold- and silver-producing areas in Lingnan. The *New Tang History* (Xin Tang shu) section on geography (*dilizhi*) recorded that Yongzhou has a "gold mine" (*jin keng*).[53] A decree from Emperor Tang Dezong (742–805) specifically highlighted Yongzhou's gold mine when he ordered that frontier area mining activity be overseen to thwart "greedy behavior," presumably from local inhabitants.[54]

Regarding gold production in the Song period, Zhou Qufei's *Notes from the Land beyond the Passes* noted that there were many gold mines in the *dong* between Yongzhou and Đại Việt, and they produced more than other counties of the Song empire.[55] There are multiple accounts through the latter years of the dynasty of how the Song court enthusiastically pursued gold mining in Yongzhou. The *History of the Song Dynasty* describes a gold mine (*jinchang*) in Yongzhou.[56] During Song Renzong's Jingyou reign period (1034–1038), the Song court surveyed the mineral deposits in every circuit of the empire, and Yongzhou ranked first among all prefectures with an estimated deposit of 704 *liang* of gold.[57] In 1074 the Guangnan West Circuit military commissioner (*jinglusi*) reported that "the Yongzhou area *dong* produce gold, and I recommend that local officials manage these gold mines on the Song court's behalf. Within five years' time, the gold obtained would equal 250,000 strings (*min*) of copper cash."[58]

The Southern Song metropolitan circuit fiscal commissioner (*jingdian zhuanyunsi*) in a memorial to the court reported that "Yongzhou . . . has produced a total of 2,046 *liang* of gold. The gold gathered here is in large nuggets and need not be refined through smelting."[59] The Song *Gazetteer of Jianwu* (Jianwu zhi), as preserved in the *Yongle Encyclopedia* (Yongle dadian) noted that "gold comes from two rivers, produced near the Right River [You Jiang] township, but the most precious gold was produced by the Left River's [Zuo Jiang] Yongfeng market."[60] This text also specified that "silver was produced in the Left River's Wancheng Prefecture [modern-day Guangxi border area] at many different sites."[61] It is important to note here that the work of mining was conducted largely by indigenous labor, and Dong World elite also realized the value of these natural resources, so local officials needed to provide adequate compensation when the Song attempted to wield influence over these sites.

In 1081 the Guangnan West Circuit's military commissioner reported that "an official gift to the amount of 65,000 one thousand–coin strings [*guan*] of copper cash was given when the Xu clan chief asked for a loan, and he repatriated the prefectural territory [presumably seized in a local confrontation] in return."[62] Li Tao noted that the Dong World elite profited by this arrangement, and the chief then focused on defending this territory "against banditry" (i.e., the marauding of other Dong World chiefs). Following this arrangement, the profits of Yongzhou's mining enterprise were used to set up gold mines in the neighboring *dong*, and each year, 3,200 *liang* in gold was purchased by the Song court.[63]

In addition to the gold found along the Sino-Vietnamese frontier area, there were many sites of gold and silver mining at the center of the Dali kingdom, although the Song appeared to have less access to these mineral resources than they did to Dali's herds of horses.[64] The mineral resources of the Dong World were one more reason for Song imperial interest in maintaining a foothold on its periphery, but until the period of Mongol administration of this politically fragmented area, northern authorities such as the Song often had to work through the Dong World's powerful local elite to gain access to its riches.

The Song Administrative Landscape in the Dong World

The Song empire engaged with polities and stateless communities along its entire frontier, comprised of a range of social orders from sedentary farmers to seminomadic pastoralists, and from shifting agriculturalists to migrant coastal foragers. In encounters with the Dong World along the Song's southwestern and southern periphery, communities sustaining themselves on all these modes of agricultural production were present. While the northern frontier posed a constant threat to the Song's military security, these Dong World communities loosely allied with the Dali kingdom no longer sought territorial conquest, but instead engaged with the Song court through trade negotiations.[65] Song officials, as noted earlier, faced violent unrest at the local level, but this violence was often sparked by efforts by indigenous elite to gain economic advantage in dealings with Song authorities.

Song borderland administration was divided into jurisdictions that covered major transportation routes between the trilateral links between the Song, Dali, and Đại Việt centers of power. Yongzhou Prefecture was located at the center of the Song's Guangnan West Circuit, and the prefecture provided administrative oversight for the southwest portion of the empire.[66] If representatives of the Dali kingdom, the Luodian kingdom, the Ziqi kingdom, the Temo Circuit, or the Đại Việt kingdom wished to reach Song authorities, they all needed to pass through Yongzhou. The region had always been home to a high concentration of distinct indigenous communities. The *History of the Song Dynasty* account states that "Yongzhou wields influence over a total of forty-four *jimi* prefectures, five *jimi* counties, and eleven *dong*."[67] These *jimi* prefectures, counties, and *dong* settlements were under the authority of the five garrisons of Taiping, Hengshan, Yongping, Guwan, and Qianlong, respectively. Of these garrisons, Hengshan, "with command over sixty settlements and two counties," was the primary military command center.[68] A major market and transit node within Yongzhou, the Hengshan garrison was located on the north bank of the Right River, in what is today Tiandong County, Guangxi Zhuang Autonomous Region. Zhou Qufei wrote the following, "If those in China wish to connect with the southwestern indigenes, they must do so through Yongzhou's Hengshan garrison."[69] Hengshan was established during the Renzong emperor's reign (1010–1063), although it was briefly overthrown during the uprising of Nùng Trí Cao and his followers.

Although the official horse trade was Hengshan's most important commercial activity, trade in the private sector was also quite prosperous. Members of the various indigenous communities and resident Han settlers (*shengmin*) were engaged in trading their local specialties, as well as a wide range of daily necessities, cultural commodities, and luxury items. Every year from December to the following April was the busiest trading season at the Hengshan garrison, marking the time when "barbarian" horses arrived with other goods. In addition to selling horses, the indigenous traders brought musk (*shexiang*), barbarian goats (*huyang*), "long-crowing" roosters (*changmingji*), pounded felt blankets (*pizhan*), Yunnan knives, and various local medicinal herbs. Song merchants in return sold patterned silk fabric (*zengjin*), leopard pelts (*baopi*), books, and a variety of manufactures to the Dong World traders.[70] In 1173 the Dali ruler Duan Zhixing (r. 1172–1200) sent a twenty-three-person trading party led by the envoys Li Guanyinde, Dong Luijinhei, and Zhang Banruoshi to the Hengshan garrison. These envoy merchants proposed that they trade horses for the appropriate amount of steel bowls (*gangqi bingwan*), opaque glass bowls (*liuli wan*),[71] pots (*hu*), red sandalwood (*zitan*), gharuwood incense (*chenxiang shui*),[72] licorice (*gancao*), abalone (*Haliotis*) (*shijueming*), stalagmites (*jingquanshi*),[73] litharge (*mituoseng*),[74] Hong clams (*xiangha*), sea clams (*haiha*), and various medicinal herbs.[75] A dazzling array of items was available at the Hengshan garrison marketplace.

Local disturbances to trade on the periphery of the Song empire could be devastating. Hong Mai's (1123–1202) *Records of the Listener* (Yi jian zhi) described the aftermath of banditry in this manner:

Supplies for the Jingjiang Prefectural Militia's storehouse accumulated like a great pool of water. So many bolts of gold brocade had been collected that they lost their uniqueness, and as a result, local officials appointed to maintain the storehouse compensated themselves from its treasures to lessen the burdens of their post. The commander of the prefecture withdrew from public service, having devoted himself to study. At the same time there were two corpses lying in a nearby ditch, located side-by-side and already beginning to decay. There were bolts of rough silk cloth [*juan*], jumbled together and beginning to spoil. After being unable to gather them together, we heard that thieves had come periodically and entered through a breach in the wall, barely large enough to pass through. To get into the storehouse, the first thief pushed his way headfirst through the opening, at which point the thieves concealed themselves within. Because many of those from this post had already perished, Zhang Gong was made the local leader.[76]

Whether due to administrative malfeasance, rural violence, or general neglect, the trade routes along the Dong World's periphery were often at risk of collapse.

The earlier collapse of the Tang imperial order allowed for the emergence of a variety of local responses to frontier unrest, including various Dong World militia systems. By the Song period there were hereditary chiefs in frontier areas, noted in the Song official sources as regional chiefs (*cishi*), prefects (*zhizhou*), district magistrates (*zhixian*), valley settlement administrators (*zhidong*), headmen (*zongshou*), chiefs (*shouling*), *dong* leaders (*dongzhu*), headpersons (*toujiao*), defense officials (*fangeshi*), and subordinate military officials (*zhihuishi*) as well as patrol officials (*xuneshi*) and "native regional chiefs" (*tu cishi*).[77] The unstable political conditions of this heavily militarized region afforded local leaders an elevated status in their engagement with representatives of the Song court in their home region.

Song officials posted to borderlands positions also engaged directly with rulers of the Dong World polities referenced earlier in this study, noting that access to the trade offered by these states necessarily passed through territory over which the Song exercised only nominal control. The prefect of Jingjiang (modern-day Guilin) in Guangnan West Circuit, Zhang Shi (1133–1180), described the "bridled and haltered" prefectures on the periphery of the Guangnan West Circuit in his essay "Remembrances of the Pavilion Wall at the Jingjiang Prefectural Residence" (Jingjiangfu ting bi timingji).[78] He wrote, "beyond but encircling these prefectures are the small barbarian kingdoms of Luodian, Ziqi, Temo, and Baiyi. Beyond them is also Giao Chỉ and Dali, to which some of the prefectures owe allegiance."[79] In his book *Well-Balanced Records of the Cassia Sea* (Guihai yuheng zhi), then resident of Jingjiang Prefecture and Guangnan transit inspector (*Jingjiangfu bing Guangxi jinglue anfushi*) Fan Chengda (1126–1193) described the frontier peoples as follows, "beyond the Nanjiang River [You Jiang], there are kingdoms that go by these names: Luodian and Ziqi; and circuits by these names: Luokong, Temo, Baiyi, and Jiudao. All of them have become tribal areas and all are located near Nanzhao [i.e., the Dali kingdom]."[80] In the accounts of both officials, Ziqi and Luodian are described as "kingdoms" (*guo*), which is a significant acknowledgement of their regional influence, given that the Song court had not established tributary relationships with these polities.[81] It is also important to note that the local Song officials accepted that their authority could not rival the influence wielded by the Dali rulers in this borderlands region.

Tales of Song Official Engagement with the Dong World

During the Five Dynasties period, the regional loyalties of locally born officials were tested by competing elite.[82] The example of Guangzhou native Pan Chongche (?–?) illustrates this point well. A native of Xianning County in what is today's Guangzhou, Pan first served under the Southern Han ruler Liu Yan (r. 917–942) as aide to the palace domestic service (*neishisheng jucheng*) and he was, according to his *History of the Song Dynasty* biography, well-read in the literature of military arts.[83] Pan became an accomplished military commander in the Southern Han campaigns to consolidate power along the south China coast. After the Southern Han commander Wu Huai'en (?–?) had successfully captured Guizhou Prefecture (modern-day

Guilin) on behalf of the regime from the local warlord Liu Shizheng (?–?), Pan replaced Wu as chief administrator in this region.[84]

Readers should note that in these same Southern Han campaigns, the kingdom's expansion southward was halted by the local ruler of Giao Châu Ngô Quyền, which marked the beginning of an autonomous polity occupying modern-day northern Vietnam. When the Southern Han ruler Liu Chang (r. 958–972) took the throne, Pan participated in additional efforts to wield influence over the territory northwest of his administered region. However, as the *History of the Song Dynasty* account notes, "Liu Chang became suspicious of Pan Chongche" and when he dispatched his envoy Xue Chongyu (d. 971) to Pan's administrative seat, he discovered that Pan had surrounded himself with "more than one hundred entertainers in beautiful dress, [and would] play the jade flute and drink wine long into the night, while ignoring his military and political responsibilities."[85] Liu Chang became furious and demanded that Pan Chongche return to the capital and surrender his military appointment, which depressed Pan. When the Song armies began their conquest of south China, the Southern Han ruler again called on Pan to take a military post, ordering him to lead fifty thousand troops to form a defensive line at the He River.[86] Pan's command was not effective, and when his forces were defeated Liu Chang's regime and the Southern Han came to an end. Song Taizu offered an amnesty to Pan Chongche, who was assigned a post in Hunan's Ruzhou Prefecture, where he died soon thereafter.

When Fan Min (936–981), who served as the Song dynasty's first prefect of Yongzhou, was in communication with the Southern Han's final ruler Liu Chang, he faced problems in bringing cultural conformity to the Dong World communities nominally under his influence. Fan complained to the court at Kaifeng that the local shamanistic ritual practices were excessive and crude, and that even though those residents suffering from sickness remained, chickens and pigs were slaughtered in substantial numbers to placate numerous spirits. Fan banned the wasteful practices and distributed medicine to those in need to secure the loyalty of his new subjects.[87] This effort was not appreciated by the former Southern Han (917–971) prefect of Rongzhou, Deng Cunzhong, who assembled a local militia of twenty thousand men and laid siege to Yongzhou for seventy days. In 980 Fan Min led local troops in the defense of Yongzhou. Fan Min was grievously wounded, but he managed to dispatch an envoy to Guangzhou and Song forces soon arrived to break the siege. The court sent a small delegation that carried Fan away by sedan chair for medical treatment, and he retired from government service.[88]

The next Yongzhou prefect was the Kaifeng "insider" Hou Renbao (?–980), who had earlier served the court as erudite of the court of imperial sacrifices (*taichang boshi*). Hou Renbao would die during a failed Song invasion of the Đại Cồ Việt kingdom under its ruler Lê Hoàn, an invasion which Hou himself had planned and strenuously advocated to the Song court.[89] After a period of administrative indecision, during which Kaifeng left the position empty, Yin Huangshang received his appointment as Yongzhou prefect in 992. Yin served in this position until he was relieved by the more seasoned official Cao Keming, referenced at the beginning of this chapter.[90] During the reign of Song emperor Zhenzong, Cao became deputy commissioner of imperial larder (*gongbeiku fushi*) and prefect of Yongzhou.[91] At this time he pacified and annexed the thirty-six *dong* of the Two River region (Left and Right rivers) by summoning the local chiefs to his official residence in Yongzhou in an effort to gain their loyalty and trust (*yuyi enxin*).[92]

In that same year, in honor of the emperor's birthday celebration (*chengtian jie*; December 2), Cao assembled his forces in public, at which he appeared in court attire and seemed visibly moved by the ceremony. When Cao heard the news that the Ruhong garrison was isolated and facing external threats, Cao Keming ordered the leader of the Two River region, the Tai-speaking chief Huang Zhongying, to assemble a militia to attack the threatening forces; Huang had the attackers' leader Lu Mujian beheaded in the marketplace.[93] Cao suppressed the mutiny led by the commander (*jiao*) Chen Jin of the "Sea of Serenity" Army (Chenghai Jun) in Yizhou (near modern-day Hechi, Guangxi). At this time, the Yu River had overflowed its banks, and the nearby garrison and citadel was destroyed. Cao assembled an indigenous work crew of corvée labor (*dingfu*), who felled numerous trees and lashed rafts together to connect both banks of the river, and the defenders reached the outer banks of the citadel. The defenders then raised numerous battle flags on top of their massive raft. Chen's army stood on top of the city wall and prepared to defend the captured citadel, recruiting three thousand militia from the surrounding *dong*. Huang was able to gain assistance from 1,500 Dong World militia, reaching out for reinforcements from Xiangzhou (modern-day Laibin, Guangxi). Huang then met with Cao Keming and agreed to consolidate their troops. This combined force next advanced to Guizhou, where the Song army encountered the indigenous forces and defeated them conclusively, beheading more than four hundred rebels.[94]

To repay Cao Keming for his meritorious deeds, the Song emperor Zhenzong transferred Cao to the position of supervisor-in-chief (*duda tizhu*) in Jiangnan West Circuit (Jiangnan Xilu), Huainan West Circuit (Huainan Xilu), as well as Liangzhe Circuit (Liangzhelu). Cao used his court support to consolidate local influence. Among the captured rebel militia, Cao recruited capable soldiers who could be enticed to join his forces. Cao used funds from the official treasury to award gifts in return for oaths of loyalty from these captives, and he managed to increase his forces by over a thousand men.[95] Later, when the local prefect of Jiangning Prefecture Zhang Yong heard news of Cao's successes, Zhang gave him a gift of four hundred thousand cash. Cao also gained the support of the Dong World chiefs of Pingzhou and Chenzhou.[96]

In 1016 Cao Keming was permitted to serve as both chief military inspector and military commissioner for ten Dong World prefectures.[97] He received this honor for successfully containing a revolt by the leadership of the Fushui Native Prefecture.[98] Following the campaign, a tale of Cao Keming's interaction with local chiefs first circulated. At this time, a Dong World chief presented Cao as a gift of "mountain valley medicine" (*xidong yao*), claiming that people struck with poisoned arrows could drink this medicine and not die. Cao Keming asked the chief how one tested the efficacy of the medicine, and the chief replied that one should use chickens and dogs as test subjects. In response Cao Keming said, "When you try it, use people" (*dang shi yi ren*). He then took a poisoned arrow and pierced the chief's thigh with the weapon. He gave the chief the medicine to drink, but the chief died. At this point, the gathered followers of the chief were frightened by the outcome and fled.[99]

During the winter of 1016–1017, a military expedition in the Dong World region was initiated by the Song authorities. In this military campaign forces from the Guangnan East Circuit, led by Military Commissioner Wang Wenqing and Military Director-in-Chief (*Dujian*) Ma Yu, left the Tianhe Garrison, located near the Tianhe District of modern-day Guangzhou, and traveled east. Forces on the west side of the Dong World frontier area, led by Cao Keming and his adjunct Yang Shouzhen, left from the Camphor Mountains (Zhang Ling) of Huanzhou. In the region between Wang's and Cao's respective regions, the mountain routes were treacherous, and dense forests slowed the campaign's advance.[100] The incoming Song forces also were subject to harassment from the region's Dong World militia, who were skilled in the use of crossbows. Wang's forces fought with all their might, and managed to score several victories against indigenous forces. According to the *History of the Song Dynasty* account, the Song court was encouraged by this military success and wanted to recruit local leaders and annex more of the Dong World territory into the Song empire.[101] Repeatedly, the court dispatched imperial decrees, calling on Cao Keming to advance aggressively, but Cao feared penetrating deeply into the contested Dong World territory. Cao sent many requests for Wang and his forces to slow their advance. When Wang's forces assembled at Ru Pass (ru men), the Dong World defenders thwarted the Song forces' advance and Wang was unable to enter. After a delay of several days, Cao Keming entered Fushui Prefecture, where he met with the Dong World prefect Meng Chenggui and others to gain their loyalty.[102] Shortly after that meeting, Cao Keming joined forces with other Dong World prefects in attacks on the neighboring *dong*, thereby wielding influence over the region mentioned previously. Cao memorialized the Song court to request that military units in Guangnan West and Guangnan East Circuits be reorganized under the title Loyal and Brave Army (Zhonggan Zhun).[103]

As a particularly effective representative of imperial power and authority in the Dong World frontier area, Cao Keming was awarded numerous promotions to handle local matters throughout the empire. After quelling the disturbance in Fushui, Cao was transferred to Chuzhou (located in modern-day Anhui) as prefect. Cao Keming's career is portrayed as a singular success story in frontier management. It would be rare to read of such a string of successes for the Song officials who followed Cao in their frontier service.

Borderlands service during and after the Song-Đại Việt conflict of 1075 and 1076 included some resourceful officials. In 1069 Xie Jicheng, a Jinjiang native, received a court appointment to the coastal prefecture Lianzhou.[104] Facing unrest from the Dong World elite in coastal prefectures west of Lianzhou, Xie Jicheng dispatched troops to put down the uprising. Xie then ordered the reinforcement of fortifications and the moat surrounding the citadel at the port of Hepu, and he equipped the local militia with proper weaponry. Through this military upgrade of Lianzhou and its trading port at Hepu, Xie made the prefecture a primary point of frontier area contact with the Song court. Shortly thereafter, Xie was reassigned to Yongzhou, where more than a thousand militia were garrisoned. The *Collected Essential Documents of the Song Dynasty* (Song hui yao) notes that Xie recruited Dong World militia to his forces at Yongzhou and gave them additional training. Because these Dong World troops were accustomed to the local climate, they were better able to thrive in this environment, unlike troops relocated from the interior of the Song empire. Following the 1075 border conflict with Đại Việt, Xie Jicheng advocated in a memorial to Kaifeng for the establishment of a temple honoring the service and martyrdom of fallen Yongzhou prefect Su Jian, under the honorific name Su Zhongyong.[105] In 1089 Xie had erected a stele at Yongzhou, titled "In Honor of Gao Zhu, Li Xiaozhong, and four others from Nanxi Mountain" to honor those Dong World leaders who assisted the Song in the conflict with Đại Việt forces.[106] When Xie died in office several years later, Emperor Zhezong ordered the construction of a temple in his honor. Effective Song borderlands officials required court recognition to serve as examples to others. Matters of social welfare also occupied Song officials. Deng Xiaolian, a native of Qujiang, received the position of deputy prefect of Yongzhou and served at the height of Yongzhou's importance as a horse market for the Southern Song when trouble from the periphery of the Dong World came with raids on the herds by local militia.[107] In response to local instability, Deng exhausted his personal resources to build a granary to supply the community and increased the salaries of many Dong World officials and staff, who had not received enough under the existing payment system.[108]

Trade became a major factor in the trilateral relationship in this period by the end of the Northern Song dynasty. In 1117 the Song emperor Huizong granted the Dali ruler Duan Heyu (r. 1108 and 1147) the grand honorific titles Glorious Grand Master with the Golden and Purple Trim (Jinzi Guanglu Daifu), Honorary Acting Minister of Works (Jianjiao Sikong), Yunnan Governor-General (Yunnan Jiedushi), Pillar of the Kingdom (Shangzhuguo), and King of Dali (Dali Guowang).[109] These titles in terms of honorific status were equal to the titles granted in the same period to the Vietnamese Lý court. This shift indicated that matters along the Song-Jin frontier area to the north had become so unstable that cross-border trade had been eliminated. The Song court was in desperate need of new trade partners. In 1118 Yan Ying memorialized the throne, reporting that the Đại Việt kingdom had "acted respectfully" since the Song-Lý border war, and so Yan requested that the imperial edict blocking their trade be rescinded. Earlier, the Guangnan West Circuit military commander (*shuai*) Zeng Bu (1036–1107) had petitioned the court, requesting that the coastal prefectures Qinzhou and Lianzhou each be permitted to established horse post stations (*yi*), and the court ordered that Đại Việt representatives be permitted to conduct trade at these stations.[110] Thereafter, Yan Ying received court authority, along with the Guangnan transportation deputy (*Guangxi zhuangyun fushi*) Wang Bo to administer trade with the Đại Việt kingdom from these locations.[111] The change in tributary status and the lessening of trade restrictions didn't assist the Huizong court in its failed attempts to thwart Jurchen conquest. Nevertheless, the states inside and outside the Dong World region adjusted to their heightened degree of interaction with the Song regime, following the Jin victory.

In the transition to the Southern Song court, trilateral relations through the Dong World and its neighbors changed quite dramatically. Under the Shaoxing Peace Treaty (Shaoxing Heyi), negotiated in 1141, the relationship was confirmed with the Jin as the "lord" and the Southern Song as the "vassal." This change had a profound effect on the relationship between the Song and the polities located in the Dong World. The Song court was compelled to recognize the enhanced independent status of both the Dali and Đại Việt kingdoms.[112] In 1164 the Southern Song court of Song Xiaozong (1127–1194), granted an imperial seal to the Đại Việt ruler, Lý Thiên Tộ (Lý Anh Tông, 1136–1175), changing the Song name for Đại Việt in the official correspondence from Jiaozhi (a colonial Han reference) to Annan (a colonial Tang reference), and recognizing Lý Anh Tông as the "King of Annan" (Annan Guowang).[113] As the Song court had already enhanced the status of the Dali kingdom in relations with Lin'an, the Đại Việt and Dali kingdoms had both been integrated into a Song-centered East Asian regional system.[114]

The Song borderlands official continued to manage local affairs in this changed regional environment. Jiang Yunji (1104–1167), a native of Jiangdong Village, first served as commandant (wei) in Liucheng (Liuzhou), where he was mainly responsible for local miliary defense during the period of conflict between the Song and the Jin.[115] Jiang successively served court appointments in the Guangnan region before being promoted to prefect of Shaozhou (modern-day Pingle County, Guangxi). According to official sources, Jiang's predecessor had pursued policies that harmed the people, and Jiang was able to change these practices. Jiang was again moved around the borderlands region during his ascent in rank and he was finally promoted in 1165 to prefect of Yongzhou, serving concurrently as military commissioner (anfushi) of Yongguan. Jiang Yunji inherited from his predecessor a tense relationship with the Dong World inhabitants of the region, who were responsible for conducting the important business of horse trading. Local officials and military leaders used their power to conduct unequal transactions and to oppress and exploit the indigenous inhabitants. Jiang managed to calm tensions and restore the large volume of trade that passed through the Yongzhou region. In 1167, Jiang Yunji died while still serving in Yongzhou at the age of sixty-three.[116]

Although his career would end under the cloud of scandal, Yu Dan was the next Song official to receive appointment as Yongzhou prefect. Yu Dan had in the spring of 1142 served as Jizhou (modern-day northeast Jishui

County, Jiangxi) defense commissioner (*fangyushi*) before the Song court dispatched him to Yongzhou for the purpose of purchasing horses.[117] At the time, the ailing Song court was in desperate need of a new source of horses in its continuing battle with the Jin cavalry. During the Jianyan reign period (1127–1130), the investigating censor (*jiancha yushi*) Hu Shunzhi (1083–1143) was sent to Yongzhou to look into allegations that Yu Dan had accumulated a stash of spoils from trade for personal profit.[118] Yu at that time also held the title of Guangnan West Circuit military commissioner (*jinglueshi*), so this alleged breach of conduct by Yu Dan was seen by the court to have strategic implications. Taking over for the disgraced Yu Dan in 1167, Mo Shixian, native of Dayu, was appointed as Yongzhou's military administrator of the revenue section (*sihu canjun*) and concurrently as prefect of Yongzhou.[119] Presumably, Mo Sixian sorted out the financial mess in Yongzhou, because Mo then served in these positions from 1168 until 1173, at which time Yao Ke (?–?) took over as Yongzhou prefect. Yao Ke, unfortunately, had his own critics.

Shortly after Yao took office, the high-ranking court official Zai Zhi approached the throne with the question "Is it true that the new Yongzhou prefect Yao Ke doesn't yet know how to buy a horse?" (*Xin cha zhi Yongzhou Yao Ke wei zhineng ban mai ma fou*).[120] The answer to this inquiry must have been unsatisfactory, because Yao Ke only served from 1173 to 1175. He was replaced by former Bingzhou prefect Shi Liangbi, who had been dispatched by the court to take the Yongzhou position with assistance from the Jingjiang prefect Zhang Shi.[121] The political environment in the frontier area soon became less of a concern to the distant Song court with the arrival of the next Yongzhou prefect Wu Jing (1125–1183), about whom much has been written in this book.

Wu Jing was a native of Xiuning in Huizhou Prefecture (now part of Anhui). Like his brother Wu Fujiang, Wu Jing excelled in his formal studies, and they were collectively known as "the two Wu of the Eastern Yangzi region" (Jiangdong er Wu). In 1157 Wu Jing received his *jinshi* degree, and was appointed as a military officer (*wei*) of Yin County in Mingzhou Prefecture (located in modern-day Zhejiang). In 1166 Wu Jing was appointed magistrate of Anren County (modern-day Hunan), and in 1174 he was transferred to Yongzhou for his first Dong World borderlands appointment. In 1178 Wu Jing was given a joint position as prefect of Yongzhou and acting Guangnan West Circuit military commissioner. Because his parents had reached old age, he soon left public service in Yongzhou to care for them and begin his second career as a teacher. At this time he began to refer to his residence as "Bamboo Island" (Zhuzhou) and Wu Jing took on students, who referred to him as Master Zhuzhou. In 1180 he took the position as Taizhou prefect and continued to perform mourning rites for his parents. In 1183 Wu Jing died at the age of fifty-nine years. Wu Jing's time along the southern frontier area was short, but his observations, as mentioned at the beginning of this chapter, reveal an acute understanding of the challenging task in expressing imperial authority so far from the center of imperial power.

The next series of local officials served short undistinguished appointments in rapid succession. Yao Kuo, native of Zhangxi, received the appointment of Yongzhou prefect in 1181 and served in this position until 1183.[122] Chen Shiying, native of Yongjia, located in modern-day Zhejiang, was appointed Yongzhou prefect in 1184 and served only until 1185, at which point the emperor Song Xiaozong ordered him to leave this post to take responsibility for the Salt Monopoly.[123] Zhang Cixie, native of Pucheng, located in modern-day northern Fujian, became prefect of Yongzhou in 1186, where he remained for a single year, leaving in 1187. Later in 1187 Wang Kan took the position of Yongzhou prefect, but he was cashiered (*fangba*) in the same year.

After Wang Kan's disastrous term, Song officials in Yongzhou appeared to improve in quality. Yan Minde, native of Qingjiao, took the position of Yongzhou prefect the same year Wang Kan was cashiered; he remained in this position until 1194.[124] He later served as the Yongzhou military governor (*anfushi*). Following Yan Minde, Yao Zhu served as Yongzhou prefect from 1194 to 1196. In the spring of 1191 Yao Zhu, then prefect of Jingzhou (modern-day Hunan Miao Autonomous Region) had memorialized the Song court, stating, "I note that the Guangnan West Circuit has this year not yet given my prefecture its annual budget of two hundred thousand cash, which next year will be three hundred thousand cash. Past practice was to allow the Hunan-Guangnan general administration [*Hu Guang zongling*] to handle these budgetary matters. In accordance with original practice, tea was offered for the money allocated. However, each year this prefecture must submit its share of taxation to the Hunan-Guangnan general administration. I ask that in subsequent years the allowed amount in taxes from this prefecture be lessened."[125] The emperor then ordered that the Hunan-Guangnan general administration follow Yao Zhu's request for annual funding and from this point Jingzhou could rely on regular funding each year from taxes. That same year the Song emperor sent the following edict: "Among the local militia are persons with dubious or outright criminal motives. According to the practices of Yuanzhou [modern-day Jiangxi Qiang Autonomous County, Hunan], this region should not be linked to Jingzhou." Prefect Yao then memorialized the throne, "this prefecture is comprised of numerous *dong*, including Man and Yao, and it's located twenty *li* from Yuanzhou. That region has long been a source of worry for my prefecture. For that reason, we have assembled a large native militia force. Therefore, I ask that with the example of Yuanzhou, we not join that region to this prefecture." The Song court made this recommendation its own order.[126] Local Song officials were able at that time to employ Dong World militia forces against neighboring Dong World communities, but the court was constantly worried about their imperial representatives misreading the motives of Dong World collaborators.

The next official to take the position of Yongzhou prefect was Chen Daji, a native of Yongjia, located in modern-day southern Zhejiang, who began his service in 1196. Chen only served for one year in this position before he was transferred to the position of Xiangzhou prefect and then again in 1204 to the position of Hengzhou prefect, where he was engaged for a decade in pursuing the "bandits" Hou Guang and Li Jianliu, who defied Song court influence in Yulin and Guizhou.[127] Another official You Jiang took over for Chen as Yongzhou prefect in 1197, but he only served for one year. This constant turnover of appointed officials must have had an impact on the Dong World elite, but the sources don't give us detailed information about their specific responses. "Banditry," as described by Song observers, would indicate that local actors saw the spotty presence of representatives of the distant Southern Song court as an opportunity to carve out individual spheres of influence and profit.

The court in Lin'an seemed to recognize the problem, because it subsequently sent a tough official in the form of Chen Liangbiao, a native of Fuzhou's Changle District (modern-day Fujian), who served as Yongzhou prefect from 1198 to 1203, with mixed results. The regular army forces were stationed in Yongzhou by the imperial court, and civilian prefects also served as military officers. Chen Liangbiao as Yongzhou prefect tried a legal case and sentenced the prisoner to one hundred strokes of the cane. When the prisoner almost died, Chen Liangbiao's political critics at court accused him of disregarding criminal law and of unreasonable harshness in his application of punishments. Chen's critics then accused the prefect of official corruption, which, they alleged, had caused the Yongzhou army to go without food and salary, forcing the soldiers to plunder the surrounding villages and threatening mutiny.[128] Chen was dismissed and Zheng Hanzhang served as Yongzhou prefect from 1204 to 1205, without encountering the troubles faced by his predecessors.

The frontier area positions continued to be staffed with officials for short periods, even as the region had been increasingly destabilized by the advance of Mongol forces elsewhere in the empire. Cui Yuzhi (1158–1239), a native of White Deer Garrison (Bailu Ying), Ningdu County, became prefect of Yongzhou in 1206, but he served in this position for just one year.[129] Xie Mingzhi, native of Longxi, then served as Yongzhou prefect until 1209.[130] In that same year he was succeeded by Xie Jicheng, who served as Yongzhou prefect from 1209 to 1211, and Xie was followed by Liao Shuzheng, who served as Yongzhou prefect from 1211 to 1213. Chen Guangzu, native of Xianyou (in modern-day Fujian), then took over the position of Yongzhou prefect from 1213 to 1215, and he had more of a local impact, as recorded in court chronicles. Chen Guangzu was the son of Chen Xizao (d. 1177), a well-known Southern Song military hero who had died in battle.[131] When Chen took the prefect position in Yongzhou, he was simultaneously appointed to the position of judicial commissioner (*tixing*) in Guangnan East Circuit. This appointment resulted in Chen having authority over the entire south China coastal region. The court may have granted him expanded authority, because Chen had earlier written a local administration treatise *The Troubles of Qinzhou* (Qin xu bian), in which he warned against the congregation of Liao people around the Qinzhou area.[132] During his administration of Yangzhou, he ordered the construction of the Xinxunxi Temple for the Daoist faithful. Such beneficence had a financial impact on Chen Guangzu, because he also lost money to the amount of three thousand strings of coins (*min*) when providing the military of Yongzhou with a granary (*lin*). Chen had a limited tax base on which he could depend, but for his efforts, upon retirement, he received the honorific position of Gentleman for Court Service (Chaofeng Lang).

Rapid turnover among prefects continued to be the norm. Liu Yuangang served as Yongzhou prefect from 1215 to 1218. Zheng Xiao took over from Liu Yuangang as Yongzhou prefect in 1218, but he ceded the position in the same year to Dong Daolong, who served from 1218 to 1221. Lin Zhen, a Fuqing native, served as Yongzhou prefect from 1221 to 1223.[133] Liu Xueqiu served as Yongzhou prefect from 1223 to 1228. Liu Xueqiu had much experience serving at the prefectural level, where he engaged in ordering the construction and renovation of local academies. He also spread his own teachings at these local schools. Unfortunately for Liu, he succumbed to an unknown epidemic that had affected the Yongzhou area, which brought an end to this scholar's service.[134] Lin Yingzhou served as Yongzhou prefect from 1229 to 1233. Tang Rong served as Yongzhou prefect from 1234 to 1237. While serving as prefect, Tang Rong dispatched troops to defend against a military intrusion from the Đại Việt; according to Chinese accounts, Rong was able to contain this invasion. Wang Taichong served as Yongzhou prefect from 1238 to 1239.[135] Following a revolt of local militia, Wang, together with Ezhou's campaign commander (*dutong*) Zhang Tixing, seized the three prefectures of Yongzhou, Binzhou, and Rongzhou back from the rebels.[136] The region around the Dong World was becoming increasingly unstable and the military skills of local Song officials were frequently tested.

Dai Yi, native of Minxian and known for his success in building ramparts and walls around the city of Nankang (modern-day Ganzhou, Jiangxi) while he served there, was appointed Yongzhou prefect from 1239 to 1244.[137] There are no records of Yongzhou prefects who served in the final years of the

Song dynasty, but records show that Cao Chen received the appointment as Yongzhou acting magistrate (*xuanhualing*) in 1272, followed by Huang Ziwen, who was appointed to the same position in 1275. At this point the Song imperial presence disintegrated in the face of the Mongol advance.

■

The greatest challenges faced by Song officials in positions along the southern and southwest frontier area of the empire can be placed in broad categories. First, many borderlands officials lacked local knowledge or even severed connections with local sources of this information, which led to a lack of trust on both sides. Second, trade issues became political issues and vice versa. Last, a lack of cooperation with partners around the Dong World often amplified local problems or complicated solutions to local issues. The tenure of many borderlands officials appointed by the Song court were cut short for one or more of the reasons mentioned in this chapter.

General trouble in the borderlands region occurred for two main reasons. First, frontier area tensions stemmed from political changes at the political center (i.e., the Kaifeng court). If the individual efforts made by border officials lacked support from the central government, or the efforts were misunderstood, local officials didn't have the resources to forge ahead with their own plans. Moreover, communications were slow between the central court and the Dong World frontier area, particularly west of the Leizhou Peninsula. Second, the Song empire's southern neighbors had different agendas in addressing Dong World-related issues of security or trade. These differences included a range of local relationships and different practices of political culture, as well as security concerns that were shaped by perceived threats and personal ambitions.

FIVE
THE DONG WORLD IN THE FACE OF MONGOL EXPANSION

The rapid Mongol expansion and military conquest of much of Eurasia in the mid-thirteenth century was a challenge that tested the political stability of both large and small states across the entire region. More often than not, encounters with the Mongol forces resulted in the collapse and disintegration of these polities, but total defeat was not always the outcome. Following the Mongol attacks on southwestern China, the Đại Việt kingdom prevailed under these conditions; the Dali kingdom, in contrast, did not.

Trade was the most significant factor in shaping the relations of particular Dong World local elite with distant courts, while strategic concerns of political and military survival included late Song local intelligence gathering.[1] The Huang clan would serve both Vietnamese and Chinese authorities in the protracted period of conflict with the Mongols, and direct contact with local leaders extended across the Sino-Vietnamese frontier. The Southern Song official Li Zengbo (1198–1265) noted that the Siming Prefecture's (southern Guangxi) administrator Huang Bing (Hoàng Bính), a leader of the aforementioned Huang clan, had long maintained contact with the Đại Việt court, having married all his daughters into the Lý ruling family. These close ties would have a lasting impact on the political loyalties of the region's inhabitants.

An example of the influence of local alliances occurred in the autumn of 1256. Facing the first Mongol invasion of Đại Việt, a defecting member of the Vietnamese royal house, Prince Trần Doan, tried to flee the kingdom. He was captured by Prefect Huang at Siming Prefecture and returned to the Đại Việt court. While retreating from the Mongols' second attempted invasion in late 1285, a contingent of the Yuan forces pulled back to Siming, only to be surrounded and attacked by Huang's descendants, still loyal to the Trần court. The cooperation between Siming prefect Huang Bing, his clan, and the Đại Việt court provides a window through which we may glimpse the implementation of local frontier alliances and evaluate the military and logistical assistance offered by local leaders in this region.

We also see in Huang Bing's service to both the Song and the Đại Việt courts a shift in the Huang clan's regional status, which was strongly influenced by changes in the primary trade routes passing through this region. Changing trade networks in the Tongking Gulf region had a direct influence on the status of the coastal, as well as more inland, indigenous elite residing between the Song and Đại Việt states. Through the early Song, the coastal area between Jiaozhi and Qinzhou shifted from the status of a regional hub of trade to a local hub, as the primary trade route shifted eastward to Guangzhou. In the period directly after the conclusion of this shift in trade status, the largely autonomous Huang clan of the Upper Tongking Gulf (Longzhou-Qinzhou-Yongzhou) region became simultaneously more dependent on interactions with both Song local representatives and the Đại Việt court and more integral to the trade activities and local intelligence gathering, at that time being conducted in their home region. These local elite were mutually dependent on the two neighboring authorities, but they were increasingly indispensable in the resolution of problems that plagued both the Song and Đại Việt along this section of the two states' shared frontier.

The Dali Response

Two years after ascending to the throne as Great Khan (Kaghan) in 1251, Borjigin Möngke (1208–1259) chose his brother Khubilai Khan (1215–1294) to develop an offensive strategy to the south, avoiding the Song Army's main line of defense. Khubilai and his advisers soon announced a plan to attack and defeat the Dali kingdom, thereby bringing men and material resources through the southwest to encircle Song defenses prior to an all-out invasion of the Chinese empire. Mongol forces had sought to attack Dali in 1248, in part from routes that passed through neighboring Tibet (Tufan) after that kingdom had surrendered to Möngke's armies, but Song forces based in Sichuan had driven back this attempted invasion.[2] In the autumn of 1253, Khubilai ordered one of his generals, Uriyangqadai (1202–1272), eldest son of Chinggis Khan's leading general Subetai (1176–1248), to assemble an army of one hundred thousand men in the region of modern-day Henan. The summer of the following year the forces under Uriyangqadai were assembled in Lintao (present-day northwest Gansu) for military training.[3] At the same time, a second Mongol military commander, Wang Dechen (1222–1259), arrived from Jiading (modern-day Leshan, Sichuan) to join Khubilai's forces.

That September, Khubilai assembled his conscripted army in Lintao and launched a three-pronged attack on Dali. Uriyangqadai's forces took a westerly route across Sichuan's Hongyuan-Ruo'ergai grasslands along the eastern end of the Tibetan Plateau. A second force led by Uriyangqadai's son Aju (1227–1287), together with Wang's forces as well as soldiers from the defeated Jurchen Jin kingdom, passed east through Tuocheng (modern-day Hanyuan, Sichuan), crossed the Dadu River, and then traveled south along the ancient Qingxi Road. Khubilai's army took a more central route from Lintao and traveled south over six hundred miles to arrive in Dali by way of the Jinsha River, the headwaters of the Yangzi River. Before leaving Lintao, Khubilai, in standard Mongol fashion, sent an emissary to the Dali court to demand that its leadership surrender prior to the outbreak of fighting. The Dali ruler Duan Xingzhi (r. 1251–1253) refused to negotiate, and his prime minister Gao Xiang (d. 1253) had the Mongol envoys executed.[4] Scholars have argued that court affairs were at this point largely in the hands of the ethnic Bai clan leaders Gao Xiang and his brother Gao He (or Gao Mu), and that Duan Xingzhi may have had little control over this self-defeating response to the Mongol request.[5] Instead, the Dali military shored up its defenses along the Jinsha River, stationing the forces of General You Qian in the high mountain passes, through which the Mongol army would be forced to traverse when arriving from Sichuan.

In the late autumn of 1253, Uriyangqadai again sent an envoy delegation to the Dali court to negotiate their surrender, once more unsuccessfully.

When the delegation arrived at the Dong World Bai-led Daguo garrison (Daguo zhai), the local commander surrendered, while his nephew refused to do so and barricaded himself inside the garrison. In the course of the fighting, the garrison was destroyed and the nephew killed, but the resistance movement did not spread among the local community.[6] Local conflicts continued in this manner, with some Dong World chiefs and their supporters submitting to the Mongol armies, while others continued to resist. The *History of the Yuan Dynasty* (Yuanshi) account also noted that Uriyangqadai's forces attacked all local leaders who failed to ally themselves with the Mongol campaign.[7] In early December, the Dali standing army and Mongol forces engaged in their first confrontation. The Mongols under Uriyangqadai assembled across the Jinsha River from the Dali army near Zhongdian. Confronted with the Mongol armies' crossing the Jinsha River, the local Mosuo chieftain submitted his forces to Mongol control.[8] In an important strategic move, Khubilai ordered the further conscription of militia from nearby tribes (most likely ethnically Naxi and Mosuo) in present-day Lijiang to create a lateral force for the attack on Dali's main force. Khubilai's chief assistant and military adviser Bayan (Boyan; 1236–1295) then launched a daring nighttime crossing of the Jinsha River on inflated rafts made of sheepskin to surprise the Dali commander Gao Taixiang's army.[9] This attack left Gao and his subordinates in a precarious situation, and they hastily retreated to the Dali capital near Erhai Lake.

Khubilai's central group of Mongol forces was able to continue south to subdue the territories of first Jianchuan and then Langong (modern-day Eryuan), both located slightly northwest of Erhai Lake.[10] These territories both submitted (*neifu*) to Mongol control and may also have contributed local troops to the conquering army. The eastern group crossed the Jinsha River and joined forces with the western group to work together to attack Dali's main army with the intention of completely annihilating Dali. Khubilai's combined forces achieved victory and occupied the Dali capital on December 15 without mass destruction and death when he was able to have an agreement forged between his assistant Yao Shu and the Dali court. Duan Xingzhi and Gao Xiang both fled, but Gao was soon captured and beheaded for his role in killing the Mongol envoys.[11] Duan fled to Shanchan (the Dali military prefecture with control over the modern-day Kunming region), where he found allies among those clan leaders who resided on or near the Song frontier.[12] This residual force continued to resist the Mongol advance for two years until Shanchan was conquered and the former Dali ruler captured.

In autumn 1255, Uriyangqadai seized the Shanchan garrison at modern-day Kunming, taking Duan Xingzhi prisoner and causing Duan's vanguard of twenty thousand soldiers to surrender unconditionally. The entire Dali region was now under Mongol control, and it was with the help of certain indigenous groups that Khubilai Khan's forces were able to achieve their victory. John Herman notes that most of the local elite who elected to serve the Mongols had not held positions of authority within the Dali political order.[13] The Mongol invasion of Yunnan brought in a Mongol overseer to supervise the leadership of Duan Xingzhi and the conquered Dali court.[14] Bin Yang notes that the Duan clan was recruited to assist with the further invasions of the Burmese kingdom of Pagan (1044–1287) and the initially successful attack on the Trần in Đại Việt, which will be discussed later in this chapter.[15] The Mongols established commanderies throughout the formerly autonomous kingdom and displaced the overarching authority of the Duan. Still, space remained for local self-rule. The leadership of the Ziqi kingdom would continue their resistance until the kingdom's conquest in 1260.

Khubilai and his military commanders quickly adopted a general policy of leniency toward the conquered population in the capital to appease the people, achieve stability, bring order, and reduce support for remaining Dali resistance in the vicinity. Although the Mongols may have secured the Duan clan's service through conquest, there were many local leaders who still resisted their advance.[16] Khubilai named Uriyangqadai governor of the entire region, and the Mongol general was soon actively seeking allies among the various upland chiefs of the territory (now named Yunnan) to secure final victory for the Mongols. The stele "Khubilai Khan's Pacification of Yunnan" (Shizu ping Yunnan bei), raised in the aftermath of the campaign, spelled out the Mongol army's attention to ethnic differences among those who supported and those who resisted the Mongol advance, stating,

Soon after seizing Shanchan, Uriyangqadai received the Dali ruler Duan Xingzhi's offer of surrender. Uriyangqadai made it clear that the former Dali ruler would not be killed. The Yuan army then advanced into the tribal areas to subdue the thirty-seven clans of the Wuman, those upland *dong* settlements of eastern Yunnan that were allied with the Dali leadership.[17] With tribal assistance from these conquered peoples, Uriyangqadai's forces attacked Jiaozhi [Đại Việt], capturing its capital [Thăng Long] and taking control of the Temo District's thirty-six mountain valley *dong*, the lands of the "Gold Teeth" [Jinchi], the Bai, the Yi, the "Luo spirits" [Luogui; i.e., Wuman elite of Luodian], and the various Dong World tribes of [modern-day Myanmar] — all in succession were brought under Mongol rule.[18]

The Song Response: Commissioner Li and Prefect Huang (Hoang)

With an increasing number of hostile encounters between Song and Mongol armies, the Song court struggled to cope with an advancing enemy in the south under very difficult circumstances. Guangxi's geographical environment involved a unique topography filled with steep hills located close to the rivers, undulating ridges and peaks, and numerous passes and unfamiliar channels, the defense of which was not easy. Good military intelligence in such unrelenting terrain was absolutely necessary.[19] The circulation of intelligence information involved strengthening communication channels between Lin'an (Hangzhou) and the office of the Guangnan West Circuit military commissioner in Jingjiang Prefecture (modern-day Guilin), and on communication between Yongzhou and Jingjiang. Having ignored the southern frontier for most of his reign, the Lizong emperor (r. 1224–1264) was finally forced to take a strategic interest in developments throughout this region. In early 1239 the Song court received a memorial from Chen Long, the military commissioner in Sichuan who reported that Mongol forces had plans to sweep down the Dadu River in an invasion of the Dali kingdom, after which the Mongols would be free to attack the Song's "soft underbelly." Upon receiving the report, the Song court ordered Xu Qingsuo,

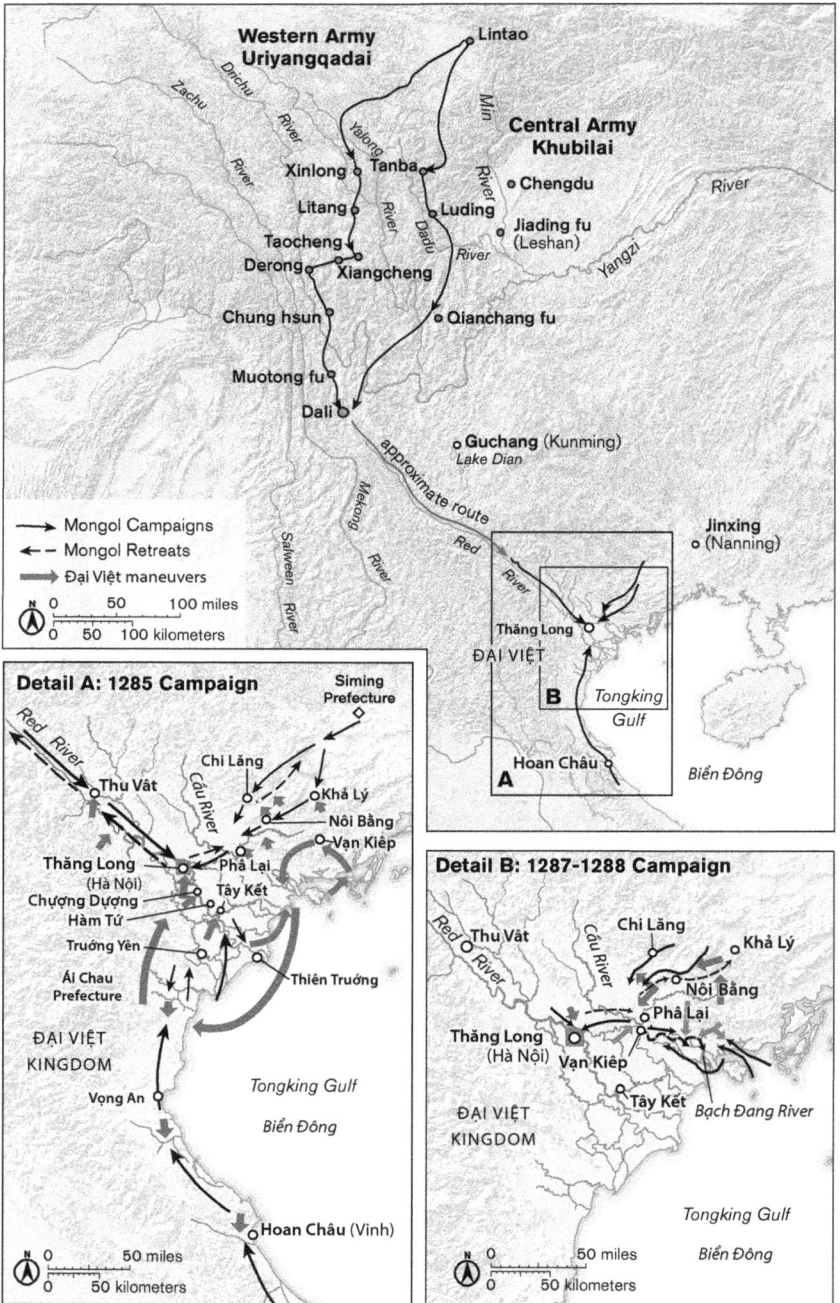

Mongol Military Campaigns in the Dong World

then serving as Guangnan's military commissioner, to prepare the southern frontier to brace against the expected assault.[20] Following the Mongols' probing attacks on Dali several years later, the Song court was compelled to make the defense of the Guangnan West Circuit a much higher priority. In 1244 Mongol armies had captured Jiuhe Township, killing its defender, the Dali prince Gao He, as mentioned earlier. When the Song court received this news, imperial troops from the Jinghu Circuit (modern-day central Hunan) were ordered in 1245 to relocate to the Guangnan West Circuit to fortify its defenses.[21] When Mongol troops made no additional advances into the region, many of these troops were returned to their home garrisons.

Li Zengbo, who had earlier served as military commissioner to the circuits of Huainan East and West (modern-day central Jiangsu and Anhui), was a leading choice of the Song court for an effective local administrator. Li's selection indicated how important the defense of Guangnan had become for the Song's survival. In 1249 the court appointed Li Zengbo as military commissioner for Guangnan residing at Jingjiangfu Military Prefecture, as well as transport commissioner (*zhuanyun shi*) for the circuit, with oversight of the region's fiscal and military matters. The court charged Li with the following tasks: dispatching spies for intelligence gathering throughout the region, with a particular focus on fostering strong cooperation between the Sichuan and Jinghu circuits; forging a formal alliance with the Dali kingdom to provide the Song empire with a vital buffer zone; repairing city walls and irrigation works while reequipping local militia; dispatching reliable local commanders to strategic garrisons, including Hengshan and Yongping, as a means of forging ties with indigenous Dong World elite; and, finally, organizing militia groups consisting of both Han settlers and Dong World communities to produce a first line of defense against the anticipated Mongol invasions.[22] In 1257 the Song emperor specifically ordered Li Zengbo to assemble troops stationed between Yongzhou and Yizhou and to take control of local militia from the *jimi* aboriginal settlements in that region. In the late autumn of that year, Li Zengbo took the additional position as pacification commissioner (*anfu dashi*) for Jinghu South Circuit.[23] This appointment was likely intended to better coordinate the local defenses of Guangnan and Jinghu once the Dali kingdom had fallen to the Mongols and no longer provided an opportunity for a separate alliance. In the summer of 1260 Li Zengbo left these positions with his official transfer back north, where he remained until his death four years later, but Li learned much from these years of frontier service. As Huang Kuan-chung notes, when Li Zengbo served as the administrator of Jingjiangfu Military Prefecture, the Guangxi situation was quite dire, and he had to bear the heavy responsibility for the defense of Sichuan and the Jinghu South Circuit. In the course of fighting with the Mongols and recovering Xiangyang, he came to understand the Mongols very well.[24] One of the lessons that Li Zengbo learned was to rely on the Dong World elite, including the Huang, for military support and local knowledge in this dire situation.

During the late Southern Song period, intelligence gathering along the southern frontier became a critical concern for the court at Lin'an, and the strategy for intelligence gathering involved borderlands cooperation. In the spring of 1255, after the Mongol forces had conquered the Dali kingdom, the Song court began to request intelligence from the Trần court on the movements of Mongol troops in the region.[25] In the autumn of 1257, following a request from Lin'an for better intelligence, Li Zengbo instructed the Guangxi military commissioner Yin Yingfei (*jinshi* 1241) to send envoys to the Đại Việt kingdom. Yin Yingfei sent Liao Yangsun to the Trần court "using books and currency to gain access to the rulers of Giao."[26] Huang Kuan-chung notes that Li Zengbo in this instance was gathering intelligence from the petty merchants who traveled between the Dong World river valley communities from Yongzhou to Qinzhou to sell their wares.[27] Li Zengbo, along with his fellow local representatives of the Song empire, desperately sought support in the effort to prevent the Mongols from opening a southern front in their campaign to topple the Song state, and the indigenous leadership of the Upper Tongking Gulf occupied a strategic route that linked the Song with the potential allies in the Đại Việt kingdom. At the dynasty's end, it appeared that the Jingjiangfu Military Prefecture was the linchpin to the southern resistance to the Mongol advance. When Jingjiangfu was finally overrun in 1276, all the remaining loyal prefectures and commandaries of the Guangnan East and West circuits submitted to the Mongol invaders.[28]

As the leader of the Huang (Hoàng) clan's home region in this period, Huang Bing's (Hoàng Bình) administrative service to the distant northern court became increasingly important to Song authorities as local alliances shifted with the Mongol armies' advance. Until 1249, Song authorities at Yongzhou were using gold to buy local horses for their cavalry from indigenous traders along the frontier region.[29] However, following the first Mongol invasion of Đại Việt in the 1250s, Mongol commanders made their own inroads with these indigenous communities and were also able to develop good relations with many indigenous leaders in the Yunnan-Guizhou region.[30] This fact created a great deal of frustration at the Lin'an court and caused the Song leadership to fear a greater threat from Mongol incursions if military reconnaissance in the aboriginal regions were to be cut off. This severance of local ties, in fact, caused the Guangnan horse trade to dry up after 1255.[31] There were other indigenous leaders, such as Xu Zongyi, who chose, as Huang Bing did, to cooperate with the Song in repelling Mongol advances. Li Zengbo was forced to call upon these remaining Dong World allies, including the Huang clan at Siming, to shore up local defenses and to seek out vital local military intelligence. The Huang clan's role in local trade may have diminished, but their authority within the Song empire was renewed through this new role.

The military situation Li faced during his search for local allies was dire. In the period in which he acted as the chief military officer for both the Jinghu South Circuit and Guangnan West Circuit, Mongol soldiers twice invaded Guangxi. In the summer of 1258, in an initial assault, Mongol horsemen rode through the Temo Circuit, home region of the Nùng clan, into Song territory to engage Song forces at Yongzhou's East Gate (Dong Men) and Kunlun Pass before retreating to Yunnan. The Mongol advance is estimated to have caused the mass defection of more than seven thousand men of the approximately twenty-six thousand local troops garrisoned in Guangnan West Circuit. Sickness took many more; by the winter of that year the garrison at Yongzhou lost three thousand men to illness.[32] The

1258 invasion of the Mongols also caused shock in the Đại Việt kingdom. On December 7, the Mongol army captured the Đại Việt's Phú Linh Prefecture, and pushed forward to capture the Song territories of Longzhou and Anding (today part of Du'an County). At this stage in the war, Li Zengbo gave the order to Huang Bing and another Dong World official, Li Zongcheng, to meet with and debrief two Đại Việt officials surnamed Nguyễn and Trần, respectively, regarding Mongol military movements, as well as to take a statement from a local Song witness Wang Dai. All of this information was presented in detail to Emperor Lizong.[33] As noted earlier, during the period Mongol forces occupied Đại Việt, Li Zengbo depended on military intelligence on Mongol troops, which was gathered by Dong World persons who would travel between Đại Việt and Yongzhou to inform Song authorities.[34] Huang Bing, who had family members who had married into the Trần royal household, was well-placed for providing this direct contact for Li Zengbo and his fellow Song representatives.

The Đại Việt Response

Three decades before the threat of Mongol invasion became a concern for the Vietnamese court, serious challenges to the political order had come from within. When the final male ruler of the Lý dynasty, Huệ Tông, died and left no son, his daughter Lý Chiêu Hoàng took charge of state affairs. But Trần Thủ Độ (1194–1264), acting through his nephew, who was Lý Chiêu Hoàng's husband, took control of court administration. In 1225, after eliminating the remaining Lý clan members vying for the throne, Thủ Độ set the political foundation for the new Trần dynasty.[35] In early 1242, the Song emperor Lizong (1205–1264) sent an edict to the new "Prince of the State of Annan" (Annan Guowang), Trần Thái Tông (1218–1277), ordering that the honorific title "Successful Official Who Follows the Example of Loyalty and Obedience and Guards the Symbols of Authority," originally granted to the Lý dynastic rulers, should have two additional characters "Preserves Propriety" (Shouyi).[36] In the summer of 1258, Lizong sent out an edict declaring that the unorthodox dynastic change at the Trần court, in which Trần Thái Tông appointed his son Trần Hoảng (1240–1290) emperor as Trần Thánh Tông and promptly "retired" as "senior emperor," was un-fathomable and that the Sino-Vietnamese frontier region should be readied militarily. However, the Song presented no further inquiries regarding the abrupt transfer of power that had occurred in Đại Việt. There were more pressing issues to attend to with the Mongols' southern advances.

Following the conquest of the Dali kingdom, the Mongol forces turned their attention to Đại Việt and the surrounding region, launching attacks on the kingdom on three occasions: in 1257–1258, 1284–1285, and 1287–1288. It is important to note here the use of former Dali forces in these southern campaigns, even in the little-discussed first campaign. The final ruler of Dali, Duan Xingzhi, now a Mongol puppet official, ordered his younger brothers Xin Zhiri (n.d.) and Xin Yifu (n.d.) to assemble a Cuan and Bo indigenous militia army of twenty thousand men to serve as the vanguard force for the eventual Mongol assault on the Song. The *History of the Yuan Dynasty* (Yuanshi) account notes that Xin Zhiri had the surname Duan, yet his family had long served the powerful Gao clan. Those indigenous militia units not joining Uriyangqadai in his attack on the Song's southern frontier were ordered to launch the first attack on Đại Việt.[37] The Đại Việt frontier was the site of many forces, Mongol, Han, and indigenous, jockeying for position in the period leading up to the Mongols' final southern assault on the Chinese empire. In Li Zengbo's account *Continued Draft of the Manuscript from the Scholar's Chamber* (Kezhai zagao yi xu gao), the Song local administrator noted that the Song's *jimi* Siming Prefecture and the Đại Việt kingdom had long been close, because the Siming prefect Huang Bing had maintained contact with the Thăng Long court for some time, and his daughters had all married into the Lý ruling family. Men on both sides of the larger Huang clan had received Vietnamese government positions.[38] This assembly of troops caused a disturbance when in autumn 1256 Prince Trần Doãn, son of the second Trần queen Thuận Thiên (1216–1248), tried to flee the kingdom, but was captured by Prefect Huang at Siming and returned to the Đại Việt court.[39] This cooperation of Siming authorities with Đại Việt, forged through the marriage alliances, would be significant in the later Mongol campaigns when it appears that the Trần court was able to rely on military and logistical assistance from local militia in this region.

In late 1257, Khubilai Khan sent a force of several thousand Mongols and upland Yi militia under the command of Uriyangqadai south into Trần territory, engaging with the Việt forces of Trần Thái Tông on January 17, 1258, at Bình Lệ Nguyên along the Cà Lồ River in modern-day Vĩnh Phúc Province.[40] Following the strategic retreat of the Trần forces north to Phủ Lỗ, Uriyangqadai pressed his army forward in an assault on the Đại Việt capital, Thăng Long. However, the Vietnamese struck back at the invaders from the eastern Red River Delta, harassing and finally driving out the Mongol-led armies, aided by local forces, including upland allies. When a detachment of Mongol soldiers arrived at Qúy Hoa garrison, at the heart of Tai-speaking clan power during Nùng Trí Cao's effort at autonomy two centuries earlier and negotiated away from the Song following the 1075 frontier war, the Dong World garrison commander Hà Bổng Chiêu led his Dong World militia in an ambush on these troops, causing a significant defeat.[41]

In the absence of Uriyangqadai's forces, the former Dong World elite of eastern Dali and the frontier kingdoms rallied for an anti-Mongol resistance that would last the next ten years. Eventually, during the summer of 1259, the Mongol court called for Uriyangqadai's forces to pull back from Đại Việt and move northward, joining other Mongol forces the next year near Tanzhou (modern-day Changsha, Hunan). The target of the Mongol military became once again the Southern Song. In 1260 Uriyangqadai assembled an army of three thousand Mongol cavalry and ten thousand upland militia troops from western Guangxi, Guizhou, and eastern Yunnan, including peoples once closely allied with the Dali court. This Mongol force attacked Song defenses from the south, passing through modern-day Guilin in Guangxi to strike the Hengshan garrison and push forward from Tanzhou. A second expedition against Đại Việt waited until after Khubilai Khan had established his own rule against all opposition and set up his court in Beijing in 1260 (then called Dadu, the "Great Capital"). Initially, it appeared that the Yuan court under Khubilai might leave Đại Việt in peace. The ruler declared, "All ceremonies and customs [pertaining to Đại Việt] should follow precedent," and in 1261 the Trần court sent tributary envoys to Dadu, at which time Khubilai Khan enfeoffed the Vietnamese ruler Trần Thánh Tông (r. 1258–1290) as "King of Annan."[42] The Yuan at this time only requested that Đại Việt send a tribute mission once every three years, but thereafter the Mongol court repeatedly dispatched emissaries with "imperial edicts on all matters."[43] Trần Thánh Tông had not asked the Yuan emperor for permission to take the throne when he did so, and the Trần court continued to maintain tribute relations with the Southern Song until shortly before that dynasty's collapse in 1279. All this was cause for Khubilai Khan's dissatisfaction.

The Mongols, having taken the throne of China, looked to wield influence over the sea lanes of maritime Southeast Asia, this time with their sights set on the conquest of Đại Việt's southern coastal neighbor, Champa (Zhancheng). In 1279, Khubilai appointed a trusted Tangut-Mongol military commander Sogetu (Suodu, d. 1285) to the position of provincial secretary (*zuo cheng*) in the port of Quanzhou "to spread word of the Yuan's founding" to the various Southeast Asian kingdoms.[44] In 1281 a large Mongol naval fleet was sent to Champa, capturing the capital Vijaya in the same year. The Cham king Indravarman V escaped into the mountains. Meanwhile, the Đại Việt court declined requests from the Yuan to assist with these southern expeditions. It may be that the Mongols also wished to prevent a joint anti-Yuan effort by Southern Song exiles and Đại Việt. Huang Fei cites the displaced scholar Zheng Sixiao (1241–1318) with his observation that in the early Yuan "many civilian and military officials [of the fallen Song] went into exile abroad, took up official service in Champa, married into the ruling elite in Jiaozhi [Đại Việt], or left to drift abroad in distant kingdoms."[45] For all these reasons, Khubilai began to increase pressure on the Trần court.

In the summer of 1283, the Mongol emperor sent the Uighur official Ariq Qaya (1227–1286) to the Trần capital with an imperial request for help from Jiaozhi (Đại Việt) with troops and provisions for the expedition against Champa.[46] At this time the newly enthroned Vietnamese emperor Trần Nhân Tông (r. 1279–1308), with help from his father the senior ruler Thánh Tông, again refused to offer assistance, and the Vietnamese court instead readied its troops, including local militia and former Song soldiers.[47] In the summer of 1284 Nhân Tông's uncle Trần Quốc Tuấn (1226–1300), most famously known by his honorific title of the Hưng Đạo Prince, readied local troops at Đông Bộ Đầu Wharf, located outside modern-day Hà Nội, to prepare for the capital's defense.[48] His preparations were certainly in order, because Khubilai's court soon took the Vietnamese court's refusal as a reason to attack. In the fall of 1284, Khubilai's son Toghan (d. 1285) commanded troops from Jinghu to approach and camp on the frontier with Đại Việt at Lộc Châu. In December, an envoy, Trần Phủ, returned to the Vietnamese court to report that Khubilai had ordered Toghan, along with his trusted commanders, senior minister Pingzhang Ali and Ariq Qaya, to enter Đại Việt under the pretext of launching the conquest of northern Champa, but instead to divide forces for an invasion of Đại Việt.[49] The Mongol forces split into two groups, one attacking by land and one attacking by sea from the south. The account in *Complete Book of the History of the Great Việt* famously notes that when Trần Nhân Tông first heard of the attack, he assembled all his trusted advisers, including the senior ruler, for a banquet to solicit their advice, at which time "all called for an attack, a myriad spoke as if with one voice."[50] Trần Quốc Tuấn issued his proclamation "Dispatch to All My Officers" (Dụ chư tỳ tướng hịch văn), which is now famous as a battle cry for the assembled Trần nobility calling for retaliation, citing as inspiration to his men the example of Uriyangqadai's overthrow of the Dali kingdom and the subsequent campaigns through southern China.[51]

At the start of this second invasion, Toghan's collective force pursued two routes in the attack on Đại Việt. Those troops following the land route from Lạng Sơn at the Động Bản Pass encountered and defeated its Vietnamese defenders, resulting in the death of the Vietnamese commander Tần Sầm. Once the Yuan forces were within the pass, Toghan ordered the troops split into six battalions to attack the forces of Trần Quốc Tuấn from separate directions. Six days into the invasion, the Yuan forces had seized the upland garrisons at Vĩnh Châu, Nội Bàng, Thiết Lược, and Chi Lăng, but the Yuan commander did not see any advantage in advancing farther and instead pulled back to the Vạn Kiếp garrison, located in Chí Linh County (now Hải Hưng Province).[52] After these encounters, the senior ruler Trần Thánh Tông, who had reentered the battlefield personally, ordered his land forces under the Thánh Vũ Army commander and his naval forces to assist Trần Quốc Tuấn. Avoiding a direct encounter with the Yuan forces, Quốc

Tuấn turned for support to the militia assigned to the coastal circuits of Hải Đông, Vân Trà, and Ba Điểm, calling on local commanders to offer their best troops as his vanguard before escaping south by sea.[53] Quốc Tuấn also rallied militia and logistical support from surrounding upland districts to supply his troops while he was in hiding.[54] Meanwhile, the Yuan forces continued to advance on Thăng Long. The account in *History of the Yuan Dynasty* (Yuanshi) notes that Trần Thánh Tông along the Phú Lương River (or Cầu River, which was likely an alternative name for the Hồng River) "gave the order that vessels along the [southern] banks of the river should erect a wooden stockade" as a defense against the Yuan army.[55] This defensive measure did little to slow the Mongols' momentum, and when the Yuan armies had crossed the Phú Lương River, they faced the gates of Thăng Long, and the forces led by Thánh Tông and Nhân Tông fell back. The next day, Toghan entered the capital to find an empty palace. The Trần forces continued to regroup on their estates deeper in the Red River Delta.

At this point in the campaign, the Yuan commanders Li Bangxian and Liu Shiying ordered the construction of garrisons and courier stations and dispatched troops to patrol the frontier areas to prevent Vietnamese troops from returning. Land-based troops led by Toghan's son Toru Puhua with Poluo Hada'er and sea-based forces led by Li Heng and Wu Ma'er, among others, continued to pursue Trần Quốc Tuấn. Early in the winter of 1285, Toghan's warships landed troops near Đà Mạc (in modern-day Bắc Ninh), capturing and executing General Trần Bình Trọng (1259–1285), whose defensive efforts allowed the two Trần rulers to retreat safely. Trần troops had had "Death to the Tartars" (*Thát Đát*) tattooed on their arms, a slogan that infuriated the Yuan troops, who massacred the first wave of defenders they faced.[56] However, local resistance to the Yuan advance was widespread. As the Yuan official Zhang Bang noted about the Trần defenders, "all the kingdom's commanderies and counties, if faced with an outside invasion, would fight to the death, or should their military strength be inadequate, they were permitted then to flee to the mountain areas, where they would forge ahead and not accept defeat in the struggle."[57] The Hưng Phúc Temple stele, located to the south in An Duyên Township, Quảng Hùng Commune, Thanh Hoá Province, is concrete evidence of this coordinated local resistance. The 1860 reengraved temple tablet commemorates the defense of Thanh Hoá *lộ* in late 1284 against the armies of Sogetu, who had led the sea-borne force south in this invasion attempt.[58] According to this account, a mid-ranked village official (*đại toát đại liêu ban phục*), Lê Cong Mạnh, in the summer of 1284 led the local resistance to the Mongols. Following a protracted and bloody struggle, the Yuan forces entered the village in early 1285. As the stele reports,

> Midway through 1284, the "northern caitiffs" [*hulu*; i.e., Mongol forces] came south. The caitiff prime minister Sogetu led his army to our kingdom by a sea route and met with the forces of Đại Việt at Cổ Khê [modern-day Kính Village, Quảng Xương Commune, Quảng Hùng District, Thanh Hoá Province]. The marquis [Trần Quốc Toản] led a force of local people to resist the attackers at Cổ Bút Village, where the two sides engaged in battle, but the caitiffs repeatedly refused to withdraw.[59]

However, defeat in this battle did reveal political fissures in the Trần ruling house. In the midst of the fighting, imperial family member Trần Kiện, son of Prince Trần Quốc Khang (1237–1300); Trần Kiện's retainer and later historian Lê Tắc; Prince Trần Ích Tắc (1254–1329), younger brother of the senior ruler Trần Thánh Tông and uncle of the king; as well as prominent nobility including Văn Chiêu, Prince Trần Lộng, Phạm Cụ Địa, Lê Diễn, and Trịnh Long fled the battlefield.[60] Trần Ích Tắc, Trần Kiện, Trần Tú Ái, and Trần Văn Lộng defected to the Mongols.[61] The *Complete Book* notes that uplanders were among those who attempted to avenge this betrayal. Before Toghan was able to send his captives north to Dadu, the Lạng Giang Dong World chieftains (*thổ hào*) Nguyễn Thế Lộc and Nguyễn Lĩnh, among others, attacked the Ma Lục garrison, where the captives were being held. Quốc Tuấn's own slave Nguyễn Địa Lô shot Trần Kiện dead. Lê Tắc threw the defected prince's lifeless body on the back of a horse to escape in the night, burying him some distance from the fort.[62]

By late spring, the northern Vietnamese weather gradually began to change and so did the fortunes of the Trần defenders. The Yuan general Sogetu replenished his army with Dong World militia from the Yunnan region, numbering some five hundred thousand men, along with troops from the Champa campaigns.[63] However, the Trần military leaders chose to fight these numbers with new tactics. Quốc Tuấn led his well-supplied army of local militia back to the Vạn Kiếp River. Together with the forces of the Dong World chieftain Nguyễn Lu (n.d.), then based at the Yongping garrison in southern Guangxi, Quốc Tuấn engaged in skirmishes with the Yuan forces. The prince employed guerrilla tactics, such as a "scorched earth" defense to deprive the Mongols of supplies. Yuan troop casualties increased, due to logistical difficulties and the fact that foraging proved insufficient. In the well-known battle of Hàm Tử Pass, a contingent of Yuan troops was defeated by a Trần force consisting of former Song troops and Dong World militia.[64] Within a month's time, Toghan decided to pull his troops back into China to Siming Prefecture in Guangnan West Circuit. However, the Siming region was surrounded with local forces still loyal to the Trần court, descendants of the local chieftain mentioned earlier in this chapter. In the midst of crossing the Vạn Kiếp River, the Yuan military was ambushed by Vietnamese forces. Many among the Yuan forces drowned or died in battle, including General Li Heng, who was struck by a poisoned arrow upon arriving in Siming.[65] The Yuan forces to the south under Sogetu were soon caught in transit by Cham forces, and Sogetu himself was killed.[66] In June, Toghan led a small residual force under his command to escape the region, but this Yuan military conquest had ended in failure.

Another invasion effort was organized by the Yuan court in early 1286, but the campaign was abandoned after less than a month of military action. However, this did not mark the end of Khubilai Khan's efforts to subdue Đại Việt. By early 1287, Khubilai had devised a new plan. The Yuan emperor enfeoffed Thánh Tông's younger brother Trần Ích Tắc as "King of Annan" to replace his nephew Nhân Tông as the new ruler of Đại Việt.[67] This was the reason given for the third invasion attempt. The Yuan court sent a new expeditionary force under Abači (Abachi), comprised of seventy thousand Mongol and Han troops and five hundred warships from the provinces of Huai, Jiangxi, and Huguang; six thousand troops from Yunnan; and fifteen thousand Dong World "Li militia" (*Li bing*) from outlying frontier regions. Zhang Wenhu (n.d.), son of former pirate and Yuan maritime commissioner Zhang Xuan (n.d.), Fei Gongchen (n.d.), and Tao Daming (n.d.) were entrusted with transporting 170,000 men by sea to enter Đại Việt by various routes.[68] The supreme commander for this force was again Toghan, likely wishing to appease his father following the earlier failed campaign.

In late autumn of 1287, the local Trần official Trịnh Xiển reported to the court that Mongol troops under Prince Atai had seized the garrison at Phú Lương Pass.[69] Soon thereafter, the Yuan general Cheng Pengfei (n.d.) and his Mongol counterpart Beiluoheda'er joined the attack with their Han soldiers, accompanied by local forces from Yongping, now a subdued ally of the Mongol empire. The Yuan admirals Omar (n.d.) and Fan Ji (n.d.) launched their assault on Đại Việt from the sea. Fan and Omar encountered more than four hundred Vietnamese naval vessels at An Bang Bay, located southwest of modern-day Hạ Long Bay at the mouth of the Bạch Đằng River, and defeated this fleet. Despite Trần opposition, Cheng and Beiluoheda'er captured the garrisons guarding the three passes at Lão Thử, Hãm Sa, and Tì Trúc.[70] In December, Toghan arrived at Mao La Harbor, at which point Trần Quốc Tuấn retreated. In order to prevent Quốc Tuấn from assembling troops again at Vạn Kiếp, and thereby blocking the escape route of the Yuan army, Toghan commanded Cheng and Oquqči to construct a sturdier fortification to defend Vạn Kiếp. He also ordered Omar and Abači to take separate water and land routes for an attack on the Trần capital. Shortly thereafter, Toghan led his armies across the Phú Lương River and once again captured Thăng Long.[71] This time, after the Yuan had taken the capital, they wantonly engaged in burning and looting. The fourteenth-century Chinese account *Records of Travels through An Nam* (Annan xingji) notes that when Yuan troops entered the Vietnamese capital, they "set fire to the government offices, robbed the graves of the people's ancestors, held captive or killed young and old in their homes, destroyed the material possessions of the common people, and engaged in all types of ruthless conduct and all manner of evil."[72] By early 1288, the forces led by Trần Quốc Tuấn and his son were on the run and things looked dire for the Trần resistance.

However, when Zhang Wenhu and his provisioning fleet arrived at the coast in late 1287, the Mongols encountered Vietnamese warships.[73] A successful battle with the Mongols at Vân Đồn Island turned the tide of the fighting and split the invading army.[74] In the ensuing battle, Zhang's fleet became lost and subsequently dumped a large portion of its rice supply at sea before escaping to Qiongzhou near modern-day Haikou on Hainan Island. Due to high winds, Fei Gongchen's provisioning fleet was unable to enter Đại Việt waters, and he returned to Qiongzhou to join Zhang. The lack of provisions and the weather's gradual warming, reminiscent of the past failed campaign, caused considerable worry among the Yuan military commanders.[75] Toghan ordered Omar and Fan Ji to retreat by sea, and in March Toghan decided to lead all the land forces in retreat from the region. However, the Vietnamese army had deployed its military forces of more than thirty thousand men to guard Nữ Nghe Pass and Khâu Cấp Hill and block the Yuan army's northern exit. Subsequently, the Vietnamese army launched a major counterattack. When the Mongol fleet approached the capital by way of the Bạch Đằng River, Trần Quốc Tuấn's soldiers used Ngô Quyền's (897–944) famous iron-tipped pole defense of 938 to trap the fleet in the river at low tide for a second time with great success. The *DVSKTT* account notes that so many Yuan troops were drowned or killed, the river ran red in the midst of the battle.[76] Fan Ji's entire force was destroyed on the Bạch Đằng, while Abači contracted a malarial infection and had to retreat, and finally died in Chengdu. Omar's forces were still located to the north and Toghan, himself struck by a poisoned arrow, had retreated to Siming. The Yuan military faced another defeat. Soon thereafter, Trần Nhân Tông sent a delegation to Dadu to present tribute and once again request vassal status, as well as ordering the release of all Mongol prisoners of war.[77] The Vietnamese tribute delegation offered the Yuan court a small amount of gold and an apology for its "sins."

That the local frontier communities were able to provide greater assistance to the Trần than they could to the Dali court may be argued from another angle. Huang Fei believes that local uprisings of the early Yuan dynasty indirectly benefitted the Đại Việt kingdom. According to Yuan official records, in 1284 the Jiangnan-based Xiangting Uprising (Xiangting Er Qi) involved more than two hundred rebel groups until 1290, when it was noted that more than four hundred groups were active throughout the southeast.[78] In the face of so many rebel uprisings, the Yuan court had transferred part of its military to these areas to crack down on dissent, thus weakening the power of the Yuan army during the Đại Việt campaigns.[79]

Perhaps, but in any case, the Yuan military appeared to learn the lesson belatedly that widespread local support for any expeditions against the Đại Việt kingdom would be absolutely necessary. In 1289 the Chengdu Protectorate military commander Liu Delu memorialized Khubilai with the following request, "I wish to take a force of five thousand men to demand the surrender of the southwestern communities of the 'Eight Indigenous Militarized Regions' (Ba Fan Shun Yuan Xuan Wei Si) in order to invade and conquer Jiaozhi."[80] Liu received approval from Khubilai for the plan, but nothing more. The Mongols further planned attacks in 1291 and 1293, but with the death of Khubilai Khan in 1294, these plans were never realized. After Chengzong (Temür Öljeytü Khan; r. 1294–1307) came to the throne, the Yuan court implemented the conciliatory policy of "great forgiveness, far and near" (*dasi she you, wu wen yuanjin*), while the Vietnamese court too adopted a matching policy of "great forgiveness" (*kuanyou*) regarding its northern neighbor.[81] The Đại Việt kingdom subsequently continued to act as a tributary vassal throughout the Yuan dynasty.

■

Even after the fall of the Song, the Huang clan, then in the service of the Vietnamese court, continued to serve the anti-Mongol cause. In the aftermath of the second Yuan invasion of Đại Việt in 1285, many Yuan troops died while retreating through the Huang clan home region, including the Tangut general Li Heng, who had played an important role as military commander in the final battle with the remnant forces of the Song, only to be struck by a poisoned arrow upon arriving in Siming Prefecture.[82] Even after the southern frontier was finally pacified by Yuan forces, the Huang clan proved unapologetic. When the local leader Huang Shengxu was able to assemble military forces from both sides of the frontier, he launched a uprising in 1292 with twenty thousand supporters. After the Mongol court sent the military commander Cheng Pengfei to put down the unrest, Huang

Taiping Fu City Wall, Chongzuo, Guangxi (Ming period)

fled south into the Đại Việt kingdom.[83] In the fall of 1318, the local frontier leaders Huang Fafu and He Kai launched another revolt that required the intervention of Mongol troops.[84] However, local resistance from the Huang clan in Siming did not continue forever. In 1329 the local elite Huang Ke-shun would serve the Yuan court as route commander (*zongguan*) for the Siming Prefecture, and that year responsibly brought tribute to the court at Dadu.[85] Loyalty on the Sino-Vietnamese frontier was a complicated matter, and this remained the case well into the modern era.

Rulers of the Dali kingdom were confronted with their own Dong World problems when the Duan clan sought to defend against the advancing Mongol forces. Although the surrounding clans were willing to ally themselves with the Duan when all could benefit from protection and trade advantages, the Mongols' superior military powers completely transformed the landscape and left open the possibility of new political alignments for the local chiefs without severe repercussions. The Đại Việt leadership, in contrast, could rally local *dong* chiefs to the defense of the Vietnamese court, because the fortunes of even uplands local communities were more clearly linked to the Trần imperial family than to the threatening invaders. Defending one's own territory meant choosing to defend the Trần dynastic order as well. In such a situation, the Sinitic model of centralized power, dependent on status conferred by one's participation in the political order, formed a bulwark against institutional disintegration in the face of hegemonic power. The Việt leadership had borrowed the best of the northern administrative tradition and utilized it to gain the loyalty of indigenous neighbors and thereby fend off the powerful outsiders. By the early 1360s the Trần official Phạm Sư Mạnh would note in a poem describing the Vietnamese side of the frontier in modern-day Lạng Sơn: "The barrier mountain's strong points determine our strategy. Streams, mountain torrents, and a screen of tribesmen provide a far-flung [defense]."[86] The Trần official regards the reliability of a first line of defense by indigenous communities to be similar to that of the rugged terrain of their home region.

Indigenous communities joined conflicts on one side or the other for their own reasons. Dali's chiefs saw their advantage with the Mongols, while Đại Việt's chiefs remained firm for the Trần. Just as the Lý rulers had utilized the Tang pattern of dreams and tales to separate themselves from the north, the Trần applied northern administrative practices to draw the chiefs on their frontier to their side. The Trần leaders even venerated the spirit of the eighth-century upland chieftain Phùng Hưng (761–802), among the court's most revered deities, to bring this supernatural source of power into the service of the kingdom.[87] Dali was unable to do this. In this way, the southern Sinitic frontier remained stretched from north of the Red River Delta to south of the Yunnan-Guizhou Plateau, reaching the edge of the mountain slopes leading into the northern mainland of Southeast Asia.

The connection between the Southwest Silk Road and the Dong World entered a new phase with the fall of the Dali kingdom, although the indigenous elite of the *dong* fought to retain autonomy in matters of trade and local administration after the initial advance of the Mongol military. The political landscape of the Dong World region—modern-day southwest China—was transformed by the Mongol invasion. When Chinggis Khan had earlier questioned his central military adviser Guo Baoyu (d. ca. 1226) about an invasion plan, Guo replied, "The Central Plains of north China are vast, and the region cannot be suddenly taken, but the southwest barbarians' able-bodied population is available for conscription. You would be advised to take this territory first, in order to make use of its strategic location and its gold [and other natural resources], otherwise you will be frustrated in your efforts."[1] Ögedei Khan (1186–1241) in 1235 dispatched troops to attack the Jingxiang region (in modern-day Hubei, between Xiangfan and Wuhan) and Sichuan and met strong resistance from the Southern Song forces. After this event, the Mongol khanate sent troops to scout the situation in the Dali kingdom. As the region that flanked Southern Song territory, Dali was therefore targeted for conquest. Mongol intelligence sources reported that throughout Dali "the chiefs have all scattered, furiously competing with one another, while seeking weapons and supplies while the common people are being trampled in this conflict," and so the Mongol advance was launched.[2]

After Khubilai Khan had subdued the Dali kingdom, he left Uriyangqadai to deal with the aftermath while part of his army returned north. In 1259,

Uriyangqadai led several thousand cavalry troops and ten thousand locally conscripted soldiers to attack Guangxi's Hengshan garrison. Following a victorious assault on Hengshan, his forces continued eastward, attacking Guizhou, Xiangzhou, Jingjiangfu, Chenzhou, and Yuanzhou. Proceeding in this direction, his army arrived at Tanzhou (modern-day Changsha), and laid siege to the city. Having heard that Khubilai had led his army across the river to Ezhou (modern-day Wuchang, Hubei), Uriyangqadai ordered his troops to join forces with the army of Khubilai. Uriyangqadai's attack had largely achieved the Mongol court's strategy of "aiming for the soft belly" (*wo fu zhi ju*).[3] Subduing the northern half of the Dong World was key to the Mongol force's victory over the Song.

The Yuan court's implementation of the "native officials" (*tuguan*) system eventually brought the Mongol leadership a more effective way to rule the native communities in the Dong World under their control. The court appointment of twenty-four surveillance commissioners and the establishment of many pacification commissions (*xuanweisi*) through the region, along with the implementation of the Yuan's *tuguan* system, was an active effort to forge a new relationship between central authorities and the many *zhixi* clan branches of the borderlands Dong World elite. The complex process of creating an effective web of relationships linked to a power center located beyond the native communities of the Dong World was bound to have periods of success and failure. Historian Fang Tie argues that implementation of the *tuguan* system, and its subsequent replacement with the *tusi* (local rule) system, allowed the Yuan court authority to reach deeply into remote areas of the Dong World, as well as to train the local elite to exercise greater loyalty to Yuan court.[4] However, although a new relationship was forged for communication and surveillance, the historical record contains many instances in which the Dong World communities continued to act in ways the central court would have judged insubordinate or disloyal. The greater change in relations came later in the Ming period, during which the influx of Han settlers caused Dong World interactions to be more directly tied to a frontier management implemented from distant courts. In this period the Dong World elite played an important role in the resistance to the early fifteenth-century Ming occupation of the Đại Việt kingdom, as well as the founding of the Latter Lê dynasty (1428–1788). Even during the decline in Lê authority, the rise of Mạc power, and the feuding between rival Trịnh and Nguyễn lowland clans, Dong World upland elite participated for their own purposes in the political struggle.

The Manchu-led Qing court (1644–1911) initially treated the Dong World on its southwestern frontier as a region beyond direct control, but once the conquest of China's interior had been completed, the new Manchu leadership turned back to a program of expansion into the southwest. The Manchu conquest of the Ming in the north had opened Yunnan Dong World communities to thrive within the mountain valleys through the second half of the seventeenth century. The Ming general Wu Sangui (1612–1678) had invited Manchu forces to enter China through the Great Wall to the northeast to drive out rebels in Beijing. The Manchu gave three semiautonomous dominions in southwest China to Chinese military defectors, including Wu, who ordered mining activity to be resumed in the lands in Yunnan and Guizhou that he controlled.[5] The final chapter in regional pacification didn't come until the War of the Three Feudatories (1673–1681), when Qing troops defeated the armies of Wu Sangui and the other two Ming defectors. Local chiefs were instrumental in assisting Qing forces with this military campaign.[6]

By the mid-Qing the court began to pay significantly more attention to frontier management than did the courts of all preceding dynasties. This is the period that initiated the court policy of *gaitu guiliu* ("reforming the native and returning to the regular"). In the 1720s, the Yongzheng emperor's (r. 1723–1735) stress on centralized bureaucratic control resulted in a major change in policy toward the southwest's Dong World communities and local chieftains, replacing the *tusi* with regular bureaucratic officials. Yongzheng proclaimed in edicts his strong belief that *tusi* clan leaders were local tyrants who sold the local people's land and oppressed the local communities. Beginning from the mid-1720s, Yongzheng and his chief lieutenant in the southwest, Ortai (E'ertai; 1680–1745), actively reduced the number of *tusi* across the region over the course of a decade.[7] By this point, however, the population of the southwest frontier had begun to increase rapidly, largely as a result of migration. There was also a rise in the number of new towns, due to population growth and economic developments. For example, the government's implementation of the *gaitu guiliu* policy in Dongchuan, Wumeng, and Zhenxiong (eastern Yunnan) caused a large portion of the local inhabitants under *tusi* chieftains to flee north to the Jinsha River's Liangshan region in southwest Sichuan.[8] As a result, displaced Han settlers poured into the previously mentioned area to open up lands for agriculture, mining, and the production of charcoal. Gradually, the Han population in the area outstripped the number of Dong World peoples. However, as the Qing's failed campaign in 1769 to conquer the Burmese Konbaung state (1752–1885) illustrates, the southwestern frontier was not fully cowered by Manchu authority.[9] Nevertheless, as Yunnan became a more integral part of the Qing empire, its outside contacts became secondary to its links with provinces in the empire's interior. Eventually, Yunnan's official contacts with neighboring kingdoms were maintained as routes used by tributary missions. Private caravan trade supplied only local or regional markets in Burma, Sichuan, and Tibet.[10] In this way the terminus for the Southwest Silk Road became the Dong World itself, while maritime links with lands controlled by colonial European powers had long since eclipsed overland connections in terms of volume of trade.

The middle of the nineteenth century saw anti-Qing revolts across the northern Dong World, from the Christian Taiping (1850–1864) in the east to the Miao (1854–1873) in the center, and the Muslim Panthay/Du Wenxiu Uprising (1856–1873) in the west. After the First Opium War in the mid-nineteenth century, Western powers in China accelerated their expansion into the Qing interior. In the second half of the century, the British entered the Irrawaddy Plain while the French approached from the Red River Delta, cutting their way into the southwest and southeast flanks of the Qing frontier, respectively. Following the Second Opium War, French colonial authorities took a strong interest in China's southwestern frontier area. Caravans of Yunnanese traders would soon transport goods along routes from the Indochinese Union (Vietnam, Cambodia, and Laos). This movement of an external authority into the frontier region threatened to cause further instability, and Qing officials scrambled for a suitable response. On July 2, 1909, the newly appointed Yunnan-Guizhou governor-general (*zongdu*), Shen Bingkun (1862–1913), memorialized the court that a close cultural bond should be forged with the most marginal areas of the empire. Shen wrote,

> Yunnan began the process of becoming civilized comparatively late, and all along the border there are numerous *tusi* headsmen. Often because of language differences, these people feel estranged from the people residing in the empire's interior. Earlier efforts to educate this population were not successful. I plan to investigate the circumstances surrounding the native *tusi* governance in these frontier areas; only the three prefectures of Yongchang, Shunning, and Pu'er have been administered directly from the provincial governor's office. At this time, I will revive education as a means to bring peace and stability and establish academies in these three prefectures for this purpose.[11]

Time had run out for the Qing dynasty to implement lasting official reforms, but similar educational changes were in place by the fall of the dynasty in 1911. In the early Republican period, Tai-speaking merchants attempted to reap the benefits of expanded infrastructure and new educational institutions while protecting their spheres of local authority, even after the Republican-era government with Han merchant support began to retract local privileges given to Tai elite in an earlier period. The experience of Tai merchants was in contrast with the "disempowered development" that Kham merchants on the periphery of the Tibetan Plateau were subject to after the Qing establishment of the Sichuan-Yunnan Frontier Affairs Commission in 1905, under the mercenary Qing official Zhao Erfeng (1845–1911).[12]

In the southernmost reaches of the Dong World, the Qing government claimed special rights in northern Vietnam and pressured the colonial French forces to withdraw.[13] The anti-French violence launched by the rebel Black Flags, and their leader Liu Yongfu's (Lưu Vĩnh Phúc; 1837–1917) hereditary title bequeathed by the Nguyễn court of the Tự Đức emperor (r. 1847–1883), echoed similar upland alliances with a lowland Vietnamese court that date back a thousand years. In the escalating violence that became the Sino-French War (1883–1885), French forces in 1884 used the port of Hải Phòng to launch an attack on the Qing navy anchored in the harbor of the southern Chinese city of Xiamen (then called Amoy). The decisive French victory ensured that the French would continue their expansion unchallenged. The Treaty of Tianjin signed in the aftermath of the war established the Border Demarcation Commission, to which both French and Chinese delegations were assigned. On July 4, 1885, the new twelve-year-old Nguyễn ruler Hàm Nghi fled to the Central Highlands, where he called for popular opposition to the French. However, the resistance came much too late. Hàm Nghi was captured by the French and exiled to Algeria. Opposition continued for several more years, but on June 25, 1887, the Sino-French Treaty was signed to accept the newly surveyed markers for a fixed border through the lower half of the Dong World between the Qing empire and the French Tonkin Protectorate.

The new colonial order was firmly in place, the ancient Sino-Vietnamese tributary relationship was shattered, yet the eleventh-century land border between these two states had hardly moved. While there were cases in which frontier area settlements petitioned to be included on a particular side of the new political boundary—such as the return to Qing administration for the residents of the "Golden Dragon Aboriginal Grotto" (Kim Long Động) after seventy years of being listed as a Lê dynasty "bridled and haltered" region—most of the Dong World settlements continued to interact locally as they had prior to the border negotiations. For more than one thousand years, neighboring regimes had interacted with polities large and small throughout the vast region of the Dong World, but none had completely dominated its territory or quashed the ambitions of its leaders without leaving the smallest space for contestation and negotiation.

In a 2020 study, historian Charles Patterson Giersch examines the late Qing period of transformation of merchant culture in Yunnan, when there was a Weberian rationalization of commercial activity. During this time, leading families found high social status as traders while fostering educational institutions to promote their community's values. Giersch argues that Yunnan merchants in this period developed a "business culture" that contained pragmatic training in business matters with the moral education retained in a traditional Neo-Confucian learning.[14] Nationwide intellectual trends that had a local impact included elements of "evolutionary thinking, industrialization, and progress toward modern nationhood," which for reform-mind merchants on the borderlands included a drive to establish sovereignty defined by international legal standards and outright control of frontier area communities.[15] Giersch raises the fascinating point that indigenous elite had already reached beyond the Qing government representatives and Han merchants to launch efforts to "modernize" the borderlands region, noting that one Tai *saopha* had early on sponsored local youth to study commerce in Japan.[16] This forward thinking, however, would not permit these indigenous elite to remain on the vanguard of economic and social change without subordinating themselves to Han-led institutions of reform.

The political turmoil of the first half of the twentieth century both loosened external control (in chaotic times) and tightened it (as the lowland states asserted themselves). Outside actors attempted at times to revive an autonomous Dong World in the period of postimperial state-building. After the fall of the Qing, warlords, such as Cai E (1882–1916) of the Yunnan clique (Dianxi), took control of much of the region.[17] Nationalist leaders suppressed these efforts at autonomy when they took power again after Yuan Shikai's countercoup failed in 1916. The Dong World's strategic geographic location continued in times of crisis to protect its autonomy. In World War II, the Nationalist Party under Chiang Kai-shek used Yunnan as an anti-Japanese base. When the Japanese began occupying French Indochina in 1940, the Burma Road that linked Kunming and the outside world with unoccupied China grew increasingly vital as much of the essential support and materiel were imported from the west. Likewise, in Mainland Southeast Asia, forces working for independent and autonomous states saw their segments of the frontier communities (as carved out by the colonial powers) forming part of the newly recognized geobody of their nations. The frontier communities recognized by the British (Shan, Kachin, Lahu,

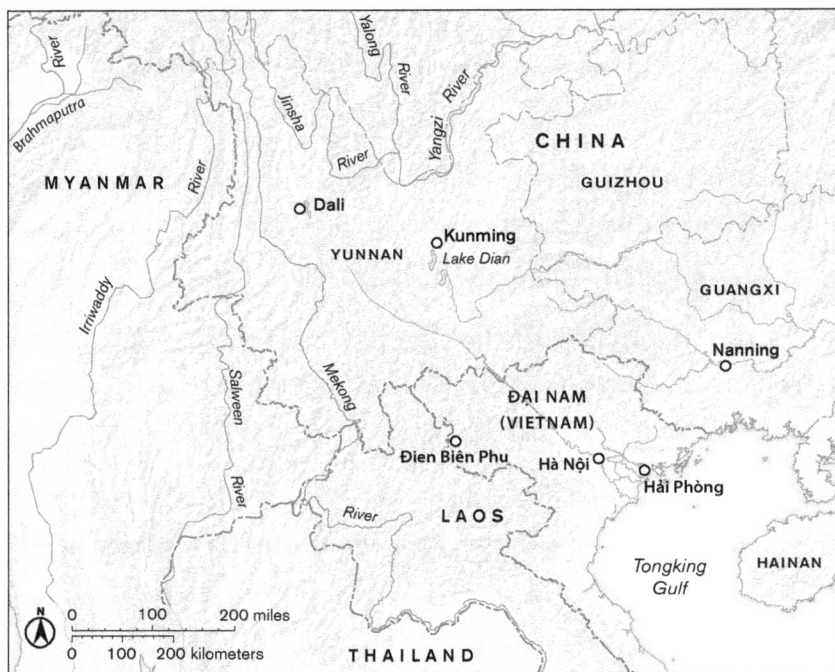

The Modern Region of Southwestern China and Mainland Southeast Asia

Wa, etc.) on the southwest of the Dong World utilized this connection to maintain their authority in their own valleys, as the Communist Party of Burma also operated there.[18]

The Chinese Nationalist and Communist regimes, though taking different approaches, both sought to assimilate the Dong World communities into the Chinese nation and play positive roles in the formation of their own modern nation states. Giersch's discussion of the end of the local authority of Tai elite provides a bookend on this study of the emergence of this elite a thousand years earlier. Commenting on the balance between natural and social factors that direct economic change, Giersch writes, "We need to realize that . . . the fixed aspects of geography, including climate, terrain, and natural resources, are important to making some regions and communities more prosperous than others, but so too are the historical events and human institutions that structure access to and exploitation of these resources."[19] The ethnic dimension of Giersch's study draws on the long history of China's southwest as a politically and economically autonomous region. The leading merchant families—the Dong, Yan, Yang, Yin, and the Cen—had maintained elite status in the area since the Three Kingdoms period, as described in this study. Giersch described in his book the point at which these local elite lost their last vestiges of independent authority. To illustrate this argument Giersch focused on several Tai-speaking merchants, in particular Fang Kesheng, a descendant of Tai elite from the Sino-Burmese frontier area. Having served as a delegate in 1947 to the first People's Participatory Conference, Fang returned to Yunnan to assist with the economic transformation of his home region and to quell any attempts by local elite to resist the modernizing effort of corporate interests that Fang concluded would bring an invigorating energy to local communities. Giersch demonstrated how Fang and other reform-minded elite were instead sidelined as the new Communist state privileged Han-led business interests treated local peoples as obstacles to be removed in the effort to create a more modern Yunnan. Some Dong World elite, whose ancestors entered the region with the thirteenth-century Mongol consolidation of power, found themselves targets of state aggression in post-1949 efforts to exercise lowland power. The Shadian incident (*Shadian shijian*), a 1975 uprising of ethnic Hui residents in the township of Shadian during the Cultural Revolution, ended in a military-led massacre of 1,600 civilians, including three hundred children. The local Muslim Hui community had demanded religious freedom, and Beijing responded with force by dispatching People's Liberation Army troops to regain local control. Tensions remain for many members of this community, which itself is the historical result of outside forces bringing a new order to the Dong World.

In post–World War II changes, independent regimes have risen across the southwest borderlands and have sought to consolidate their portions of this world as defined by the modern international borders. The Vietnamese joined with the People's Republic of China (PRC) in following the Stalinist nationalities model to define the ethnic minorities, both upland and frontier peoples, and to set up autonomous regions for self-governance. Geographer Christian Lentz describes the physical and social complexity of the upland region around Điện Biên Phu, located directly to the south of the Tai-speaking region Giersch describes, and Lentz also notes how local elite had thwarted many lowland governmental efforts to impose direct control over the Black River Region through the period of French colonial rule and anticolonial resistance.[20] Lentz describes how the Việt Minh military annexation of the Black River Region with local Tai elite support, which culminated in the famous siege of French military forces at Điện Biên Phu in 1954, was a very different process from the effective administration of the same region as the Democratic Republic of Vietnam's Northwest Zone, and he examines various challenges in socializing this borderlands territory within the larger Vietnamese geobody. In this example from the other side of the Sino-Vietnamese borderlands, we can see a similar scenario of upland-lowland cooperation for one cause giving way to local resistance to state-led intervention that largely served the interests of the lowland centers of power. One must also note the actions of other upland Dong World inhabitants, such as the many Hmong (Miao-Yao) who joined US forces to oppose the lowland Vietnamese intrusions into their territory in Laos and lost in 1975. The Democratic/Socialist Republic of Vietnam (DRV/SRV) has worked to integrate the frontier territories in its northern and northwestern mountains, while still battling the Chinese there in 1979.

Overall, across both the northern and southern sectors of the southwest borderlands, state efforts to displace local rule by frontier chieftains and to apply direct control has continued through the second half of the twentieth century into the twenty-first. Today, the Dong World region has again become integral to the commercial and communication network linking the heartland of the Chinese state to the markets of Southeast Asia, as was the case in ancient times. As a massive infrastructure project presented as part of the Belt and Road Initiative, a network of new railway links beginning in Kunming and ending in Singapore is currently under construction at immense cost—financially and environmentally—for all participants.[21] Areas of this Dong World region that once maintained trade contact, but resisted lowland political intrusion, are again linked to distant markets and have become a popular destination for faraway tourists. Since World War II, the effect of earlier integration with neighboring states undermined any dreams of lasting political autonomy, while promised economic develop-ment with lowland investment came at a slow pace. The Belt and Road Initiative has brought greater commitment to economic development in China's border areas, but these initiatives haven't often included an equal commitment to the cultural autonomy of the indigenous communities of these regions. Perhaps this new phase in the relationship between the Dong World and its lowland neighbors will finally bring these promised changes.

APPENDIX 1
RECONSTRUCTED
ROUTES

The Two Main Branches of the Southwest Silk Road

One branch of the Southwest Silk Road, the Old Yak Route (Gu Maoniu Dao), extended from Chengdu southwest across the Sichuan Basin to the foothills of the Ming Mountains.[1] Traders then traveled farther southwest to Qingyi (modern-day Ya'an), a town located on a tributary of the Min River (Min Jiang), which is itself a tributary of the Yangzi. The town was an important center for horse trade with connections through the Tibetan Plateau.[2] From Qingyi one traveled to Yandao (modern-day Yingjing) in the valley of the Jinsha River (Jinsha He), winding southwest through mountain passes to Maoniu (modern-day Hanyuan), moving southward through a connected system of valleys to Lingguan (modern-day Yuexi), past Xide, through Qiongdu to Huiwu Prefecture (modern-day Huili County), due southwest along the Jinsha, through the modern-day industrial town of Panzhihua, once a market town and a "central travel node" at the confluence of the Jinsha River and the Yalong River (Yalong Jiang), both tributaries of the Yangzi, through the Panxi Valley to Sanjiang (modern-day Dayao) and finally west to Dali on Lake Erhai.

The second route was called the Five "Foot" Route (Wuchi Dao) and the Old Bo People's Route (Gubo Dao) in the Qin dynasty, the Southern Yi People's Route (Nanyi Dao) in the Han, and the Stone Gate Route (Shimen Dao) or the Zangke People's Route (Zangke Dao) by the Sui period.[3] Travelers on this route passed south from Yibin to Nanguang Prefecture (modern-day Gaoxian County), past the three-way convergence of the

Min River (Min Jiang), Jinsha River (Jinsha He), and Yangzi River. Here was also the site of the Yun and Lian "loose rein" (*jimi*) prefectures (modern-day Yunlian County). At this point the route begins to head southwest downstream along the Heng River (Heng Jiang) valley through Stone Gate Pass (Shimen Guan) or modern-day Dousha Pass (Dousha Guan), Great Pass (Da Guan), overland to Zhuti (modern-day Zhaotong).[4] The trade route then proceeded farther southwest to Weixian (modern-day Qujing). Weixian was located within the Shicheng Commandary (Shichengjun) under the authority of the Dali kingdom. This route then passes through Guchang (modern-day Kunming) and the area around Lake Dian (Dianchi), and finally on to Dali.

The Ancient Road of the One Hundred Yue/Việt

From the Hengshan garrison, one day's voyage took travelers to the first postal station in Gutian County, located in the modern-day Dahe Village, Nabi Township, Youjiang District, Baise City.[5] Records do not survive as to who administrated this region. From Gutian County one traveled north to Guile Prefecture, located in Yongle Township and part of Baise's Youjiang District. Guile Prefecture was territory under the authority of the Nùng (Nong) clan, who sought control as an extension of their power base in Temo District (more about this region later in the chapter). In 1062, as tensions along the Sino-Vietnamese borderlands began to rise, the post–Nùng Trí Cao Rebellion clan leader Nùng Tông Đán claimed control over Guile Prefecture, among other *jimi* regions. Once he took control he appointed officials to administer these regions, giving gifts for their service in the form of plow cattle, salt, and bolts of cloth.[6] These *jimi* prefectures include: Tangxing Prefecture,[7] Suidian Prefecture,[8] Qiyuan Prefecture,[9] Sicheng Prefecture,[10] Guna Dong Settlement,[11] Anlong Prefecture,[12] the Liao Ferry Crossing (Liaodukou) at Fengcun Mountain,[13] Shangzhan,[14] Bowen Ridge,[15] Luofu Prefecture,[16] to the edge of Ziqi kingdom's periphery, which goes by the name Moju.[17] In another three day's travel, one reaches the center of the Ziqi kingdom, passing through Ziqi's four walled cities (or Sicheng). Four additional days took one to the Dali kingdom's Shicheng Commandary (modern-day Qujing).[18] Shicheng was known to Zhou as "Gucheng."[19] In three more days, one reaches the Dali kingdom's edge at the place called Shanchan Military Prefecture. Another six days finally brought travelers to the center of the Dali kingdom.[20] Five days from the Dali kingdom was the kingdom of Pagan (Pugan), from where it was not much farther to western India (Tianzhu). The Irrawaddy River (Yuni He) obstructs this route. It was passable, but not without risk. Zhou Qufei noted that the journey took a total of thirty-two days. Although it was difficult to trace the place names for this route, one can speculate how the trip was conducted.

Eastern and Western Routes
through the Dong World to Đại Việt

Yang Zuo described the eastern route as the Mulberry Road (Sang Dao). From Sichuan one traveled to central Yunnan, boarding a ferry on the Nanpan River (Nanpan Jiang) at a point west of Mile County (in today's Honghe Hani and Yi Autonomous Prefecture) and following the river until it passed through the southeast corner of Yunnan at Wenshan. At this point travelers journeyed downstream on the Bàn Long (Coiled Dragon) River via Tuyên Quang to Hà Nội. This body of water may be the modern-day Sông Lô River, but its modern identity is difficult to confirm. From the western route, one traveled from Sichuan to Dali in western Yunnan and then traveled along the Red River to Hanoi, and from Hanoi to the Tongking Gulf and its maritime connections. The western route was the oldest waterway connecting Yunnan and northern Mainland Southeast Asia.[21]

APPENDIX 2
LOCATING
THE DONG WORLD

Dali Kingdom's Territory

The Dali kingdom's eastern frontier bordered the Tongchuan Fulu Circuit and Guangnan West Circuit; its western frontier abutted the present-day Kachin state of Myanmar. Its southern frontier touched on modern-day Laos and Vietnam, while the northern frontier extended to the Dadu River, which Song authorities established as the border. Within the Dali kingdom there were eight prefectures: Yongchang (present-day Baoshan, Yunnan), Tengchong (modern-day Tengchong, Yunnan), Muotong (modern-day Heqing, Yunnan), Huichuan (modern-day Huili, Sichuan), Jianchang (present-day Xichang, Sichuan), Nongdong (present-day Yao'an, Yunnan), Weichu (present-day Chuxiong, Yunnan), and Shanchan (present-day Kunming, Yunnan). There were also three commandaries: of Shanju (modern-day Yongsheng, Yunnan), Shicheng (present-day Qilin District, Qujing City, Yunnan), and Dongchuan (present-day Huize, Yunnan).[1]

The "Nine Rivers" Tai Homeland

As noted in Nguyễn Chí Buyên's edited volume, the ancestral homeland of the Tai-speaking Dong World communities was described as the region where the "nine rivers" meet. According to Nguyễn Chí Buyên, these rivers were: the Nậm Tao River (Hồng River), the Nậm Ta River (Đà River), the Nậm Ma River (Mã River), the Nậm Công River (Mekong River), the Nậm U River, the Nậm Nua River, the Nậm Na River, and two more rivers in

China that could not be determined by modern geographers. The Nam Nua River flows through Điện Biên Phủ and into the Nậm U River in the region of Thượng Lào (Muong Khoua, northern Laos), and the Nậm Na River flows from south Yunnan into the Đà River in Mường Lay and Thuận Châu (Sơn La).[2]

GLOSSARY

Languages included in the glossary include Arabic (A), Burmese (B), Chinese (C), Mongol (M), Sanskrit (S), Sogdian (So), Tibetan (T), Uighur (U), and Vietnamese (V).

A Pei (C) 阿佩

Abači (M) / Abachi (C) 阿巴赤

Achang (C) 阿昌

Aí (V) 愛

Ải Chi Quan (V) 支棱關

Ailao (C) 哀牢

An Ao (C) 安鰲

An Bang (C) 安邦

An Bình (V) 安平

An Đức (V) 安德

An Dương Vương (V) 安陽王

An Ji (C) 安濟

An Lushan (C) / Roχšan (So)
    安祿山

An Nam (V) / Annan (C) 安南

An Quan (C) 安銓

An Viễn (V) 安远

An Yu (C) 安宇

Anawrahta (B) / Anulutuo (C)
    阿奴律陀

Anchang (C) 安昌

Anfu (C) 安復

anfu dashi (C) 安撫大使

anfushi (C) 安撫使

Anlong (C) 安龍

Annan Duhufu (C) 安南都護府

Annan dutong shi (C) 安南都統使

Annan Guowang (C) 安南國王

Annan jinglueshi (C) 安南經略使

Annan xingji (C) 安南行記

Annan xuanweisi (C) 安南宣慰司

Anning (C) 安寧

Anren (C) 安仁

Anshun (C) 安順

Anuo (C) 阿諾

Anxi (C) 安西

Anyang (C) 安陽

Anzhou (C) 安州

Aqi (C) 阿齊

Ariq Qaya (U) / Alihaiya (C)
    阿里海牙

Atai (C) 阿台

Atun (C) 阿屯

Âu Lạc (V) 甌駱

âu mục (V) 州牧

Awu (C) 阿吾

Ba (C) 巴

Ba Điểm (V) 巴點

Bà Hoàng đại vương (V) 婆皇大王

Bắc (V) 北

Bắc Giang (V) 北江

Bắc tặc (V) 北賊

Bác Tam (V) 博三

Badi (C) 巴底

Ba Fan Shun Yuan Xuan Wei Si (C) 八番順元宣慰司

Bai Yue Gudao (C) 百越古道

Baibaxifu (C) 八百媳婦

Baide (C) 百德

Bailiang (C) 百梁

Bailu ying (C) 白鹿營

Baiman (C) 白蠻

Baise (C) 百色

Baizhang (C) 百丈

Baizhou (C) 白州

Baling (C) 巴鈴

Bàn Đạo Kiềm (V) 盤道鉗

Ban Liang (C) 班良

Bán Ngân (V) 半銀

ban xian (C) 阪險

Bàng Hà (V) 旁河

Banna (C) 版納

Bantao (C) 板桃

Báo cực truyền (V) 報極傳

Bảo Lạc (V) 保樂

Bảo Thắng (V) 保勝

Baoheding (C) 寶合丁

baopi (C) 豹皮

Baoshan (C) 保山

Bát Đam (V) 八耽

Bazi (C) 壩子

Beijing (C) 北京

Beiluoheda'er (C) 字羅合答兒

Benna Fatanna (C) 奔那伐檀那

Bi Chengzhe (C) 必程者

Biaoguo (C) 膘國

Bigan Shan (C) 碧玗山

Bình Di (V) 平夷

Bình Hoàng (V) 平皇

Bình Lâm Châu (V) 平林州

Bình Nguyên (V) 平原

Bình Vương (V) 平王

Binzhou (C) 賓州

Bishu manchao (C) 避暑漫抄

Bo (C) 焚

Bonan Dao (C) 博南道

Boshi (C) 博是

Bố Trí (V) 佈置

Bouyei (C) 布依

Bowen (C) 博文

Boyan (C) 伯顏

boyichang (C) 博易場

bu tingming (C) 不聽命

bu zu zheng (C) 不足徵

Bulang (C) / Palaung (B) 布朗

buluo (C) 部落

Cai Cộng Đại Vương (V) 蓋共大王

Cai E (C) 蔡鍔

Cai Jing (C) 蔡經

Cai Xi (C) 蔡襲

Caise Shalin (C) 彩色沙林

caixiang (C) 宰相

Cẩm Điền Bộ (V) 錦田步

Cảm Hoá (V) 感化

Cảm Thành (V) 感誠

Cangwu (C) 蒼梧

Canzhi zhengshi (C) 參知政事

Cao Bằng (V) 高平

Cao Chen (C) 曹陳

Cao Keming (C) 曹克明
Cao Lỗ (V) 高魯
cao shi (C) 草市
Cao Thông (V) 高通
Ceheng (C) 冊亨
Celeng (C) 策楞
Cen Jilu (C) 岑繼祿
Cen Yingchen (C) 岑映宸
Chai Chun (C) 柴椿
Chama Dao (C) 茶馬道
Changhuazhou (C) 昌化州
Changle (C) 長樂
changmingji (C) 長鳴雞
Changqing (C) 長慶
Chaofeng Lang (C) 朝奉郎
Chaolie daifu (C) 朝列大夫
châu (V) 州
Chen Boshao (C) 陳伯紹
Chen Daji (C) 陳大紀
Chen Fu (C) 陳孚
Chen Guangqian (C) 陳光前
Chen Guangzu (C) 陳光祖
Chen Jin (C) 陳進
Chen Liangbiao (C) 陳良彪
Chen Long (C) 陳隆
Chen Shiying (C) 陳士英
Chen Shu (C) 陳書
Chen Tan (C) 陳檀
Chen Wenche (C) 陳文徹
Chen Xizao (C) 陳希造
Cheng Kuan (C) 程寬
Cheng Pengfei (C) 程鵬飛
Cheng Zhuo (C) 成卓
Chengdu (C) 成都
Chenghai Jun (C) 澄海軍
chenghuang miao (C) 城隍廟
chengtian jie (C) 承天節

Chengzhou (C) 成州
Chengzong (C) 成宗
chenxiang shui (C) 沉香水
Chenzhou (C) 辰州
Chi Lăng (V) 枝陵
Chí Linh (V) 至靈
Chí Thành (V) 至誠
Chiêu Văn (V) 昭文
Chongde Dian (C) 崇德殿
Chongqing (C) 重慶
Chongsheng (C) 崇聖
Chongzhou (C) 充州
Chu (V) 朱
Chu (C) 楚
Chu Ái (V) 周愛
Chu Nhai (V) 朱崖
chuanqi (C) 傳奇
Chuanqin (C) 川秦
Chuan Shan xuanfu fushi (C)
    川陝宣撫副使
Chunqiu (C) 春秋
Chuxiong (C) 楚雄
Chuxiong Yizu Zizhizhou (C)
    楚雄彝族自治州
Chuzhou (C) 滁州
ci wai fei you ye (C) 此外非吾有也
Cili (C) 慈利
cishi (C) 刺史
ciyi susang badong bumao zhidi (C)
    賜以宿桑八峒不毛之地
Cổ Bút (V) 古筆
Cổ Khê (V) 古溪
Cổ Loa (V) 古螺
Cổ Phật (V) 古拂
Cuan (C) 爨
Cuan Baozi Bei (C) 爨寶子碑
Cuan Da Bei (C) 爨大碑

Cuan Hongda (C) 爨弘達

Cuan longyan Bei (C) 爨龍顏碑

Cuan man (C) 爨蠻

Cuan ren (C) 爨人

Cuan Shen (C) 爨深

Cuan Xi (C) 爨習

Cui (C) 崔

Cui Chengsi (C) 崔乘嗣

Cui Yuzhi (C) 崔與之

Cung Hoàng (V) 恭皇

Đa Bảo (V) 多寶

da jiangjun pao (C) 大將軍炮

Da Lun xu (C) 大倫墟

Da Zhongguo (C) 大中國

Dachanghe (C) 大長和

Dadian (C) 大甸

Dadu (C) 大都

Daduhe (C) 大渡河

Daguan (C) 大關

Daguo zhai (C) 打郭寨

Dahe (C) 大和

Dai (C) 傣

Đại Cồ Việt (V) 大瞿越

Dai Fu (C) 戴孚

Đại La (V) 大羅

Đại Nam (V) 大南

Đại Nguyên Lịch (V) 大元歷

Đại Than (V) 大灘

Đại Thông (V) 大通

đại toát đại liêu ban phục (V)
大撮大僚班服

Đại Việt (V) 大越

Dai Yao (C) 戴耀

Dai Yi (C) 戴翼

dajie (C) 大捷

Dali (C) 大理

Dali fu zhi (C) 大理府志

Dali Guo (C) 大理國

Dali Guowang (C) 大理國王

Dalian Dong (C) 大廉洞

Dalishan (C) 大黎山

dâm tự (V) 淫祠

Dameng (C) 大蒙

Daming (C) 大名

Đản Nãi (V) 但乃

dang shi yi ren (C) 當試以人

Đặng Thạnh Vương (V) 鄧盛王

Danjia (C) 蜑家

dansha (C) 丹砂

đạo (V) 道

Đào Đại Di (V) 陶代彝

Đào Tông Nguyên (V) 陶宗元

Đào Tử Kì (V) 陶子奇

Daohua (C) 導化

Daolao (C) 倒老

Daonian (C) 倒捻

Daqin Poluomen (C) 大秦婆羅門

Dashuai (C) 大帥

Datianxing (C) 大天興

Datong (C) 大通

Dayao (C) 大姚

Dayining (C) 大義寧

Dayu (C) 大庾

Dazhong (C) 大中

Dazhong Xiangfu (C) 大中祥符

Dechang (C) 德昌

Dehong (C) 德宏

Deng Cunzhong (C) 鄧存忠

Deng Pi (C) 鄧闢

Deng Xiaolian (C) 鄧孝廉

Dengjiang (C) 澄江

Dengtan (C) 遵賧

Di Qing (C) 狄青

Dian (C) 滇

Dianbo Gudao (C) 滇僰古道

Dianchi (C) 滇池

Dianhe (C) 滇河

dianhua (C) 點化

Dianshi (C) 滇史

Dianxi (C) 滇系

Dianyue (C) 滇越

Dianyue Chengxiang (C) 滇越乘像

Didiao (C) 抵掉

Điển Châu (V) 田州

dilizhi (C) 地理志

ding (C) 丁

Ding Wenjiang (C) 丁文江

dingfu (C) 丁夫

Đinh (V) 丁

Đinh An (V) 丁安

Đinh Củng Viên (V) 丁拱垣

Đinh Liệt (V) 丁列

Định Nguyên (V) 定源

Đinh Văn Thản (V) 丁文坦

Đỗ Anh Vũ (V) 杜英武

Đỗ Kiên Nhất (V) 杜堅一

Đỗ Kim (V) 都金

Đỗ Quốc Kế (V) 杜國計

Đỗ Thiện (V) 杜善

động (V) 峒

dong (C) 洞, 峒

    alternate form of same character

Dong (C) 董 surname

Động Bàn Pass (V) 洞板隘

Đông Bộ Đầu (V) 東步頭

Đông Các (V) 東閣

Dong Changling (C) 董昌齡

Đông Chinh (V) 東征

Đông Đang (V) 同登

Dong Daolong (C) 董道隆

Dong Guan Han ji (C) 東觀漢記

Dong Jin (C) 東晉

Dong Lan (C) 董蘭

Đông Lan Đại Vương (V) 東蘭大王

Dong Luijinhei (C) 董六斤黑

Dong Tianzhu(C) 東天竺

Dong'an (C) 東安

Dongcan (C) 棟蠶

Dongchuan (C) 東川

dongding (C) 峒丁

dongmen (C) 東門

Dongxie (C) 東謝

Dongxing (C) 東興

dongzhu (C) 洞主

Dou (C) 斗

dou shao (C) 豆杓

Dousha Guan (C) 豆沙關

Douzhou (C) 竇州

Du Changhui (C) 杜長惠

Dụ chư tỳ tướng hịch văn (V) 諭諸裨將
    檄文

Du Huidu (C) 杜慧度

Dữ tả hữu nghị sự (V) 與左右議事

Du Tianhe (C) 杜天合

Du Wenxiu (C) 杜文秀

Du Zengming (C) 杜僧明

Du'an (C) 都安

Duan (C) 段

Duan Geng (C) 段哽

Duan Heyu (C) 段和譽

Duan Hui (C) 段暉

Duan Jingzhi (C) 段敬芝

Duan Siping (C) 段思平

Duan Sizong (C) 段思聰

Duan Sushun (C) 段素順

Duan Xingzhi (C) 段興智

Duan Yanzhen (C) 段彦貞

Duan Yu (C) 段譽
Duan Zhixing (C) 段智興
Duan Zibiao (C) 段子標
Dực Thánh (V) 翊聖
duda tizhu (C) 都大提舉
dudu (C) 都督
duhu (C) 都護
duhufu (C) 都護府
Dujian (C) 都監
Dulao (C) 都老
Dunianzi (C) 都念子
Dunrenyi (C) 敦忍乙
Dương Bối (V) 楊貝
Dương Đạo (V) 陽導
Dương Minh (V) 陽明
Dương Tự Minh (V) 楊嗣明
dutong (C) 都統
duxunjian (C) 都巡檢
Duyuanshuai (C) 都元帥

E'ertai (C) 鄂爾泰
Enping (C) 恩平
Erhai (C) 洱海
Erhe (C) 洱河
Ezhou (C) 鄂州

fan bi (C) 藩蔽
Fan Chengda (C) 范成大
Fan Ji (C) 樊楫
Fan Min (C) 範旻
Fan Tao (C) 樊韜
Fan Zhuo (C) 樊綽
Fang Yi (C) 方異
fangba (C) 放罷
Fang'eshi (C) 防遏使
Fangfan (C) 方蕃
Fanglin (C) 芳林

Fanluoshi (C) 蕃落使
fanzhen (C) 蕃鎮
fashu (C) 法術
Fei Gongchen (C) 費拱辰
Fei Shen (C) 費沈
Feng Jiayi (C) 鳳伽異
Fengbi (C) 豐琵
Fengcun (C) 鳳村
Fengguojun Jiedushi (C)
    奉國軍節度使
Fengquan (C) 風全
fengshi (C) 奉使
fengsu ming (C) 風俗名
Folangji (C) 佛郎機
Foya (C) 佛牙
fu (C) 府
Fuchang (C) 富昌
Fuqing (C) 福清
fushi (C) 副使
Fushui (C) 撫水
Fuzhou (C) 涪州 Tang-period district
    near modern-day Chongqing
Fuzhou (C) 福州 city in Fujian Province
fuzhou (C) 符咒 script on Daoist
    talismans

gaitu guiliu (C) 改土歸流
gancao (C) 甘草
gangqi bingwan (C) 鋼器並碗
Ganzhou (C) 贛州
Gao (C) 高
Gao He (C) 高和
Gao Mu (C) 高禾
Gao Pian (C) 高駢
Gao Qizhuo (C) 高其倬
Gao Shengtai (C) 高升泰
Gao Xiang (C) 高祥

Gao You (C) 高誘

Gao Zhu Li Xiaozhong deng si ren Nanxi Shan timing (C) 高鑄李孝忠等四人南溪山題名

Gaoming (C) 嶠名

Gaoshang (C) 高尚

Gaoxian (C) 高縣

Gaoxing (C) 高興

Gaoyao (C) 高要

Gaozhou (C) 高州

Gaozong (C) 高宗

Ge Hong (C) 葛洪

Ge Luofeng (C) 閣羅鳳

Ge Luojia (C) 閣風迦

Ge Men Xuan Zan She Ren (C) 閣門宣贊舍人

gejue (C) 隔絕

Gemeilu (C) 箇沒盧

Gengma (C) 耿馬

Gia Định (V) 嘉定

Giao Châu (V) 交州

Giao Chỉ (V) 交趾

giáp (V) 甲

Giáp Thừa Quý (V) 甲承貴

Gong Yin (C) 龔蔭

gongbeiku fushi (C) 供備庫副使

gongjin (C) 貢錦

gongma (C) 貢馬

Gongzhou (C) 龔州

Guan (C) 貫

Guan Zhong (C) 觀仲

guanchashi (C) 觀察使

Guanggu (C) 管故

Guanghan (C) 廣漢

Guangnan (C) 廣南

Guangnan Xilu (C) 廣南西路

Guangxi (C) 廣西

Guangxi Jinglue Anfusi (C) 廣西經略安撫司

Guangxi zhuangyun fushi(C) 廣西轉運副使

Guangyiji (C) 廣異記

Guangzhou ji (C) 廣州記

Guanhe (C) 關河

Guannan (C) 關南

Guanyin (C) 觀音

Gubao (C) 谷保

Gubodao (C) 古僰道

Guchang (C) 谷昌

Gudang Dong (C) 古黨洞

Gui (C) 嶲 ancient ethnicity

Gui (C) 圭 jade tablet

gui (C) 桂 cassia

gui (C) 鬼 spirit

gui shi (C) 鬼市

Gui Zhongwu (C) 桂仲武

Guiguan (C) 桂管

Guihai Yuheng Zhi (C) 桂海虞衡志

Guihua (C) 歸化

Guile (C) 歸樂

Guilin ku man (C) 桂林庫滿

Guinan Wang (C) 桂南王

Guizhou (C) 桂州 (south central China)

Guizhou (C) 貴州 (southern China)

Guizhou tujing xinzhi (C) 貴州圖經新志

guizhu (C) 鬼主

Guna Dong (C) 古那洞

guo (C) 國

Guo Baoyu (C) 郭寶玉

Guo Kui (C) 郭逵

Guo Yongyuan (C) 郭永元

Guozhu (C) 國主

Gusen (C) 古森

Gutian (C) 古天
Guwan (C) 古萬
Guyongbu (C) 古勇步
Guzi (C) 孤子

Hạ Bộ (V) 下步
Hà Bổng Chiêu (V) 何俸招
Hà Nội (V) 河內
Hà Trắc Tuấn (V) 何昃俊
Hải Đông (V) 海東
Hải Dương (C) 海陽
Haicang (C) 海滄
haiha (C) 海蛤
Hãm Sa (V) 陷沙
Han Chengdi (C) 漢成帝
Han Gaozu (C) 漢高祖
Han Hedi (C) 漢和帝
Hàn Lâm (V) 翰林
Han Wudi (C) 漢武帝
Han Xiaozong (C) 漢肅宗
Hani (C) 哈尼
Hanlin Xue (C) 翰林學
Hanman Jun (C) 捍蠻軍
Hanyuan (C) 漢源
Hao Yu (C) 郝裕
He Chengtian (C) 何承天
Hẻ Trưởng (V) 奚長
Hechi (C) 河池
Hedong (C) 河東
Hejiang (C) 賀江
Heman (C) 和蠻
Hengjiang (C) 橫江
Hengshan (C) 橫山
Hengshan zhai (C) 橫山寨
Hengyang (C) 衡陽
Hengzhou (C) 橫州
Hepu (C) 合浦

Hetuo Man (C) 鶴拓蠻
Hezhou (C) 河州
Hiến Tông (V) 憲宗
Hiếu (V) 孝 filial piety
Hiệu (V) 號 art name
Hiếu Tôn Quốc Hoàng (V) 孝尊國皇
Hồ Quý Ly (V) 胡季犛
Hoa Lư (V) 華閭
Hoài Đạo (V) 懷道
Hoan (V) 驩
Hoàng (V) 黃
Hoàng A Xã (V) 黃亞社
Hoẳng Chân (V) 宏真
Hoàng Công Toản (V) 黃公纘
Hoàng Đức Lương (V) 黃德梁
Hoàng Kim Cúc (V) 黃金菊
Hoàng Kim Mãn (V) 黃金滿
Hoàng Kim Nguyên (V) 黃金元
Hoàng Phúc Vệ (V) 黃福衛
Hoàng Triều Quan Chế (V) 皇朝官制
Hoàng Tư Vinh (V) 黃思荣
Hoàng Văn Đồng (V) 黃文桐
hoàng-đế (V) / huangdi (C) 皇帝
Hồng Đức (V) 洪德
Hong Mai (C) 洪邁
Honghe Hani zu yizu zizhizhou (C)
    紅河哈尼族彝族自治州
Honglu (C) 鴻臚
Hongshui (C) 紅水
Hongzhi (C) 弘治
Hou Guang (C) 侯廣
Hou Han shu (C) 後漢書
Hou Renbao (C) 候仁寶
Hu (C) 胡 surname
hu (C) 壺 pot or jar
Hu Guang zongling (C) 湖廣總領
Hu Hong (C) 胡宏

Hu Shunzhi (C) 胡舜陟
Hu Zhishi (C) 胡知事
hua min (C) 化民
Hua Yi zhixu (C) 華夷秩序
Huai (C) 淮
Huaibei (C) 淮北
Huainan (C) 淮南
Huainan Xilu (C) 淮南西路
Huan (C) 驩
Huang Bing (C) / Hoàng Bình (V) 黃炳
Huang Boshan (C) 黃伯善
Huang Boyun (C) 黃伯蘊
Huang Changguan (C) 黃昌瓘
Huang Changmian (C) 黃昌沔
Huang Chengqing (C) 黃承慶
Huang Fafu (C) 黃法扶
Huang Keshun (C) 黃克順
Huang Lin (C) 黃璘
Huang Qianyao (C) 黃乾曜
Huang Shaodu (C) 黃少度
Huang Shaogao (C) 黃少高
Huang Shaoqing (C) 黃少卿
Huang Shengxu (C) 黃聖許
Huang Zhongying (C) 黃眾盈
Huang Ziwen (C) 黃子文
Huangdong (C) 黃洞
Huangjin Zhi Luan (C) 黃巾之亂
Huangshi (C) 黃石
Huanjiang Maonanzu Zizhixian (C)
　環江毛南族自治縣
Huanzhou (C) 環州
Hui'an (C) 惠安
Huichang (C) 會昌
Huichuan (C) 會川
Huili (C) 會理
Huitong (C) 會同
Huitong Guan (C) 會同館

Huiwu (C) 會無
Huizhou (C) 徽州
Hulonghaiya (C) 忽籠海牙
hulu (C) 胡虜
Hùng (V) 雄
Hưng Hiếu (V) 興孝
Hưng Hoá (V) 興化
Hưng Hóa xứ phong thổ lục (V)
　興化處風土錄
Hưng Nhượng (V) 興讓
Hunqilan (C) 渾乞濫
hương (V) 鄉
Huotou (C) 火頭
Hữu Giang (V) 右江
Huxin (C) 忽辛
huyang (C) 胡羊
huyện (V) 縣
Hy Dương (V) 矣揚

ji (C) 髻
Jiabo (C) 价博
Jiading (C) 嘉定
Jiajing (C) 嘉靖
Jiamolübo (C) 迦摩縷波
Jian Yan yilai chaoye zaji (C)
　建炎以來朝野雜記
jiancha yushi (C) 監察御史
Jianchang (C) 建昌
Jianchuan (C) 劍川
Jiang Jin (C) 蔣瑾
jiang xi (C) 江西
Jiang Yunji (C) 蔣允濟
Jiangdong (C) 江東
Jiangdong er Wu (C) 江東二吳
jiangjun (C) 將軍
Jiangling (C) 江陵
Jiangnan Xilu (C) 江南西路

Jiangning (C) 江寧

Jiangtou (C) 江頭

jianjiao (C) 檢校

Jianjiao Sikong (C) 檢校司空

Jianlong (C) 建隆

Jianning (C) 建寧

Jianshan (C) 監山

Jianshui (C) 建水

jianshui shezhou (C) 監稅攝州

jiansi (C) 監司

Jianwu zhi (C) 建武志

jianya (C) 監押

Jianyan (C) 建炎

Jianzhou (C) 建州

Jiao (C) 交 ancient term
    for northern Vietnam

jiao (C) 校 military field officer

jiaohua (C) 教化

Jiaozhi (C) 交趾

Jiaozhi ji (C) 交趾記

Jiaozhou (C) 交州

Jiaozhou ji (C) 交州記

Jiayin (C) 甲寅

Jiazhou (C) 嘉州

jiedushi (C) 節度使

jifeng zhi jingcao, ban dang shi cheng
    chen (C) 疾風知勁草, 板蕩識誠臣

jimi (C) 羈縻

jin (C) 斤 weight

Jin (C) 晉 dynastic title

jin (C) 帛 silk

jin keng (C) 金坑

jin zhuang (C) 金裝

Jin Ziguang Lu Daifu (C) 金紫光祿大夫

jinbo (C) 金帛

jinchang (C) 金場

Jinchi (C) 金齒

Jinchi Baiyi (C) 金齒百夷

Jingchu (C) 荊楚

Jingde (C) 景德

jingdian zhuanyunsi (C) 京畿轉運司

Jingdong Yizuzizhhixian (C)
    景東彝族自治縣

Jinghu (C) 荊湖

Jinghu Zhancheng (C) 荊湖占城

Jingjiang (C) 静江

Jingjiangfu (C) 静江府

Jingjiangfu bing Guangxi jinglue anfushi
    (C) 静江府並廣西經略安撫使

Jingjiangfu ting bi timingji (C)
    静江府廳壁題名記

jinglue anfuci (C) 經略安撫司

jinglueshi(C) 經略使

Jingman Jun (C) 静蠻軍

Jingpo (C) / Kachin (B) 景頗

jingquanshi (C) 井泉石

Jingxiang (C) 荊襄

Jingyou (C) 景祐

Jingzhou (C) 靖州

Jinjiang (C) 晉江

Jinkang (C) 晉康

Jinle (C) 金勒

Jinning (C) 晉寧

Jinshahe (C) 金沙河

jinshi (C) 進士

Jinuo (C) 基諾

Jinzi Guanglu Daifu (C) 金紫光祿大夫

Jishui (C) 吉水

Jiu Tang shu (C) 舊唐書

jiu zhi bu xiu Man Yi, wei qi wu
    guan yu xian zhi ye (C)
    舊志不修蠻夷, 謂其無關於縣志也

Jiudao (C) 九道

Jiuhe (C) 九和

Jiuzhou (C) 九州 nine provinces of
  ancient China
Jiuzhou (C) 舊州 Guangxi township
Jizhou (C) 吉州
Jizhou fangyushi (C) 吉州防禦使
juan (C) 絹
jueming (C) 爵命
juming jing (C) 舉明經
jun (C) 君 chief
jun (C) 郡 administrative unit
Junlian (C) 筠連
junqi ju (C) 軍器局
junwang (C) 郡王
Junxian (C) 郡縣
Junyan zhi ze chen chubai (C)
  君言至則臣出拜
junying (C) 軍營
Junzhou (C) 郡州
juren (C) 舉人

kai nanzhong (C) 開南中
Kainan (C) 開南
Kang Senghui (C) 康僧會
Kangzhou (C) 康州
Kezhai Zagao Yi Xu Gao (C)
  可齋雜稿一續稿
Kezhou (C) 珂州
Khai Hoàng (V) 開皇
Khai Thiên (V) 開天
Khâm định Việt sử Thông giám cương
  mục (V) 欽定越史通鑑綱目
Khâu Cấp (V) 丘急
Khâu ôn (V) 丘溫
Khâu Sầm (V) 邱岑
Kiến Sơ (V) 建初
Kim Hoa Bộ (V) 金華步
Kim Khê (V) 金谿

Kim Long Động (V) 金龍峒
Kim Pha (V) 金坡
Kinh (V) 京
Kính Quang (V) 敬光
Kính Trình (V) 敬呈
kuanyou (C) 寬宥
Kuicheng tujing (C) 夔城圖經
Kuiwang (C) 虧望
Kuizhou (C) 夔州
Kuizhou duhufu changshi (C)
  夔州都督府長史
Kunchuan (C) 昆川
Kunlun (C) 崑崙
Kunmi (C) 昆彌
Kunming (C) 昆明
Kunming Chi (C) 昆明池

La (V) 羅
La Luân (V) 羅倫
Lạc (V) 雒
Lạc Long (V) 貉龍
Lading (C) 剌定
La'e (C) 剌俄
Lahu (C) 拉祜
Laibin (C) 來賓
Lam Sơn Động Chủ (V) 藍山峒主
Lâm Tây (V) 臨西
Lan Qin (C) 蘭欽
Lan Yu (C) 藍玉
Lạng Châu (V) 諒州
Lạng Giang (V) 諒江
Lạng Sơn (V) 諒山
Langqiong (C) 浪穹
Langqu (C) 莨渠
Lao (C) 獠
Lào Cai (V) 老街
Lão Thử (V) 老鼠

lao zu (C) 老祖

Laosicheng (C) 老司城

Laqiu (C) 剌秋

Lê (V) 黎

Lê Cong Mạnh (V) 黎公孟

Lê Diễn (V) 黎演

Lê Duy Kỳ (V) 黎維祺

Lê Duy Phổ (V) 黎維溥

Lê Hoàn (V) 黎桓

Lê Khắc Phục (V) 黎克復

Lê Lợi (V) 黎利

Lê Mục (V) 黎目

Lê Niệm (V) 黎念

Lê Tắc (V) 黎崱

Lê Thánh Tông (V) 黎聖宗

Lê Thọ Vực (V) 黎壽域

Lê Trọng Đà (V) 黎仲佗

Lê Tuân (V) 黎荀

Lê Văn Nhận (V) 黎文認

Lê Văn Thắng (V) 黎文勝

Leiman (C) 雷蠻

Leli (C) 樂里

Leshan (C) 樂山

Li (C) 俚 rustic

Li (C) 李 surname

Li Bangxian (C) 李邦憲

Li bing (C) 黎兵

Li Boxiang (C) 李伯祥

Li Buweng (C) 李布翁

Li Cui (C) 李漼

Li Cunxu (C) 李存勗

Li Deyu (C) 李德裕

Li Fang (C) 李昉

Li Guanyinde (C) 李觀音得

Li Heng (C) 李恒

Li Hongjie (C) 李弘節

Li Jianliu (C) 李藍六

Li Jinxing (C) 李金星

Li Jiukui (C) 李九葵

Li Mei (C) 李梅

Li Panwang (C) 李盤王

Li Qian (C) 李謙

Li shuai (C) 俚帥

Li Sidao (C) 李思道

Li Siyan (C) 李思衍

Li Tianbao (C) 李天保

Li Xiangen (C) 李仙根

Li Xianggu (C) 李象古

Li Xingjian (C) 李行簡

Li Yu (C) 李栻

Li Yuanxi (C) 李元喜

Li Zengbo (C) 李曾伯

Li Zhen er nian shi'er yue (C)
利貞二年十二月

Li Zhi (C) 李治

Li Zhuo (C) 李琢

Li Zichong (C) 李紫琮

Li Zongcheng (C) 李宗城

Lian (C) 蓮

Liang Chu (C) 梁楚

Liang Feng (C) 梁奉

Liang Sanqi (C) 梁三岐

Liang shu (C) 梁書

Liang Wang (C) 梁王

Liang Yao (C) 梁耀

Liang Zeng (C) 梁曾

Liang Zibin (C) 梁子賓

Liangshan (C) 凉山

Liangzhelu (C) 兩浙路

Lianzhou (C) 廉州

Liao Dian (C) 廖殿

Liao Shuzheng (C) 廖叔政

Liao Yangsun (C) 廖揚孫

Liaodukou (C) 獠渡口

Liaoge (C) 了薥

libu youshilang (C) 禮部右侍郎

Lịch Triều Hiến Chương Loại Chí (V) 歷朝憲章類誌

Licheng (C) 鯉城

Liexian zhuan (C) 列仙傳

Lili cuan (C) 禮例纂

liluo (C) 籬落

lin (C) 廩 granary

Lin (C) 林 surname

Lin Maosheng (C) 林茂昇

Lin Xiyuan (C) 林希元

Lin Yingzhou (C) 林应周

Lin Zhen (C) 林振

Lin'an (C) 臨安

ling qi (C) 令旗

Lingguandao (C) 靈關道

Lingwai daida (C) 嶺外代答

Lingyun (C) 凌雲

lingzhang (C) 伶長

Lĩnh Nam chích quái liệt truyện (V) 嶺南摭怪列傳

linh tích (V) 靈跡

Lintao (C) 臨洮

Linyi (C) 林邑

Linzhang (C) 臨漳

Lishui (C) 麗水

Lisu (C) 倮倮

Liu Bei (C) 劉備

Liu Chang (C) 劉錩

Liu Che (C) 劉徹

Liu Da (C) 劉炟

Liu Delu (C) 劉德祿

Liu Geping (C) 劉格平

Liu Mian (C) 劉勔

Liu Shang (C) 劉尚

Liu Shiying (C) 劉世英

Liu Shizheng (C) 劉士政

Liu Shizhong (C) 劉時中

Liu Tingzhi (C) 劉庭直

Liu Wenhui (C) 劉文輝

Liu Xiang (C) 劉翔

Liu Xueqiu (C) 劉學裘

Liu Yan (C) 劉龑

Liu Yongfu (C) 劉永福

Liu Yuan (C) 劉源

Liu Yuangang (C) 留元剛

Liu Zhang (C) 劉璋

Liu Zhen (C) 劉珍

Liu Zongyuan (C) 柳宗元

Liucheng (C) 柳城

liuli wan (C) 琉璃碗

Liushi (C) 六事

Liuzhou (C) 柳州

Lizhou (C) 黎州

Lizong (C) 理宗

Lô (V) 瀘 river name

lộ (V) 路 circuit

Lộc Châu (V) 祿州

Lôi Hỏa (V) 雷火

Lộng (V) 弄

Long Biên (C) 龍編

Long Độ (V) 龍度

Long Nhãn (V) 龍眼

Long Thành (V) 龍城

Long Yige (C) 龍異閣

Longfan (C) 龍蕃

Longhe (C) 龍和

Longjin (C) 龍令

Longlin (C) 隆林

Longquanshui (C) 龍泉水

Longsu (C) 隴蘇

Longxi (C) 龍溪

Lu Anxing (C) 盧安興

Lu Jia (C) 陸賈

Lu Mujian (C) 陸木前

Lu Qingsun (C) 路慶孫

Lu Xun (C) 盧循

Luanzhou (C) 巒州

Lục Nam (V) 陸南

Lucheng (C) 潞城

Lüeyang (C) 略陽

Lufeng (C) 祿丰

Lugu (C) 瀘沽

Luliang (C) 陸良

Lulu Man (C) 盧鹿蠻

Luo An (C) 羅安

Luo gui (C) 羅鬼

Luo Ping (C) 羅平

Luocheng (C) 羅城

Luodian (C) 羅殿
    ancient kingdom title

Luodian (C) 羅甸
    county in Guizhou

Luodou Dong (C) 羅竇洞

Luofan (C) 羅蕃

Luofu (C) 羅扶 prefecture in Guangxi

Luofu (C) 羅浮 township
    in Guangdong

Luokong (C) 羅孔

Luoluo (C) 羅羅

Lương Như Hộc (V) 梁如鵠

Lương Thế Vinh (V) 梁世榮

Luoshi Guiguo (C) 羅氏鬼國 ancient
    kingdom title

Luoshi Guiguo (C) 羅施鬼國 alternate
    version of ancient kingdom title

Luoxing (C) 裸形

Luozhou (C) 羅州

Luozuoguan (C) 羅佐關

Lüping (C) 祿平

Lưu Kỳ (V) 劉記

Luxi (C) 瀘西

Luzhou (C) 陸州 Tang period
    prefecture in Guangxi

Luzhou (C) 祿州 Tang period
    prefecture in Guizhou

Lý (V) 李 surname

lý (V) 理 envoy

Lý Anh Tông (V) 李英宗

Lý Bí / Lý Bốn (V) 李賁

Lý Can Đức (V) 李乾德

Lý Chiêu Hoàng (V) 李昭煌

Lý Công Uẩn (V) 李公蘊

Lý Đạo Thành (V) 李道成

Lý Dương Hoán (V) 李陽煥

Lý Huệ Tông (V) 李惠宗

Lý Huy (V) 李暉

Lý Kế Nguyên (V) 李繼元

Lý Nghiệt (V) 李梟

Lý Nhân Tông (V) 李仁宗

Lý Nhật Tôn (V) 李日尊

Lý Ông Trọng (V) 李翁仲

Lý Phật Mã (V) 李佛瑪

Lý Phật Tử (V) 李佛子

Lý Phục Man (V) 李服蠻

Lý Phúc Trị (V) 李福治

Lý Tế Xuyên (V) 李濟川

Lý Thái Tổ (V) 李太祖

Lý Thánh Tông (V) 李聖宗

Lý Thiên Tộ (V) 李天祚

Lý Thường Kiệt (V) 李常傑

Ma (C) 馬

Ma Chu (C) 馬楚

Ma Duanlin (C) 馬端臨

Ma Lục (V) 麻六

Ma Suofei (C) 馬鎖飛

Ma Yu (C) 馬玉
Ma Yuan (C) 馬援
Maguan (C) 馬關
Maimaci (C) 買馬司
Malong (C) 馬龍
Man (C) / Mán (V) 蠻
Man Yi (C) 蠻夷
Mangshi (C) 芒施
Manhao (C) 蔓亳
Manli (C) 蠻利
manzi (C) 蠻子
Mao Bowen (C) 毛伯溫
Mao La (C) 茅羅
Maoniu (C) 氂牛
Maozhou (C) 茂州
Matijusi (C) 馬提舉司
Mậu Hợp (V) 茂洽
Meng Chang (C) 孟昶
Meng Chenggui (C) 蒙承貴
Meng Gong (C) 孟珙
Meng Jian (C) 蒙薦
Meng Yuanlao (C) 孟元老
Meng Zhixiang (C) 孟知祥
Menglian (C) 孟連
Mengman (C) 夢蠻
Mengshe (C) 蒙舍
Mengsui (C) 蒙嶲
Mengzi (C) 蒙自
Mi (C) 彌
Mian (C) 緬
mian de shu qian li (C) 緜地數千里
Mian guozhu (C) 緬國主
min (C) 民 people
Min (C) 緡 string of copper cash
Ming (C) 明
Ming shilu (C) 明實錄
Mingshi (C) 明史

Mingzhou (C) 明州
Minhou (C) 閩侯
Minjiang (C) 岷江
Minxian (C) 閩縣
mituoseng (C) 蜜陀僧
Mo Chun (C) 莫淳
Mo Shixian (C) 莫士先
Mo Tingmo (C) 莫延慕
Mo Xun (C) 莫潯
Moju (C) 磨巨
Móng Cái (V) 芒街
Mosuo (C) 摩娑
Mu Ying (C) 沐英
mục (V) 牧
Muli (C) 木裡
Muluodian (C) 木羅甸
Muotong (C) 謀統
Muyi Huailai (C) 慕義懷徠
Mỵ Châu (V) 媚珠

Na (C) 納
Na Sầm (V) 那岑
Nabi (C) 那畢
Nai'ai (C) 乃愛
Nalading (C) 訥剌丁
Nam (V) 南
Nam Cương (V) 南疆
Nam Nguyên (V) 南源
Nam Tấn (V) 南晉
Nam Thiên (V) 南天
Nam Tiến (V) 南進
Nam Việt (V) / Nan Yue (C) 南越
Nan Qi shu (C) 南齊書
Nan shi (C) 南史
Nandingzhou (C) 南定州
Nanfuzhou (C) 南扶州
Nanguang (C) 南廣

Nanhai Wang (C) 南海王

Nanhezhou (C) 南合州

Nanjing (C) 南京
city in Jiangsu Province

nanjing (C) 南境 southern frontier

Nankang (C) 南康

Nanliu (C) 南流

Nanman (C) 南蠻

Nanning Zhou (C) 南寧州

Nantong (C) 南通

Nanxie (C) 南謝

Nanyidao (C) 南夷道

Nanyue Wang (C) 南越王

Nanyue Zhi (C) 南越志

Nanzhao (C) 南詔

Nanzhou yiwuzhi (C) 南州異物志

Nasir al-Din (A) / Nasulading (C)
納速剌丁

neifu (C) 內附

neishisheng jucheng (C) 內侍省局丞

neishu (C) 內屬

Ngô Quyền (V) 吳權

Ngô Sĩ Liên (V) 吳士連

Ngô Văn Sở (V) 吳文楚

Ngũ Hoa (V) 五華

Ngũ Hoa Trại (V) 五花寨

Ngưu Hống (V) 牛吼

Ngụy Danh Cao (V) 偽名高

Nguyễn (V) 阮

Nguyễn Bẫu (V) 阮培

Nguyễn Cư Đạo (V) 阮居道

Nguyễn Địa Lô (V) 阮地爐

Nguyễn Đức Hoan (V) 阮德懽

Nguyễn Lĩnh (V) 阮領

Nguyễn Lu (V) 阮盝

Nguyễn Nghĩa Toàn (V) 阮義全

Nguyễn Ngọc Hán (V) 阮玉漢

Nguyễn Ngọc Huân (V) 阮玉勛

Nguyễn Nhạc (V) 阮岳

Nguyễn Nộn (V) 阮嫩

Nguyên Quang Bình (V) 阮光平

Nguyên Thanh (V) 元清

Nguyễn Thế Khôi (V) 阮世魁

Nguyễn Thế Lộc (V) 阮世祿

Nguyễn Trãi (V) 阮廌

Nguyễn Văn Hàn (V) 阮文翰

Nguyễn Văn Phúc (V) 阮文富

nhân (V) 仁

Nhật Lạc (V) 日落

Nhật Tân (V) 日新

Như Tích (V) 如昔

Ning Changzhen (C) 寧長真

Ningdu (C) 寧都

Ningzhou (C) 寧州

Ninh Sóc (V) 寧朔

Ninuojiangshui (C) 彌諾江水

niuhuang (C) 牛黃

Nội Bàng (V) 內旁

nội loạn (V) 內亂

Nông Công Phái (V) 農公派

Nong Jincheng (C) 儂金澄

Nong Jinle (C) 儂金勒

Nong Jinyi (C) 儂金意

Nong Zhongwu (C) 儂仲武

Nongdong (C) 弄棟

Nongmin (C) 農民

Noulading (C) 耨剌丁

Nữ Nghe (V) 女兒

Numoudian (C) 怒謀甸

Nùng (V) / Nong (C) 儂or 獽

Nùng Dân Phú (V) 儂民富

Nùng Hạ Khanh (V) 儂夏卿

Nùng Lượng (V) 儂亮

Nung Tôn Lộc (V) 儂全錄

Nùng Tông Đản (V) 儂宗亶
Nùng Tông Đán (V) 儂宗旦
    alternate characters

Ögedei Khan (M) / Wokuotaihan (C) 窩闊台汗
Omar (M) / Wuma'er (C) 烏馬兒
ơn (V) 恩
Ông Phúc (V) 翁富
Ông Thân Lợi (V) 翁申利
Ouyang Wei (C) 歐陽頠
Ouyang Yan (C) 歐陽戩

Pan Chongche (C) 潘崇徹
Panyu (C) 番禺
Panyue (C) 盤越
Panzhihua (C) 攀枝花
Panzhou (C) 潘州
paodai(C) 袍帶
Pei Hangli (C) 裴行立
Peng Jian (C) 彭瑊
Peng Jingxuan (C) 彭景巡
Peng Shiyan (C) 彭師晏
Phạm Cụ Địa (V) 范巨地
Pham Minh Tự (V) 範明字
Phạm Sư Mạnh (V) 范師孟
Phạm Thuần Hậu (V) 范純厚
Phan Hoành Diệu (V) 潘宏耀
Phan Huy Chú (V) 潘輝注
phò mã (V) 駙馬
phủ (V) 府
Phù Đổng (V) 扶董
Phù Lan (V) 扶蘭
Phù Linh (V) 富令
phủ lộ tư (V) 府路司
Phú Lương (V) 富良
Phù Vạn (V) 扶萬

Phúc Hoà (V) 覆和
Phùng Chân (V) 馮振
Phùng Hưng (V) 馮興
Pi Luoge (C) 皮羅閣
ping li dong (C) 平俚洞
Pingle (C) 平樂
Pingma (C) 平馬
Pingshan (C) 屏山
Pingxiang(C) 憑祥
pingzhang (C) 平章
Pingzhang Ali (M) 平章阿剌
pizhan (C) 披氈
Poluo Hada'er (C) 孛羅哈達兒
Poyang (C) 番陽
Pu Lu (C) 普露
Pu'an (C) 普安
Pucheng (C) 浦城
Pudong (C) 浦東
Pu'er (C) 普洱
Pugan (C) 蒲甘
Puli (C) 普里 Puri, India
Puluomen lu (C) 婆羅門路
Puzhou (C) 蒲州
Pyu (C) 驃

Qi (C) 杞
Qi Jiguang (C) 戚繼光
qian (C) 錢 cash
Qian (C) 黔 Guizhou
Qiang (C) 羌
Qianlong (C) 遷隆 village in Guangxi
Qianlong (C) 乾隆 Qing emperor
qianzhen (C) 乾貞
Qianzhou (C) 黔州
Qiao Chen (C) 喬臣
Qiaoma (C) 巧馬
qijiawang (C) 奇嘉王

Qin (C) 秦

Qin Jiang (C) 欽江

Qin Shihuangdi (C) 秦始皇帝

Qin Xu Bian (C) 欽恤編

Qing (C) 清

Qinghai (C) 青海

Qingjiang (C) 靜江

Qingjiao (C) 青礁

qingping guan (C) 清平官

Qingshilu (C) 清實錄

Qingxiguandao (C) 清溪閞道

Qingyi (C) 青衣

Qinzhou (C) 欽州

Qiongbu (C) 邛部

Qiongdu (C) 邛都

Qiongye (C) 邛笮

Qiongzhou (C) 瓊州

Qitaituoyin (C) 乞台脫因

Qiu He (C) 丘和

Qiu zhang (C) 酋長

Qixian (C) 祁鮮

Qiyuan (C) 七源

Quận Tầm (V) 郡尋

Quang Bính (V) 光昺(昞)

Quảng Nguyên (V) 廣源

Quảng Oai (V) 廣威

Quảng Phúc (V) 廣福

Quảng Yên (V) 廣安

Quanzhou (C) 泉州

que (C) 闕

que dian (C) 闕典

Qujiang (C) 曲江

Qujing (C) 曲靖

Qulizhao (C) 渠斂趙

Quốc Hoàng (V) 國皇

Qúy Hoa (V) 歸化

Quỷ Môn Quan (V) 鬼門關

Rangshui (C) 瀼水

Ren Guan (C) 任官

Rixuan (C) 日烜

Rong (C) 容

Rongcheng Wang (C) 戎成王

Rongshuzhou (C) 戎數州

ru bantu (C) 入版圖

ru xue (C) 儒學

Ruhong (C) 如洪

Ruili (C) 瑞麗

Rumen (C) 如門

Ruxi (C) 如昔

Ruzhou (C) 汝州

sách (V) 冊

San Guo (C) 三國

Sandu Shuizu Zizhixian (C)
　　三都水族自治縣

Sanjiang (C) 三縫

Sanshi (C) 三史

sanshiqi bu huimeng bei (C) 三十七部
　　會盟碑

Sanxingdui (C) 三星堆

Sanya (C) 三衙

Sanzhen (C) 三陣

Shadian shijian (C) 沙甸事件

Shali (C) 沙梨

Shan (C) 撣

Shan Jidi (C) 閃繼迪

Shan Yinglei (C) 閃應雷

Shan Zhongtong (C) 閃仲侗

Shan Zhongyan (C) 閃仲儼

Shanchan (C) 鄯闡

Shang Di (C) 上帝

Shangguo (C) 上國

Shanghai (C) 上海

Shangshu (C) 尚書

Shangzhan (C) 上展
Shangzhuguo (C) 上柱國
Shanju (C) 善巨
Shanshi (C) 閃氏
Shao Pu (C) 邵溥
Shaoguan (C) 韶關
Shaoxing (C) 紹興
Shaoxing Heyi (C) 紹興和議
Shaozhou (C) 昭州
shen (C) 神
Shen Bingkun (C) 沈秉堃
shen qiang (C) 神槍
Shen Quanqi (C) 沈佺期
Shen Zhaoqian (C) 沈肇乾
Shendan (C) 申賧
Shengmachuan (C) 升麻川
shengmin (C) 省民
shengyi (C) 生夷
shenji jiangjun (C) 神機將軍
shenji ying (C) 神機營
Shenli (C) 沈黎
shenma (C) 神馬
Shennong (C) 神農
shenyan baowu (C) 申嚴保伍
Shenzong (C) 神宗
shexiang (C) 麝香
Shexue (C) 社學
shi (C) 絁
Shi Liangbi (C) 石良弼
Shi Xie (C) 士燮
Shicheng (C) 石城
Shichengjun (C) 石城郡
shidafu (C) 士大夫
Shidi (C) 十低
Shidong (C) 拓東
Shifan (C) 石蕃
shijian (C) 世見

shijueming (C) 石決明
shilang (C) 侍郎 administrative title
Shilang (C) 施浪 Tang period ethnic
   group in Yunnan
Shilong (C) 世隆
Shiluo (C) 時羅
Shimen Dao (C) 石門道
Shimenguan (C) 石門關
Shiqi (C) 石碕
Shiqu (C) 石渠
Shixiu (C) 時休
Shiyijian (C) 世壹見
shizi (C) 世子
Shizu ping Yunnan bei (C)
   世祖平雲南碑
shou chen (C) 守臣
Shoutian Sheng Dawang (C)
   守天聖大王
Shu (C) 蜀
Shu Han (C) 蜀漢
shu zhe zai dao zhi qi ye (C) 書者載道
   之器也
shuai (C) 帥
shuaici (C) 帥司
shuangchong chenshu (C) 雙重臣屬
Shuangtou dong (C) 雙頭洞
Shuangzhou (C) 雙州 or 瀧州
shuli (C) 屬吏
Shumanta (C) 梳蠻塔
shumi fushi (C) 樞密副使
Shun (C) 舜
Shun'an (C) 順安
Shunning (C) 順寧
si dong (C) 四峒
Sicheng (C) 泗城
Sichuan (C) 四川
Sifang Guan (C) 四方館

sihu canjun (C) 司戶參軍

sikong (C) 司空

Sile (C) 思勒

sili xiaowei (C) 司隸校尉

Silin (C) 澌廩

Siling (C) 思陵

Siming (C) 思明

sixing (C) 四姓

Sơn La (V) 山喇

Song (C) 宋

Song Dao (C) 宋道

Song hui yufu (C) 宋揮玉斧

Song Huizong (C) 宋徽宗

Song Lizong (C) 宋理宗

Song Min (C) 宋敏

Song Ningzong (C) 宋寧宗

Song Renzong(C) 宋仁宗

Song Shenzong (C) 宋神宗

Song shu (C) 宋書

Song Yingzong (C) 宋英宗

Song Zhenzong (C) 宋真宗

Songshou (C) 宋壽

Songzhu (C) 宋主

soushuai (C) 叟帥

Sri Vijaya (S) / Sanfoqi (C)
　　三佛齊

Su Jian (C) 蘇緘

Sử Ký (V) 史記

Su Xian (C) 蘇憲

Su Zhongyong (C) 蘇忠勇

Su Zuo (C) 蘇佐

Suanzhi'erwei (C) 算只兒威

Sui shu (C) 隋書

Suidian (C) 睢殿

Sun Gongqi (C) 孫公器

suo gui buzhi yin re bianshi (C)
　　所貴不致引惹邊事

Suodu (C) 唆都

Tả Giang (V) 左江

taichang boshi (C) 太常博士

taifu (C) 太傅

Taigong (C) 太公

Taihe cheng (C) 太和城

Taiping (C) 太平

Taiping huanyuji (C) 太平寰宇記

Taiping xu (C) 太平墟

Taiping yulan (C) 太平御覽

taishou (C) 太守

Taizhou (C) 太州

Taizu (C) 太祖

Tam Đảo (V) 三島

Tan (C) 壇

Tan Bi (C) 譚必

Tan Chuo (C) 坦綽

Tan Daoji (C) 檀道濟

Tần Sầm (V) 秦岑

Tan Xiu (C) 談修

Tanan Wang (C) 拓南王

Tang Daizong (C) 唐代宗

Tang Dezong (C) 唐德宗

Tang Gaozong(C) 唐高宗

Tang Meng (C) 唐蒙

Tang Muzong (C) 唐穆宗

Tang Rong (C) 唐容

Tang Wude (C) 唐武德

Tang Xianzong (C) 唐憲宗

Tang Xiaozong (C) 唐肅宗

Tang Xuanzong (C) 唐玄宗

Tang Yizong (C) 唐懿宗

Tangchang (C) 蕩昌

Tangxing (C) 唐興

Tangzhou (C) 唐州

tanmachijun (C) 探馬赤軍

Tao Bi (C) 陶弼

Tao Daming (C) 陶大明

Tập Hiền (V) 集賢

Tây Nùng (V) 西農

Temo (C) 特魔

Temo Dao (C) 特磨道

Temo xidong sanshiliu (C) 特磨溪洞三十六

Tengchong (C) 騰衝

Tengzhou (C) 滕州

Thạch Lâm (V) 石林

Thạch Mật (V) 石蜜

Thái Nguyên (V) 太原

Thân Cảnh Phúc (V) 申景福

Thân Lợi (V) 申利

thần nhân (V) 神人

Thân Nhân Trung (V) 申仁忠

Thân Thừa Quý (V) 申承貴

thản xước (V) / tanchou (C) 坦綽

Thảng Do (V) 儻猶

Thăng Long (V) 昇龍

Thanh Hoá lộ (V) 清化路

thành hoàng (V) 城隍

Thánh Vũ (V) 聖羽

Thát Đát (V) 殺韃

Thất Nguyên (V) 七源

Thất Tộc Phiên Thần (V) 七族藩臣

Thiền (V) 禪

Thiên Đức (V) 天德

Thiên Nam Động Chủ (V) 天南峒主

Thiên Nam Dư Hạ Tập (V) 天南餘暇集

Thiên Nam Hoàng Đế Chi Bảo (V) 天南皇帝之寶

Thiết Lược (V) 鉄略

thổ (V) 土

thổ hào (V) 土豪

thổ thần (V) 土神

thủ lịnh (V) 首令

thử sứ (V) 刺史

Thục Phán (V) 蜀泮

Thương (V) 滄

Thượng Đế (V) 上帝

Thượng Nguyên (V) 上原

Thường Tân (V) 常新

Thụy Hương (V) 瑞香

Tì Trúc (V) 茨竹

Tian (C) 天

Tian Sishuang (C) 天駟爽

Tianbao (C) 天寶

tianbing (C) 天兵

Tianci (C) 天賜

Tiandong (C) 田東

Tianfu (C) 天福

Tianhe (C) 天河

Tianjian (C) 天監

Tianjiang (C) 天將

Tianlin (C) 田林

Tianzhou (C) 田州

Tielang (C) 貼浪

tizhu (C) 提舉

tizhu dongding (C) 提舉峒丁

Tô Bách (V) 蘇百

Tô Hiến Thành (V) 蘇憲城

Tô Lịch (V) 蘇歷

Tô Mậu (V) 蘇茂

Toghan (M) / Tuohuan (C) 脫驩

Tôn (V) 尊

toujiao (C) 頭角

touren (C) 頭人

Trà Hương (V) 茶鄉

trại (V) 寨

trấn (V) 鎮 garrison township

Trần (V) 陳 surname

Trần Bình Trọng (V) 陳平仲

Trần Công (V) 陳公
Trần Di Ái (V) 陳遺愛
Trần Đình Huyên (V) 陳廷暄
Trần Hoảng (V) 陳晃
Trần Ích Tắc (V) 陳益稷
Trần Kiện (V) 陳鍵
Trần Lộng (V) 陳弄
Trần Minh Tông (V) 陳明宗
Trần Nhân Tông (V) 陳仁宗
Trần Nhật Duật (V) 陳日燏
Trần Nhật Huyên (V) 陳日烜
Trần Phủ (V) 陳甫
Trần Quang Khải (V) 陳光啟
Trần Quốc Khang (V) 陳國康
Trần Quốc Tảng (V) 陳國顙
Trần Quốc Tuấn (V) 陳國峻 (Hưng
    Đạo 興道 posthumous honorific
    name)
Trần Thái Tông (V) 陳太宗
Trần Thánh Tông (V) 陳聖宗
Trần Thủ Độ (V) 陳守度
Trần Tú Ái (V) 陳秀嗳
Trần Tự Khánh (V) 陳嗣慶
Trần Văn Lộng (V) 陳文弄
Trễ Nguyên (V) 虒源
tri châu (V) 治州
Trí Chi (V) 智之
Triệu (V) 趙
Triệu Trí Chi (V) 趙智之
Trịnh Đình Toản (V) 鄭廷瓚
Trịnh Kỳ (V) 鄭旗
Trịnh Long (V) 鄭隆
Trịnh Xiển (V) 鄭闡
Trisong Detsen (T) / Chisongdezan (C)
    赤松德贊
Trưng (V) 徵
Trương (V) 張

Trường Sinh (V) 長生
tu cishi (C) 土刺史
tu da shi (C) 圖大事
Tư Đức (V) 嗣德
Tư Lãng (V) 思琅
Từ Liêm (V) 慈廉
tu xiancheng (C) 土縣承
tu xun jian (C) 土巡檢
tu yi (C) 土夷
tu zhifu (C) 土知府
Tufan (C) 吐蕃
tuguan zhifu (C) 土官知府
Tundong (C) 屯洞
tuntian (C) 屯田
tuo tai huan gu (C) 脫胎換骨
Tuodong (C) 拓東
Tuohe (C) 馱河
Tuohuan (C) 脫歡
Tuoluhe (C) 馱盧河
tusi (C) 土司
Tuyên Hoá (V) 宣化
Tuyên Quang (V) 宣光

Uẩn (V) 溫
Uriyangqadai (M) / Wuliang Getai(dai)
    (C) 兀良合臺(帶)

Văn (V) 文
Văn Chiêu (V) 文昭
Vân Đồn (V) 雲屯
Văn Dương (V) 文陽
Vạn Hạnh (V) 萬行
Vân Hội (V) 雲會
Vạn Kiếp (V) 萬劫
Văn Lang (V) 文郎
Vạn Nhai (V) 萬崖
Vân Trà (V) 雲茶

Vi (V) 章

Vị Long (V) 渭龍

Vi Phúc Quản (V) 章福琯

Vị Thiệu Khâm (V) 章紹欽

Vị Thiệu Tự (V) 章紹嗣

Vi Thủ An (V) 韋守安

Việt (V) 越

Việt điện u linh tập (V) 粵甸幽靈集

Việt điện u linh tập lục toàn biên (V) 粵甸幽靈集錄全編

Việt Sử Lược (V) 越史略

Vĩnh An (V) 永安

Vĩnh Châu (V) 永州

Vĩnh Thông (V) 永通

Vĩnh Tuy (V) 永綏

Vũ Đức (V) 武德

Vũ Lặc (V) 武勒

Vũ Nhĩ (V) 武珥

Vũ Ninh (V) 武寧

Wa (C) 佤

wai (C) 外

wai yi (C) 外夷

wan kou chong (C) 碗口銃

Wan Nu (C) 萬奴

Wan'an (C) 萬安

Wancheng (C) 萬承

Wang Anshi (C) 王安石

Wang Bo (C) 王蕃

Wang Dai (C) 王戴

Wang Jian (C) 王鑒

Wang Junhou (C) 王君侯

Wang Kan (C) 王侃

Wang Mang (C) 王莽

Wang Mansheng (C) 王蠻盛

Wang Quanbin (C) 王全斌

Wang Shangyong (C) 王尚用

Wang Taichong (C) 王太衝

Wang Wenqing (C) 王文慶

Wang Xian (C) 王先

Wang Xiangzhi (C) 王象之

Wang Xuance (C) 王玄策

Wang Yinglin (C) 王應麟

Wangqi (C) 王氣

Wangren (C) 王人

Wangyan (C) 妄言

Wanli (C) 萬曆

Wanshou Guan (C) 萬壽觀

wei (C) 尉 officer

Wei (C) 魏 surname

Wei Jinglan (C) 韋敬簡

Wei Qixiu (C) 韋齊休

Wei Yue (C) 韋悅

Weichu (C) 威楚

Weining (C) 威寧

Weixian (C) 味縣

Weiyuan (C) 威遠

Weizhou (C) 威州

Wen Fangzhi (C) 溫放之

Wen Liang (C) 文良

Wendan (C) 文單

Wengzhong (C) 翁仲

Wengzhong Junhe (C) 翁仲君何

Wenshan (C) 文山

wo fu zhi ju (C) 斡腹之舉

Wozhu (C) 窩主

Wu (C) 吳

Wu Chengfei (C) 武承斐

wu da yuan shuai (C) 五大元帥

Wu Fu (C) 吳福

Wu Fujiang (C) 吳俯講

Wu Huai'en (C) 吳懷恩

Wu Huan (C) 伍環

Wu Jing (C) 吳儆

Wu Ju (C) 伍舉

Wu Ma'er (C) 烏馬兒

Wu Sangui (C) 吳三桂

Wu Shan (C) 巫山

wu wenxian (C) 無文獻

Wu Xing Fan (C) 五姓番

Wu Zongli (C) 吳宗立

wu zu (C) 五族

Wuchidao (C) 五尺道

Wudeng (C) 勿鄧

Wuding (C) 武定

Wu'e (C) 勿惡

Wufeng hu xiansheng wenji (C) 五峰胡
先生文集

wuju (C) 武舉

Wuling (C) 武陵

Wuman (C) 烏蠻

Wuman buluo sanshiqi (C) 烏蠻部落
三十七

Wuning Dajun (C) 武寧將軍

Wuping (C) 武平

Wuxingfan (C) 五姓蕃

Wuyang (C) 勿陽 prefecture in Guangxi

Wuyang (C) 武陽 prefecture in Sichuan

Wuzhou (C) 梧州

xi an shi zhi lou xi (C) 洗安氏之陋習

Xi Jiang duhu (C) 西江督護

Xi Rong (C) 西戎

Xia Lei (C) 下雷

Xiancheng (C) 鄉城

Xiang Zhi (C) 相支

xiangha (C) 香蛤

xianglao zhi koushi (C) 鄉老之口實

Xiangting Er Qi (C) 相挺而起

Xiangyang (C) 襄陽

Xiangzhou (C) 相州 Tang prefecture

in Henan

Xiangzhou (C) 象州 Tang prefecture
in Guangxi

Xianning (C) 咸寧

Xiantong (C) 咸通

Xianyang (C) 咸陽

Xianyou (C) 仙遊

Xianyu Zhongtong (C) 鮮于仲通

Xiao Cheli (C) 小車里

Xiao Mai (C) 蕭勣

Xiao Xi Tian (C) 小西天

Xiaozong shilu (C) 孝宗實錄

Xiapu (C) 霞浦

Xiaxi (C) 下溪

xích (V) 尺

Xichang (C) 西昌

Xichong (C) 滕充

Xichuan (C) 西川

Xide (C) 喜德

Xidian-Tianzhu Dao (C) 西滇天竺道

xidong (C) 谿峒

xidong yao (C) 溪洞藥

xidongsi (C) 溪峒司

Xie Jicheng (C) 謝季成

Xie Mingzhi (C) 謝明之

xie shu (C) 邪書

Xiemoti (C) 些摩徒

Xihu (C) 西滬

Xikang (C) 西康

Xin cha zhi YongzhouYao Ke wei
zhineng ban mai ma fou (C)
新差知邕州姚恪未知能辦買馬否

Xin Jian (C) 辛讜

Xin Tang shu (C) 新唐書

Xin Yifu (C) 信宜福

xin zheng (C) 新政

Xin Zhiri (C) 信直日

Xin'an (C) 新安

Xinan Tongchuan Fulu (C) 西南渔川
府路

Xinchang (C) 新昌

Xing Can (C) 行參

Xing yuan (C) 姓苑

Xing'an (C) 興安

Xing'an wen shi zi liao (C) 興安文史資
料

Xingning (C) 興寧

Xingren (C) 興仁

Xingzhong (C) 興中

Xinning (C) 新寧

Xinuluo (C) 細奴邏

Xinxunxi (C) 新灞溪

Xinzhou (C) 新州

Xiongcuo (C) 雄挫

xipi jia'anpei (C) 犀皮甲鞍轡

Xiping (C) 西平

Xirong (C) 西戎

Xiu shijian zhili (C) 修世見之禮

Xiuning (C) 休寧

Xiyidao (C) 西夷道

Xiyu (C) 西域

Xizhan (C) 細氈

Xizhao (C) 西趙

Xizhou (C) 巂州

xu (C) 墟

Xu Dao (C) 除道

Xu Nanyue zhi (C) 續南越志

Xu Qingsuo (C) 徐清叟

Xu Tixie (C) 使徐惕

Xu Yuanyu (C) 許元育

Xu Zizhi tongjian (C) 續資治通鑑

Xu Zongyi (C) 許忠義

xuanfushi (C) 宣撫使

xuanhualing (C) 宣化令

Xuantong zhengji (C) 宣統政紀

xuanweisi (C) 宣慰司

Xue Chongyu (C) 薛崇譽

xuming (C) 虛名

Xun Fazhao (C) 荀法超

Xun Fei (C) 荀斐

xun jian guan yi (C) 巡檢官宜

Xun Jiang (C) 荀匠

Xunchuan Man (C) 尋傳蠻

Xundian (C) 尋甸

xun'eshi (C) 巡遏使

xunjian (C) 巡檢

Xunjiansi (C) 巡檢司

Xunzhou (C) 潯州 Tang prefecture
in Guangxi

Xunzhou (C) 順州 Song borderlands
prefecture in southern Guangxi

Xuong Giang (V) 昌江

Xuyi (C) 盱眙

Ya'an (C) 雅安

Yaghan Tegin (M) / Yehan dejin (C)
也罕的斤

Yan Ben (C) 彥賁

Yan Da (C) 燕達

Yan feng si (C) 驗封司

Yan Minde (C) 顏敏德

Yan Ying (C) 燕瑛

Yan Zhen (C) 嚴鎮

Yandao (C) 嚴道

Yang (C) 楊

Yang An (C) 陽旻

Yang Changhui (C) 楊長惠

Yang Lin (C) 楊林

Yang Shouzhen (C) 楊守珍

Yang Zhaojie (C) 楊兆傑

yanjiang bu bingchuan, li mushan (C)

沿江布兵船, 立木栅
Yanjin (C) 鹽津
Yanyuan (C) 鹽源
Yanzhong (C) 延眾
Yao Jun (C) 姚俊
Yao Ke (C) 姚恪
Yao Kesheng (C) 姚恪盛
Yao Kuo (C) 姚廓
Yao Zhu (C) 姚桀
Yao'an (C) 姚安
Yaoman (C) 猓蠻
Yazhou (C) 雅州
Yedu (C) 筰都
Yelang (C) 夜郎
Yên Sinh (V) 安生
Yexiantiemu'er (C) 也先帖木爾
Yi (C) 彝 ethnonym for a southwestern ethnic group
Yi (C) 夷 general ethnonym
Yi (C) 鎰 unit of weight
yi (C) 驛 postal station
Yi jian zhi (C) 夷堅志
yi que (C) 詣闕
yi yi ping yi (C) 以夷平夷
Yibin (C) 宜宾
Yidi (C) 夷地
yihua (C) 夷化
Yiliang (C) 宜良
Yimouxun (C) 異牟尋
Yin (C) 鄞
Yin Huangshang (C) 尹黄裳
Yin Yingfei (C) 印應飛
Yingdi (C) 營底
Yinghan (C) 岑映翰
Yingjing (C) 滎經
Yingqi (C) 嬰齊
Yinjin shi (C) 引進使

Yinsheng (C) 銀生
yinshi yanzei (C) 引師掩賊
yishuai (C) 夷帥
Yiwang fu (C) 義王府
Yixi (C) 以熙
Yixibuxue (C) 亦奚不薛
Yizhou (C) 宜州 prefecture in Guangxi
Yizhou (C) 益州 prefecture in Sichuan
Yizu (C) 彝族
Yong Youdiao (C) 雍由調
Yongchang (C) 永昌
Yongchang Dao (C) 永昌道
Yongfeng (C) 永豐
Yongguan (C) 邕管
Yongjia (C) 永嘉
Yongle (C) 永樂
Yongle dadian (C) 永樂大典
Yongli (C) 永曆
Yongning (C) 永寧
Yongping (C) 永平
Yongxing Jun (C) 永興軍
Yongzheng (C) 雍正
Yongzhou (C) 邕州
Yongzhou Dao (C) 永州道
you chengxiang (C) 右承相
you weimingzhe (C) 有違命者
Youjiang (C) 右江
Youyi Guan (C) 友誼關
Youzhou (C) 有州
Yu (C) / Uất (V) 鬱
Yu Dan (C) 俞僬
Yu di ji sheng (C) 輿地紀勝
yu fu (C) 玉符
Yu shu lou (C) 御書樓
Yuan (C) 元
Yuan Zi (C) 袁滋

Yuanfeng (C) 元豐

Yuanhe (C) 元和

Yuanhe junxianzhi (C) 元和郡縣志

Yuanhui (C) 元徽

Yuanzhou (C) 員州 prefecture in Guangxi

Yuanzhou (C) 沅州 prefecture in Hunan

Yudijisheng (C) 輿地紀勝

Yuedanchuan (C) 越賧川

Yueqiong (C) 越檮

Yuexizhou (C) 越析州

Yuexi (C) 越西

Yuezhou (C) 越州

Yulin (C) 欝林

Yulüshu (C) 玉律術

Yumi buchuan (C) 語秘不傳

Yun (C) 筠

Yunihe (C) 淤泥河

Yunlian (C) 筠蓮

Yunnan (C) 雲南

Yunnan fu (C) 雲南府

Yunnan ji (C) 雲南記

Yunnan Jiedushi (C) 雲南節度使

Yunnan tong zhi (C) 雲南通志

Yunnan xingji (C) 雲南行記

yushi daifu (C) 御史大夫

Yushibu (C) 於矢部

Yuwen Heitai (C) 宇文黑泰

yuyi enxin (C) 諭以恩信

Yuyuan (C) 俞元

Zai Zhi (C) 宰執

zaixiang (C) 宰相

Zanghedao (C) 牂牁道

Zangke (C) 牂牁 (柯)

Zangzhou (C) 牂州

Zeng Bu (C) 曾布

Zeng Gun (C) 曾袞

zengjin (C) 繒錦

zha fu (C) 劄付

zhan (C) 甎

zhan ji (C) 氊屬

Zhancheng (C) 占城

zhang (C) 丈

Zhang Bang (C) 張榜

Zhang Banruoshi (C) 張般若

Zhang Cixie (C) 張次髙

Zhang Gong (C) 張公

Zhang Hanxing (C) 張漢興

Zhang Lidao (C) 張立道

Zhang Qian (C) 張騫

Zhang Shi (C) 張栻

Zhang Shou (C) 張首

Zhang Tixing (C) 張提刑

Zhang Wenhu (C) 張文虎

Zhang Xingjian (C) 張行簡

Zhang Xuan (C) 張瑄

Zhang Yong(C) 張詠

Zhang Yue (C) 張岳

Zhangfan (C) 張蕃

Zhang Ling (C) 樟嶺

Zhangxi (C) 長溪

Zhangzhou (C) 漳州

Zhanla (C) 占蜡

Zhanyi (C) 霑益

Zhao (C) 趙 surname

zhao (C) 召 imperial decree

zhao (C) 詔 alternate form of zhao

Zhao Chang (C) 趙昌

Zhao Erfeng (C) 趙爾豐

Zhao Gui (C) 趙灵

Zhao Kuangyin (C) 趙匡胤

Zhao Rukuo (C) 趙汝适

Zhao Shi (C) 趙始

Zhao Shu (C) 趙曙
Zhao Tuo (C) 趙佗
Zhao Xie (C) 趙禼
Zhao Yun (C) 趙昀
Zhaoqing (C) 肇慶
Zhaotong (C) 昭通
Zhaozhou (C) 昭州
Zhejiang (C) 浙江
Zhelinzhou (C) 羈林州
zhen (C) 鎮
Zhen Congyu (C) 真崇鬱
Zhenan Wang (C) 鎮南王
Zheng Hanzhang (C) 鄭漢章
Zheng He (C) 鄭和
Zheng Hui (C) 鄭回
Zheng Sixiao (C) 鄭思肖
Zheng Xiao 鄭蕭
Zheng Xiong (C) 鄭熊
Zhengde (C) 正德
Zhennan (C) 鎮南
Zhennanwang (C) 鎮南王
Zhenyuan (C) 貞元
Zhi Kai (C) 智開
Zhide (C) 至德
zhidong (C) 知洞
zhiguai (C) 志怪
zhihuishi (C) 指揮使
zhishi (C) 指使
zhixi (C) 支系
zhixian (C) 知縣
zhizhou (C) 知州
Zhong Tiandu (C) 中天竺
Zhonggan Zhun (C) 忠敢軍
Zhongguo (C) 中國
Zhongguo Renmin Zhengzhi Xieshang
    Huiyi (C) 中國人民政治協商會議

Zhongguo ren min zheng zhi xie shang
    hui yi Guangxi Xing'an xian wei yuan
    hui wen shi zi liao wei yuan hui (C)
    中國人民政治協商會議廣西興安縣
    委員會文史資料委員會
Zhonghe (C) 中和
Zhongqing lu (C) 中慶路
Zhongqinglu ruxueji (C) 中慶路儒學記
Zhongshuling (C) 中書令
Zhongxing (C) 中興
Zhongyue Wang (C) 中越王
Zhou Enlai (C) 周恩來
Zhou Shixiong (C) 周世雄
Zhou Wenyu (C) 周文育
Zhou Zongshi (C) 周宗奭
Zhu De (C) 朱德
Zhu Gui (C) 朱貴
Zhu San Taizi (C) 朱三太子
Zhu Shengfei (C) 硃勝非
Zhu Xi (C) 朱熹
Zhu Yigui (C) 朱一貴
Zhu Youlang (C) 朱由榔
Zhu Yuanzhang (C) 朱元璋
Zhu Zhen (C) 朱震
Zhu Zhou (C) 竹洲
zhuangyunshi (C) 轉運使
Zhuangzong (C) 莊宗
zhuanyu fushi (C) 轉運副使
zhubu (C) 主簿
Zhuge Liang (C) 諸葛亮
Zhuge Yuansheng (C) 諸葛元聲
Zhuhou (C) 諸侯
Zhulan (C) 朱蘭
Zhuti (C) 朱提
Zhuyazhou (C) 朱崖州
zhuza (C) 駐紮

Ziqi (C) 自杞

zitan (C) 紫檀

Zizhi tongjian (C) 資治通鑑

zongdu (C) 總督

zongguan (C) 總官

zongling (C) 總領

zongshou (C) 總首

zongzhi tuben (C) 宗支圖本

Zu Liangfan (C) 祖良范

Zuining (C) 最寧

Zuizhou (C) 檇州

zuo cheng (C) 左丞

Zuo You liangjiang (C) 左右兩江

zuo zhenfu (C) 佐鎮撫

Zuodouyaya (C) 左都押衙

NOTES

Abbreviations

ANCL	Lê Tắc, *Annam Chỉ Lược*
DTXYJJZ	Xuan Zang, *Da Tang Xiyu ji jiao zhu*
DVSKTB	Ngô Thì Sĩ, *Đại Việt sử ký tiền biên*
DVSKTT	Ngô Sĩ Liên, *Đại Việt sử ký toàn thư*
HHS	Fan Ye, *Houhanshu*
JTS	Liu Xu, *Jiutang shu*
KDDNHDSL	*Khâm định Đại Nam hội điển sự lệ*
KDVSTGCM	*Khâm định Việt sử thông giám cương mục*
LTHCLC	Phan Huy Chú, *Lịch triều hiến chương loại chí*
LWDD	Zhou Qufei, *Lingwai daida*
SHY	Xu Song, *Song hui yao ji gao*
TPYL	Li Fang, *Taiping yulan*
VSCMTY	Đặng Xuân Bằng, *Việt sử cương mục tiết yếu*
VSL	Anon., *Việt sử lược*
XTS	Ouyang Xiu, *Xintang shu*
XZZTJ	Bi Yuan, *Xu Zizhi tongjian*
ZFZ	Zhao Rukuo, *Zhu fan zhi*
ZZTJCB	Li Tao, *Xu Zizhi tongjian changbian*

Introduction

1. See Schafer, *Vermillion Bird*, 48–78, 277n21, 278n78, 347; and Churchman and Baldanza in Anderson and Whitmore, *China's Encounters on the South and Southwest*. J. L. Weinstein, *Empire and Identity in Guizhou*, 21, notes that "*cuengh (zhuang)* means 'narrow, flat-bottomed river valleys in the mountains,'"

"a self-appellation used by the ancient Tai-speaking inhabitants of northern Guangxi"; perhaps this was the original form of what has become the term *dong*. For Yunnan, Bin Yang speaks of *bazi*, "small fertile basins and valleys"; B. Yang, *Between Winds and Clouds*, 25–26, 148, 151.

2.   Influential borderlands studies of other regions and other periods include Brooks, *Captives and Cousins*, and Radding, *Wandering Peoples*. For the modern period, please see Brown, *A Biography of No Place*.

3.   Abulafia and Berend, *Medieval Frontiers*, xi.

4.   Abulafia and Berend, *Medieval Frontiers*, xiv.

5.   Sahlins, *Boundaries*, xv.

6.   *Dong*, usually translated as "grotto," actually means "mountain valley settlement."

7.   White, *The Middle Ground*, xiii.

8.   For a discussion of the meaning of the term *dong*, see Churchman, "Where to Draw the Line?," 65, and Baldanza, "A State Agent at Odds with the State," 171–72; see also Baldanza, *Ming China and Vietnam*, 122–23; Churchman, *The People between the Rivers*, 21; Fan Chengda and Hargett, *Treatises of the Supervisor and Guardian of the Cinnamon Sea*, li–lii.

9.   Moseley, *The Consolidation of the South China Frontier*, 12.

10. Scott, *The Art of Not Being Governed*.

11. Scott, *The Art of Not Being Governed*, 13–14.

12. Tambiah, *World Conqueror and World Renouncer*.

13. James A. Anderson and John K. Whitmore, *China's Encounters on the South and Southwest*, vii.

14. Nguyễn Chí Buyên et al., eds., *Nguồn Gốc Lịch Sử Tộc Người Vùng Biên Giới Phía Bắc Việt Nam*, 55.

15. Tapp, "The Han Joker in the Pack" in *Critical Han Studies*, ed. Mullaney, 153; Brindley, *Ancient China and the Yue*, 31.

16. Nguyễn Chí Buyên et al., eds., *Nguồn Gốc Lịch Sử Tộc Người Vùng Biên Giới Phía Bắc Việt Nam*, 55.

17. Chin, "Antiquarian as Ethnographer," 128.

18. Anderson, "Treacherous Factions," 194.

19. Wolters, *History, Culture, and Region in Southeast Asian Perspectives*, 27.

1. Southwest Silk Road and the Dong World

1.   Polo, *The Travels of Marco Polo*, 177–81.

2.   Huo, *Xinan kaogu yu Zhonghua wenming*, 220. Qiang is an ethnonym used in

first-century Han sources to describe peoples the borderlands between modern-day western China and Tibet. Chinese scholars often directly connect the peoples referenced in these sources and the modern Chinese national minority identified as Qiang, but this direct connection remains in dispute. For a description of the historical Qiang, see Mote, *Imperial China*, 169.

3. The Lancang River is the upstream name of the Mekong River in China, the headwaters of which are in Qinghai. The Jinsha River is the upstream name of the Yangzi River in China. As archaeologist Huo Wei notes, burial sites reached from areas of eastern Tibet, along the Yajiang River in the Tibetan prefecture of Ganzi to areas of central Sichuan near the city of Ya'an, and finally the Deqinyongzhi burial sites of northwest Yunnan the tombs found in Nagu township of central Yunnan's Tonghai County. Huo, *Xinan kaogu yu Zhonghua wenming*, 220.

4. From chap. 2 in B. Yang, *Between Winds and Clouds*.

5. Sima Qian, *Shiji*, 116:2995–96.

6. Sima Qian, *Shiji*, 123:3166.

7. Yuan, *The Sinitic Civilization*, 279.

8. Sage, *Ancient Sichuan*, 143–44. Cited in Herman, "The Kingdoms of Nanzhong," 244.

9. Herman, "The Kingdoms of Nanzhong," 244.

10. Herman, "The Kingdoms of Nanzhong," 244.

11. An alternate form of this name in the sources was Zangke.

12. Kunming referred to the Dali area in the Western Han, the Yanyuan area of modern-day Sichuan, established by Tang Gaozu in 619, and the modern city of Kunming from the Yuan dynasty on. See Xu Jiarui, *Dali gudai wenhua shigao*, 40. What is now Kunming was in the Western Han period called Zuizhou. The city was known as Shidong during the Nanzhao period. See Xu Jiarui, *Dali gudai wenhua shigao*, 43.

13. Giersch, *Asian Borderlands*, 30.

14. *HHS*, 177.

15. Xu Jiarui, *Dali gudai wenhua shigao*, 56.

16. Zhou and Ding, eds., *Sichou zhi lu da cidian*, 748.

17. Zhang Zhongshan, *Zhongguo sichou zhi lu huobi*, 139.

18. B. Yang, "Horses, Silver, and Cowries," 281–82.

19. Clunas, *Art in China*, 18–19.

20. Wang Fangqing, *Weizheng Gong Jian Lu, juan* 3; Wu Jing, *Zhenguan zheng yao, juan* 5.

21. Wu Jing's phrase was "jifeng zhi jingcao, ban dang shi cheng chen." See Wu Jing, *Zhongguo di wang xue*, 201.

22. Personal correspondence with Professor Marc Gilbert. See Heiss and Heiss, *The Story of Tea*, 11. See also L. Wang, *Tea and Chinese Culture*, 149–50.

23. Sen, *Buddhism, Diplomacy, and Trade*, 171.

24. Sen, *Buddhism, Diplomacy, and Trade*, 174.

25. Chen Jiarong, *Gudai nanhai diming huiyi*, 541; *XTS*, 50:1152.

26. The Vụ Ôn Mountains, also known as the Vụ Thấp Mountains, are today called the Vụ Quang Mountains and are located in Vụ Quang District, Hà Tĩnh Province. Chinese scholars once placed the location of Wendan on the site of modern-day Vientiane, but the precise location of this kingdom's center has more recently been disputed. See Shen Fuwei, "Wedan guo yu Zhujiang guo xin-lun," 100–114. Cited in Fang Tie, "Tang Song liang chao zhi zhongnan bandao jiaotong xian de bianqian," xx.

27. *XTS*, 150:6283.

28. *XTS*, 50:1152.

29. Fan Ye notes in the *Hou Han Shu* that Liu Zhen's (fl. 2nd cent.) historical compilation *Dong Guan Han Ji* used the character *tan* for the Shan kingdom's name. See *HHS*, 80:2851.

30. *HHS*, 80:2851.

31. *HHS*, 80:2851. See also Duan Yu, *Nanfang sichou zhi lu yanjiu lunji*, 127.

32. *TPYL* 2:767:7a.

33. *DTXYJJZ*, vol. 10.

34. Zhou and Ding, eds., *Sichou zhi lu da cidian*, 745.

35. *XTS*, 150:6248.

36. Zhou and Ding, eds., *Sichou zhi lu da cidian*, 740.

37. Sharma, *Early Medieval Indian Society*, 257

38. Gray and Overby, "Introduction," 2.

39. Needham and Wang, *Science and Civilization in China*, 2:428.

40. As Sen notes, although Tangzong's court may have initiated a project to translate the *Daode Jing* in Sanskrit, and a 648 Tang embassy to Kāmarūpa may have presented this translated text as one of its gifts to the South Asian court, extant sources do not include clear conformation of a direct connection between one event and the other. Sen, *Buddhism, Diplomacy, and Trade*, 46.

41. Sen, *Buddhism, Diplomacy, and Trade*, 45.

42. Wu, "Xinan Sichou zhi lu yanjiu de renshi wuqu." 39.

43. Zhou and Ding, eds., *Sichou zhi lu da cidian*, 740.

44. For a recent discussion of this debate, see Dien, *Six Dynasties Civilization*, 395–97.

45. Sen, *Buddhism, Diplomacy, and Trade*, 239.
46. Borchert, "Worry for the Dai Nation," 109.
47. Bo, *Miandian shi*, 29. Cited in Li Xiaomei, "Nazhao, Daliguo he Miandian de Biaoguo, Pugan wang chao de guanxi," 177.
48. Mao, D., *Miandian Shi*, 30.
49. Li Xiaomei, "Nazhao, Daliguo he Miandian de Biaoguo, Pugan wang chao de guanxi," 177.
50. Duan Yuming, *Dali guoshi*, 332–33.
51. Toghto, *Songshi*, 412:12379.
52. Toghto, *Songshi*, 412:12380.
53. Goody, *The Oriental, the Ancient, and the Primitive Systems of Marriage and the Family in the Pre-Industrial Societies of Eurasia*, 362.
54. Scott, *The Art of Not Being Governed*, xx.
55. Backus, *The Nan-chao Kingdom and T'ang China's Southwestern Frontier*, 7.
56. Shi Di, *Shenhua yu fazhi*, 132.
57. Shi Di, *Shenhua yu fazhi*, 132.
58. Shi Di, *Shenhua yu fazhi*, 132.
59. Tapp, *The Hmong of China*, 146.
60. Meng Yuanlao's (fl. 1120s) *Dongjing Menghua lu*, vol. 6:2b. Accessed June 22, 2021, https://ctext.org/wiki.pl?if=gb&chapter=655186.
61. *SHY, Fanyi* 5:31
62. For another example, see Anderson, "Pearls and Power," 223–36.
63. Administered by a civilian supervisor (*tizhu*) with a constable (*xunjian*) and other officers posted here. Hengshan was located a seven-day trip from Yongzhou. See Chen Yirong, "Baiyue gudao de lishi wenhua kaocha," 107.
64. Curtin, *Cross-Cultural Trade in World History*, 108.
65. For a more detailed description of Hepu's role in the Maritime Silk Road, please see Gilbert, "Paper Trails."
66. Wink, *Al-Hind, the Making of the Indo-Islamic World*, 342.
67. Shaffer, "Southernization," 15–16.

2. Nanzhao and Dali Kingdoms as Multiethnic States

1. Because the high overhanging cliffs on each side of the river resemble two sides of a massive doorway, the pass was originally called "Stone Gate." In the Yuan period the pass was renamed Luozuo Pass (Luozuo Guan) and it retained this name through the Ming dynasty. In the Qing period the name Dousha came

from the Yi language pronunciation of *dou shao*, which referred to a local clan name. See Ding, *Zhongguo diming cidian*, 210.

2. Giersch, *Asian Borderlands*, 52.

3. For such views, please see Lewis, *China's Cosmopolitan Empire*, and Backus, *The Nan-chao Kingdom and T'ang China's Southwestern Frontier*.

4. Giersch, *Asian Borderlands*, 22.

5. Anderson, *The Rebel Den of Nùng Trí Cao*.

6. Shen, Xu, *Zhongguo xinan dui waiguan xishi yanjiu*, 130–31.

7. Lombard and Aubin, *Asian Merchants and Businessmen in the Indian Ocean and the China Sea*, 288. See also Xiangming Chen, *As Borders Bend*, 202.

8. Evans, Hutton, and Kuah, *Where China Meets Southeast Asia*, 210.

9. Sen, *Buddhism, Diplomacy, and Trade*, 174.

10. Sima Qian, *Shiji*, 123:3166. Cited in part in Nguyễn et al., eds., *Nguồn Gốc Lịch Sử Tộc Người Vùng Biên Giới Phía Bắc Việt Nam*, 84–85. See also Taishan Yu, "A History of the Relationship between the Chinese Dynasties and the Western Regions," 23.

11. The elephant breeding ground was located in modern-day Honghe Hani and Yi Autonomous Prefecture (Honghe Hani Zu Yizu Zizhizhou) and the southwestern areas of Yunnan. See Nguyễn et al., *Nguồn Gốc Lịch Sử Tộc Người Vùng Biên Giới Phía Bắc Việt Nam*, 84–85.

12. Sima Qian, *Shiji*, 123:3166.

13. Sima Qian, *Shiji*, 116:2997. See Wade, "The Polity of Yelang and the Origins of the Name 'China,'" 38.

14. Catherine Churchman contends that these conventional ethnonyms from imperial sources do not refer to specific ethnic groups, but rather the people associated with Bronze drum culture by Han chroniclers. See Churchman, *The People between the Rivers*, 9.

15. James Chamberlain contends that historical linguistic analysis provides evidence that the Li-Lao (or Rei-Kra) had entered the eastern Dong World prior to the Warring States period. See Chamberlain, "Kra-Dai and the Proto-History of South China and Vietnam," 50.

16. Clifford, "Traveling Cultures," 101; Clifford, *Returns*, 76.

17. The Bo people and the Yi people are both ethnic groups with strong historical ties to the Cuan clan.

18. The specific species is *S. nigrum* subsp. *nigrum*. See Zumbroich, "The Origin and Diffusion of Betel Chewing," 109. Other scholars contend that the plant was a type of black pepper. See Chandra and Jain, *Foundations of Ethnobotany*, 98.

19. Wang Yongqiang et al., eds., *Zhongguo shaoshu minzu wenhuashi tudian xinan juan*, 113.

20. Yang Jialuo, *Xin jiao ben Sanguo zhi*, 43:1045.

21. Swain, "Native Place and Ethnic Relations in Lunan Yi Autonomous County, Yunnan," 176.

22. Giersch, *Asian Borderlands*, 30.

23. Located near the modern-day city of Qujing in eastern Yunnan.

24. Located near modern-day Yiliang in Yunnan.

25. From this period we have inscriptional evidence of powerful local leadership in the form of two stelae now located in the courtyard of a Qujing Middle School: the "Cuan Baozi Stele" (Cuan Baozi Bei) and the "Cuan Longyan Stele" (Cuan Longyan Bei). See Wang Yongqiang et al., eds., *Zhongguo shaoshu minzu wenhuashi tudian xinan juan*, 123.

26. Qujing Municipal Historical Committee, *Qujing wenshi ziliao*, 7.

27. Wang Yongqiang et al., eds., *Zhongguo shaoshu minzu wenhuashi tudian xinan juan*, 123.

28. Wang Yongqiang et al., eds., *Zhongguo shaoshu minzu wenhuashi tudian xinan juan*, 123.

29. Wang Yongqiang et al., eds., *Zhongguo shaoshu minzu wenhuashi tudian xinan juan*, 123.

30. Feng, *Kaogu xuelun wenji*, 140.

31. Wang Yongqiang et al., eds., *Zhongguo shaoshu minzu wenhuashi tudian xinan juan*, 123.

32. Lin Chaomin, *Lin Chaomin wenji*, 223.

33. Mathieu, *A History and Anthropological Study of the Ancient Kingdoms of the Sino-Tibetan Borderland*, 411.

34. Toghto, *Songshi*, 186:6317.

35. Wei Zheng, *Sui shu*, 45:1241. Event noted in Giersch, *Asian Borderlands*, 31.

36. Wang Yongqiang et al., eds., *Zhongguo shaoshu minzu wenhuashi tudian xinan juan*, 123.

37. Stuart-Fox, *A Short History of China and Southeast Asia*, 49.

38. Giersch, *Asian Borderlands*, 31.

39. Wang Yongqiang et al., eds., *Zhongguo shaoshu minzu wenhuashi tudian xinan juan*, 123.

40. Smith, *Taxing Heaven's Storehouse*, 82.

41. *XTS*, 222:6267.

42. Wang Yongqiang et al., eds., *Zhongguo shaoshu minzu wenhuashi tudian xinan juan*, 123.

43. *XTS*, 222:6267.

44. Michaud, *Historical Dictionary of the Peoples of the Southeast Asian Massif*, 174. See also Aikhenvald and Dixon, *Areal Diffusion and Genetic Inheritance Problems in Comparative Linguistics*, 237.

45. Backus, *The Nan-chao Kingdom and T'ang China's Southwestern Frontier*, 66.

46. *Manshu*, Chinese Text Project, 4:63. The *XTS* account records the place name Kainan as "Guannan."

47. *Manshu*, Chinese Text Project, 4:63.

48. *Manshu*, Chinese Text Project, 4:63.

49. Bryson, *Goddess on the Frontier*, 24.

50. Zhang Qizhi, Zhang Guogang, and Yang Shusen, *Sui Tang Song shi*, 182–83.

51. Pan, *Son of Heaven and Heavenly Qaghan*, 259.

52. Lewis, *China's Cosmopolitan Empire*, 153.

53. Lewis, *China's Cosmopolitan Empire*, 155.

54. Lewis, *China's Cosmopolitan Empire*, 156.

55. Zhang Yunxia, "Rujia wei xiang zai Nnanzhao shehui de chuanbo," 12.

56. Du, *Tongdian*, 1:87.

57. Lin Chaomin, *Tangdai Yunnan de Han wenhua*, 169.

58. Zhang Yunxia, "Rujia wei xiang zai Nanzhao shehui de chuanbo," 14.

59. Lewis, *China's Cosmopolitan Empire*, 77.

60. Bryson, *Goddess on the Frontier*, 15.

61. *JTS*, 197:5281.

62. Pan, *Son of Heaven and Heavenly Qaghan*, 259. Zhou and Ding, eds., *Sichou zhi lu da cidian*, 759.

63. *JTS*, 197:5281.

64. Pan, *Son of Heaven and Heavenly Qaghan*, 325.

65. Nanzhao Dehua Bei (The Nanzhao Dehua Stele).

66. Song Lian, *Yuanshi*, 58:1457.

67. Li Qiuhua, "Tianbao zhanzheng hou Nanzhao de kuozhang ji yingxiang," 102, 104.

68. Li Qiuhua, "Tianbao zhanzheng hou Nanzhao de kuozhang ji yingxiang," 102, 104.

69. Bryson, *Goddess on the Frontier*, 30.

70. Lewis, *China's Cosmopolitan Empire*, 158.

71. Lewis, *China's Cosmopolitan Empire*, 158.

72. *JTS*, 197; 5281.

73. Zhou and Ding, eds., *Sichou zhi lu da cidian*, 757.

74. Lewis, *China's Cosmopolitan Empire*, 64.
75. Pan, *Son of Heaven and Heavenly Qaghan*, 336.
76. Xu Songshi claims that the "Yellow Grotto Barbarians," as well as Nùng Trí Cao and his followers, all belonged to the modern-day Zhuang ethnic group. Cited in Xu Songshi, *Yue jiang liu yu renmin shi*, 72. See also Schafer, *The Vermilion Bird*, 66.
77. Backus, *The Nan-chao Kingdom and Tang China's Southwestern Frontier*, 103–4.
78. Pan, *Son of Heaven and Heavenly Qaghan*, 341.
79. Pan, *Son of Heaven and Heavenly Qaghan*, 342.
80. Pan, *Son of Heaven and Heavenly Qaghan*, 342.
81. Li Yinbing, "*Manshu* ji qi shiliao jiazhi," 2.
82. Gordon Luce in his 1961 translation of this text notes that the *Manshu* was widely consulted during the Song period, but that the text appears to have disappeared by the Ming. See Oey and Luce, *The Man Shu*, 1.
83. Lewis, *China's Cosmopolitan Empire*, 158. Pan, *Son of Heaven and Heavenly Qaghan*, 342–44.
84. Li Yinbing, "*Manshu* ji qi shiliao jiazhi," 2.
85. Qujing Municipal Historical Committee, *Qujing wenshi ziliao*, 2–3.
86. Li Weizhen, "Daliguo yu Jiaozhi li chao de junshi zhiheng guanxi tanjiu," 154.
87. Fang Tie, "Dali guo de minzu zhidi he duiwai zhengce," xx.
88. Tambiah, *World Conqueror and World Renouncer*.
89. Toghto, *Songshi*, 496:14241.
90. *XTS*, 50:1151.
91. Nguyễn Chí Buyên et al., *Nguồn Gốc Lịch Sử Tộc Người Vùng Biên Giới Phía Bắc Việt Nam*, 88–89.
92. *XTS*, 150:6282.
93. *ZFZ*, 1:1.
94. I have used James Hargett's translation of this passage. See Fan Chengda and Hargett, *Treatises of the Supervisor and Guardian of the Cinnamon Sea*, 18.
95. "Hưng Hóa xứ phong thổ lục" (Account of Hưng Hóa's local customs), in *Hưng Hóa phong thổ chí*, 84. Cited in Nguyễn Chí Buyên et al., *Nguồn Gốc Lịch Sử Tộc Người Vùng Biên Giới Phía Bắc Việt Nam*, 89–90.
96. Nguyễn Chí Buyên et al., *Nguồn Gốc Lịch Sử Tộc Người Vùng Biên Giới Phía Bắc Việt Nam*, 98.
97. Nguyễn Chí Buyên et al., *Nguồn Gốc Lịch Sử Tộc Người Vùng Biên Giới Phía Bắc Việt Nam*, 98.
98. Nguyễn Chí Buyên et al., *Nguồn Gốc Lịch Sử Tộc Người Vùng Biên Giới Phía Bắc Việt Nam*, 98–99.

99. Li Weiwei and Wan Xuebo, "*Lüe guo shixing heping mulin youhao waijiao zhan-lüe de yuanyin tan lüe*, 10.

100. *XZZTJ*, 4:4b.

101. Li Weiwei and Wan Xuebo, "*Lüe guo shixing heping mulin youhao waijiao zhan-lüe de yuanyin tan lüe*, 10.

102. Meng Zhixiang was general of the Latter Tang who established the Latter Shu kingdom during the Five Dynasties period. The date noted in the *Dianshi* account doesn't appear to agree with Meng's biography.

103. Duan Yuming, *Dali guoshi*, 313.

104. Duan Yuming, *Dali guoshi*, 313.

105. Li Weiwei and Wan Xuebo, "*Lüe guo shixing heping mulin youhao waijiao zhan-lüe de yuanyin tan lüe*," 10.

106. Li Weizhen, "Daliguo yu Jiaozhi li chao de junshi zhiheng guanxi tanjiu," 150–51.

107. Li Weizhen, "Daliguo yu Jiaozhi li chao de junshi zhiheng guanxi tanjiu," 150.

108. Li Weizhen, "Daliguo yu Jiaozhi li chao de junshi zhiheng guanxi tanjiu," 151.

109. Modern scholars Li Xiaobin and Yuan Lihua carefully outlined the possible origins of the communities described as the "Golden Teeth." As Li and Yuan write, there "are basically two kinds of viewpoints. Firstly, most De'ang history scholars point out that the Golden Teeth, the Black Teeth, Mang Man and Bai Yi were synonyms of the Dai, which was the dominant ethnic group in the establishment of the Jinchi kingdom, based on the development of ethnic origins, customs and culture (Fang 1998: 19–21; You 1994: 187, 315; Jiang 1983: 97–99). Secondly, the Jinchi were not the ancestors of the Dai people, but it was a general term for the Wa-De'ang Language Branch in the Song and Yuan Dynasties. Meanwhile, the Golden Teeth were the ancestors of the Benglong (De'ang), Bulang and Wa people, who were the dominant nationalities in establishing the Jinchi kingdom (Yunnan Editorial Team 1987: 2)." Cited in Li Xiaobin and Yuan Lihua, "Historical Inheritance and the Construction of Historical Identity of Ethnic Groups in Mountainous Regions of Yunnan," 44.

110. Li Weizhen, "Daliguo yu Jiaozhi li chao de junshi zhiheng guanxi tanjiu," 152.

111. *DVSKTT*, 2:243.

112. Li Weizhen, "Daliguo yu Jiaozhi li chao de junshi zhiheng guanxi tanjiu," 152.

113. Li Weizhen, "Daliguo yu Jiaozhi li chao de junshi zhiheng guanxi tanjiu," 152.

114. Regarding this place name, the late scholar Fan Honggui wrote that in the Viet-namese chronicles *Việt Sử Lược* and *Khâm định Việt sử Thông giám cương mục* "the place of the fighting between the two kingdoms is named Kim Hoa Bộ 金華步 or Kim Hoa Bộ 金花步. Kim Hoa Bộ was classified as a *bộ* 步 ('position'),

which should be like the toponym 'Guyongbu' ('*Manshu*' volume 1) that historically described the location in a river basin, such as Hạ Bộ and Cẩm Điền Bộ
(*DVSKTT* Ngoại Kỷ, Quyển 5). Kim Hoa Bộ was located in Fanglin Prefecture,
indicating that this prefecture was located along a river." Cited in Fan, *Nong
Zhigao yanjiu ziliao ii*, xx.

115. *DVSKTT*, 2:151.
116. Fang Guoyu notes that Yang's name is also recorded in *Việt Sử Lược* as Du
     Changhui. See Fang, *Zhongguo xinan lishi dili kaoshi*, 1:700.
117. Li Weizhen, "Daliguo yu Jiaozhi li chao de junshi zhiheng guanxi tanjiu," 152.
118. The Dực Thánh Prince was the younger brother of Lý Công Uẩn. *DVSKTT*
     2:152. See Duan Yuming, *Dali guo shi*, 329. See also Li Weizhen, "Dali guo yu
     Jiaozhi li chao de junshi zhiheng guanxi tanjiu," 152–53.
119. Duan Yuming, *Dali guoshi*, 329.
120. Li Weizhen, "Daliguo yu Jiaozhi li chao de junshi zhiheng guanxi tanjiu," 153.
121. *SHY*, 4/30:7728.
122. *DVSKTT*, 2:152.
123. *SHY*, 4/30:7728.
124. *DVSKTT*, 2:152.
125. Li Weizhen, "Daliguo yu Jiaozhi li chao de junshi zhiheng guanxi tanjiu," 153.
126. Anderson, "China's Southwestern Silk Road in World History."
127. Faure, *Emperor and Ancestor*, 45.
128. Backus, *The Nan-chao Kingdom and Tang China's Southwestern Frontier*, 163.
     Cited in Wicks, *Money, Markets, and Trade in Early Southeast Asia*, 51.
129. Toghto, *Songshi*, 300:14072.
130. Fang Guoyu, *Zhongguo xinan lishi dili kaoshi*, 697–99.
131. The region administered by Dali's Zuining garrison in the southeastern part
     of the kingdom includes the western and southern portions of Temo Circuit,
     including Maguan County (modern-day Wenshan Prefecture). The area around
     Maguan County was at that time adjacent to and contested by the three domi-
     nant states: the Dali, the Đại Việt, and the Song.
132. Li Weizhen, "Daliguo yu Jiaozhi li chao de junshi zhiheng guanxi tanjiu," 155.
     See also Duan Yuming, *Dali Guoshi*, 45–46.
133. Only Chinese sources include the suggestion that the child changed his name to
     Triệu Trí Chi. Traditional Vietnamese accounts retain the name Ông Thân Lợi.
     Other titles attributed to him are Bình Hoàng and Bình Nguyên Đại Tướng.
134. *SHY*, 4/30:7735.
135. Li Xinchuan, *Jianyan yi lai chao ye zaji*, 752.

136. *DVSKTT*, 4:222–23.

137. Li Weizhen, "Dali guo yu Jiaozhi li chao de junshi zhiheng guanxi tanjiu," 155. See also Duan Yuming, *Dali guoshi*, 46.

138. Li Weizhen, "Dali guo yu Jiaozhi li chao de junshi zhiheng guanxi tanjiu," 155. See also Duan Yuming, *Dali guoshi*, 46.

139. You, "Zhengquan shiqi xinan bian jiang de minzu difang zhengquan," 55–62.

140. Longfan (Dragon Barbarian) was an ethnonym coined by the Song court for one of the ruling clans of Luodian. Doubtless, the clan did not identify itself in this manner.

141. Toghto, *Songshi*, 496:14241.

142. Toghto, *Songshi*, 496:14241. Such a personal audience with the emperor seems unlikely, given the protocol of that time.

143. Toghto, *Songshi*, 496:14241.

144. Guo and Wang, "The Significant Reform of the Administrative System in the National Borderlands in the Early Yuan Dynasty through the Evolution of the Areal Distribution of the Tribes of Five Surnames and Eight Surnames in the Song and Yuan Dynasty," 82–91.

145. *Guizhou tujing xinzhi*, 1:xx. Cited in You, *Zhonghua minzu fazhan shi*, 456.

146. Toghto, *Songshi*, 414:857.

147. Guo and Wang, "The Significant Reform of the Administrative System in the National Borderlands in the Early Yuan Dynasty through the Evolution of the Areal Distribution of the Tribes of Five Surnames and Eight Surnames in the Song and Yuan Dynasty," 82–91.

148. *Yizu jianshi*, 97. Cited in Bai Xingfa, "Ziqi guoshi shi kao shu," 37.

149. Bai Xingfa, "Ziqi guoshi shi kao shu," 38.

150. Bai Xingfa, "Ziqi guoshi shi kao shu," 38. This is my translation, but one can also see Jim Hargett's translation of this passage in Fan and Hargett, *The Supervisor and Guardian*, 189.

151. Bai Xingfa, "Ziqi guoshi shi kao shu," 38.

152. *VSL*, 161.

153. Li Weizhen, "Dali guo yu Jiaozhi li chao de junshi zhiheng guanxi tanjiu," 155. See also Duan Yuming, *Dali guoshi*, 46.

154. Toghto, *Songshi*, 300:14072.

155. Toghto, *Songshi*, 300:14072. See also *Songshi*, 186:4565.

156. Toghto, *Songshi*, 162:2235. Cited in Fang, "Tang Song liang chao zhi Zhongnan bandao jiaotong xian de bianqian," 106.

157. Fang, "Tang Song liang chao zhi Zhongnan bandao jiaotong xian de bianqian," 106.

158. *LWDD*, 51:122.

159. Toghto, *Songshi*, 186:4565.

160. Toghto, *Songshi*, 300:14072.

161. Toghto, *Songshi*, 300:14073.

162. Toghto, *Songshi*, 186:4565.

163. Toghto, *Songshi*, 186:4565.

164. Toghto, *Songshi*, 186:4565.

165. Anderson, "Trade Relations between the Đại Việt Kingdom and the Song Empire," 244.

166. Toghto, *Songshi*, 186:4565.

167. Faure, *Emperor and Ancestor*, 45.

168. Backus, *The Nan-chao Kingdom and Tang China's Southwestern Frontier*, 163; Wicks, *Money, Markets, and Trade in Early Southeast Asia*, 51.

169. *XTS*, 241:1.

170. Lewis, *China's Cosmopolitan Empire*, 158.

3. Đại Việt Kingdom's Engagement with the Dong World

1. Đàm, *Chính Sách Dân Tộc*, 5. The original quotation is as follows, "Nước Việt Nam là một. Dân tộc Việt Nam là một. Sông có thể cạn, núi có thể mòn, song chân lý ấy không bao giờ thay đổi."

2. Lentz, *Contested Territory*, 219–20.

3. Nguyễn et al., eds., *Nguồn Gốc Lịch Sử Tộc Người Vùng Biên Giới Phía Bắc Việt Nam*, 24.

4. The origins of the Văn Lang kingdom are deeply embedded in the Vietnamese nationalist narrative of the legendary Hùng kings (Hùng Vương); collaborating evidence for this polity is not substantial. Văn Lang is a Sino-Vietnamese term for this polity, which challenges the singular Tai origins for the state, at least as described in premodern Chinese and Vietnamese sources. See Maspero, "Études d'histoire d'Annam," and Ferlus, "Formation of Ethnonyms in Southeast Asia," 4.

5. Lã, "Quanh vấn đề An Dương Vương Thục Phán hay là truyền thuyết 'Cẩu chúa cheng vua' của đồng bào Tày." See also Kelley, "Tai Words and the Place of the Tai in the Vietnamese Past," 138.

6. Kelley, "Tai Words and the Place of the Tai in the Vietnamese Past," 138–39.

7. Churchman, *The People between the Rivers*, 34.

8. Đàm, *Chính Sách Dân Tộc*, 7–8.

9. Đàm, *Chính Sách Dân Tộc*, 9.

10. Đàm, *Chính Sách Dân Tộc*, 11.

11. Đàm, *Chính Sách Dân Tộc*, 9.

12. Đàm, *Chính Sách Dân Tộc*, 10.

13. Đàm, *Chính Sách Dân Tộc*, 10.

14. Đàm, *Chính Sách Dân Tộc*, 12.

15. Đàm, *Chính Sách Dân Tộc*, 12.

16. Đàm, *Chính Sách Dân Tộc*, 12.

17. These clans were the Bế, the Hà, the Hoàng, the Ma, the Nguyễn, the Nùng, and the Vy. See Anderson, *The Rebel Den of Nùng Trí Cao*, 164–65.

18. Hoàng Xuân Hãn, *Lý Thường Kiệt*, 85.

19. According to Nguyễn Chí Buyên, the Vi clan occupied the regions of Tú Lăng, Lộc Châu, Tư Bình (Guangxi), and Tô Mậu Prefecture (modern-day Đình Lập, Lạng Sơn). See Nguyễn et al., eds., *Nguồn Gốc Lịch Sử Tộc Người Vùng Biên Giới Phía Bắc Việt Nam*, 74.

20. Đàm, *Chính Sách Dân Tộc*, 18.

21. *XTS*, 222:6329. See also Anderson, "Commissioner Li and Prefect Huang," 37.

22. *XTS*, 222:6329.

23. *XTS*, 222:6330.

24. *XTS*, 222:6330.

25. *XTS*, 222:6330.

26. *XTS*, 222:6330.

27. *XTS*, 222:6330.

28. *XTS*, 222:6330.

29. *XTS*, 222:6330.

30. *XTS*, 222:6332.

31. *XTS*, 222:6332.

32. Taylor, *The Birth of Vietnam*, 240.

33. Đàm, *Chính Sách Dân Tộc*, 18.

34. Hoàng Xuân Hãn, *Lý Thường Kiệt*, 87.

35. Maspero, "Études d'histoire d'Annam," 37. Maspero notes that by the middle of the twelfth century the second kind of collective *châu* appears from the sources to have been renamed *trấn*. Cited in James A. Anderson and John K. Whitmore, *China's Encounters on the South and Southwest*, 113.

36. Hoàng Xuân Hãn, *Lý Thường Kiệt*, 89.

37. Hoàng Xuân Hãn, *Lý Thường Kiệt*, 97–98.

38. Anderson, *The Rebel Den of Nung Tri Cao*, 53.

39. Sometimes these alliances extended beyond this temporal realm. According to

the local history *Cao Bằng thực lục*, at the end of the Ma Chu dynasty (927–951) in the Twelve Warlord period, a Trần clan chief named "Duke Trần" (Trần Công) succeeded in controlling Ninh Sóc (modern-day Cao Bằng). Trần Công had a wife from the Hoàng clan, and their son was named Trần Triệu (*Cao Bằng thực lục*, 10b). According to the legend, Trần Triệu would develop physical features of the deer his mother loved to eat, but she raised him with great care. Trần Triệu's sons Trần Kiên and Trần Quý grew up to be spirit hunters and took their swords everywhere in search of demons. During the Lê dynasty, the court posthumously appointed Trần Kiên as Cai Cộng Đại Vương and Trần Quý as Đông Lan Đại Vương and established temples in their honor in Thanh Lâm in Cao Bằng. See Vũ and Phạm, *Việt Nam, kho tàng dã sử*, 342.

40. Hoàng et al., *Văn hoá truyền thống Tày-Nùng*, 82.
41. Lã, *Chế độ thổ ty Việt Nam*, 4.
42. Anderson, *The Rebel Den of Nung Tri Cao*, 76.
43. *DVSKTB*, 273.
44. Hoàng Xuân Hãn, *Lý Thường Kiệt*, 84.
45. Đàm, *Chính Sách Dân Tộc*, 19.
46. *KDVSTGCM*, 306.
47. Đàm, *Chính Sách Dân Tộc*, 19–20; Hoàng Xuân Hãn, *Lý Thường Kiệt*, 98.
48. *VSL*, 2/7b. Cited in Kelley, "Tai Words and the Place of the Tai in the Vietnamese Past," 144. See also Anderson, *The Rebel Den of Nùng Trí Cao*, 77.
49. Hoàng Xuân Hãn, *Lý Thường Kiệt*, 98.
50. *DVSKTT*, 258.
51. *KDDNHDSL*, 358.
52. Hoàng Xuân Hãn, *Lý Thường Kiệt*, 99.
53. *KDDNHDSL*, 398.
54. Đàm, *Chính Sách Dân Tộc*, 20.
55. Fang Tie, "Jian lun xinan sichou zhi lu," xx.
56. Yang Zuo, *Yunnan mai ma ji*, 117.
57. Li Weizhen, "Daliguo yu Jiaozhi li chao de junshi zhiheng guanxi tanjiu," 153.
58. Li Weizhen, "Daliguo yu Jiaozhi li chao de junshi zhiheng guanxi tanjiu," 153–54.
59. Li Weizhen, "Daliguo yu Jiaozhi li chao de junshi zhiheng guanxi tanjiu," 154.
60. Đàm, *Chính Sách Dân Tộc*, 20.
61. *DVSKTT*, 243.
62. *DVSKTT*, 260.
63. *DVSKTT*, 274. See also Nguyễn Thanh Bình, "Dai Viet Diplomatic Relations with Neighboring Countries under Lý Dynasty," 60.

64. *DVSKTT*, 228.

65. *DVSKTT*, 295. The *DVSKTT* account gives the place-name as Nông Prefecture.

66. *DVSKTT*, 302.

67. *DVSKTT*, 306.

68. *DVSKTT*, 112.

69. *DVSKTT*, 242.

70. *DVSKTT*, 243.

71. The younger brother of Lý Mỗ and Lý Công Uẩn.

72. The *Việt sử lược* account refers to him as Đỗ Trường Huệ.

73. *DVSKTT*, 244.

74. *DVSKTT*, 244.

75. The *Việt sử lược* account refers to Đại Nguyên Lịch as Đại Quang Lịch. *DVSKTT*, 246.

76. *DVSKTT*, 253–54.

77. Đàm, *Chính Sách Dân Tộc*, 22.

78. Lý Thái Tông's poem "Dữ tả hữu nghị sự" in *Thơ văn Lý Trần*, 248–52. See also *DVSKTT*, 248.

79. *DVSKTT*, 255.

80. *DVSKTT*, 258.

81. *Cao Bằng thực lục*, A. 1129–Hán Nôm, 4b. I have written at length about the Tai-speaking chief Nùng Trí Cao in my first monograph, but some mention of his role in Dong World politics bears repeating in this study.

82. *ZZTJCB*, 18:395.

83. *SHY*, Fanyi 5/73.

84. The location of the prefecture Thất Nguyên in *Khâm Định Việt Sử Thông Giám Cương Mục* is described this way: "during the Lý dynasty this prefecture was called Thất Nguyên, during the Lê dynasty it was called Thất Tuyền, and now [during the Nguyễn period] it is the Thất Khê District in Lạng Sơn." Cited in *KDVSTGCM*.

85. According to *KDVSTGCM*, Tư Lang Prefecture was located between Quảng Nguyên and Thất Tuyền. As noted in this text, "to the north of Thất Khê [formerly Thất Nguyên], there is Hạ Lang District of Cao Bằng Province, which in ancient times was called Tư Lang Prefecture." Cited in *KDVSTGCM*.

86. *ZZTJCB*, 18:396. *SHY*, Fanyi 5/73. See also Anderson, *The Rebel Den of Nùng Trí Cao*, 75.

87. Anderson, *The Rebel Den of Nùng Trí Cao*, 68.

88. *Cao Bằng thực lục*, 5a.

89. Anderson, *The Rebel Den of Nùng Trí Cao*, 90.

90. *DVSKTT*, 263.

91. *Cao Bằng thực lục*, 7a.

92. Anderson, *The Rebel Den of Nung Tri Cao*, 96.

93. Hoàng Xuân Hãn, *Lý Thường Kiệt*, 121.

94. *Cao Bằng thực lục*, 7a.

95. *Cao Bằng thực lục*, 9b.

96. Hoàng Xuân Hãn, *Lý Thường Kiệt*, 230–31.

97. Đàm, *Chính Sách Dân Tộc*, 25–26.

98. Đàm, *Chính Sách Dân Tộc*, 24.

99. *DVSKTT*, 277.

100. Lê and Phạm, "Cuộc Kháng Chiến Chống Tống Thế Kỷ XI," 109–17.

101. Lê and Phạm, "Cuộc Kháng Chiến Chống Tống Thế Kỷ XI," 109–17.

102. Anderson, *The Rebel Den of Nung Tri Cao*, 141.

103. Hoàng Xuân Hãn, *Lý Thường Kiệt*, 133–34.

104. Lê Thành Khôi, *Histoire du Viet Nam*, 159.

105. *DVSKTT*, 278.

106. *ZZTJCB*, 273:6679.

107. Toghto, *Songshi*, 17:289; *DVSKTT*, 278.

108. Toghto, *Songshi*, 17:289. Modern PRC sources contend that the site of the Peng clan's Xizhou Prefecture is the region of Laosicheng, which is an archaeological site in Sicheng Village, Lingxi Township, Yongshun County, Hunan. Other sources place Xizhou within modern-day Guangxi. A modern website devoted to the Peng clan contends that the family ruled their native Xixiang Prefecture from Peng Jian's adoption of the leadership role under the Latter Tang ruler Zhuangzong (Li Cunxu; r. 923–926) court in 923, shortly before the Song conquest of the Northern Zhou kingdom until the capitulation to Qing authorities of Peng Jingxuan in 1728. Accessed December 30, 2019, http://www.worldpeng .org/content/?1437.html.

109. *DVSKTT*, 278.

110. Today, there is a temple in Lũng Đính Village (Bản) in the northern region of Trùng Khánh (Cao Bằng), which is said to be the place to worship Hoàng Lục.

111. *ZZTJCB*, 277:6767.

112. *ZZTJCB*, 277:6774.

113. *ZZTJCB*, 277:6767.

114. Lê and Phạm, "Cuộc Kháng Chiến Chống Tống Thế Kỷ XI," 115.

115. Lê and Phạm, "Cuộc Kháng Chiến Chống Tống Thế Kỷ XI," 115.

116. Lê and Phạm, "Cuộc Kháng Chiến Chống Tống Thế Kỷ XI," 115.

117. Lê and Phạm, "Cuộc Kháng Chiến Chống Tống Thế Kỷ XI," 115.

118. Anderson, *The Rebel Den of Nùng Trí Cao*, 142.

119. *DVSKTT*, 278; Lê and Phạm, "Cuộc Kháng Chiến Chống Tống Thế Kỷ XI," 117.

120. Lê and Phạm, "Cuộc Kháng Chiến Chống Tống Thế Kỷ XI," 115.

121. Lê and Phạm, "Cuộc Kháng Chiến Chống Tống Thế Kỷ XI," 115.

122. Anderson, *The Rebel Den of Nùng Trí Cao*, 143.

123. Đàm, *Chính Sách Dân Tộc*, 26–27.

124. *KDVSTGCM*, 358.

125. *LTHCLC*, 279.

126. Sun, *Shuo zhoubian lishi hua jiangyu bianqian*, 659.

127. Lu, *Zhongguo jindai bianjie shi*, 823; Sun, *Shuo zhoubian lishi hua jiangyu bianqian*, 659.

128. Sun, *Shuo zhoubian lishi hua jiangyu bianqian*, 659.

129. Anderson, *The Rebel Den of Nùng Trí Cao*, 145–46.

130. *VSCMTY*, 134.

131. Sun, *Shuo zhoubian lishi hua jiangyu bianqian*, 659.

132. *KDVSTGCM*, 396.

133. *DVSKTT*, 313; *VSCMTY*, 129.

134. *DVSKTT*, 312; *VSCMTY*, 129.

135. *VSCMTY*, 129–31.

136. *DVSKTT*, 320.

137. *VSCMTY*, 172.

138. *DVSKTT*, Tập II, 46.

139. Đàm, *Chính Sách Dân Tộc*, 21.

140. *DVSKTT*, 40.

141. *DVSKTT*, Tập II, 115–16.

142. The Cao Bằng region in the early Lê dynasty was ruled as the Taiyuan commandary. During the Quang Thuận (1460–1469) reign period of Lê Thánh Tông, the region became a part of the Ninh Sóc Circuit, of which Cao Bằng was one of three regions. It was contested in the period of Mạc domination under Ming protection, and became part of the Mạc kingdom and in the kingdom's later period, the only territory directly controlled by the Mạc. In 1668 the territory returned to the Lê court under Emperor Huyền Tông (1663–1671) when it was administered for successive regimes as a township with four prefectures: Thạch Lâm, Quảng Uyên, Thượng Lãng, and Hạ Lãng. Cited in *An Nam Tạp Chí*, 27a.

143. Cao Bằng Television, "Thông tin về các Lễ hội trên địa bàn thành phố Cao Bằng năm 2018."

144. *DVSKTT*, 4:315.

145. *DVSKTT*, 4:316.

146. Đàm, *Chính Sách Dân Tộc*, 21.

4. Borderlands Engagement in the Song Period

1. Wu Jing, *Zhuzhou ji*, 1a–1b. See also Wu, "Lun Yongzhou hua Waizhuguo," *Quan Songwen*, 224:56.

2. Wu Jing used the antiquated Tang designation for Vietnam: the "Pacified South."

3. Wu Jing, "Lun Yongzhou hua Waizhuguo," *Quan Songwen*, 224:56.

4. Hengshan Township in modern-day Luchuan County, Guangxi.

5. Wu Jing, "Lun Yongzhou hua Waizhuguo," *Quan Songwen*, 224:56.

6. Anderson, *The Rebel Den of Nùng Trí Cao*, 42.

7. For the accusations, see Lorge, *War, Politics and Society in Early Modern China, 900–1795*, 32.

8. Lorge, "The Rise of the Martial," 134.

9. Zhao, *Wenwu zhi jian*, 20. Cited in Ng, "Su Jian shihuan shengya kao shu," 114–15.

10. Toghto, *Songshi*, 272:9318.

11. Toghto, *Songshi*, 272:9318.

12. *SHY*, zhiguan, 47/14.

13. Hucker wrote that the capital security commissioner (*huangchengshi*) was "a kind of secret service agency entrusted with maintaining peace and order in the dynastic capital, headed by a military officer or a eunuch having the Emperor's personal trust." See Hucker, *A Dictionary of Official Titles in Imperial China*, 261; Li Zhiliang, *Song liang Guang dajun shouchen yiti kao*, 333.

14. Tan Qilong, *Tanshi zongpu*, 152.

15. "Memorial from the Prefect of Jingjiangfu Council," Zhang Shi (1133–1180), in Wang Sen and Zhu Bian, eds., *Yuexi cong zai*, 4:26a–26b.

16. Chen Changqi, *Guangdong tong zhi*, 388; 23a.

17. Chen Changqi, *Guangdong tong zhi*, 388; 23a.

18. Blench, "The Spread of the Horse into Southeast Asia," 2; Bagley, *Ancient Sichuan*, 39; Wade, "The Horse in Southeast Asia prior to 1500 CE," 162; Clarence-Smith, "Breeding and Power in Southeast Asia Horses, Mules, and Donkeys in the Longue Durée," 32–33.

19. Lan, *Xinan lishi wehua dili*, 442

20. Qiongye is a shorthand for the Han-period southwestern Dong World (*nanyi*) regions of Qiongdu and Yedu. Sima Qian, *Shiji*, 129:3261. Cited in Lan, *Xinan lishi wehua dili*, 443. See also Xie, "Ye tan wu chi dao de kaitong ji qi dui xinan yi diqu shehui fazhan de yingxiang," 162–68.

21. Sima Qian, *Shiji*, 116: 2993. Cited in Lan, *Xinan lishi wehua dili*, 443.

22. *HHS*, 86:2847.

23. Lan, *Xinan lishi wehua dili*, 443.

24. Fan Zhuo, *Manshu*.

25. Smith, *Taxing Heaven's Storehouse*, 24.

26. Lan, *Xinan lishi wehua dili*, 443.

27. *LWDD*, 349.

28. Toghto, *Songshi* 198:5800.

29. Fan Chengda, *Fan Chengda biji liu zhong*, 106.

30. Li Xinchuan, *Jianyan yi lai chao ye zaji*, 428.

31. Liu, "Ziqi guo kaolue," 78–83.

32. The "Shaoxing Horse-Breeding Station," in Wang Yinglin's (1223–1296) encyclopedic work *Sea of Jade* (Yu hai), 79:394. Cited in Bai Xingfa, "Ziqi guoshi shi kao shu," 38.

33. Bai Xingfa, "Ziqi guoshi shi kao shu," 38.

34. *LWDD*, 186.

35. As Hok-Lam Chan noted, the Jurchen leadership had once been a great provider of horses in the north. But the Jurchen had noted in its horse trade with the Qidan (Liao) the importance of projecting military power, so that by the time of the Jurchen chief Yingge (1053–1103), they had stopped sending horses to the Liao court. The Song attempted to purchase horses from Jurchen sources as early as 961, but this trade ended in 991 when the Liao cut off trade, and the Song had little access to Jurchen horses after that period. See Chan, "Commerce and Trade in Divided China," 142–43. Smith, *Taxing Heaven's Storehouse*, 279.

36. *LWDD*, 349.

37. Toghto, *Songshi*, 198:4956.

38. Toghto, *Songshi*, 198:4956.

39. Toghto, *Songshi*, 198:4956.

40. An *yi* was a unit of weight equal to twenty or twenty-four *liang*.

41. At this time, a bolt of brocade sold for four hundred *yi* and rough silk (*shi*) sold for four thousand *yi*.

42. Toghto, *Songshi*, 198:4956.

43. Ma Rong, *Yongle dadian fangzhi jiyi*, 2856.

44. Toghto, *Songshi*, 198:4956.

45. Toghto, *Songshi*, 186:4565.

46. *SHY, bing*, 22/22.

47. *SHY*, 7155.

48. Li Xinchuan, *Jianyan yi lai chao ye zaji*, 18:427.

49. *Sima Guang, Zizhi Tongjian*, 113:2.

50. Toghto, *Songshi*, 198:4956.

51. Toghto, *Songshi*, 198:4956.

52. Carlin-type gold is found as fine participles in other minerals, such as pyrite, and it must be separated from these minerals by chemical means rather than sifting. Foster, *Gold Metallogeny and Exploration*, 219; Cui et al., "Copper Mineralization in the Western Longbohe Area, SE Yunnan, China: A Comparison with the Shengquan Copper Deposit, Vietnam," 369; Wang and Groves, "Carlin-Style Gold Deposits, Youjiang Basin, China," 909; Lei et al., "Current Gold Prospecting in China," 298–320.

53. *XTS*, 10:184.

54. *JTS*, 150:4012.

55. *LWDD*, 6:269.

56. Toghto, *Songshi*, 162:2240.

57. Zhu Wenhui and Wang Yuanlin, "Songdai Guang nanxi lu de san da bo yi chang he Hainan Dao de duiwai maoyi," 14.

58. Ma Duanlin, *Wenxian tongkao*, 180.

59. Zhou Hui, *Qingbo zazhi*, 357.

60. Ma Rong, *Yongle dadian fangzhi jiyi*, 2862.

61. Ma Rong, *Yongle dadian fangzhi jiyi*, 2862.

62. *ZZTJCB*, 312: 7573.

63. *ZZTJCB*, 312:7573.

64. Vogel, *Marco Polo Was in China*, 248.

65. Anderson and Whitmore, eds., *China's Encounters on the South and Southwest*, 7.

66. Cui Yuzhi, *Song chengxiang Cui Qingxian gong quan lu*, 8:94.

67. Toghto, *Songshi*, 977:2240.

68. Wang Xiangzhi, *Yudi jisheng*, 106:3242–43.

69. *LWDD*, 51:122–23.

70. *LWDD*, 87:193.

71. A variety of Arab glassware. See Wheatley, "Geographical Notes on Some Commodities in Sung Maritime Trade," 244.

72. Gharuwood incense was native to both Mainland and Island Southeast Asian kingdoms in the Song period, but the best quality came from the Upper Malay Peninsula. See Wheatley, "Geographical Notes on Some Commodities in Sung Maritime Trade," 236.

73. Reference found in Shibata and Koyas, *An English and Japanese Dictionary*, 796. Stalagmites, like stalactites, were collected for the medicinal use of their mineral deposits. See Fan Chengda and Hargett, *Treatises of the Supervisor and Guardian of the Cinnamon Sea*, 29–30.

74. Litharge is natural mineral form of lead monoxide, described in the Tang period text *Bencao gangmu* as a compound used in medicine and alchemy. See Schafer, "The Early History of Lead Pigments and Cosmetics in China," 418n3.

75. *Guihai yuheng zhi Guihai yuheng zhi*, 257. Fan Chengda and Hargett, *Treatises of the Supervisor and Guardian of the Cinnamon Sea*, 225–26. See also Wu Jing, *Zhuzhou ji*, 10:257.

76. Hong, "Guilin ku man" (The full storehouse in Guilin) in *Yi jian zhi*, 11:631.

77. *SHY*, 5/103. Cited in Bai Yaotian, "Tu guan yu tusi kao bian," 27. *SHY*, 5/40; *ZZT-JCB, juan* 247.

78. Zhang Shi was an associate of the Fujian native and Neo-Confucian Lixue scholar Hu Hong (1105–1161), and wrote the forward to Hu's collected volume *Wufeng hu xiansheng wenji* (The collected works of Mr. "Five Peaks" Hu).

79. Bai Xingfa, "Ziqi guoshi shi kao shu," 38.

80. Bai Xingfa, "Ziqi guoshi shi kao shu," 38.

81. See Zhang Shi's memorial from the eleventh month of 1175, on the Ziqi kingdom in Bi Yuan's *Xu Zizhi tongjian* (Continuation of *The comprehensive mirror to aid in government*), 145:796.

82. Unless otherwise noted, the administrative and biographical information come from the Qing gazetteer Jin Hong, Qian Yuanchang, and Lu Lun, (Yongzheng period), *Guangxi Tongzhi* (Guangxi gazetteer), *juan* 51:52b–55b. Online *SKQS* (Wenyuange ed.), accessed November 20, 2011.

83. Toghto, *Songshi*: 481:13931.

84. Toghto, *Songshi*: 481:13931.

85. Toghto, *Songshi*: 481:13931.

86. Toghto, *Songshi*: 481:13931.

87. Ge, *An Intellectual History of China*, 152.

88. *XZZTJ*, 7:31.

89. *XZZTJ*, 10:51.

90. Cao Keming, a native of Baizhang District, Yazhou (modern-day Ya'an, Sichuan), received the appointment during the Jingde (1004–1008) reign period.
91. Toghto, *Songshi* 255:9317.
92. Toghto, *Songshi* 255:9317.
93. Toghto, *Songshi* 255:9317.
94. Toghto, *Songshi* 255:9317.
95. Toghto, *Songshi* 255:9317.
96. Toghto, *Songshi* 255:9317.
97. Those ten prefectures included Yizhou, Rongzhou, Guizhou, Shaozhou, Liuzhou, Xiangzhou, Yongzhou, Qinzhou, Lianzhou, and Baizhou.
98. Fushui Prefecture was located between modern-day Sandu Shui Autonomous County (Sandu Shuizu Zizhixian) in Guizhou and Huanjiang Maonan Autonomous County (Huanjiang Maonanzu Zizhixian) in Guangxi Zhuang Autonomous Region.
99. Toghto, *Songshi* 255:9317.
100. Toghto, *Songshi* 255:9317.
101. Toghto, *Songshi* 255:9317.
102. Toghto, *Songshi* 255:9318.
103. Toghto, *Songshi* 255:9318.
104. Lianzhou is modern-day Licheng, a district of Quanzhou, Fujian.
105. *SHY, li* 20/39.
106. The stele was titled "Gao Zhu, Li Xiaozhong, deng si ren Nanxi Shan timing." Guilin Shi Wenwu Guanli Weiyuanhui, *Guilin shike*, 70.
107. Qujiang is the modern-day Qujiang District of Shaoguan, Guangdong. *Nanning fu zhi* (Jiajing 43), 6:28b–29a.
108. *Nanning fu zhi* (Jiajing 43), 6:29a.
109. Toghto, *Songshi*, 488:6676.
110. The Song period Guangnan West Circuit included the following prefectures: Guizhou, Rongzhou, Yongzhou, Xiangzhou, Rongzhou, Zhaozhou, Wuzhou, Tengzhou, Gongzhou, Xunzhou, Guizhou, Liuzhou, Yizhou, Bingzhou, Kangzhou, Hengzhou, Huazhou, Gaozhou, Leizhou, Baizhou, Qinzhou, Zhelinzhou, Lianzhou, Qiongzhou, Changhuazhou, Wan'an Army, and Zhuyazhou. *SHY*, SH 19:48110.
111. Toghto, *Songshi*, 186:4564.
112. Li Weizhen, "Daliguo yu jiaozhi li chao," 149.
113. *DVSKTT*, 4:323. Toghto, *Songshi*, 488:14071.
114. Li Weizhen, "Daliguo yu jiaozhi li chao," 149.

115. Jiangdong Village is modern-day Gaoshang Township, Xing'an County, Guilin. Zhongguo Renmin Zhengzhi Xieshang Huiyi, *Xing'an wen shi zi liao*, 60.

116. Zhongguo Renmin Zhengzhi Xieshang Huiyi, *Xing'an wen shi zi liao*, 62.

117. *SHY*, *bing* 22/24.

118. Toghto, *Songshi*, 255:11670.

119. Dayu is modern-day Dayu County, Jiangxi. Lin Fu and Huang Zuo, *Guangxi tong zhi*, 51:53b.

120. Lin Fu and Huang Zuo, *Guangxi tongzhi*, 51:53b.

121. *SHY*, *shiguan* 72/18.

122. Zhangxi is modern-day Xiapu, Fujian. Lin Fu and Huang Zuo, *Guangxi tongzhi*, 51:53b.

123. *Zhejiang tongzhi*, 125:12109; Bi Yuan, *XZZTJ*, 150:824.

124. Modern-day Haicang, Zhangzhou, near Xiamen.

125. *SHY*, *zhiguan* 41/62.

126. *SHY*, *xingfa* 4/59.

127. *Zhejiang tongzhi*, 126:1231.

128. Wang Hongpeng, *Zhongguo lidai wu zhuangyuan*, 119.

129. Ningdu is modern-day Yingdi Village, Huangshi Township, Ningdu County, Jiangxi.

130. Longxi is in modern-day Fujian.

131. Huang Zhongzhao, *Hongzhi Bamin tongzhi*, 71:4827.

132. Huang Zhongzhao, *Hongzhi Bamin tongzhi*, 71:4827.

133. Fuqing is in modern-day Fujian.

134. Huang Zhongzhao, *Hongzhi Bamin tongzhi*, 64:4827.

135. Liu Kezhuang, *Houcun xian sheng da quan ji*, 155:4.

136. Liu Kezhuang, *Houcun xian sheng da quan ji*, 155:4.

137. Minxian is modern-day Minhou, Fujian.

5. Dong World in the Face of Mongol Expansion

1. Huang Kuan-chung, "*Wan Song junqing souji yu chuandi*," 136.

2. Li Tianming, *Song Yuan zhan shi*, 640.

3. Rossabi, *Khubilai Khan*, 24.

4. Rossabi, *Khubilai Khan*, 25.

5. Zhang Xilu, "Yuan shizu hu bi lie mie dali guoshi shi kao," 7.

6. Xia, *Yuandai Yunnan shi di congkao*, 108. See also Song Lian, *Yuanshi*, 4:59.

7. Zhang Xilu, "Yuan shizu hu bi lie mie dali guoshi shi kao," 5.

8. Li Tianming, *Song Yuan zhan shi*, 643.

9. Rossabi, *Khubilai Khan*, 25.

10. Shi Jianjun, "Hubilie zheng Dali luxian xinkao," 150.

11. Rossabi, *Khubilai Khan*, 25

12. In his book, John Herman named these groups as the Azhe (the Luodian kingdom), Awangren (the Ziqi kingdom), Bole, Chele, Wumeng, Mangbu, and Wusa clans. See Herman, *Amid the Clouds and Mist*, 48.

13. Herman, *Amid the Clouds and Mist*, 48.

14. Grousset, *The Empire of the Steppes*, 284.

15. B. Yang, *Between Winds and Clouds*, 93–94.

16. Herman, *Amid the Clouds and Mist*, 48.

17. John Herman identifies the Wuman collectively as the Nasu Yi ethnic group.

18. Zhang Xilu, "Yuan shizu hu bi lie mie dali guoshi shi kao," 6.

19. Huang Kuan-chung, "Wan Song junqing souji yu chuandi," 136.

20. Yang Shiqi and Huang Hai, *Lidai mingchen zouyi*. Cited in Li Tianming, *Song Yuan zhan shi*, 639.

21. Li Tianming, *Song Yuan zhan shi*, 640.

22. Li Tianming, *Song Yuan zhan shi*, 640–41.

23. Huang Kuan-chung, "Wan Song junqing souji yu chuandi," 134. See also Toghto, *Songshi*, 420:12574.

24. Huang Kuan-chung, "Wan Song junqing souji yu chuandi," 136.

25. Huang Kuan-chung, "Wan Song junqing souji yu chuandi," 142.

26. Li Zengbo, *Kezhai zagao*, 5:19.

27. Huang Kuan-chung, "Wan Song junqing souji yu chuandi," 142.

28. Li Tianming, *Song Yuan zhan shi*, 1507.

29. Li Tianming, *Song Yuan zhan shi*, 1641.

30. Huang Kuan-chung, "Wan Song junqing souji yu chuandi," 147.

31. Li Tianming, *Song Yuan zhan shi*, 1641.

32. Li Tianming, *Song Yuan zhan shi*, 1622–23.

33. Li Zengbo, *Kezhai zagao*, 5:16–17.

34. Huang Kuan-chung, "Wan Song junqing souji yu chuandi," 144–45.

35. In the *Songshi* account, Trần Cảnh (Trần Thái Tông, 1218–1277) is described as Trần Thủ Độ's son-in-law. Vietnamese accounts more accurately described Trần Cảnh as his nephew. *DVSKTT* (1984), 5:321.

36. Anderson, "Frontier Management and Tribute Relations along the Empire's Southern Border," 354.

37. Song Lian, *Yuanshi*, 166:3910. Cited in Duan Yuming, "Dali guozhun zhidu kaolüe," 34.

38. Zhang Jinlian, "Songchao yu Annan tongdao shikao," 66.

39. *DVSKTT*, 5:338.

40. *DVSKTT*, 5:339.

41. *DVSKTT*, 5:339.

42. Song Lian, *Yuanshi*, 209:4635.

43. Song Lian, *Yuanshi*, 209:4639.

44. Song Lian, *Yuanshi*, 129:3152.

45. Zheng Sixiao, *Xinshi*, 70. Cited in Huang Fei, "Lun Yuan Hubilie chao dui An-nan de zhengfa," 95.

46. Song Lian, *Yuanshi*, 209:4640.

47. *DVSKTT*, 5:354.

48. *DVSKTT*, 5:356.

49. *DVSKTT*, 5:356.

50. *DVSKTT*, 5:357.

51. Ngô, *Việt Nam Văn Học*, 104.

52. *DVSKTT*, 5:357.

53. *DVSKTT*, 5:357.

54. The upland districts listed in the *DVSKTT* account are: Bàng Hà, Na Sầm, Trà Hương, Yên Sinh, and Long Nhãn, among others (*DVSKTT*, 5:357). The *DVSKTT* account claims that two hundred thousand militiamen were assembled to converge on the Vạn Kiếp garrison.

55. Song Lian, *Yuanshi*, 209:4643.

56. *DVSKTT*, 5:358.

57. Song Lian, *Yuanshi*, 209:4644.

58. Phan et al., *Văn Khắc Hán Nôm Việt Nam*, 2:174.

59. Phan et al., *Văn Khắc Hán Nôm Việt Nam*, 2:176, 180–81.

60. *DVSKTT*, Bản Kỷ, 5:46b. Cited in Phan et al., *Văn Khắc Hán Nôm Việt Nam*, 2:174.

61. *ANCL*, 312. See also *DVSKTT*, 5:358.

62. *DVSKTT*, 5:358.

63. *DVSKTT*, 5:359.

64. *DVSKTT*, 5:359.

65. Song Lian, *Yuanshi*, 129:3159. *DVSKTT*, 5:360.

66. *DVSKTT*, 5:361.

67. *DVSKTT*, 5:361.

68. Song Lian, *Yuanshi*, 209:4647. *DVSKTT*, BK 5:362.

69. *DVSKTT*, 5:362.

70. Song Lian, *Yuanshi*, 209:4647.

71. Song Lian, *Yuanshi*, 209:4648.

72. Xu Mingshan, *Annan xingji*, preserved in *Shuofu, juan* 51. Compiled by Tao Xiongyi (1370). *Biji xiaoshuo daguan* ed. Cited in Huang Fei, "Lun Yuan Hubilie chao dui Annan de zhengfa," 96.

73. Lo, "The Controversy over Grain Conveyance during the Reign of Qubilai Qaqan, 1260–94," 282.

74. *DVSKTT*, 5:363.

75. Song Lian, *Yuanshi*, 209:4648.

76. *DVSKTT*, 5:363

77. *ANCL*, 335.

78. Chen Gaohua, *Yuanshi yanjiu lun gao*, 235.

79. Huang Fei, "Lun Yuan Hubilie chao dui Annan," 96.

80. Song Lian, *Yuanshi*, 15:320.

81. Song Lian, *Yuanshi*, 209:4650.

82. Song Lian, *Yuanshi*, 417:277.

83. Wang Sen, *Yuexi cong zai*, 27:11a.

84. Huang Chengshou, *Guangxi minzu guanxi de lishi yu xianzhuang*, 92.

85. Wei Yuan, *Yuanshi xinbian*, 13:9a.

86. Excerpt of Oliver Wolters's translation of Phạm Sư Mạnh's poem "Thượng Ngao" in Wolters and Reynolds, *Early Southeast Asia*, 216.

87. Wolters, *Monologue, Dialogue, and Tran Vietnam*, 57.

Conclusion

1. Song Lian, *Yuanshi*, 149:3521.

2. Guo Songnian, "Zhongqinglu ruxueji" (Notes on Zhongqing Circuit Confucianism), in *Dali Xingji*; Liu Wenwei, *Dianzhi, juan* 20.

3. Fang Tie, "Hubilie yu Yunnan," 34.

4. Fang Tie, "Hubilie yu Yunnan," 39.

5. Anderson and Whitmore, *China's Encounters on the South and Southwest*, 30.

6. Herman, "Empire in the Southwest," 48.

7. Anderson and Whitmore, *China's Encounters on the South and Southwest*, 32.

8. Hein and Zhao, "The Cultural Other and the Nearest Neighbor," 275–76.

9. Thant, *The River of Lost Footsteps*, 100.

10. Ma J. and Ma C., "The Mule Caravans as Cross-Border Networks," 243.

11. *Qingshilu, juan* 13, "Xuantong zhengji" in Gu Yongji, "Ming Qing shiqi Yunnan

Daizu diqu de jiaoyu fazhan ji tedian," 148; Anderson and Whitmore, *China's Encounters on the South and Southwest*, 40.

12. Giersch, *Asian Borderlands*, 97.

13. Davis, *Imperial Bandits*, 93.

14. Giersch, *Corporate Conquests*, 56.

15. Giersch, *Corporate Conquests*, 133.

16. Giersch, *Corporate Conquests*, 142.

17. Cai served as an inspiration for Zhu De (1886–1976), who later became one of the most successful military leaders of the Chinese Red Army, the forerunner to the People's Liberation Army.

18. Smith, *Taxing Heaven's Storehouse*, especially chap. 16.

19. Giersch, *Corporate Conquests*, 4.

20. Lentz, *Contested Territory*, 3.

21. For a description of this project, see Kuik, Lampton, and Ho, *Rivers of Iron*.

Appendix 1

1. In the Han period the route was called the Ling Mountain Pass Route (Lingguan Dao) or the Western Yi Indigenes Route (Xiyi Dao). In the Tang the route was called the Qingxi Mountain Pass Route (Qingxiguan Dao). See Zhou and Ding, eds., *Sichou zhi lu da cidian*, 739. For the suggested translation of *Shendu Guo* as *Sindhu*, see Chanda, *Bound Together*, 151.

2. B. Yang, "Horses, Silver, and Cowries," 298.

3. The Bo people and the Yi people are both ethnic groups with strong historical ties to the Cuan people.

4. In the region around Zhuti, the Cui clan was another powerful local family with influence over the political and the trade activities. The Cui clan's best-known patriarch, Cui Chengsi (fl. fourth century), served the Jin court during the Tai-yuan period (376–396). Cui Chengsi's tomb was unearthed in 1963, revealing a wealth of material objects and inscriptional evidence that pointed to the prominence this area had along the trade routes of that time. See Zhou and Ding, eds., *Sichou zhi lu da cidian*, 756.

5. Administered by a civilian supervisor (*tizhu*) with a constable (*xunjian*); other officers were posted here as well. Hengshan was a seven-day trip from Yong-zhou. See Chen Yirong, "Baiyue gudao de lishi wenhua kaocha," 107.

6. *SHY, Fanyi*, 5:65.

7. Tangxing is modern-day Tangxing District, located northwest of Baise in central Guangxi.

8. Suidian was located northwest of modern-day Baise.

9. Qiyuan was located in modern-day Leli Township, Tianlin District, northwest Baise. The *Lingwai Daida* notes indicated that in the Song period there were two Qiyuan prefectures (p. 123). See Chen Yirong, "Baiyue gudao de lishi wenhua kaocha," 103–4.

10. Sicheng Prefecture was located in the Yao Autonomous District of Lucheng in today's Lingyun County, Guangxi (*LWDD*, 123, notes).

11. Guna was located in Bantao Township, Tianlin District.

12. Anlong was located in Jiuzhou Township, northwest of Tianlin District.

13. Fengcun Mountain was located in Shali Township in the Autonomous Longlin District.

14. Shangzhan was located in southwestern Guizhou, in Qiaoma Township, Miao Autonomous Ceheng District.

15. Bowen Ridge was located in modern-day Xin'an Township, Anlong District.

16. Luofu was located northeast of modern-day Baling Township, northeast Xingren County.

17. Moju was located northeast of Baide Township, Xingren County.

18. The Ziqi kingdom was located in an area covering southwestern Guizhou and eastern Yunnan.

19. Gucheng is the Dali kingdom's Shicheng Commandary, located near modern-day Qujing. It was given the name Shicheng by the Meng clan and made a commandary at this time.

20. Shanchanfu is modern-day Kunming city.

21. Zhu Annu, "Lun Nanzhao Dali guo shiqi nanfang sichou zhi lu de wenhua tedian," 8.

Appendix 2

1. Toghto, *Songshi*, 496:14241.

2. *Tư liệu về lịch sử và Xã hội dân tộc Thái*, 177. Cited in Nguyễn Chí Buyên et al., *Nguồn Gốc Lịch Sử Tộc Người Vùng Biên Giới Phía Bắc Việt Nam*, 88–89.

BIBLIOGRAPHY

This section lists primary and secondary sources separately. In this work, a primary source includes all sources written prior to the twentieth century, with the exception of sources written by local historians prior to 1975 in Vietnam. Secondary sources include all works by professional scholars written since the beginning of the twentieth century.

Primary Sources

Anonymous. *Việt sử lược* 越史略 (History of the Việt; *VSL*). Translated and annotated by Trần Quốc Vượng. Hà Nội: NXB văn su dia, 1960.

Ban Gu 班固 (32–92). *Hanshu* 漢書 (History of the Han). Beijing: Zhonghua Shuju, 1962.

Bi Yuan 畢沅 (1730–1797). *Xu Zizhi tongjian* 續資治通鑑 (Continuation of *The comprehensive mirror to aid in government*). *Sibu beiyao*, vol. 264. Taipei: Taiwan Zhonghua Shuju, 1965.

Cao Bằng thực lục 高平實錄 (The veritable records of Cao Bằng). *Institute of Sino-Nom studies library number*: A. 1129. Hán Nôm Institute Manuscript.

Chen Changqi 陳昌齊 (1743–1820). Annotated by Ruan Yuan 阮元 (1764–1849). *[Daoguang] Guangdong tongzhi* [道光]廣東通志 (General gazetteer Guangdong Province). 334 *juan*. China, 1864.

Cui Yuzhi 崔與之 (1158–1239). *Song chengxiang Cui Qingxian gong quan lu* 宋丞相崔清獻公全錄 (Complete record of Song prime minister Cui Qingxian). Guangzhou: Guangdong Renmin Chubanshe, 2008.

Dai Jing 戴璟 (*jinshi* 1526) and Yue Zhang 張岳等. *Guangdong tongzhi chugao* 廣東通志初稿 (Preliminary draft of the General gazetteer of Guangdong). 40 *juan*. Beijing: Shumu Wenxian, 1988.

Đặng Xuân Bảng 鄧春榜 (1828–1910). *Việt sử cương mục tiết yếu* 越史綱目節要 (An outline history of the Việt; *VSCMTY*). Annotated by Hoàng Văn Lâu. Hà Nội: Nhà xuất bản Khoa học xã hội, 2000.

Du You 杜佑 (735–812). *Tongdian* 通典 (Comprehensive institutions). Beijing: Zhonghua Shuju, 1988.

Fan Chengda 范成大 (1126–1193). *Fan Chengda biji liu zhong* 范成大筆記六種 (Six kinds of notes from Fan Chengda). Annotated by Kong Fanli. Beijing: Zhonghua Shuju, 2002.

———. *Guihai yuheng zhi* 桂海虞衡志 (Well-balanced records of the Cassia Sea). Chengdu: Sichuan Minzu Chubanshe, 1986.

Fan Ye 范曄. *Houhanshu* 後漢書 (History of the Latter Han; *HHS*). Beijing: Zhonghua Shuju, 1965.

Fan Zhuo. *Manshu* 蠻書 (History of the southern indigenes) edited by the Palace Museum Library, translated by Walter Stanish, "Translation: Manshu/Chapter 7," Wikisource. Accessed May 17, 2020. https://en.wikisource.org/w/index.php ?title=Translation:Manshu/Chapter_7&oldid=7065038.

Fu Wanglu 傅王露 (jinshi 1715) and Li Wei 李衛. *Zhejiang Tongzhi* 浙江通志 (Complete Gazetteer of Zhejiang). 280 juan. Shanghai: Shuangwu chubanshe, 1934.

Gu Yanwu 顧炎武 (1613–1682). *Tianxia junguo libing shu* 天下郡國利病書 (Regarding the benefits and shortcomings of the empire's local administration). *Yunnan* section 2. Zongqiuerlinzhaizangban lithograph edition. Beijing: Beitu jichengju, Guangxu 27 (1901).

Guizhou tujing xinzhi 貴州圖經新志 (New illustrated gazetteer of Guizhou). 17 *juan*. Chengdu: Bashu Shushe, 2006.

Guo Fei 郭棐 (1529–1605). *Yue da ji* 粵大記 (Great record of the Yue region). Edited by Huang Guosheng 黃國聲 and Deng Guizhong 鄧貴忠. Guangzhou: Guangdong Renmin Chubanshe, 2014.

Guo Songnian 郭松年 (active 13th cent.–14th cent.). *Dali xingji* 大理行記 (Travels to Dali). Beijing: Zhonghua Shuju, 1991.

Hong Mai 洪邁 (1123–1202). *Rong zhai suibi* 容齋隨筆 (Rongzhai essays) Shanghai: Shanghai Guji Chubanshe, 1978.

———. *Yi jian ding zhi* 夷堅丁志 (Ding section of *The record of the listener*). Beijing: Zhonghua Shuju, 1985.

———. *Yi jian zhi* 夷堅志 (The record of the listener). 4 vols. Beijing: Zhonghua, 2006.

Huang Zhongzhao 黃仲昭 (fl. 1485–1491), ed. *Hongzhi Bamin tongzhi* 弘治八閩通志

(Hongzhi period general gazetteer of Bamin). 87 *juan*. Taipei: Taiwan Xuesheng Shuju, 1987.

Hưng Hóa phong thổ chí 興化風土志 (Gazetteer of Hưng Hóa). Cảnh Hưng 39 (1778) *Institute of Sino-Nom studies library number*: A.974. Hán Nôm Institute Manuscript.

Lê Tắc 黎崱. *An Nam Chỉ Lược* 安南志略 (Chronicles of An Nam; *ANCL*). Beijing: Zhonghua Shuju, 1995.

Li Fang 李昉 (925–996). *Taiping yulan* 太平御覽 (Readings of the Taiping era; *TPYL*). Song edition. Beijing: Zhonghua Shuju edition. 1998.

———. *Taiping yulan* 太平御覽 (Readings of the Taiping era; *TPYL 2*). 1000 *juan*. Jiaqing 12–17 (1807–1812) edition.

Li Jifu 李吉甫 (758–814). *Yuanhe junxian tuzhi* 元和郡縣圖志 (Treatise on all districts from the Yuanhe reign period [806–820]). Beijing: Zhonghua Shuju, 1983.

Li Shihua 黎士華 and Zhang Xianxiang 張顯相. *Pingnan xian zhi* 平南縣志 (Pingnan County gazetteer). 22 *juan*. Guangxi, 1835.

Li Tao 李燾 (1115–1184). *Xu Zizhi tongjian changbian* 續資治通鑑長編 (Continuation of *The Mirror of Government*; *ZZTJCB*). Beijing: Zhonghua Shuju, 1985.

Li Xiling 李熙齡 (*jinshi* 1829). *Yulin fu zhi* 榆林府志 (Yulin Prefecture gazetteer). 50 *juan*. Taipei: Taiwan Xuesheng Shuju, 1968.

Li Xinchuan 李心傳 (1167–1244). *Jianyan yi lai chao ye zaji* 建炎以來朝野雜記 (Miscellaneous notes on official and unofficial politics since the Jianyan reign period [1127–1130]). Beijing: Zhonghua Shuju, 2000.

Li Zengbo 李曾伯 (1198–?). *Kezhai zagao* 可齋雜稿 (Miscellaneous manuscripts of Kezhai). Taipei: Shangwu Chubanshe, 1970.

Lin Fu 林富 and Huang Zuo 黃佐, (Jiajing r.p., 嘉靖). *Guangxi tongzhi jiajing* 廣西通志嘉靖 (General gazetteer of Guangxi). 60 *juan*. Jinan: Qilu Shushe, 1997.

Ling Dizhi 凌迪知 (*jinshi* 1556). *Wan xing tongpu* 萬姓統譜 (General register of the ten thousand surnames). 140 *juan*. Taipei: Xinxing Shuju, 1971.

Liu Kezhuang 劉克莊 (1187–269). *Houcun xian sheng da quan ji* 後村先生大全集 (Complete works of Mr. Houcun). Taipei: Taiwan Shangwu Yinshuguan, 1979.

Liu Wenwei 劉文徵 (1555–1626). *Dianzhi* 滇志 (Gazetteer of Dian). 33 *juan*. Shanghai: Shanghai Guji Chubanshe, 1995.

Liu Xu 劉昫. *Jiutang shu* 舊唐書 (Old history of the Tang; *JTS*). Beijing: Zhonghua Shuju, 1975.

Liu Xun 劉恂 (10th cent.). *Lingbiao luyi* 嶺表錄異 (The records of the unusual from Lingnan). Congshu Jicheng edition. Shanghai: Shangwu Yinshuguan, 1936.

Ma Duanlin 馬端臨 (1245–1322). *Wenxian tongkao* 文獻通考 (Comprehensive investigations based on literary and documentary sources). Beijing: Zhonghua, 1986.

Meng Yuanlao 孟元老 (fl. 1120s). *Dongjing Menghua lu* 東京夢華錄 (Dreams from the Eastern Capital). Chinese Text Project online database.

Ngô Sĩ Liên 吳士連. *Đại Việt sử ký toàn thư* 大越史記全書 (Complete book of the history of the Great Việt; *DVSKTT*). *Bản in nội các quan bản—Mộc bản khắc năm chính hòa thứ 18* (1697). Hà Noi: Nhà Xuat Bản Khoa Học Xã Hôi, 1993.

———. *Đại Việt sử ký toàn thư* 大越史記全書 (Complete book of the history of the Great Việt). Edited by Chen Jinghe 陳荊和. Vol. 1. Tokyō: Tōkyō Daigaku Tōyō Bunka Kenkyūjo Fuzoku Tōyōgaku Bunken Sentā, 1984.

Ngô Thì Sĩ 吳時仕 (1726–1780) and Lê Văn Bảy. *Đại Việt sử ký tiền biên* 大越史記續編 (Continuation of *The History of the Great Viet*; *DVSKTB*). Hà Noi: Nhà xuất bản Văn hóa thông tin, 2011.

Nguyễn Hữu Cung 阮祐恭 (fl. 19th cent.). *Cao Bằng Thực Lục* 高平實錄 (Record of affairs in Cao Bằng). 1810 (Gia Long 10). *Institute of Sino-Nom studies library number*: VHc 1438. Hán Nôm Institute Manuscript.

Nguyễn Tụy Trân 阮萃珍 (fl. 20th cent.). *Đại Việt Cổ Kim Diên Cách Địa Chí Kảo* 大越古今沿革地志考 (A study of historical geography in imperial Vietnam). 1907 (Thành Thái 19). *Institute of Sino-Nom studies library number*: A. 77. Hán Nôm Institute Manuscript.

Ouyang Xiu 歐陽修 (1007–1072). *Xintang shu* 新唐書 (New Tang History; *XTS*). Beijing: Zhonghua Shuju, 1975.

Phạm An Phủ 范安甫 (fl. 19th cent.). *Cao Bằng Kí Lược* 高平紀略 (The abridged history of Cao Bằng). 1845 (Thiệu Trị 4). *Institute of Sino-Nom studies library number*: A.999. Hán Nôm Institute Manuscript.

Phan Huy Chú 潘輝注 (1782–1840). *Lịch triều hiến chương loại chí* 歷朝憲章類誌 (Categorized records of the institutions of successive dynasties; *LTHCLC*). Hà Nội: NXB Khoa học xã hội, 1992.

Qi Feng 馮琦 (1558–1603). *Songshi jishi benmo* 宋史紀事本末 (Records of the history of the Song dynasty). 109 *juan*. Taipei: Shangwu Yinshuguan, 1965.

Sima Guang 司馬光 (1019–1086). *Zizhitongjian* 資治通鑑 (Comprehensive mirror to aid in government). Beijing: Zhonghua Shuju, 1956.

Sima Qian 司馬遷 (ca. 145–ca. 86 BCE). *Shiji* 史記 (Records of the historian). Beijing: Zhonghua Shuju, 1959.

———. *Shiji* 史記 (Records of the historian). Taipei: Shangwu Yinshu Guan, 1965.

Song Lian 宋濂 (1310–1381). *Yuanshi* 元史 (History of the Yuan dynasty). Beijing: Zhonghua Shuju, 1976.

Tan Qilong 譚其龍, ed. *Tanshi zongpu* 譚氏宗譜 (Tan family genealogy). 2nd edition. Taipei: Tan Shouxin, 2003.

Toghto 脫脫 (1311–1355) et al. *Songshi* 宋史 (Official history of the Song dynasty) Beijing: Zhonghua Shuju, 1983.

Trần Huy Phác 陳輝樸 (fl. 19th cent.). *An Nam Tạp Chí* 安南雜誌 (Miscellaneous annals of An Nam) VHN manuscript. 1861 (Tự Đức 14). *Institute of Sino-Nom studies library number*: A. 2916. Hán Nôm Institute Manuscript.

Viện Sử Học, ed. *Khâm định Đại Nam hội điển sự lệ* 欽定大南會典事例 (Collected institutions of Đại Nam; *KDDNHDSL*) Tập VIII, Huế: NXB Thuận Hoá, 2004.

———, ed. *Khâm định Việt sử thông giám cương mục* 欽定越史通鑑綱目 (The imperially ordered annotated text completely reflecting the history of Viet; *KDVSTGCM*) Tập I, Hà Nội: NXB Giáo dục, 1998.

Wan Yinglin. *Yu hai* 玉海 (Jade sea). 200 *juan*. Hangzhou: Zheshiang Shuju, 1883.

Wang Fangqing 王方慶 (?–702). *Weizheng Gong Jian Lu* 魏鄭公諫錄 (Duke Wei Zheng's public remonstrance). 3 *juan*. *Sikuquanshu*, vol. 446. Taipei: Taiwan Shangwu Yinshuguan, 1979.

Wang Sen 汪森 (1653–1726), ed. *Yuexi cong zai* 粵西叢載. String-bound reprint. Beijing: Zhongguo Shudian, 1987.

———. *Yuexi wen zai* 粵西文載 (Lingnan literature). *Sikuquanshu*, vols. 365–400. Taipei: Taiwan Shangwu Yinshuguan, 1979.

Wang Xiangzhi 王象之 (*jinshi* 1196). *Yudi jisheng* 輿地紀勝 (Comprehensive description of the empire). 1849 edition. Taipei: Wenhai Chubanshe, 1962.

Wang Zhongzhao 王重昭 (1435–1508). *Ba Min tongzhi* 八閩通志 (General gazetteer of Ba Min). Beijing: Shumu Wenxian, 1988.

Wei Yuan 魏源 (1794–1857). *Yuanshi xinbian* 元史新編 (New compilation of the Yuan history). 95 *juan*. Shanghai: Shanghai Guji Chubanshe, 1995.

Wei Zheng 魏征. *Sui shu* 隋書 (History of the Sui dynasty). Beijing: Zhonghua Shuju, 1973.

Wu Jing 吳競 (670–749). *Zhenguan zheng yao* 貞觀政要 (The political program in Zhenguan times). Taipei: Sanmin Chubanshe, 2020.

———. *Zhongguo di wang xue: "Zhenguan zheng yao" bai hua ban* 中國帝王學："貞觀政要" 白話版 (A study of Chinese emperors: Vernacular edition of Wu Jing's *The Political Program in Zhenguan Times*). Translated and annotated by Ge Jingchun. Taipei: Yuanliu Chubanshe, 2003.

Wu Jing 吳儆 (1125–1183). *Zhuzhou ji* 竹洲集 (The collected works of Master Zhuzhou). Shanghai: Shanghai Guji Chubanshe, 1987.

Xu Mingshan 徐明善. *Annan xingji* 安南行記 (Records of travels through An

Nam), preserved in *Shuofu* 說郛 (The domain of texts), 51 *juan*. Compiled by Tao Xiongyi (1370). Biji xiaoshuo daguan edition.

Xu Song. *Song hui yao ji gao* 宋會要輯稿 (Collected essential documents of the Song dynasty; *SHY*). Taipei: Shijie Shuju, 1964.

Xu Tai 徐泰 (Jiajing 43, 1564). *Nanning Fu Zhi* 南寧府志 (General gazetteer of Nanning prefecture), 10 *juan*. *Tianyige cang Mingdai fang zhi xuan kan xu bian* 天一閣藏明代方志選刊續編 (Selected reprints of Ming dynasty gazetteers from the Tianyige Collection), no. 67. Shanghai: Shanghai Shudian, 1990.

Xuan Zang 玄奘 (ca. 596–664). *Da Tang Xiyu ji jiao zhu* 大唐西域記校注 (Annotated edition of *The great Tang dynasty record of the western regions*; *DTXYJJZ*). Beijing: Zhonghua Shuju, 1985.

Yang Jialuo. *Xin jiao ben Sanguo zhi* 新校本三國志 (New edition of the story of *The Three Kingdoms*). Taipei: Dingwen Shuju, 1997.

Yue Shi 樂史 (930–1007). *Taiping huanyuji* 太平寰宇記 (Universal geography of the Taiping era [976–983]). 1793 edition. Taipei: Wenhai Chubanshe, 1993.

Zeng Gongliang 曾公亮 (999–1078). *Wujing Zongyao Qianji* 武經總要前集 (First collection of the *Compendium of Important Matters from the Military Classics*). Beijing: Zhonghua Shuju, 1959.

Zeng Zaozhuang 曾棗莊 and Liu Lin 劉琳, eds. *Quan Song wen* 全宋文. (Complete Collection of Song Essays). 1st ed. Shanghai: Shanghai cishu chubanshe, 2006. Zhang Tingyu 張廷玉 (1672–1755). *Ming shi* 明史 (History of the Ming). 332 *juan*. Beijing, Zhonghua Shuju, 1974.

Zhao Rukuo 趙汝适 (1170–1231). *Zhu fan zhi* 諸番誌 (Treatises on various foreign peoples; *ZFZ*). Beijing: Zhonghua Shuju, 2000.

Zheng Sixiao 鄭思肖 (1241–1318). *Xinshi* 心史 (History of my heart) Vol. 2. Beijing: Zhongzhu Shuju Kanben, 1894.

Zhou Hui 周揮 (1126–1198). *Qingbo zazhi* 清波雜志 (Various notes from the Clear Waves). Beijing: Zhonghua Shuju, 1994.

Zhou Qufei 周去非. *Lingwai daida* 嶺外代答 (Notes from the land beyond the passes; *LWDD*). Beijing: Zhonghua Shuju, 1999.

Zhuge Yuansheng 諸葛元聲 (fl. 1581). *Dianshi* 滇史 (History of the Dian kingdom). Kunming: Dehong Minzu Chubanshe, 1994.

Secondary Sources

Abulafia, David, and Nora Berend. *Medieval Frontiers: Concepts and Practices*. Aldershot, England: Ashgate, 2002.

Aikhenvald, Alexandra, and Robert M. W. Dixon. *Areal Diffusion and Genetic Inheritance Problems in Comparative Linguistics*. Oxford: Oxford University Press, 2001.

Anderson, James A. "China's Southwestern Silk Road in World History." *World History Connected* 6, no. 1 (March 2009): 1–7. https://worldhistoryconnected.press .uillinois.edu/6.1/anderson.html.

———. "Commissioner Li and Prefect Huang: Sino-Vietnamese Frontier Trade Networks and Political Alliances in the Southern Song." *Asia Major*, 3rd series 27, no. 2 (2014): 29–51.

———. "Frontier Management and Tribute Relations along the Empire's Southern Border: China and Vietnam in the 10th and 11th Centuries." PhD diss., University of Washington, 1999.

———. "Pearls and Power: Chōla's Tribute Mission to the Northern Song Court within the Maritime Silk Road Trade Network." In *Silk Roads: From Local Realities to Global Narratives*, edited by Jeffrey D. Lerner and Yaohua Shi, 223–36. Oxford: Oxbow Books, 2020.

———. *The Rebel Den of Nùng Trí Cao: Loyalty and Identity Along the Sino-Vietnamese Frontier*. Seattle: University of Washington Press, 2007.

———. "Trade Relations between the Đại Việt Kingdom and the Song Empire in the Long Twelfth Century." *Crossroads* 19 (2020).

———. "'Treacherous Factions': Shifting Frontier Alliances in the Breakdown of Sino-Vietnamese Relations on the Eve of the 1075 Border War." In *Battlefronts Real and Imagined: War, Border, and Identity in the Chinese Middle Period*, edited by Don J. Wyatt. New York: Palgrave Macmillan, 2008.

Anderson, James A., and John K. Whitmore, eds. *China's Encounters on the South and Southwest: Reforging the Fiery Frontier over Two Millennia*. Leiden: Brill, 2015.

Aung-Thwin, Michael A. "The 'Classical' in Southeast Asia: The Present in the Past." *Journal of Southeast Asian Studies* 26, no. 1, Perspectives on Southeast Asian Studies (March 1995): 75–91.

Aung-Thwin, Michael A., and Kenneth R. Hall, eds. *New Perspectives on the History and Historiography of Southeast Asia: Continuing Explorations*. New York: Routledge, 2011.

Backus, Charles. *The Nan-chao Kingdom and T'ang China's Southwestern Frontier*. New York: Cambridge University Press, 1981.

Bagley, Robert. *Ancient Sichuan: Treasures from a Lost Civilization*. Seattle: Seattle Art Museum, 2001.

Bai Xingfa 白興發. "Ziqi Guoshi shi kao shu" 自杞國史事考述 (A review on the history of Ziqi kingdom). *Wenshan shifan gaodeng zhuanke xuexiao xuebao* 文山師範高等專科學校學報 (Journal of the Wenshan Teachers College) 121, no. 14 (December 2008): 37–43.

Bai Yaotian 白耀天. "Tu guan yu tusi kao bian" 土官與土司考辯 (Textual research on native officials and chieftains). *Guangxi difangzhi* 廣西地方志 (Guangxi gazetteer journal), no. 3 (1999): 27–32.

Baldanza, Kathlene. *Ming China and Vietnam, Negotiating Borders in Early Modern Asia.* Cambridge: Cambridge University Press, 2016.

————. "A State Agent at Odds with the State: Lin Xiyuan and the Ming Recovery of the Four Dong." In *China's Encounters on the South and Southwest: Reforging the Fiery Frontier over Two Millennia*, edited by Anderson and Whitmore. Leiden: Brill, 2015, 169–90.

Barlow, Jeffrey. "The Zhuang Minority People of the Sino-Vietnamese Frontier in the Song Period." *Journal of Southeast Asian Studies* 18, no. 2 (September 1987): 250–69.

Blench, Roger. "The Spread of the Horse into Southeast Asia: Evidence from Vernacular Names." Unpublished paper, Kay Williamson Educational Foundation, 2010.

Bo Baxin 波巴信. *Miandian shi* 緬甸史 (History of Myanmar). Beijing: Commercial Press, 1965.

Borchert, Thomas. "Worry for the Dai Nation: Sipsongpannā, Chinese Modernity, and the Problems of Buddhist Modernism." *Journal of Asian Studies* 67, no. 1 (February 2008): 107–42.

Brindley, Erica. *Ancient China and the Yue: Perceptions and Identities on the Southern Frontier, c. 400 BCE–50 CE.* London: Cambridge University Press, 2015.

Brooks, James. *Captives and Cousins: Slavery, Kinship, and Community in the Southwest Borderlands.* Chapel Hill: University of North Carolina Press, 2002.

Brown, Kate. *A Biography of No Place: From Ethnic Borderland to Soviet Heartland.* Cambridge, MA: Harvard University Press, 2004.

Bryson, Megan. *Goddess on the Frontier: Religion, Ethnicity, and Gender in Southwest China.* Stanford: Stanford University Press, 2016.

Cao Bằng Television (website). "Thông tin về các Lễ hội trên địa bàn thành phố Cao Bằng năm 2018" (Information about festivals in Cao Bằng city in 2018). Accessed October 11, 2019. http://caobangtv.gov.vn/index.php?language=vi&nv=news&op=Xa-hoi-65/Thong-tin-ve-cac-Le-hoi-tren-dia-ban-thanh-pho-Cao-Bang-nam-2018–1118.

Chamberlain, James R. "Kra-Dai and the Proto-History of South China and Vietnam." *Journal of the Siam Society* 104 (2016): 50.

Chan, Hok-Lam. "Commerce and Trade in Divided China: The Case of Jurchen-Jin Versus the Northern and Southern Song." *Journal of Asian History* 36, no. 2 (2002): 135–83.

Chanda, Nayan. *Bound Together: How Traders, Preachers, Adventurers, and Warriors Shaped Globalization*. New Haven: Yale University Press, 2007.

Chandra, S., and A. K. Jain. *Foundations of Ethnobotany: 21st Century Perspective*. Jodhpur, India: Scientific Publishers, 2017.

Chen, Jack Wei, and David Schaberg. *Idle Talk: Gossip and Anecdote in Traditional China*. Berkeley: University of California Press, 2014.

Chen, Xiangming. *As Borders Bend: Transnational Spaces on the Pacific Rim*. Lanham, MD: Rowman and Littlefield, 2005.

Chen Gaohua. *Yuanshi yanjiu lun gao* 元史研究論稿 (A compendium of research in Yuan history). Vol. 122. Beijing: Zhonghua Shuju, 1991.

Chen Jiarong 陳佳榮. *Gudai nanhai diming huiyi* 古代南海地名匯釋 (Ancient seven seas gazetteer). Beijing: Zhonghua Shuju, 1986.

Chen Yirong. "Baiyue gudao de lishi wenhua kaocha" 百越古道的歷史文化考察 (A historical and cultural study of the Baiyue ancient road). *Guangxi minzu yanjiu* 廣西民族研究 (Guangxi ethnic studies), no. 1 (2012): 103–7.

Chin, Tamara T. "Antiquarian as Ethnographer: Han Ethnicity in Early China Studies." In *Critical Han Studies: The History, Representation, and Identity of China's Majority*, edited by Thomas S. Mullaney, James Leibold, Stéphane Gros, and Eric Vanden Bussche, 128–46. Berkeley: Global, Area, and International Archive/University of California Press, 2012.

Churchman, Catherine. *The People between the Rivers: The Rise and Fall of Bronze Drum Chiefdoms, 200–750 CE*. Lanham, MD: Rowman and Littlefield, 2016.

———. "Where to Draw the Line? The Chinese Southern Frontier in the Fifth and Sixth Centuries." In *China's Encounters on the South and Southwest: Reforging the Fiery Frontier Over Two Millennia*, edited by Anderson and Whitmore. Leiden: Brill, 2015, 59–77.

Clarence-Smith, William G. "Breeding and Power in Southeast Asia Horses, Mules and Donkeys in the Longue Durée." In *Environment, Trade and Society in Southeast Asia: A Longue Durée Perspective*, edited by David Henley and Henk Schulte Nordholt, 32–45. Leiden: Brill, 2015.

Clifford, James. *Returns: Becoming Indigenous in the Twenty-First Century*. Cambridge, MA: Harvard University Press, 2013.

———. "Traveling Cultures." In *Cultural Studies*, edited by Lawrence Grossberg, Cary Nelson, and Paula A. Treichler, 96–116. New York: Routledge, 1992.

Clunas, Craig. *Art in China*. Oxford: Oxford University Press, 1997.

Cui Y., Qin D., Chen Y. "Copper Mineralization in the Western Longbohe Area, SE Yunnan, China: A Comparison with the Shengquan Copper Deposit, Vietnam." In *Mineral Deposit Research: Meeting the Global Challenge*, edited by J. Mao and F. P. Bierlein. Berlin: Springer, 2005, 369–72.

Curtin, Philip D. *Cross-Cultural Trade in World History*. Studies in Comparative World History. Cambridge: Cambridge University Press, 1984.

Đàm Thị Uyên. *Chính Sách Dân Tộc Của Các Triều Đại Phong Kiến Việt Nam — Thế Kỷ XI- Đến Giữa thế Kỷ XIX* (Ethnic policy of the feudal dynasties of Vietnam — 11th century to the mid-19th century). Hà Nội: Nhà Xuất Bản Văn Hoá Dân Tộc, 2007.

Đặng Nghiêm Vạn and Hoàng Hoa Toàn. *Bộ đội cần biết về các dân tộc ở biên giới phía Bắc* (What the army needs to know about ethnic groups along the northern border). Hà Nội: NXB QĐND, 1983.

Davis, Bradley Camp. *Imperial Bandits: Outlaws and Rebels in the China-Vietnam Borderlands*. Seattle: University of Washington Press, 2017.

Dessaint, Alain Y. *Minorities of Southwest China; An Introduction to the Yi (Lolo) and Related Peoples and an Annotated Bibliography*. New Haven: HRAF Press, 1980.

Dharwadker, Vinay, ed. *Cosmopolitan Geographies: New Locations in Literature and Culture*. New York: Routledge, 2001.

Dien, Albert E. *Six Dynasties Civilization*. New Haven: Yale University Press, 2007.

Ding Li. *Zhongguo diming cidian* 中國地名詞典 (Chinese place-name dictionary). Shanghai: Shanghai cishu, 1990.

Duan Yu. *Nanfang sichou zhi lu yanjiu lunji* 南方絲綢之路研究論集 (Research on the southern silk road). Chengdu: Ba Shushe, 2008.

Duan Yuming 段玉明. "Dali guo de zhoubian guanxi" 大理國的周邊關係 (The Dali kingdom's relations with its frontier neighbors). *Yunnan shehui kexue* 雲南社會科學 (Yunnan social sciences), no. 3 (1997): 54–64.

———. *Dali guoshi* 大理國史 (History of the Dali kingdom). Kunming: Yunnan Ethnic Publishing House, 2003.

———. "Dali guozhun zhidu kaolüe" 大理國軍事制度考略 (A study of the Dali kingdom's military organization). *Yunnan Minzu Xueyuan xuebao* 雲南民族學院學報 (Journal of Yunnan Nationalities University) 4 (1995): 33–35.

Eberhard, Wolfram. *The Local Cultures of South and East China*. Leiden: Brill, 1968.

Evans, Grant, Christopher Hutton, and Kuah Khun Kuah. *Where China Meets Southeast Asia: Social and Cultural Change in the Border Regions*. Bangkok: White Lotus, 2000.

Fan Chengda. *Treatises of the Supervisor and Guardian of the Cinnamon Sea*. Edited and translated by J. H. Hargett. Seattle: University of Washington Press, 2010.

Fan Honggui 范宏貴. *Nong Zhigao Yanjiu ziliao ji* 儂智高研究資料集 (Nong Zhigao research collection). Nanning: Guangxi Minzu, 2005.

Fang Guoyu. *Zhongguo xinan lishi dili kaoshi* 中國西南歷史地理考釋 (Textual research on historical geography of southwest China). Beijing: Zhonghua, 1992.

Fang Tie. "Dali guo de minzu zhidi he duiwai zhengce" 大理國的民族治策和對外政策 (National policies and external policies in the kingdom of Dali). In *Baizu wenhua yanjiu 2003* 白族文化研究 2003 (Bai cultural studies 2003). Vol. 4. Beijing: Minzu, 2004.

———. "Hubilie yu Yunnan" 忽必烈與雲南 (Khubilai Khan and Yunnan). *Wenshan yueyuan xuebao* 文山學院學報 (Journal of Wenshan University) 24, no. 1 (February 2011): 34–40.

———. "Jian lun xinan sichou zhi lu" 簡論西南絲綢之路 (On the southwest silk road). *Chang'an Daxue xuebao* 長安大學學報 (Journal of Chang'an University), no. 3 (2015): 114–20.

———. "Lidai zhi bian yu Yunnan di diyuan zhengzhi guanxi" 歷代治邊與雲南的地緣政治關係 (The history of frontier rule and geopolitical relations in Yunnan). *Xinan Minzu Daxue xuebao* 西南民族大學學報 (Journal of the Southwest University for Nationalities), no. 9 (2011): 5–20.

———. "Tang Song liang chao zhi zhongnan bandao jiaotong xian de bianqian" 唐宋兩朝至中南半島交通線的變遷 (Mainland Southeast Asia transit route changes in the Tang-Song period). *Shehui kexue zhanxian* 社會科學戰線 (Frontlines in the social sciences), no. 4 (2011): 101–11.

———. *Xinan Tongshi* 西南通史 (A survey history of the southwest). Zhengzhou: Zhongzhou Guji Chubanshe, 2003.

Fang Tie and Zou Jianda. "Lun Zhongguo gudai zhi bian zhi zhong bei qing nan qingxiang ji qi xingcheng" 論中國古代治邊之重北輕南傾向及其形成 (Discussion of ancient China's tendency to stress the importance of the northern frontier over the southern frontier). *Yunnan Shifan Daxue xuebao* (Journal of Yunnan Normal University), no. 3 (2006): 174–81.

Faure, David. *Emperor and Ancestor: State and Lineage in South China*. Stanford: Stanford University Press, 2007.

Feng, Han-yi and J. K. Shyrock "The historical origins of the Lolo." *Harvard Journal of Asiatic Studies* 3 (1938): 103–27.

Feng Hanji 馮漢驥. *Kaogu xuelun wenji* 考古學論文集 (Writings on archaeology). Beijing: Wenwu Chubanshe, 1985.

Ferlus. Michel. "Formation of Ethnonyms in Southeast Asia." Forty-Second International Conference on Sino-Tibetan Languages and Linguistics, Payap University, November 2009, Chiang Mai, Thailand.

Filipiak, Kai, ed. *Civil-Military Relations in Chinese History: From Ancient China to the Communist Takeover*. London: Taylor and Francis, 2014.

Fitzgerald, C. P. *The Southern Expansion of the Chinese People*. New York: Praeger, 1972. Foster, R. P. *Gold Metallogeny and Exploration*. Dordrecht: Springer Netherlands, 1993.

Fragner, Bert, Ralph Kauz, Roderich Ptak, and Angela Schottenhammer, eds. *Pferde in Asien: Geschichte, Handel und Kultur*. Vienna: Verlag der Österreichischen Akademie der Wissenschaften, 2009.

Fusao Taniguchi 谷口房男 and Bai Yaotian 白耀天. *Zhuangzu tuguan zupu jicheng* 壯族土官族譜集成 (Genealogies of native Zhuang officials). Nanning: Guangxi Minzu Chubanshe, 1998.

Gao Honglei 高洪雷著. *Zhonghua minzu de gushi* 中華民族的故事 (The story of the Chinese people). Beijing: Changjiang Wenyi, 2016.

Ge, Zhaoguang. *An Intellectual History of China*. Vol. 2. Leiden: Brill, 2018.

Ghosh, Lipi, ed. *The Southern Silk Route: Historical Links and Contemporary Convergences*. London: Taylor and Francis, 2019.

Giersch, Charles Patterson. *Asian Borderlands: The Transformation of Qing China's Yunnan Frontier*. Cambridge, MA: Harvard University Press, 2006.

———. *Corporate Conquests: Business, the State, and the Origins of Ethnic Inequality in Southwest China*. Stanford: Stanford University Press, 2020.

Gilbert, Marc. "Paper Trails: Port Cities in the Classical Era of World History." *World History Connected* 3, no. 2 (February 2006). http://www.historycooperative.org /journals/whc/3.2/gilbert.html.

Goody, Jack. *The Oriental, the Ancient, and the Primitive Systems of Marriage and the Family in the Pre-Industrial Societies of Eurasia*. Studies in Literacy, Family, Culture and the State. Cambridge: Cambridge University Press, 1990.

Gray, David, and Ryan Richard Overby. "Introduction: Tracing Tantric Traditions through Time and Space." In *Tantric Traditions in Transmission and Translation*, edited by David B. Gray and Ryan Richard Overbey. New York: Oxford Academic, 2016. Accessed August 4, 2023. https://doi.org/10.1093/acprof:oso/9780199763 689.001.0001.

Grossberg, Lawrence, Cary Nelson, and Paula A. Treichler, eds. *Cultural Studies*. New York: Routledge, 1992.

Grousset, René. *The Empire of the Steppes: A History of Central Asia.* New Brunswick, NJ: Rutgers University Press, 1970.

Gu Yongji. "Ming Qing shiqi Yunnan Daizu diqu de jiaoyu fazhan de tedian" 明清時期雲南傣族地區的教育發展的特點 (The educational development and characteristics of the Dai-inhabited areas in the Ming and the Qing dynasties). *Yunnan Shifan Daxue xuebao* 雲南師範大學學報 (Journal of Yunnan Normal University) 43, no. 2 (March 2011): 142–50.

Gu Zuyu. *Dushi fangyu jiyao* 讀史方輿紀要 (Essence of historical geography). Beijing: Zhonghua Shuju, 2019.

Guilin Shi Wenwu Guanli Weiyuanhui 桂林市文物管理委員會. *Guilin shike* 桂林石刻 (Guilin stele). Guilin: Guilin Shi Wenwu Guanli Weiyuanhui, 1979.

Guo Shengbo and Wang Ning. "The Significant Reform of the Administrative System in the National Borderlands in the Early Yuan Dynasty through the Evolution of the Areal Distribution of the Tribes of Five Surnames and Eight Surnames in the Song and Yuan Dynasty." *Guizhou Ethnic Studies* 32, no. 6 (2011): 82–91.

Gutiérrez, Ramón A., and Elliott Young. "Transnationalizing Borderlands History." *Western Historical Quarterly* 41, no. 1 (February 1, 2010): 27–53.

Hall, Kenneth. "Economic History of Early Southeast Asia." In *The Cambridge History of Southeast Asia.* Vol. 1, Part 1, *From Early Times to c. 1500*, ed. Nicholas Tarling, 183–275. Cambridge: Cambridge University Press, 1999.

Harrell, Stevan. *Cultural Encounters on China's Ethnic Frontiers.* Seattle: University of Washington Press, 1995.

———. *Perspectives on the Yi of Southwest China.* Berkeley: University of California Press, 2001.

———. *Ways of Being Ethnic in Southwest China.* Seattle: University of Washington Press, 2001.

Hein, Anke, and Deyun Zhao. "The Cultural Other and the Nearest Neighbor: Han-Nuosu Relations in Zhaojue County, Southwest China." *Asian Ethnicity* 17, no. 2 (2016): 273–93.

Heiss, Mary Lou, and Robert J. Heiss. *The Story of Tea: A Cultural History and Drinking Guide.* Berkeley: Ten Speed Press, 2007.

Henley, David, and Henk Schulte Nordholt, eds. *Environment, Trade and Society in Southeast Asia: A Longue Durée Perspective.* Leiden: Brill, 2015.

Herman, John E. *Amid the Clouds and Mist: China's Colonization of Guizhou, 1200–1700.* Cambridge, MA: Harvard University Asia Center, 2007.

———. "Empire in the Southwest: Early Qing Reforms to the Native Chieftain System." *Journal of Asian Studies* 56, no. 1 (1997): 47–74.

———. "The Kingdoms of Nanzhong China's Southwest Border Region Prior to the Eighth Century." *T'oung Pao*, 2nd series, 95, nos. 4/5 (2009): 241–86.

———. "The Mu'ege Kingdom: A Brief History of a Frontier Empire in Southwest China." In *Political Frontiers, Ethnic Boundaries and Human Geographies in Chinese History*. Edited by Don J. Wyatt and Nicola Di Cosmo. London: Routledge Curzon, 2003, 245–85.

Higiri Masumi. "Ajia-teki seisan yōshiki-ron kenkyū nitsuite" アジア的生産様式論研究について (Research on the Asiatic mode of production theory). In *Nihon no kokusaika to chiiki kenkyū no yakuwari* 日本の国際化と地域研究の役割 (The role of international and area studies in Japan). Tokyo: Tōkyō Gaikokugo Daigaku Kaigai Jijō Kenkyūjo, 1983.

Hill, Ann Maxwell. *Merchants And Migrants: Ethnicity and Trade among Yunnanese Chinese in Southeast Asia*. New Haven: Yale University Southeast Asia Studies, 1998.

History Writing Group No. 1. *Yizu jianshi* 彝族簡史 (A brief history of the Yi people). Kunming: Yunnan Renmin, 1987.

Hoàng Quyết, Ma Khánh Bằng, Hoàng Huy Phách, Cung Văn Lược, and Vương Toàn. *Văn hoá truyền thống Tày-Nùng* (Tày-Nùng traditional culture). Hà Nội: NXB Văn hoá Dân tộc, 1993.

Hoàng Xuân Hãn. *Lý Thường Kiệt. Lịch sử ngoại giao và tôn giáo của triều Lý* (Lý Thường Kiệt: History of diplomacy and history of the Lý dynasty). Hà Nội: Nhà xuất bản Sông Nhị, 1949.

Holcombe, Charles. *The Genesis of East Asia: 221 B.C.–A.D. 907*. Honolulu: University of Hawai'i Press, 2001.

Holm, David. "Linguistic Diversity Along the China-Vietnam Border." *Linguistics of the Tibeto-Burman Area* 33, no. 2 (October 2010): 1–63.

Huang Chengshou 黄成授. *Guangxi minzu guanxi de lishi yu xianzhuang* 廣西民族關係的歷史與現狀 (The history and current conditions of minority group relations in Guangxi). Beijing: Minzu, 2002.

Huang Fei. "Lun Yuan Hubilie chao dui Annan de zhengfa" 論元忽必烈朝對安南的征伐 (A discussion of the An Nam campaigns by Khubilai Khan's court). *Qiqiha'er shifan gaodeng zhuanke xuexiao xuebao* 齊齊哈爾師範高等專科學校學報 (The journal of the Qiqihar Junior Teachers College) 114, no. 2 (2010): 95–97.

Huang Kuan-chung. "Wan Song junqing souji yu chuandi—Yi *Kezhai zagao* suojian song, meng guangxi zhanyi wei" 晚宋軍情蒐集與傳遞：以《可齋雜藁》所見宋、蒙廣西戰役為例 (The collection and transmission of military intelligence in the late Song: Mongol and Song warfare in Guangxi as reflected in the *Kezhai zagao*). *Hanxue yanjiu* 漢學研究 (Sinology) 27, no. 2 (June 2009): 133–66.

Hucker, Charles O. *A Dictionary of Official Titles in Imperial China.* Stanford: Stanford University Press, 1985.

Huo Wei 霍巍. *Xinan kaogu yu Zhonghua wenming* 西南考古与中华文明 (Southwestern archaeology and Chinese civilization). Chengdu: Bashu Shushe, 2011.

Itō, Masako. *Politics of Ethnic Classification in Vietnam.* Kyoto: Kyoto University Press, 2013.

Jing Zhenguo. *Zhongguo guji zhong you guan Laozhua ziliao huibian* 中國古籍中有關老撾資料彙編 (Compilation of materials on Laos in ancient Chinese texts). Beijing: Zhongzhou Guji, 1985.

Kelley, Liam. "Tai Words and the Place of the Tai in the Vietnamese Past." *Journal of the Siam Society* 101 (2013): 55–84.

Kuik, Cheng-Chwee, David M. Lampton, and Selina Ho. *Rivers of Iron: Railroads and Chinese Power in Southeast Asia.* Berkeley: University of California Press, 2020.

Kulke, Hermann. "The Early and the Imperial Kingdom in Southeast Asian History." In *Southeast Asia in the 9th to 14th Centuries,* edited by D. G. Marr and A. C. Milner, 1–22. Singapore: Institute of Southeast Asian Studies, 1986.

Lã Văn Lô. *Chế độ thổ ty Việt Nam, tài liệu Viện dân tộc học, ký hiệu* (The chieftain system in Vietnam: Documents from the Institute of Ethnology). D.275.

———. "Quanh vấn đề An Dương Vương Thục Phán hay là truyền thuyết 'Cẩu chúa cheng vua' của đồng bào Tày." (Around the issue of An Duong Vuong Thuc Phan or the legend of "Lord cheng king" of the Tày ethnic groups). *NCLS*, no. 50 (1963).

Lan Yong. *Xinan lishi wehua dili* 西南歷史文化地理 (Historical cultural geography in southwest China). Chongqing: Xinan Shifan Daxue, 2001.

Le Bail, Hélène, and Abel Tournier. "From Kunming to Mandalay: The New 'Burma Road.'" *Asie Visions* (Paris: Centre Asia IFRI), no. 25 (March 2010): 1–46.

Le Thanh Khoi. *Histoire du Viet Nam: Des origines à 1858.* Paris, 1981.

Lê Văn Yên and Phạm Thị Hải Châu. "Cuộc Kháng Chiến Chống Tống Thế Kỷ XI" (The battle against the Song in the 11th century). *Tạp Chí Khoa Học Xã Hội Việt Nam* (Journal of Vietnamese sociology) 88, no. 3 (2015): 109–17.

Leach, Edmund. *Political Systems of Highland Burma: A Study of Kachin Social Structure.* London: Athlone Press, 1970.

LeBar, Frank M., et al., eds. *Ethnic Groups of Mainland Southeast Asia.* New Haven: Human Relations Area Files Press, 1964.

Lehman, F. K. (Chit Hlaing). "Burma: Kayah Society as a Function of the Shan-Burma-Karen Context." In *Asian Rural Societies,* edited by Julian Steward. Vol.

2 of *Contemporary Change in Traditional Society*. Urbana: University of Illinois Press, 1967, 1–101.

Lei, Shibin, Qing Min, Niu Cuiyi, and Wang Liang. "Current Gold Prospecting in China." *Acta Geologica Sinica—English Edition* 90, no. 4 (2016): 1298–320.

Lentz, Christian C. *Contested Territory: Điện Biên Phủ and the Making of Northwest Vietnam*. New Haven: Yale University Press, 2019.

Lewis, Mark Edward. *China's Cosmopolitan Empire: The Tang Dynasty*. Cambridge, MA: Belknap Press of Harvard University Press, 2009.

Li Qiuhua 李秋華. "Tianbao zhanzheng hou Nanzhao de kuozhang ji yingxiang (gongyuan 754 nian–779 nian)" 天寶戰爭後南詔的擴張及影響 (公元754年–779年) (The Nanzhao kingdom's expansion and influence after the Tianbao war (754–779). *Heilongjiang shi zhi* 黑龍江史志 (Heilongjiang history journal) 21 (2013): 102–4.

Li Qunyu 李群玉, Huang Rensheng, and Chen Shengzheng, eds. *Tang dai Xiangren shi wen ji* 唐代湘人詩文集 (Collection of Tang dynasty Hunan poetry). Changsha: Yuelu Shu She, 2013.

Li Tianming. *Song Yuan zhan shi* 宋元戰史 (History of the Song-Mongol war). Taipei: Shihuo, 1988.

Li Weiwei 李魏巍 and Wan Xuebo 萬雪波. "Lüe guo shixing heping mulin youhao waijiao zhanlüe de yuanyin tan lüe" 略國實行和平睦鄰友好外交戰略的原因探略 (Probing into the reasons for the Dali kingdom's peaceful and friendly neighboring diplomacy: Based on geopolitical interpretation). *Dali Xueyuan xuebao* 大理學院學報 (Journal of Dali University) 3, no. 3 (March 2018): 9–14.

Li Weizhen. "Daliguo yu Jiaozhi li chao de junshi zhiheng guanxi tanjiu" 大理國與交趾李朝的均勢制衡關係探究 (A probe into the balance of power between Dali kingdom and Đại Việt's Lý dynasty). *Hubei Minzu Daxue xuebao* 湖北民族大學學報 (Journal of Hubei University for Nationalities), no. 3 (2019): 148–57.

Li Xiaobin and Yuan Lihua. "Historical Inheritance and the Construction of Historical Identity of Ethnic Groups in Mountainous Regions of Yunnan: The Case of the De'ang Nationality." In *Ethnicity and Religion in Southwest China*. Edited by H. Ming and D. Lewis. New York: Routledge, 2020.

Li Xiaomei 李小梅. "Nazhao, Daliguo he Miandian de Biaoguo, Pugan wang chao de guanxi" 南詔、大理國和緬甸的驃國、蒲甘王朝的關係 (Nanzhao and Dali relations with the Pyu and Bagan kingdoms of Myanmar). *Bianjiang jingji yu wenhua* 邊疆經濟與文化 (The border economy and culture), no. 4. (2011): 176–77.

Li Yinbing 李銀兵. "*Manshu* ji qi shiliao jiazhi" 《蠻書》及其史料價值 (The book

Manshu and its valuable historical materials). *Yibin Xueyuan xuebao* 宜賓學院學
報 (Journal of Yibin University) 7, no. 3 (March 2008): 53–55.

Li Zhiliang 李之亮. *Song liang Guang dajun shouchen yiti kao* 宋兩廣大郡守臣易
替考(Study of local officials of Guangdong and Guangxi in the Song dynasty).
Chengdu: Ba Shu Shushe, 2001.

Liang Xiaoqiang 梁曉強. *Nanzhao shi* 南詔史 (History of Nanzhao). Beijing: China
Social Sciences Press, 2013.

Lieberman, Victor B. *Strange Parallels: Southeast Asia in Global Context, c. 800–1830.*
Vol. 2. New York: Cambridge University Press, 2009.

Lin Chaomin 林超民. *Lin Chaomin wenji* 林超民文集 (Collected works of Lin
Chaomin). Kunming: Yunnan Renmin Chubanshe, 2008.

———. *Tangdai Yunnan de Han wenhua* 唐代云南的漢文化 (Yunnan's Han culture
in the Tang dynasty). Kunming: Yunnan Renmin Chubanshe, 1991.

Liu Fusheng 劉復生. "Ziqi guo kaolue" 自杞國考略 (A study of the Ziqi kingdom).
Minzu yanjiu 民族研究 (Ethnic studies), no. 5 (1993): 78–83.

Lo, Jung-Pang. "The Controversy over Grain Conveyance during the Reign
of Qubilai Qaqan, 1260–94." *Far Eastern Quarterly* 13, no. 3 (May 1954):
263–85.

Lombard, Denys, and Jean Aubin. *Asian Merchants and Businessmen in the Indian
Ocean and the China Sea.* New Delhi: Oxford University Press, 2000.

Lorge, Peter. "The Rise of the Martial: Rebalancing *Wen* and *Wu* in Song Dynasty
Culture." In *Civil-Military Relations in Chinese History: From Ancient China to the
Communist Takeover*, edited by Kai Filipiak. London: Taylor and Francis, 2014,
134–43.

———. *War, Politics and Society in Early Modern China, 900–1795.* London: Taylor
and Francis, 2005.

Lu Simian 呂思勉 (1884–1957). *Yanshi zhaji* 燕石札記 (Notes about Yanshi). Taipei:
Taiwan Shangwu, 1968.

Lu Yiran 呂一燃, ed. *Zhongguo jindai bianjie shi* 中國近代邊界史 (The history of
modern China's boundaries). Vol. 2. Chongqing: Sichuan Renmin Chubanshe, 2007.

Ma, Jianxiong, and Cunzhao Ma. "The Mule Caravans as Cross-Border Networks:
Local Bands and Their Stretch on the Frontier between Yunnan and Burma." In
Myanmar's Mountain and Maritime Borderscapes, edited by Su-Ann Oh, 237–60.
Singapore: ISEAS Publishing, 2016.

Ma Rong 馬蓉. *Yongle dadian fangzhi jiyi* 永樂大典方志輯佚 (Lost gazetteers of the
Yongle dadian). Beijing: Zhonghua Shuju, 2004.

Mao, J., and F. P. Bierlein, eds. *Mineral Deposit Research: Meeting the Global Challenge*. Berlin: Springer, 2005.

Mao Ding'ang 貌丁昂. *Miandian shi* 緬甸史 (History of Myanmar). Kunming: Yunnan Institute of Southeast Asian Studies, 1983.

Maspero, Henri. "Études d'histoire d'Annam." *Bulletin de l'École française d'Extrême-Orient* 16 (1916): 1–55.

Mathieu, Christine. *A History and Anthropological Study of the Ancient Kingdoms of the Sino-Tibetan Borderland—Naxi and Mosuo*. London: Edwin Mellen Press, 2003.

Michaud, Jean. *Historical Dictionary of the Peoples of the Southeast Asian Massif*. Greenwich: Scarecrow Press, 2006.

Mignolo, Walter, Irene Siverbatt, and Sonia Saldivar-Hull. "Introduction: The Social Ecology of the Sonoran Frontier." In *Wandering Peoples: Colonialism, Ethnic Spaces, and Ecological Frontiers in Northwestern Mexico, 1700–1850*, edited by Cynthia Radding. Durham: Duke University Press, 1997, 1–18.

Miller, Lucien, and Guo Xu, trans. and eds. *South of the Clouds: Tales From Yunnan*. Seattle: University of Washington Press, 1994.

Molnar, Peter. "The Geologic Evolution of the Tibetan Plateau." *American Scientist* 77, no. 4 (1989): 350–60.

Momoki Shiro. "Military Actions and Control of Local Powers in Vietnam under the Lý Dynasty" 桃木, 至朗, ヴェトナム李朝の軍事行動と地方支配. *Southeast Asian Studies* 東南アジア研究 24, no. 4 (1987): 403–17.

———. "Nippon niokeru Betonamu zen kindai-shi kenkyū no seika to kadai—dokuritsu ōchō-ki no jidai kubun womegutte" 日本におけるヴェトナム前近代史研究の成果と課題—独立王朝期の時代区分をめぐって (Achievements and challenges in Japan in the study of premodern Vietnamese history—The period of independent dynastic rule). *Atarashii rekishi-gaku no tame ni* 新しい歴史学のために (For a new history), no. 175 (1984), 9–19.

Moseley, George. *The Consolidation of the South China Frontier*. Berkeley: University of California Press, 1973.

Mote, Frederick W. *Imperial China, 900–1800*. Cambridge, MA: Harvard University Press, 1999.

Mullaney, Thomas S., ed. *Critical Han Studies: The History, Representation, and Identity of China's Majority*. Berkeley: University of California Press, 2012.

Nanning Gudai Qingguan Lianli 南寧古代清官廉吏 (Honest officials of ancient Nanning). Nanning: Guangxi Remin Chubanshe, 2015.

Needham, Joseph, and Ling Wang. *Science and Civilisation in China*. Vol. 2, *History of Scientific Thought*. Cambridge: Cambridge University Press, 1956.

Ng Pak-sheung 伍伯常. "Su Jian shihuan shengya kao shu: Jian lun beisong wenchen canyu junshi de lishi xianxiang" 蘇緘仕宦生涯考述: 兼論北宋文臣參與軍事的歷史現象 (The life and career of Su Jian: Reexamining the issue of civil officials taking charge of military affairs). *Zhongguo Wenhua Yanjiusuo xuebao* 中國文化研究所學報 (Journal of Chinese studies), no. 56 (January 2013): 101–41.

Ngô Tất Tố. *Việt Nam Văn Học: Văn Học Đời Trần* (Vietnamese literature: The literature of the Trần period). Saigon: Nhà sách Khai Trí, 1960.

Nguyễn Chí Buyên, Hoàng Hoa Toàn, and Lương Văn Bảo, eds. *Nguồn Gốc Lịch Sử Tộc Người Vùng Biên Giới Phía Bắc Việt Nam* (History of the origins of ethnic groups of northern Vietnam's border areas). Hà Nội: Nhà Xuất Bản Văn Hóa Dân Tộc, 2000.

Nguyễn Thanh Bình. "Dai Viet Diplomatic Relations with Neighboring Countries under Lý Dynasty." *Vietnam Social Sciences* 179, no. 3 (2017): 54–63.

Oey, G. P., and Gordon H. Luce. *The Man Shu*. Ithaca, NY: Department of Far Eastern Studies, Cornell University, 1961.

Oh, Su-Ann, ed. *Myanmar's Mountain and Maritime Borderscapes* Singapore: ISEAS Publishing, 2016.

Olson, James Stuart. *An Ethnohistorical Dictionary of China*. Westport, CT: Greenwood Press, 1998.

Pan, Yihong. *Son of Heaven and Heavenly Qaghan: Sui-Tang China and Its Neighbors*. Bellingham, WA: Center for East Asian Studies, Western Washington University, 1997.

Phan Văn Các et al., eds. *Văn Khắc Hán Nôm Việt Nam* 越南漢喃銘文匯編 (Han and Nom epigraphical texts of Vietnam). Vol. 2. Taipei: Xinwenfeng, 2002.

Phan Văn Các and Claudine Salmon. *Épigraphie en Chinoise du Viêt Nam*. Vol. 1. Paris: École française d'Extrême-Orient; Hà Nội: Viện Nghiên cứu Hán Nôm, 1998.

Pines, Yuri. *The Everlasting Empire: The Political Culture of Ancient China and Its Imperial Legacy*. Princeton: Princeton University Press, 2012.

Polo, Marco. *The Travels of Marco Polo*. Edited by R. E. Latham. London: Penguin Books, 1958.

Polyakov, Gleb V., Alexander S. Borisenko, Phuong Thi Ngo, Dung Thi Pham, Anh Tuan Tran, Andrey E. Izokh, Pavel A. Balykin, and Hoa Trong Tran. *Intraplate Magmatism and Metallogeny of North Vietnam*. New York: Springer, 2015.

Qujing Municipal Historical Committee (Qujing Shi Zhengxie Wenshi Wei). *Qujing wenshi ziliao* 曲靖文史資料 (Materials on the history of Qujing). Vol. 1, Internal "neibu" documents for circulation. Qujing, Yunnan: CPPCC Literature and History Information Committee Pub, 2003.

Radding, Cynthia. *Wandering Peoples: Colonialism, Ethnic Spaces, and Ecological Frontiers in Northwestern Mexico, 1700–1850*. Durham: Duke University Press, 1997.

Rossabi, Morris. *Khubilai Khan: His Life and Times*. Berkeley: University of California Press, 1988.

Sage, Steven F. *Ancient Sichuan and the Unification of China*. Albany: State University of New York Press, 1992.

Sahlins, Peter. *Boundaries: The Making of France and Spain in the Pyrenees*. Berkeley: University of California Press, 1989.

Sakurai, Yumio 桜井由躬雄. "李朝期 (1010–1225) 紅河デルタ開拓試論：デルタ開拓における農学的適応の終末 (<特集>故水野浩一教授を偲んで)" (The Red River Delta during the Lý dynasty [1010–1225]: Special issue in memory of the late Professor Koichi Mizuno). 東南アジア研究 (Southeast Asian studies) 18, no. 2 (September 1980): 271–314.

Schafer, Edward H. "The Early History of Lead Pigments and Cosmetics in China." *T'oung Pao* 44 (1956): 413–38.

———. *The Vermilion Bird: T'ang Images of the South*. Los Angeles: University of California Press, 1967.

Scott, James C. *The Art of Not Being Governed: An Anarchist History of Upland Southeast Asia*. New Haven: Yale University Press, 2009.

Sen, Tansen. *Buddhism, Diplomacy, and Trade: The Realignment of Sino-Indian Relations, 600–1400*. Honolulu: University of Hawai'i Press, 2003.

Shaffer, Lynda. "Southernization." *Journal of World History* 5 (Spring 1994): 1–21.

Sharma, Ram S. *Early Medieval Indian Society: A Study in Feudalism*. Kolkata: Orient Longman, 2003.

Shen Fuwei 沈福偉. "Wedan guo yu Zhujiang guo xinlun" 文單國與朱江國新論 (New discussion of the Wendan and Zhujiang kingdoms). *Lishi yanjiu* 历史研究 (Historical research), no. 5 (2003): 100–114.

Shen Xu 申旭. *Zhongguo xinan dui waiguan xishi yanjiu: Yi xinan sichou zhi lu wei zhongxin* 中國西南對外關係史研究：以西南絲綢之路為中心 (History of southwest China's foreign relations: The southwest silk road as the center). Kunming: Yunnan Meishu Chubanshe, 1994.

Shi Di 師蒂. *Shenhua yu fazhi: Xinan minzu fa wenhua yanjiu* 神話與法制-西南民族文化研究 (Mythology and legality: Research of national legal culture in southwest China). Kunming: Yunnan Jiaoyu, 1992.

Shi Jianjun. "Hubilie zheng Dali luxian xinkao" 忽必烈徵大理路線新考 (New textual research on the route taken by Khubilai Khan on his expedition against the Dali kingdom). *Zhongguo lishi dili luncong* 中國歷史地理論叢 (Journal of Chinese historical geography) 24, no. 1 (January 2009): 146–58.

Shibata, M., and T. Koyas. *An English and Japanese Dictionary: Explanatory, Pronouncing, and Etymological, Containing All English Words in Present Use, with an Appendix.* 2nd rev. ed. Tokyo: Ni-shu-sha Printing Office, 1887.

Shin, Leo Kwok-yueh. *The Making of the Chinese State: Ethnicity and Expansion on the Ming Borderlands.* Cambridge: Cambridge University Press, 2006.

Smith, Paul J. *Taxing Heaven's Storehouse: Horses, Bureaucrats, and the Destruction of the Sichuan Tea Industry, 1074–1224.* Harvard-Yenching Institute Monograph Series 32. Cambridge, MA: Council on East Asian Studies, Harvard University, 1991.

Stuart-Fox, Martin. *A Short History of China and Southeast Asia: Tribute, Trade and Influence.* New South Wales, Australia: Allen and Unwin, 2003.

Sun Tingjin. *Shuo zhoubian lishi hua jiangyu bianqian.* 說周邊歷史話疆域變遷 (Discussion of the history and transformation of borderlands areas). Beijing: Zhongguo Youyi Chuban Gongsi, 2016.

Swain, Margaret. "Native Place and Ethnic Relations in Lunan Yi Autonomous County, Yunnan." In *Perspectives on the Yi of Southwest China*, edited by Stevan Harrell, 170–95. Berkeley: University of California Press, 2001.

Tambiah, S. J. *World Conqueror and World Renouncer.* Cambridge: Cambridge University Press, 1976.

Tapp, Nicholas. "The Han Joker in the Pack: Some Issues of Culture and Identity from the Minzu Literature." In *Critical Han Studies: The History, Representation, and Identity of China's Majority*, edited by Thomas S. Mullaney, 147–70. Berkeley: University of California Press, 2012.

———. *The Hmong of China: Context, Agency, and the Imaginary.* Leiden: Brill, 2003.

Tarling, Nicholas, ed. *The Cambridge History of Southeast Asia.* Vol. 1, Part 1, *From Early Times to c. 1500.* Cambridge: Cambridge University Press, 1999.

Taylor, Keith Weller. *The Birth of Vietnam.* Berkeley: University of California Press, 1991.

Thant Myint-U. *The River of Lost Footsteps: Histories of Burma.* New York: Farrar, Straus and Giroux, 2006.

Took, Jennifer. *A Native Chieftaincy in Southwest China Franchising a Tai Chieftaincy under the Tusi System of Late Imperial China.* Sinica Leidensia 70. Leiden: Brill, 2005.

Triệu, Đức Thanh, and Duy Đại Lê. *Các dân tộc ở Hà Giang.* (Ethnic groups in Ha Giang). Hà Nội: Nhà xuất bản Thế giới, 2004.

Tư liệu về lịch sử và Xã hội dân tộc Thái (Documentation on Thai history and society, social science). Hà Nội: Khoa học XH, 1997.

Turner, Sarah. *Red Stamps and Gold Stars: Fieldwork Dilemmas in Upland Socialist Asia*. Vancouver: University of British Columbia Press, 2013.

Turton, Andrew, ed. *Civility and Savagery: Social Identity in Tai States*. Richmond, Surrey: Curzon Press, 2000.

Twitchett, Denis Crispin, and John King Fairbank. *The Cambridge History of China*. Vol. 8, part 2, *The Ming Dynasty, 1368–1644*. Cambridge: Cambridge University Press, 1978.

Viện Văn Học (Institute of Literature). *Thơ văn Lý Trần* (tập I). Hà Nội: NXB Khoa học xã hội, 1977.

Vogel, Hans Ulrich. *Marco Polo Was in China: New Evidence from Currencies, Salts and Revenues*. Leiden: Brill, 2012.

Vũ, Ngọc Khánh, and Minh Thảo Phạm. *Việt Nam, kho tàng dã sử* (Vietnam: A chronicle of treasures). Hà Nội: NXB Văn hóa-thông tin, 2004.

Wade, Geoff. "The Horse in Southeast Asia prior to 1500 CE: Some Vignettes." In *Pferde in Asien: Geschichte, Handel und Kultur*, edited by Bert Fragner, Ralph Kauz, Roderich Ptak, and Angela Schottenhammer, 161–77. Vienna: Verlag der Österreichischen Akademie der Wissenschaften, 2009.

———. "The Polity of Yelang and the Origins of the Name 'China.'" In *The Southern Silk Route: Historical Links and Contemporary Convergences*, edited by Lipi Ghosh, 37–58. London: Taylor and Francis, 2019.

———. *Southeast Asia-China Interactions: Reprint of Articles from the Journal of the Malaysian Branch, Royal Asiatic Society*. Kuala Lumpur: Malaysian Branch of the Royal Asiatic Society, 2007.

Wang, Ling. *Tea and Chinese Culture*. San Francisco: Long River Press, 2005.

Wang, Q., and D. Groves. "Carlin-Style Gold Deposits, Youjiang Basin, China: Tecto-no-Thermal and Structural Analogues of the Carlin-Type Gold Deposits, Nevada, USA." *Mineralium Deposita* 53, no. 7 (2018): 909–18.

Wang Hongpeng 王鴻鵬 et al., eds. *Zhongguo lidai wu zhuangyuan* 中國歷代武狀元 (China's historical champions). Beijing: Jiefang Jun Chubanshe, 2002.

Wang Ningsheng. *Zhongguo xinan minzu de lishi yu wenhua* 中國西南的歷史與文化 (The history and culture of the ethnic groups in southwest China). Kunming: Yunnan Minzu Publishers, 1989.

Wang Wenguang and Gong Qing. "Daliguo de Wuman" 大理国的乌蛮 (The Wu-man of the Dali kingdom). *Yunnan Minzu Xueyuan xuebao* 雲南民族學院學報 (Journal of Yunnan Nationalities University) 24, no. 15 (September 2007): 86–90.

Wang Wenguang, You Weiqiong, and Zhang Meiling. *Yunnan minzu de lishi yu wen-hua gaiyao* 雲南民族的歷史與文化概要 (A summary of the history and culture of Yunnan's ethnic groups). Kunming: Yunnan Daxue Chubanshe, 2014.

Wang Yongqiang et al., eds. *Zhongguo shaoshu minzu wenhuashi tudian xinan juan* 中國少數民族文化史圖典西南卷 (An illustrated guide to the cultural history of China's minorities: The southwest volume). Nanning: Guangxi Jiaoyu Chubanshe, 1999.

Weber, Max. *Economy and Society*. Vol. 1. Berkeley: University of California Press, 1978.

Weinstein, J. L. *Empire and Identity in Guizhou: Local Resistance to Qing Expansion*. Seattle: University of Washington Press, 2014.

Wheatley, Paul. "Geographical Notes on Some Commodities in Sung Maritime Trade." In *Southeast Asia-China Interactions: Reprint of Articles from the Journal of the Malaysian Branch, Royal Asiatic Society*, edited by Geoff Wade, 1–139. Kuala Lumpur: Malaysian Branch of the Royal Asiatic Society, 2007.

White, Richard. *The Middle Ground: Indians, Empires, and Republics in the Great Lakes Region, 1650–1815*. Twentieth anniversary edition. New York: Cambridge University Press, 2011.

Whitmore, John K. "Colliding Peoples: Tai/Viet Interactions in the 14th and 15th Centuries." Unpublished conference paper, Association of Asian Studies Annual Meeting, San Diego, 2000.

Wicks, Robert Sigfrid. *Money, Markets, and Trade in Early Southeast Asia: The Development of Indigenous Monetary Systems to AD 1400*. Ithaca, NY: Southeast Asia Program, Cornell University, 1992.

Wiens, Herold. *Han Chinese Expansion in South China*. Shoe String Press, Yale University, 1967.

Wilhelm, Gábor. "The Ainu in Japan: Ethnic Identity and Cultural Definitions." *Pro Ethnologia* 11 (January 2001). https://www.erm.ee/sites/default/files/penr11.pdf.

Wink, André. *Al-Hind, the Making of the Indo-Islamic World*. Leiden: Brill, 1991.

Wolters, O. W. *History, Culture, and Region in Southeast Asian Perspectives*. Rev. ed. Ithaca, NY: Southeast Asia Program, 1999.

———. "Monologue, Dialogue, and Tran Vietnam." Unpublished manuscript, 2009.

Wolters, O. W., and Craig J. Reynolds. *Early Southeast Asia: Selected Essays*. Ithaca, NY: Southeast Asia Program, Cornell University, 2008.

Wu Zhuo. "Xinan sichou zhi lu yanjiu de renshi wuqu" 西南絲綢之路研究的認識誤區 (Erroneous identifications in southwestern silk road research). *Lishi yanjiu* 歷史研究 1 (1999): 37–49.

Xia Guangnan. *Yuandai Yunnan shi di congkao* 元代雲南史地叢考 (History and geography of Yuan period Yunnan). Shanghai: Zhonghua, 1935.

Xie Chongan 謝崇安. "Ye tan Wuchi dao de kaitong ji qi dui xinan yi diqu shehui fazhan de yingxiang" 也談五尺道的開通及其對西南夷地區社會發展的影響 (A discussion of the opening of the Wuchi road and its impact on the social development of the southwestern region). *Guizhou minzu yanjiu* 貴州民族研究 (Guizhou ethnic studies), no. 5 (2011): 162–68.

Xu Jiarui 徐嘉瑞. *Dali gudai wenhua shigao* 大理古代文化史稿 (Draft history of ancient Dali culture). Beijing: Zhongguo Shuju, 1978.

Xu Songshi 徐松石 (1900–1999). *Yue jiang liu yu renmin shi* 粵江流域人民史 (History of the peoples of southern China's river regions). Hong Kong: Shijie Shuju, 1963.

Yang, Bin. *Between Winds and Clouds: The Making of Yunnan (Second Century BCE to Twentieth Century CE).* New York: Columbia University Press, 2008.

———. "Horses, Silver, and Cowries: Yunnan in Global Perspective." *Journal of World History* 15 (September 2004): 281–322.

Yang Qianamiao. *Songdai renwu cidian* 宋代人物辭典 (Dictionary of Song persons). Baoding: Hebei Daxue Chubanshe, 2015.

Yang Shiqi and Huang Huai. *Lidai mingchen zouyi* 歷代名臣奏議. 338 *juan.* Shanghai: Shanghai Guji, 1989.

Yang Xieli 楊絜澧. *Guangxi yu diquan tu* 廣西輿地全圖 (Complete map of Guangxi). Guangzhou: Cheng Tiange, 1907.

Yang Zuo 楊佐. *Yunnan mai ma ji* 雲南買馬記 (Yunnan horse trade). Kunming: Yunnan Minzu, 2003.

Yao, Alice. *The Ancient Highlands of Southwest China from the Bronze Age to the Han Empire.* Oxford: Oxford University Press, 2016.

You Zhong 尤中. "Song hui yufu xinjie" 宋揮玉斧新解 (New assessment of the phrase "The Song wields a jade axe"). *Xixiang zhanxian* 思想戰線 (Ideological front), no. 6 (1985): 70–73.

———. "Zhengquan shiqi xinan bian jiang de minzu difang zhengquan 'zhengquan shi gui guo' he 'zi qi guo'" "政權時期西南邊疆的民族地方政權"政權施鬼國" 和"自杞國" (Local governance on the southwest border of the Southern Song dynasty in the "Lushi ghost kingdom" and the "Ziqi kingdom"). *Sixiang zhanxian* 思想戰線 (Ideological front), no. 3 (1996): 55–62.

———. *Zhonghua minzu fazhan shi* 中華民族發展史 (History of the development of the Chinese people). Vol. 2, *Liao Song Jin Yuan dai* 宋遼金元代 (Liao, Song, Jian and Yuan dynasties). Kunming: Chenguang Chubanshe, 2007.

Yu, Taishan. "A History of the Relationship between the Chinese Dynasties and the Western Regions." Sino-Platonic Papers 131 (March 2004; repr. 2013).

Yu, Ying-shih. *Trade and Expansion in Han China: A Study in the Structure of Sino-Barbarian Economic Relations*. Berkeley: University California Press, 1967.

Yuan, Hong. *The Sinitic Civilization, Book 2: A Factual History through the Lens of Archaeology, Bronzeware, Astronomy, Divination, Calendar and the Annals*. Bloomington: iUniverse, 2018.

Zhang Jinlian. "Songchao yu Annan tongdao shikao" 宋朝與安南通道試探 (A trial probe into roads for transportation in the Song dynasty and An Nam). *Dongnanya zongku* 東南亞縱庫, no. 10 (2005): 65–71.

Zhang Qizhi, Zhang Guogang, and Yang Shusen. *Sui Tang Song shi* 隋唐宋史 (Sui-Tang-Song history). Taipei: Wunan Tushu, 2002.

Zhang Shengzhen and Qin Cailuan, eds. *Zhuangzu shi* 壯族史 (History of the Zhuang people). Guangzhou: Guangdong Renmin Chubanshe, 2002.

Zhang Xilu. "Yuan shizu hu bi lie mie dali guoshi shi kao" 元世祖忽必烈灭大理国史事考 (A historical reexamination of Khubilai Khan's overthrow of the Dali kingdom). *Dali Xueyuan xuebao* 大理學院學報 (Journal of Dali University) 5, no. 3 (March 2006): 5–9.

Zhang Yunxia 張雲霞. "Rujia wei xiang zai Nanzhao shehui de chuanbo" 儒家思想在南詔社會的傳播 (The spread of Confucianism in ancient Nanzhao society). *Dali Xueyuan xuebao* 大理學院學報 (Journal of Dali University) 1, no. 1 (January 2002): 12–15.

Zhang Zhongshan. *Zhongguo sichou zhi lu huobi* 中國絲綢之路貨幣 (The currencies of the Chinese silk road). Lanzhou: Lanzhou Daxue Chubanshe, 1999.

Zhao Dongmei 趙冬梅. *Wenwu zhi jian: Bei Song wuxuanguan yanjiu* 文武之間: 北宋武選官研究 (Between civil and military: Studies on military grade officials in the Northern Song). Beijing: Beijing Daxue Chubanshe, 2010.

Zhongguo Renmin Zhengzhi Xieshang Huiyi 中國人民政治協商會議. *Xing'an wen shi zi liao* 興安文史資料 (Xing'an cultural and historical materials). Vol. 2. Zhongguo Renmin Zhengzhi Xieshang Huiyi Guangxi Xing'an Xian Weiyuanhui Wenshi Ziliao Weiyuanhui 中國人民政治協商會議廣西興安縣委員會文史資料委員會 (Chinese People's Political Consultative Conference, Guangxi Xing'an County Committee Cultural and Historical Materials Committee), 1989.

Zhonghua Xie shi zongpu gan xian juan 中華謝氏總譜贛縣卷 (The complete Chinese genealogical records of the Xie clan). Salt Lake City, Utah: Genealogical Society of Utah, 2015.

Zhou Weizhou 周偉洲 and Ding Jingtai 丁景泰, eds. *Sichou zhi lu da cidian* 絲綢之路大辭典 (Dictionary of the silk road). Xi'an: Shaanxi Renmin Chubanshe, 2006.

Zhu Annu 朱安女. "Lun Nanzhao Dali guo shiqi nanfang sichou zhi lu de wenhua tedian" 論南詔大理國時期南方絲綢之路的文化特點 (On the characteristics of the southern silk road culture in Nanzhao and Dali kingdom). *Dali Xueyuan xuebao* 大理學院學報 (Journal of Dali University) 14, no. 11 (November 2015): 8–13.

Zhu Wenhui and Wang Yuanlin. "Songdai Guang nanxi lu de san da bo yi chang he Hainan Dao de duiwai maoyi" 宋代廣南西路的三大博易場和海南島的對外貿易 (Three trading markets in Guangxi and Hainan Island's foreign trade in the Song Dynasty). *Hainan Daxue xuebao* 海南大學學報 (Journal of Hainan University) 28, no. 5 (October 2010): 14–17.

Zumbroich, Thomas J. "The Origin and Diffusion of Betel Chewing: A Synthesis of Evidence from South Asia, Southeast Asia and beyond." *eJIM, the eJournal of Indian Medicine* 1:87–140.

INDEX

Confucianism, 43, 44

Cuan clan: Eastern and Western, 37–40; emergence of, 32–34, 35–37; as ethnic group, 37–38, 210n17, 232n3; militia, 145; and the rise of the Dali and Nanzhao, 40, 49; steles, 35, 211n25; during Sui and Tang, 39–41

Cuan Hongda, 39–40

Cuan Shen, 35, 37

Cuan Xi, 35–36

Cui Chengsi, 232n4

Cui clan, 232n4

Cui Yuzhi, 131

Cultural Revolution, 165

Dachanghe regime, 49

Đại Cồ Việt kingdom, 54–58, 71; Lý dynasty, 83, 88; occupation of north by Lý, 58; relations with Dali, 55, 58, 90; Song invasion, 122; Song support for, 57–58. *See also* Đại Việt kingdom; Lý dynasty

Dai Fu, *Guangyiji* (Record of strange things in Guangnan), 48

Đại Nguyên Lịch, 87

Dai people, 214n109; Chinese national minority, 21

Đại Việt kingdom: border conflict with Song, 8, 59–60, 82, 93–99, 125, 215n131; boundary with Song, 101; cultural impacts of raids, 43; Dong World intermediaries, 4, 62; frontier administration, 80–82, 100, 102, 105, 156; local alliances, 134, 145, 156; market for pearls, 68; military intrusion in Yongzhou region, 132; Ming occupation, 158–59; Mongol attacks on,

134–35, 139, 144–46, 148–54; name of, 93; northern region, 58–59; relations with Dali, 7–8, 54–55, 60–61, 65, 85, 87; relations with Mongols under Khubilai, 146–47; relations with Song, 8–9, 54, 117, 142; relations with Southern Song, 127, 147; resistance to Mongols, 150–54, 156; ruling families, 82–83, 218–19n39; sea attacks, 152–53; as Song trading partner, 126; trade routes to, 25, 171; trading port, 85; transfer of power from Lý to Trần, 144–45; tributary relations with Yuan, 147, 153–54. *See also* An Nam; Đại Cồ Việt kingdom; Lý dynasty; Sino-Vietnamese borderlands; Song–Đại Việt borderlands conflict; Trần dynasty

Dai Yi, 132

Dalhi (Dunrenyi) kingdom, 19

Dali kingdom: attack by Pagan ruler, 21; creation of, 31, 49, 52, 59; Dong World interactions, 4, 57, 59, 62, 69; Duan leadership, 31, 49, 53, 60, 118, 136, 137–39, 145, 155–56; ethnic groups, 49, 52; fall of, 9, 31, 49, 157; gold and silver mining, 116; Han influence, 13–14; influence in borderlands, 120; interclan power struggle, 60; military conflict with Đại Cồ Việt, 55–58; and Mongol expansionism, 134, 135–39, 148, 155–56, 157; nonaggression policy, 53–54; prefectures and commandaries, 173; relations with Đại Việt, 7–8, 54–55, 60–61, 65, 85, 87; relations with Song, 22, 54, 58, 59, 69, 112–15, 117, 127, 141; religious traditions in, 20; request for Chinese texts, 114–15; seized by

Yongzhou, 128; Ziqi kingdom, 65, 103–4, 110–11, 114

horses, 74; as tribute, 57, 66–67. *See also* horse trade

Hou Guang, 130

Hou Han Shu (Fan Ye), 19, 208n29

Hou Renbao, 82, 122

Hu Hong, 226n28

Hu Shunzhi, 112, 128

Hua-Yi order (*Hua Yi zhixu*), 59

Huang Bing (Hoàng Bính), 134–35, 143, 144, 145

Huang Boshan, 79

Huang Boyun, 79

Huang Changguan, 77

Huang Changmian, 77

Huang Chengqing, 77

Huang (Hoàng) clan, 9, 70, 75–78; marriage alliances with Đại Việt, 145; relations with Song and Đại Việt, 134–35, 142, 143, 145, 154–55; tribute to Yuan court, 155

Huang Fafu, 155

Huang Fei, 147, 153

Huang Keshun, 155

Huang Kuan-chong, 142

Huang Lin, 66, 67

Huang Qianyao, 76–77

Huang Shaodu, 77

Huang Shaogao, 77

Huang Shaoqing, 77

Huang Shengxu, 154–55

Huang Zhongying, 122–23

Huang Ziwen, 133

huangchengshi (capital security commissioner), 107, 223n13

Huệ Minh (monk), 65

Hui ethnic group, 165

Hunan-Guangnan general administration, 130

Hưng Đạo Prince. *See* Trần Quốc Tuấn

Hưng Hiếu Prince, 101

Hùng kings, 217n4

Hưng Nhượng Prince (Trần Quốc Tảng), 100–101

Hưng Phúc Temple stele, 149–50

Huo Wei, 207n3

Huyền Tông, Emperor, 222n142

Imperially Ordered Annotated Text Completely Reflecting the History of Viet, 56, 83–84, 214n114

incense, 118, 226n72

India Route, 16–17, 34

Indochinese Union, 160

Indravarman V of Champa, 147

intelligence gathering, 8, 105, 134, 135, 139, 141–42, 143, 144

Japanese occupation of French Indochina, 163

Jiang Jin, 95

Jiang Yunji, 127

Jianwu Gazetteer, 112, 116

jimi regions. *See* bridled and haltered regions

Jinchi Baiyi (Golden Teeth Baiyi), 49, 55, 139, 214n109

Jingdong, 52

Jingjiangfu Military Prefecture, 142

Jinning, 37. *See also* Qujing (Weixian)

Ju berry sauce, 34, 210n18

Juidao people, 51

Jurchen Jin dynasty, 62, 126–27, 136

www.ingramcontent.com/pod-product-compliance
Lightning Source LLC
Chambersburg PA
CBHW031412270326
41929CB00010BA/1420